To Teena and Rudy,
With gratitude for your
friendship and warmest best
wishes — Steve
18 Nov. 2004

A War of a Different Kind

A WAR OF A DIFFERENT KIND

Military Force and America's Search for Homeland Security

STEPHEN M. DUNCAN

Naval Institute Press
Annapolis, Maryland

Naval Institute Press
291 Wood Road
Annapolis, MD 21402

Library of Congress Cataloging-in-Publication Data
Duncan, Stephen M.
    A war of a different kind : military force and America's search for
homeland security / Stephen M. Duncan.
        p. cm.
    Includes bibliographical references and index.
    ISBN 1-59114-220-2 (alk. paper)
        1. United States—Military policy. 2. United States—Armed
Forces. 3. Civil defense—United States. 4. War on Terrorism, 2001–
5. Terrorism—Prevention—United States. I. Title.
    UA23.D824 2004
    363.35'0973—dc22

                                                    2003019333

Printed in the United States of America on acid-free paper ∞
11 10 09 08 07 06 05 04   9 8 7 6 5 4 3 2
First printing

To my grandchildren—Tyler Duncan, Tristan Kyle, Charles Marcus, Anna Luella, Julia Danielle, and Christopher Stephen—with my prayer that they will be able to spend their childhoods pursuing childish delights and that when they become adults, they will not have to worry about the security of our home.

And to their grandmother—my beloved Luella—a gift from God, who made our home in this world a sanctuary where only love and happiness resided and who now lives in total joy in our heavenly home.

In times of peace and prosperity cities and individuals alike follow higher standards because they are not forced into a situation where they have to do what they do not want to do. But war is a stern teacher; in depriving them of the power of easily satisfying their daily wants, it brings most people's minds down to the level of their actual circumstances.

Thucydides, *Peloponnesian Wars, III,* 82

Contents

Preface

Saturday 8 June 1991 was a hot day in the nation's capital. The temperature was in the high eighties and the ever present humidity was quickly noticed by visitors from New England and the West. No one seemed to be complaining. There was too much excitement in the air.

The Stars and Stripes flew from hotels, government buildings, private automobiles, public buses, and small sticks carried by endless groups of people. Yellow ribbons were tied around trees and a broad selection of available poles. The public grounds between the U.S. Capitol building and the Washington Monument had been transformed into a sand-colored carnival setting. The object of fascination in the morning by adults and children alike had been a seven-block-long display of some of the weapons that had been used in the recently completed Persian Gulf War against Iraq. Dozens of military vehicles and aircraft could be seen and touched. Soldiers, sailors, marines, and airmen in battle dress uniform were everywhere.

The U.S. Park Service estimated that approximately 800,000 people had jammed into Washington, D.C., that day. The *Washington Post* would later describe the day as being unlike any day since the end of World War II. The purpose of the celebration was to officially welcome home the 550,000 U.S. troops who had achieved the magnificent victory in Operation Desert Storm. The highlight of the celebration was a two and one-half mile victory parade proceeding down Constitution Avenue. It ended after the last troops marched past the Vietnam Veterans Memorial and across the flag-bedecked Memorial Bridge.

I was sitting on one of the temporary bleacher seats that are set up for large affairs in Washington. My beloved late wife Luella, who had seen me leave for the Vietnam theater of operations twenty-six years earlier and only ten days after we were married, sat beside me. We were joined by senior civilian colleagues who were serving with me in the Pentagon. Across the street, President George H. W. Bush, Secretary of Defense Dick Cheney, and others watched the parade from the presidential reviewing stand.

Newspapers and books later reported certain cold facts about the parade. Some 8,800 veterans marched down the boulevard at a scheduled pace of 116 steps per minute. Few had ever marched for a president. The flyover of eighty-three aircraft included E-3 AWACS and the now famous F-117A Stealth Fighter.[1] The treads of the 67-ton M1A1 Abrams tanks and the 30-ton Bradley fighting vehicles made deep cuts in asphalt softened by the sun's rays. The $12 million cost of the celebration was criticized by some because the District of Columbia faced financial difficulties.[2]

Statistics, however, did not begin to tell the real story. That story had been told earlier over several decades by the actions of many of the heroes who were now marching past. One such hero was Lt. Gen. Fred Franks, USA, holder of a Ph.D., who marched on a prosthetic leg as the result of having lost his leg below the knee from a grenade wound during the Vietnam War. Fred had commanded the U.S. Army's VII Corps, the armor and infantry force that had smashed into southern Iraq and then turned east in the famous "left hook" envelopment maneuver that resulted in the destruction of much of Iraq's Republican Guard. Another such hero was Brig. Gen. John Hopkins, USMC, who had also received a major combat wound in Vietnam. John had been a boxing instructor when I was a midshipman at the U.S. Naval Academy in the early 1960s and he had hosted my prewar visit to the U.S. Marine Corps' combined armed training base in the desert at Twenty-Nine Palms, California. In Operation Desert Storm, John had commanded the 7th Marine Expeditionary Brigade, the first significant U.S. ground force to reach the combat area. There had been no victory parade at the conclusion of either the Vietnam War or the Cold War, so it was particularly poignant to watch people who had devoted their entire adult lives to the security of the United States finally receive a small measure of gratitude from their fellow countrymen.

As the troops, bands, flags, battle streamers, and guidons passed in front of me, I reflected upon the remarkable events of the previous two years and the implication of those events for the future. The Cold War was over. The Soviet Union no longer existed. The Communist East Bloc's Warsaw Pact had been disbanded. The regime of General Manuel Antonio Noriega had been dislodged from Panama. The naked, brutal invasion of Kuwait by Saddam Hussein's forces had been reversed. Democratic governments and market economies were replacing totalitarian regimes and state economies in Eastern Europe and South America.

Could it be that despite Plato's admonition that only the dead have seen the end of war, Americans could now look forward to at least one or two generations of peace? In their 1968 book, *The Lessons of History*, Will Durant and Ariel Durant asserted that in the 3,421 years of recorded history, only 268 had been free of war. Military historians know that since 1783 the United States has sent sizeable forces into harm's way every twenty years.[3] But, there now seemed to be grounds for believing that the prospects for breaking that vicious cycle were good. Just that morning, President Bush had stood near the Tomb of the Unknowns at Arlington National Cemetery with the families of 390 Americans who had died during Operations Desert Shield and Desert Storm. After looking out at the many attendees who were crying, Bush had said that he hoped "this time was the last time."[4] Was it reasonable to hope that our children and their children would be able to live without fear of another clash of arms?

I remembered vividly the drills of my elementary school when children were taught how to seek protection from a nuclear weapon delivered by a communist adversary. Families talked about backyard bomb shelters and those who could afford them had constructed them. My entire life had been centered on or shadowed by the prospect of war. Only five years after my father and uncle had returned home after World War II, U.S. forces had been mobilized and sent to the front lines of the Korean War. When I was twenty-one years old and a midshipman at the U.S. Naval Academy, the world had come dangerously close to a nuclear Armageddon during the Cuban missile crisis of October 1962. Less than two years after my graduation from the academy, I left San Diego on an amphibious flagship for my first tour of duty in the Vietnam war zone. That experience was followed by service in Vietnam as a weapons officer aboard a small ship that provided close-in gunfire support of U.S. ground troops. Eighteen years in the U.S. Naval Reserve during the Cold War preceded my appointment to senior policy positions at the Department of Defense during the presidencies of Ronald Reagan and George H. W. Bush. I had walked on the hallowed soil at Yorktown, Normandy, Corregidor, Inchon, Quang Ngai, and many other battlegrounds where American warriors had died to protect our freedom. Only one U.S. Naval Academy class had lost more of its members to combat in Vietnam than my own. I had seen firsthand the destruction of war.

Now, the United States was the world's only superpower. No armed forces in the world could match our war-fighting capabilities. In his 6 March 1991 address to Congress shortly after the cease-fire, President Bush had declared that the victory in the Gulf War belonged "to the finest fighting force this nation has ever known in its history." No nation could match our economic power. For 215 years, the U.S. experiment in democracy had demonstrated its vitality and durability.

Perhaps we could, at last, turn most of our swords into plowshares. In a highly discussed article written in 1989,[5] Francis Fukuyama asserted that the collapse of ideologies such as hereditary monarchy, fascism, and communism, and the consequent consensus concerning the legitimacy of liberal democracy as a system of government, meant an end to war. We did not know then what John Keegan, one of the world's most highly respected military historians, would say some seven years later, but most Americans would have nodded their agreement with his conclusion that while man is a volatile and risk-taking species, he is also a rational one, and that "the worst of war is now behind us and . . . mankind, with vigilance and resolution, will henceforth be able to conduct the affairs of the world in a way that allows war a diminishing part."[6] Perhaps we really had achieved what John Adams could only hope for when he declared in his 1780 letter to his wife Abigail: "I must study politics and war that my sons may have liberty to study mathematics and philosophy. My sons ought to study mathematics and philosophy, geography, natural history, naval architecture, navigation, commerce, and agriculture in order to give their children a right to study paintings, poetry, music, architecture, statuary, tapestry, and porcelain."[7]

Each time I began to wonder whether human development had finally reached the point where all disputes could be resolved in courts of law or through some other civilized mechanism, however, I remembered the ironic words of Winston Churchill decades earlier. Writing after the fact about the miscalculations and ineptness that led to the tragedy of World War I, he reflected upon all of the danger signals and the many mechanisms that had failed to prevent that conflagration: "It is nothing. It is less than nothing. It is too foolish, too fantastic to be thought of in the twentieth century. . . . No one would do such things. Civilization has climbed above such perils. The interdependence of nations in trade and traffic, the sense of public law, the Hague Convention, Liberal principles, the Labour Party, high finance, Christian charity, common sense have rendered such nightmares impossible. Are you quite sure? It would be a pity to be wrong. Such a mistake could only be made once—once for all."[8]

Still, only a bold and most insightful American could have predicted in 1991 that only ten years later, the first direct attack on the U.S. homeland since the War of 1812 would take the lives of 3,062 innocent victims, cause damage to the U.S. economy measured in billions of dollars, and strike new fear into the hearts of millions. In the early 1990s few people seriously contemplated the possibility that within a very short period of time, a small group of people or even an individual would have the capability, as well as the desire, to inflict unprecedented grief and suffering on innocent Americans through the unprovoked use of weapons of mass destruction. Few government leaders in 1991 would have agreed with Robert Kaplan, a veteran observer of wars, political upheaval, and Third World poverty: "[I]n a world in which democracy and technology are developing faster than the institutions needed to sustain them—even as states themselves are eroding and being transformed beyond recognition by urbanization and the information age—[the U.S. foreign policy of the future] will be the art . . . of permanent crisis management."[9] Fewer leaders still could have foreseen that in only eleven years a future White House Office of Homeland Security would find it necessary to issue a five-level system of graduated terrorism threat assessments for the continental United States. Almost no one anticipated that in only a decade, a U.S. president would declare in a State of the Union Address that the nation was at war, that the civilized world faced unprecedented dangers, and that the first decade of the twenty-first century would be decisive in the history of liberty.[10]

No institution of American life has been more affected by the tragic events of 11 September 2001 than the U.S. Armed Forces. The nature and rules of warfare have changed dramatically as have the ways in which the U.S. government seeks to protect the American public. No longer can U.S. military power be limited to the projection of forces to hot spots outside our country's own borders. Now, we have to worry about *homeland* security. Now, we have to expect combat aircraft flying patrols above U.S. cities and soldiers in battle dress uniform guarding parts of our domestic infrastructure. No longer is the defense of the United States carried out solely by men and women in military uniform. Now, civilian hospitals, firemen, law enforcement, and other first responder personnel, state and local officials, volunteers, nongovernmental organizations, and many others are also on the front lines of defense.

No longer is the national security strategy of the United States focused almost exclusively upon the handful of nations that pose a potential military threat to U.S. interests. No longer are the lines between foreign and domestic conflict, between war and crime, between the military and the civilian, as clear and distinct as they used to be. Now, we must worry about hidden cells of terrorists trained to kill large numbers of innocent Americans and to attack the very foundations of our economic power. Now, we must worry about transnational criminal organizations, which control large sums of money and may soon have the capability of controlling or capturing a country's government to further their goals. No longer can our strategy rest upon the traditional national elements of military, diplomatic, and economic strength. Now, domestic law as well as the laws of war must be considered. Now, the jurisdiction, resources, capabilities, and even the politics of the fifty states and hundreds of local communities are involved. No longer can Americans enjoy almost total security and unfettered freedom to promote the "general welfare" that is referred to in the Preamble to the U.S. Constitution. Now, primary attention must be given by all citizens to another objective referred to in the Preamble: providing for the "common defense."

The complete story of America's urgent first efforts to protect itself from what is arguably the most complex threat to the nation's security in its history—a threat that is likely to be present for as far as we can see—has yet to be fully lived, so it obviously cannot yet be fully told. Any book written now will undoubtedly appear elementary and incomplete by future historians better able to provide dispassionate analyses of events long past and policies long changed. There is, however, much to be said about a review at an early stage of this new and very different kind of war, providing a "snapshot in time." If our future efforts are to be successful, we must first understand where we are now and from whence we have come.

It is impossible to separate politics and the war policies of the government, or the "higher conduct of the war" on terrorism, including the defense of the U.S. homeland, from the military operations that constitute an important although not exclusive part of the means adopted to attain the ends of the policies.[11] Thus, while the objective of this book is to examine the impact of the new war upon our country's armed forces and the role of military force in homeland security, I have necessarily had to consider political factors, including the government's priorities and conduct.

While researching and writing the book, I have benefited greatly from discussions with many current and former government and military officials. I am also thankful for the assistance of Mrs. Stephanie Guerrero and Mrs. Michelle Perdue, who assisted me in the preparation of the manuscript. The views expressed herein are mine alone and do not necessarily represent the positions or policies of the Department of Defense or the U.S. government.

My perspective is somewhat unique. From 1989 to 1993 I had the privilege of serving both as assistant secretary of defense and as the senior Department of Defense official responsible for the implementation by the U.S. Armed Forces of President George H. W. Bush's national drug control strategy and the new counterdrug missions that had been given to the armed forces by law. In assigning the counterdrug responsibility to me, then Secretary of Defense Dick Cheney had relied on an organizational model similar to the position of assistant to the president for homeland security, a position that, as vice president, he subsequently recommended to President George W. Bush shortly after the terrorist attacks of 11 September 2001. It was my job to "coordinate" counterdrug policy and operations within the Department of Defense (DoD); to "integrate" DoD policy with that of other federal executive branch departments and agencies, and with the governors of all of the states and territories; and to develop and manage DoD counterdrug programs and an associated budget of approximately $1.2 billion. Those of us who were involved in the effort learned—on a daily basis—the challenges of coordinating the policy preferences of many senior officials, of integrating DoD policy and operations culture with the many autonomous departments and agencies and fifty sovereign states, and of keeping a clear view of the important differences between military operations and military support of operations conducted by federal, state, and local law enforcement agencies.

In 1997 I published *Citizen Warriors*, a book about the recent history of U.S. reserve forces and their participation in the 1990–91 Persian Gulf War against Saddam Hussein. Many of my former government colleagues in the administration of President George H. W. Bush, who were the subject of discussion in that book, are now senior officials in the administration of President George W. Bush. Many military officers with whom I worked during 1989–93 now occupy some of the most senior positions in the U.S. Armed Forces. While many of the challenges we faced in 1990–91 had to be confronted again in the first months after the 11 September terrorist attacks, in this new war of a different kind, today's policy makers must resolve complex problems we could not foresee even ten years earlier.

The danger that the United States now faces is unprecedented. In many ways, we are still unprepared for it. The potential consequences of large-scale terrorist attacks had long been understood, but until 11 September 2001 the probability of such attacks was generally considered low or even theoretical. In a government that must deal with finite resources for national security, resources for which there is always strong political competition in times when danger is not immediately apparent, priorities are established. Prior to 11 September the highest priority was only given to threats that were considered most likely to result in armed conflict. Now, we must fight a new and different kind of war even as we continuously update the war strategy, change the governmental structure of many of our national security organizations, take all prudent measures to prevent future attacks, and prepare for the protection and/or treatment of large numbers of people in the event of such attacks. We do not have the luxury of time. At any moment, the United States could face circumstances involving casualties beyond our most horrific imaginations.

Once again, Americans in military uniform will be called to bear the brunt of war. To be sure, many others will make sacrifices in the global war against terrorism and in the protection of our homeland, but almost certainly U.S. military personnel will face the greatest danger and incur the most casualties. They and their families will make the greatest sacrifices. Once again, an unprepared United States has found it necessary to provide leadership in a global conflict that affects many other nations.

It is helpful in times like these to remember that other peoples in other times have faced similar mortal dangers and that the quality and energy of our response to the new dangers we face will be nothing less than a measure of our national vigor and character. So it was in 1939 when a weak Britain faced mortal peril at the hands of a nation with which the empire had engaged in war only twenty years earlier at the cost of a million dead. The unflinching words of Winston Churchill about those circumstances are no less inspiring today than when they were written: "Once again defense of the rights [of Britain] outraged and invaded by unprovoked aggression, forced us to draw the sword. Once again we must fight for life and honor against all the might and fury of the valiant, disciplined and ruthless German race. Once again! So be it."[12] So be it.

A War of a Different Kind

1

The Unthinkable

[N]ight fell on a different world.

—President George W. Bush, Address to Congress,
20 September 2001

Almost eight months into the first year of the new millennium, most Americans were focused on routine as well as important domestic matters. Gloomy economic news and the resulting increase in public pessimism had triggered new debate on Wall Street and in Congress about how to respond. Speculation was growing that an anticipated report from the National Academy of Sciences would contain recommendations that differed significantly from the new Bush administration's policy regarding federal funding of human embryo cell research. The cover of a *Time* magazine asked, "Where Have You Gone, Colin Powell?" One of its articles explored the thesis that the secretary of state's star was shining "less brightly than expected."[1] Editorialists were engaged with questioning the proper

1

balance between interdiction/law enforcement and prevention/treatment in the war on drugs. The disappearance of a congressional intern and the continuing denial of knowledge about the disappearance by the California congressman for whom she had worked and with whom she had had an affair, was still receiving national attention. Sports fans were awaiting a decision by former NBA star Michael Jordan about whether to make a comeback with a team that had won only nineteen of eighty-two games the previous season.

At the Pentagon, efforts were under way to carry out the ambitious plans of the recently elected president. In a 23 September 1999 campaign speech at the Citadel in Charleston, George W. Bush had called for defense leaders to challenge the status quo and envision "a new architecture of American defense for decades to come." In an important article a few months later, Dr. Condoleezza Rice, who would become Bush's national security advisor, had asserted that "the next president should refocus the Pentagon's priorities on building the military of the 21st century rather than continuing to build on the structure of the Cold War. U.S. technological advantages should be leveraged to build forces that are lighter and more lethal, more mobile and agile, and capable of firing accurately from long distances."[2] She identified four key priorities that should be addressed by the next administration, one of which was "to deal decisively with the threat of rogue regimes and hostile powers, which is increasingly taking the forms of the potential for terrorism and the development of weapons of mass destruction."[3] A respected academic who would soon be appointed to the Pentagon's internal Defense Policy Board had written after the election that U.S. military forces suffered from several serious, long-term problems. "The first," Eliot Cohen argued, "is strategic. American strategy still relies on a Cold War–derived understanding of military power and fails to focus on the challenges of the new century: *homeland defense*, a rising China, and what can only be termed 'imperial policing.'"[4]

After the 2000 elections, a multitude of military analysts ventured forth with their own prescriptions. Most seemed to focus, at least implicitly, on the question of whether to engage or contain nations that had the potential to become a great-power challenger to U.S. interests. Two members of the Senate

Armed Services Committee offered seven principles for shaping a new national security strategy, including a policy of "realistic restraint" in the use of U.S. military force.[5] Gen. Tony Zinni, USMC, the commander-in-chief of the U.S. Central Command, argued the inevitability of U.S. military forces being engaged in humanitarian operations, peacekeeping, peace enforcement, and other nontraditional military missions. He categorically rejected the 1980s Weinberger-Powell doctrine, which had urged the use of U.S. combat forces only as a last resort, only for vital U.S. interests, only if there was reasonable assurance of public support, only if overwhelming force was used, only if the political and military objectives were clear, only if an exit strategy was in place, and only if the intent was to win.[6]

This was not the first time in recent years that U.S. political and military leaders had reassessed the nation's defense strategy and our country's role in what was being referred to as the "post–Cold War world." Since the collapse of the Soviet Union in 1991 several significant assessments had been made of the military posture of the United States. Each had its strengths and weaknesses, but all had been criticized because they failed to reflect all the perceived changes in the international security environment.

When George H. W. Bush assumed the presidency in January 1989 the first breezes of the later storm winds of change in the security environment were already being felt. Mikhail Gorbachev's *perestroika* and *glasnost* were the subject of intense discussion. On 12 May 1989 the president declared that it was time to move beyond a foreign policy of the containment of communism to "a new policy for the 1990s—one that recognizes the full scope of the change taking place around the world."[7] As the months passed, worldwide political change seemed to accelerate. On 25 August the Solidarity movement gained power in Poland, thus becoming the eastern bloc's first noncommunist government. On 9 November the East German government opened the Berlin Wall. On 29 December Václav Havel, a former leading opponent of communism in Czechoslovakia, was elected his country's president.

In 1990 the worldwide political upheaval continued. On 11 March the Lithuanian parliament declared independence from the Soviet Union. On

18 March the first free elections were held in East Germany. On 4 May the Latvian parliament declared independence. In his March 1990 statement of the national security strategy, the president described the change in the international landscape as "breath-taking in its character, dimension, and pace." The "familiar moorings of post-war security policy," he said, were being loosened "by developments that were barely imagined years or even months earlier."[8]

On 2 August 1990 President Bush hoped to start building momentum for substantial changes in both the defense strategy and the size and shape of the U.S. Armed Forces. In remarks prepared earlier for delivery in Aspen, Colorado, during a visit by Margaret Thatcher, Britain's prime minister, the president declared, "We are entering a new era: The defense strategy and military structure needed to ensure peace can and must be different." Fate intervened to obscure his words. Early in the morning of the same day, two armored divisions and a mechanized infantry division of the Iraqi Republican Guard attacked targets in Kuwait. Commando teams and a special operations force attacked other targets. The United States soon turned from the complexities associated with the end of the Cold War to those associated with the conduct of a hot one eight thousand miles away. The military intervention was called Desert Storm.

Work in the Pentagon became intense. Even as a military force of more than a half million troops and its logistical support was being transported to Saudi Arabia for the armed conflict against Iraq, efforts continued to shape and reduce the overall size of the military force structure that would be included in the president's defense budget recommendations to Congress in January 1991. Since the early months of 1990 a major policy debate on the subject had been taking place. In my official capacity as the assistant secretary of defense for reserve affairs, I was in the middle of the debate. A major factor influencing the discussions was the congressional mandate contained in section 1101 of the National Defense Authorization Act for Fiscal Year 1990; it required the secretary of defense to convene a study group to consider several issues, including the "optimal structure of military forces required to meet the threat."[9] An interim report had to be submitted to Congress by 15 September 1990 and the final report was due 31 December.

Opinion within Congress on what the study was really supposed to accomplish was mixed. Some members had an almost naive hope for a recommendation that would be quantitatively based and so rational and free of political bias and value judgments as to constitute some sort of inevitable truth. Others were merely seeking support for their own views. As discussed elsewhere,[10] complex decisions about the design of a nation's armed forces inevitably involve judgment. There is no mathematical formula that will guarantee a perfect military strategy or a perfect size, shape, and active/reserve mix of military forces. The exercise of judgment necessarily requires choices among competing factors and interests, all of which entail some risk.

Eventually, the Bush administration recommended to Congress a force referred to as a "base force"; it was defined as that force structure below which the nation should not go if the United States wanted "to retain superpower status."[11] The general idea was to reduce the military forces by approximately 25 percent and to maintain a relatively vigorous tempo of operations until further developments made it clear that the long-standing Soviet threat really had dissipated. In round numbers, the proposed force would include 12 active army divisions and 8 Army National Guard or reserve divisions; 450 navy ships, including 12 aircraft carriers; 16 active U.S. Air Force tactical fighter wings and 12 Air National Guard or reserve tactical fighter wings along with modernized airlift capability in the air force; 3 active U.S. Marine Corps division/air wing teams; and undefined numbers of special operations forces. The base force recommendations quickly became obsolete. On Christmas Day 1991 Mikhail Gorbachev resigned and the Soviet Union ceased to exist. The ambiguity to which President Bush had referred earlier instantly became greater.

Soon after the Clinton administration assumed office in January 1993, Les Aspin, Clinton's secretary of defense, commenced what became known as the bottom-up review (BUR). Agreeing that the new post–Cold War security environment was "more complicated, more ambiguous, and constantly changing" and asserting that a national defense was needed to meet "the *real* dangers of the new era," the BUR attempted to select "the right strategy, force structure, modernization programs, and supporting industrial base and infrastructure" for the new era.[12] The recommendations of the BUR were presented to Congress on 1 September 1993.

The key factor in the BUR, just as it had been to a great extent in the base force recommendations, was "the number of major regional conflicts (MRCs) for which the United States had to prepare."[13] The recommended force structure from the BUR, scheduled to be achieved by 1999, would, so Aspin argued, "achieve decisive victory in two nearly simultaneous MRCs."[14] It included 10 active army divisions and 37 Army National Guard brigades (15 with enhanced readiness); 346 navy ships, including 11 active aircraft carriers and 1 reserve/training carrier;[15] 13 active air force tactical fighter wings and 7 Air National Guard or reserve tactical fighter wings; and 3 active marine expeditionary forces.[16]

Members of Congress and many reformers outside of the government, however, remained frustrated with continuing interservice rivalry and what was perceived to be a combination of institutional inertia and a lack of vision by Pentagon leaders. The slowness of change was not the result of intentional resistance so much as cultural factors, such as a reluctance to reduce current readiness to meet current threats in order to develop future readiness for future threats. Eliot Cohen described the cause of the inertia: "Having won its wars cheaply (if not decisively), buttressed by formal and informal lobbies that understand their interests well, and led by competent but harried men and women who have neither the time nor the inclination to question their institutions' methods of doing business, the military will resist transformation."[17]

After making a formal finding that the BUR was insufficient "on several points, including (A) the assumptions underlying the strategy of planning to fight and win two nearly simultaneous major regional conflicts; (B) the force levels recommended to carry out that strategy; and (C) the funding proposed for such recommended force levels,"[18] and concluding that a more comprehensive review was needed, Congress took action. The National Defense Authorization Act for Fiscal Year 1997, which became effective on 1 October

1996, contained a "Military Force Structure Review Act of 1996" subsection. Originally sponsored as an amendment by Senator Joseph Lieberman, the legislation established a quadrennial defense review (QDR) process.

Designed to force each new administration to review the nation's defense program at the beginning of its term of office, the new law required the current secretary of defense, "in consultation with the Chairman of the Joint Chiefs of Staff," to complete a comprehensive examination of the defense program in 1997.[19] In order to obtain an independent (i.e., outside of the Pentagon) nonpartisan evaluation of the work of the QDR, the legislation authorized a nine member National Defense Panel. The duties of the panel were to assess both the results of the QDR and to submit a variety of possible force structures of the U.S. Armed Forces through the year 2010 and beyond. Not later than 15 May 1997 the secretary of defense was required to submit to Congress a report of the results of the QDR, including the panel's assessment of it.

In a message that accompanied his 1997 submission of the QDR report, new Secretary of Defense William S. Cohen declared that the nation could not expect to "comprehend fully or predict the challenges that might emerge from the world beyond the time lines covered in normal defense planning and budgets."[20] Having determined that the United States must continue to be engaged globally, that is, the country must exercise "strong leadership in the international community" and retain the goal of being capable of winning two major theater wars nearly simultaneously, Cohen recommended a transformation of the U.S. Armed Forces. This was defined vaguely as an exploitation of "the potential of information technologies and [the] leverage [of] other advancing technological opportunities [that would] transform warfighting."[21]

Only policy analysts who had operated in Washington for years could have anticipated the enormous fallout from Cohen's use of the word *transformation* in referring to changes needed within the country's armed forces. The term quickly became the new buzzword of the Pentagon, congressional staffers, and defense contractors.[22] Favorite weapons systems were called transformational in the hope of receiving continued funding for them. Possible new approaches to warfighting were dubbed transformational as if the mere assignment of the term would substitute for merit that was otherwise lacking. The term was soon in danger of losing all meaning.

The concept behind the term, however, had real substance. For years, it had been widely accepted that the same revolution in communications and information technology that had changed business, for example, the emergence of computerized or program trading in the securities industry, could radically change the way future wars are fought. Improvements were being made in the processing power of computers, the integration of surveillance sensors, and the development of a global communications network. Reductions in the cost of precision deep-strike weapons were being achieved. Space-based navigation, new ultra-smart munitions, robotics, stealth aircraft, nanotechnology, and new naval ship designs were becoming available. These and other technological developments were occurring at an accelerating pace. The combination of such developments and the arrival of new kinds of threats created opportunities to meet future military requirements with greater effectiveness at less cost. Some commentators defined transformation in formal terms, for example, "change in the structure of command, control, training, readiness, doctrine, technology, and organization for combat,"[23] while others saw it more generally as "a continuous process of preparedness for handling the battlefield of today and forecasting what will be on the battlefield of tomorrow."[24] Precise definition was less important than the idea of flexibility, adaptiveness, and receptivity to new thinking.

At the same time that transformation was beginning to be widely discussed, new ideas about warfighting were also gaining traction. In March 1997 the U.S. Army conducted a war-fighting exercise at its national training center in the Mojave Desert. It tested key concepts of its experimental (digitized) Force XXI for the 21st Century. Every vehicle and dismounted element in the 1st Brigade, 4th Infantry Division (Mechanized), the army's first digitized ground force, was outfitted with communications systems and computers capable of acquiring, exchanging, and employing digital information throughout the battlefield. Monitors constantly updated the locations of all friendly and known (exercise) enemy locations. The following month Adm. Jay Johnson, the chief of naval operations, delivered an address that described "a fundamental shift from what we call platform-centric warfare to something we call network-centric warfare."[25] The new form of warfare would enable the U.S. Navy to make "a shift from attrition-style warfare to a much faster and more effective warfighting style characterized by the new concepts of speed of command and self-synchronization."[26]

On 1 December 1997 the National Defense Panel released its report. It was refreshingly candid. The panel members asserted that there was "insufficient connectivity between strategy on the one hand, and force structure, operational concepts, and procurement decisions on the other" in the QDR's report. Too much, the panel concluded, was focused on "the *unlikely* contingency that two major wars will occur at almost the same time." This approach "focuses significant resources on a *low-probability scenario*, which consumes funds that could be used to reduce risk to our long-term security."[27]

In words that would have much greater resonance after 11 September 2001, the panel declared, "One of the salient features of U.S. security in 2010–2020 will be a much larger role for *homeland defense* than exists today."[28] We can assume, the nine members of the panel said, "that our enemies and future adversaries have learned from the Gulf War," that they "will look for ways to match their strengths against our weaknesses," and that they will "actively seek existing and new arenas in which to exploit our perceived vulnerabilities."[29] This new *asymmetric* threat would likely involve an adaptive adversary (no specific potential enemy was identified) who would "attack our will to fight, employ imaginative tactics and techniques, deny access to forward locations, exploit [weapons of mass destruction (WMD)] technology, target fixed installations and massed formations, move the fight to urban areas, and combine approaches for even greater synergy."[30] To provide a homeland defense against this new threat, the panel broadly recommended the use of DoD assets to "advise and assist law enforcement in combating terrorist activities," the incorporation of "all levels of government into managing the consequences of a WMD-type attack," preparation of the reserve components of the armed forces "to support consequence management activities," and other measures.[31]

The concept of *asymmetric* warfare is almost as old as warfare itself. No competent combatant wishes to meet the strength of his enemy if he can attack his enemy's vulnerabilities. In Sun-Tzu's *Art of War,* written around 512 BC and recognized as China's most profound military treatise, the king of the powerful state of Wu asked Sun-Tzu: "The enemy is courageous and unafraid, arrogant and reckless. His soldiers are numerous and strong. What should we do?" In reply, Sun-Tzu said: "Even though they are numerous, they can be taken. The Tao for attacking the arrogant is to not engage their advance front."[32] His ideas about conflict included such concepts as surprise, deception, fluidity of action, speed, and the use of strength against weakness.

Similar ideas were present eight decades later in the Peloponnesian war. Writing recently about that part of the conflict that broke out in 431 BC, Donald Kagan, a respected student of the war, asserted, "Sparta's self-assurance rested on an old thinking, and overlooked the fact that [several measures taken by the Athenian empire] amounted to what we today would call a revolution in military affairs. They permitted a new style of warfare against which traditional methods would be ineffectual."[33] The nineteenth-century Prussian general and military theorist Karl von Clausewitz also spoke of the universal desire to take the enemy by surprise: "Surprise . . . becomes the means to gain superiority, but because of its psychological effect it should also be considered as an independent element."[34] In his classic *Strategy,* B. H. Liddell Hart traced the use of the indirect approach through centuries of warfare. He crystallized the history of war into two simple maxims, the first of which is to avoid a direct attack upon a strong enemy who is firmly in position.[35]

Americans alive at the time of the Japanese attack on Pearl Harbor understand fully the effect of the element of surprise in war. A more relevant American experience, however, is Vietnam. How could a backward, poor country like North Vietnam take on a superpower with the military capability of the United States? Gen. Vo Nguyen Giap, the former North Vietnamese army chief and architect of both the Viet-Minh victory over the French at Dien Bien Phu in 1954 and the struggle against the United States, provided the answer in a series of interviews in 1990 and 1991. "You know we had very few weapons and were very backward," he said, "so how could we win? It was thanks to our creativity."[36] "A Soviet marshal once asked me . . . how many infantry divisions, tank divisions, artillery divisions I had. How much aviation. If we had fought like that, we would have been beaten in less than two hours, but we fought differently, and we won."[37] To respond that U.S. forces did not lose the war militarily and that the war ended as it did only because the American people wearied of a conflict that dragged on under ineffective political leadership, is not to deny the truth of Giap's comments.

In more recent years, these ideas had been advanced and improved upon by an unsung former fighter pilot. His contributions to the art of war would be characterized by a former commandant of the U.S. Marine Corps as rivaling those "of the greatest military minds."[38] In the mid-1970s, John Boyd developed the concept of a "time-based theory of conflict."[39] Borrowing from Sun-Tzu, Boyd asserted that a war of attrition in battle should be avoided; the intent should be to "shatter cohesion, produce paralysis, and bring about the collapse of the adversary by generating confusion, disorder, panic, and chaos."[40] Some of Boyd's followers, a small group of military reformers, later urged defense leaders to focus on what was called "fourth-generation warfare."[41] It is said that asymmetric operations are not per se the same as fourth-generation warfare, but that the former are "a defining characteristic" of the latter.[42] The reformers had long asserted that the "ubiquity of [fourth-generation warfare] requires enormous changes in military capabilities (training, doctrine, and weapons)."[43]

Such concepts were ignored by the Clinton administration. Although the administration, as it was coming to a close, claimed knowledge of "new threats and dangers—harder to define and more difficult to track—[gathering] on the horizon,"[44] it was being heavily criticized for the absence of any sense of urgency and for its lack of progress in responding to the new threat of a surprise attack by terrorists using a weapon of mass destruction. The failures of leadership that occurred during the Clinton administration are discussed in the next chapter.

But there were also other factors that contributed to a lack of progress. The Department of Defense's process for developing strategy and translating it into planning guidance to shape programs and budgets was thought by some to be broken.[45] Certainly, it needed improvement. Fear of change generally by the military services was another problem, as was each service's fear of the erosion of its individual culture. The short tenure of senior military leaders was also relevant. "Most people are naturally concerned that nothing goes wrong on their watch," declared Andrew Krepinevich, an analyst of the transformation effort. "They also want to point to clear accomplishments when they depart [and one] suspects that they are loathe to start something whose fate will depend upon the good will of their successors."[46]

In the absence of a new strategic formula by political leaders for the use of U.S. military power, military leaders were attempting to think about the use of the armed forces in ways not dependent upon known threats and doctrines. In 1996 the chairman of the Joint Chiefs of Staff released a document titled *Joint Vision 2010*. It was followed in 2000 by *Joint Vision 2020*. The documents were described as broad "conceptual templates" to guide the transformation of the armed forces. They attempted to project the kinds of forces and capabilities required in the future across the full spectrum of conflict that could be reasonably contemplated, from peacekeeping to major war. The idea presented was that U.S. military power would be based upon a "system of systems" that would "concentrate long-range firepower, instead of massing battle platforms against key enemy nodes. American firepower would be brought to bear concurrently rather than sequentially to cause the quick collapse of an enemy's resolve. The key concepts involved going beyond individualization and mass to emphasize speed and information."[47] The documents did not purport to suggest a specific strategy.

After George W. Bush was inaugurated in January 2001 the feelings of anticipation at the Pentagon were palpable. After all, unlike his predecessor, the new president had at least served briefly in military uniform. The new vice president had served very ably as secretary of defense during the Persian Gulf War in 1990–91 and was quickly emerging as a de facto prime minister. Colin Powell, the new secretary of state, had been a very visible and active chairman of the Joint Chiefs of Staff during Operations Desert Shield and Desert

Storm. Donald Rumsfeld, the new secretary of defense, had served as President Richard Nixon's ambassador to the North Atlantic Treaty Organization (NATO) and as secretary of defense under President Gerald Ford in 1974–75.

Frank Carlucci, the last secretary of defense in the Reagan administration and a Princeton wrestling teammate of Rumsfeld, characterized him as a quick study full of talent. Henry Kissinger, secretary of state while Rumsfeld was at the Pentagon, said that Rumsfeld could "adopt strategic doctrine to a new situation."[48] Both Kissinger and Carlucci declared that Rumsfeld would not only shape the U.S. Armed Forces to meet the new threats, but would build a consensus to do it.[49]

The problems of strategy and resources that the new team inherited were formidable. RAND, a research and analysis institution with close ties to the Department of Defense, had recently sponsored a study by a large bipartisan panel of defense experts, many of whom were about to join the new administration. Even ten years after the end of the Cold War, the panel acknowledged that the United States was still struggling to understand what must be done abroad to support U.S. interests and values, what the limits of power are, and what the country could do to shape the kind of world in which we want to live. The RAND panel advocated "selective global leadership" in foreign and defense policy. In practical terms, that would mean striking a difficult financial balance between short-term military readiness and long-term modernization of operating force structure and aging weapon and support platforms.[50]

Among the academicians, current and former government officials, think tank theorists, editorial leaders of the media, defense industry lobbyists, and others who constitute the policy elite of the country, there was little doubt that another broad review of the country's role in the world was necessary. One scholar described the situation. "This is an extraordinary moment in modern history," said John Ikenberry, "that in many ways is absolutely unique, where one country, the United States, has overriding power in all aspects of international life, from unmatched military prowess, unprecedented economic dynamism, to an unrelenting cultural appeal."[51] The question at the core of vigorous dispute within policy circles was as yet unanswered. Should U.S. supremacy be maintained, with all of the costs and burdens associated with the maintenance of international power, or should the nation use its influence and resources to strengthen international institutions and other democratic nations? Jeffrey W. Legro had recently used a contemporary analogy to describe the posture of the ongoing debate: "The international saga of the United States since World War II is like a variation on the script from the movie 'The Gladiator.' We entered the arena reluctantly but once inside vanquished all challengers. Now we stand alone inside the Coliseum, victorious and sword in hand, but with little idea now about what to do with Rome. What's more, we're not even very sure where the exit signs leading out of the Coliseum are located."[52]

As the Bush administration began its work, followers of the ongoing debate were surprised at early grumblings from the Department of Defense, although some was predictable. Even before the new administration had assumed office, efforts to privatize many tasks performed by military personnel and to bring modern business techniques to the department had been met with strong skepticism. Russ Bennett, an active duty critic, identified some of the trendy new buzzwords: "regionalization, mergers, realignments, outsourcing," terms he characterized as "more applicable to a Fortune 500 company than the Navy."[53] Claiming that the navy had muted into an organization more about preserving civilian jobs and propping up key defense industries than it is about sailors or combat readiness, he asked, "So, what if the trendy concept of outsourcing functions results in the eradication of a few thousand shore billets for sailors? It *did* create some civilian jobs, might have earned some legislators a few votes and I'm sure some fastidious (yet clueless) accountant can show how it'll save money (someday)."[54] Memories of the disastrous 1960s Pentagon leadership of Robert S. McNamara and his band of "Whiz Kids" also made suspect all promises to run the military establishment like a profit-seeking business. Such suspicions were not ameliorated when one savvy journalist began referring to DoD as "Pentagon, Inc."[55] or when defense industry executives were appointed as the new secretaries of the army, navy, and air force.

Few informed students of defense matters, however, doubted the need for strong leadership at the Pentagon and far more effective management. In

remarks delivered at the Pentagon on 10 September 2001, Rumsfeld characterized the Pentagon bureaucracy as "an adversary that poses a threat, a serious threat, to the security of the United States of America." Criticizing the
Pentagon's business processes, regulations, financial systems, acquisition organization, and redundant staffs, he compared them to modern business practices.
"Successful modern businesses," he said, "are leaner and less hierarchical than
ever before. They reward innovation and they share information. They have
to be nimble in the face of rapid change or they die. Business enterprises die
if they fail to adapt and the fact that they can fail and die is what provides the
incentive to survive. But governments can't die, so we need to find other incen-
tives for bureaucracy to adapt and improve."[56]

Improved defense management, however, was less central to the immediate needs of the nation than was the continuing need for a new national security strategic vision. It was already clear that events would not await a leisurely
development of a new strategy. Western European and Russian leaders had
already expressed opposition to the President Bush's plans to renegotiate or
to abandon the 1972 Anti-Ballistic Missile Treaty and to develop a national
missile defense system. There was concern that the European Union's plan for
a rapid-reaction force of sixty thousand troops for peacekeeping and other
crises would be at the expense of European support of NATO. President Bush
had also expressed a desire to withdraw U.S. troops from the Balkans, where
several thousand soldiers were stationed in Bosnia and Kosovo, an idea also
opposed by the Europeans.

Tensions with China were even greater. During his 2000 campaign, Bush
had rejected the idea of China as a strategic partner. He had suggested that
he would treat China more like a competitor and even a future adversary and
would give greater support to Taiwan. The conflict over China's April detention of the twenty-four crew members of a U.S. reconnaissance plane that
was forced to land in Chinese territory after colliding with a Chinese fighter
aircraft over the South China Sea had been resolved reasonably quickly, but
leaders of the two countries had not had time to explore common ground on
other matters.

In the Middle East, the new administration had inherited a seemingly insolvable Israeli-Palestinian crisis. International support for economic sanctions against Iraq was dwindling even though Saddam Hussein was continuing to refuse the admission of United Nations (UN) weapons inspectors. The Korean peninsula was demanding attention; North Korea was aggressively engaged in the export of weapons systems. The Himalayan region of Kashmir was a sensitive potential flash point in the ongoing dispute between Pakistan and India. Both countries were developing improved nuclear weapons. Specific concern existed about the possibility of a conflict between factions of the military in coup-prone Pakistan, which could result in Islamic fundamentalist groups in the country having access to its nuclear arsenal. In Japan, there was strong local opposition to the presence of U.S. troops in Okinawa. In Colombia, Marxist rebels financed by the illegal drug trade had placed the government in a precarious position. The Bush administration would soon have to decide what kind of assistance to provide.

In this context the Bush administration launched a major review of U.S. global strategy. Attention had been immediately focused on the new secretary of defense because it was DoD's recommendations that were likely to influence strategy development most heavily. President Bush had come to office in a historically unprecedented close election and he had no foreign policy experience. On the day after his inauguration, David Broder, a nationally syndicated columnist, pointedly asserted, "The most striking thing about the new President is that he is, by any measure, one of the least experienced figures in the upper ranks of his own administration."[57]

Donald Rumsfeld had accepted his challenges without hesitation. During his confirmation hearing he observed that the Pentagon faced a "massive reorganization" so that it can better defend the United States against twenty-first century threats. Although the task would be "enormously complex," he promised a review more sweeping than the quadrennial defense review. He boldly stated, "It is not a time to preside and tweak and calibrate what's going on." It is, he said, time "to start this transformation and see that it is continued."[58]

Turning the bold promises into reality would necessarily require many hard choices. Some future challenges were already apparent. How would the administration reconcile its plan for a large tax cut with (1) its call for an expensive missile defense system, the modernization of aging weapons systems and equipment, a military pay raise, and improvements in military housing and changes mandated by Congress in the military retirement and health care systems, and (2) the competing needs of Medicare, Social Security, and education? How could the administration make the required early program decisions on major weapons systems before coherent national security and military strategies were in place to provide a basis for making policy and budgetary trade-offs? How would the administration reconcile the grueling and historically unprecedented operational tempo of recent years (thirty-seven separate deployments of military force between 1991 and 1999, an average of one deployment every eleven weeks) with a military force that was 40 percent smaller than what existed when Bush's father took the oath of office in 1989? The defense budget had been reduced in real terms (adjusted for inflation) from $302.3 billion in 1992 to $274.8 billion in 2000.

While these and other important questions remained to be answered, the seriousness that the administration placed on its review of strategy was soon apparent. The generally accepted gap between current strategy and resources was between $60 to $90 billion per year. The armed services had warned that training and maintenance would have to be cut if an infusion of $8 billion was not made in the near term. Despite campaign rhetoric of "eight years of neglect" of the military under the Clinton administration and vice presidential candidate Cheney's highly publicized campaign promise to the military that "help is on the way," however, less than three weeks after assuming office President Bush decided not to seek an immediate boost in defense spending. "It's incumbent upon those of us in the Executive Branch," he told congressional Republicans, "to present to you a blueprint about what the military ought to look like and what the priorities ought to be."[59] "You may like it, you may not like it," he added, "but good appropriations will really only occur if there is a strategic vision."[60] Speaking to reporters, he said, "I want to know what's the plan? What is the long-range vision for the military?"[61]

Neither operational nor budgetary pressures could alleviate one major obstacle to the development of a new long-range vision: the absence of developers. A recurring fact of political life in the transition between one administration and its successor is the inordinate amount of time required to select, investigate, nominate, and confirm the presidential appointees who will become the formulators of policy in the new administration. The first secretary of the army in the Clinton administration did not assume office until ten months after Clinton's inauguration. Before a new administration's policy team arrives, the new secretary of defense has no choice but to rely upon temporary holdovers from the previous administration, career civil servants, and outside consultants. The first two groups will have participated in policy formulation for the outgoing administration and can rarely be expected to bring fresh insight, energy, or enthusiasm to the task of developing a completely new strategic vision.

One developer available to Rumsfeld was Andy Marshall, the seventy-nine year old chief of the Pentagon's office of net assessment. A civil servant, Marshall had earned his reputation as the Pentagon's resident iconoclast and foremost futurist.[62] Controversial because of his outspoken criticism of many of the assumptions upon which U.S. Cold War strategy had been based, Marshall had never even been spoken to by Clinton's first secretary of defense. A strong believer in the military advantages of stealth, speed, and advanced information technology rather than industrial age systems that used material superiority to defeat enemies by direct assault, Marshall had argued that superior information, including rapid computer processing and a profusion of ground, air, and space sensors—not massed troops or overwhelming fire power—will determine the victor on future battlefields. In his view, technology would permit the location and destruction of important targets before an enemy can react.[63] Despite, or perhaps because of his decade-long relationship with Rumsfeld, Marshall's unconventional views could be expected to draw fire. One unidentified person involved in the strategic review process predicted that the opposition of the military services to Marshall's ultimate recommendations was "likely to be fierce."[64] Speculation abounded that in the same sense that a Republican hardliner like Richard Nixon was able to forge an opening to communist China in 1972, a new conservative Republican administration would be able to force the deep military reform that many thought was necessary.

Tension about the implications of the strategic review began mounting at the Pentagon less than eight weeks into the new administration. No one had any insider knowledge about the new defense secretary. Some felt that he was "too confident in himself and too distrustful of his subordinates in the military."[65] There was a blackout of information about the substance of the review and who would participate in the assessment. There was no guidance from Rumsfeld to senior officers about how to proceed or even a request for new data. A rumor mill began, "of proportions rarely seen at the Pentagon, even since the advent of email and a 'bizarre antagonism' between . . . Rumsfeld and the uniformed military."[66] Commentators on the "guerilla strategic review" identified limited options for the administration: (1) significant increases in defense spending, (2) a combined alteration of the current strategy of being able to fight two major regional conflicts almost simultaneously and a reduction in peacekeeping and other operational commitments, which would permit cuts in the number of troops, (3) cancellation of major new weapons programs, or (4) an unpopular combination of the three approaches.[67]

Obstacles to the review were also the subject of increasing attention. A member of the House Armed Services Committee observed that bureaucratic self-interest, armed service tradition, and congressional resistance were enormous.[68] A pro-defense think tank noted that there was no Cold War threat, that Bush had not received a mandate for change similar to the one received by President Ronald Reagan in 1980, and that domestic political opposition to the cancellation of favored weapons programs were likely to determine most outcomes.[69] Others criticized the temporary team Rumsfeld had put together for the review as nothing more than "a hit-or-miss pack of outside consultants, Beltway Bandits, bureaucratic hopefuls, and retired generals," some of whom were thought to have questionable links to interested stakeholders in the debate.[70]

Rumsfeld's desire to exclude the defense industry from the review was generally supported. The reason was obvious. There was much less understanding of his effort to keep Congress and senior military leadership at arm's length.

Rumsfeld needed to receive candid advice and to consider all options. He would have to defend his ultimate policy decisions. A well-known fact of political life in Washington is that those who are not at least consulted about a matter will almost certainly fear and even presume an outcome with which they have violent disagreement.

In his September 1999 speech at the Citadel candidate George W. Bush had defined the current security threats to the United States in general terms, but he had clearly recognized that the protection of the country's homeland was now a matter of great importance. "Once a strategic afterthought," he had declared, "homeland defense has become an urgent duty." He further noted that biological, chemical, and nuclear weapons can now be delivered "not by ballistic missiles, but by everything from airplanes to cruise missiles, from shipping containers to suitcases." Defense analysts were continuing to warn in 2001 that hostile nations and even non-state groups operating outside of the framework of international relations would inevitably seek ways in the future to undermine U.S. strength by attacking its vulnerabilities.[71]

Most of the recent analysis, however, had focused on the most dangerous weapons that might be used by a weaker adversary, especially the nuclear, biological, and chemical weapons of mass destruction (WMD), or on the means by which such weapons might be delivered. The proliferation of missile technology was of particular concern after the release of the 15 July 1998 report of a commission chaired by Rumsfeld, then a private citizen. The nine commissioners had agreed unanimously that "[c]oncerted efforts by a number of overtly or potentially hostile nations to acquire ballistic missiles with biological or nuclear payloads pose a growing threat to the United States" and that the threat to the United States posed by the emerging capabilities "is broader, more mature and evolving more rapidly than has been reported in estimates and reports by the Intelligence Community."[72] North Korea, Iran, and Iraq were specifically identified as countries developing the new capabilities. A subsequent report of the commission had warned of a possible "space Pearl Harbor" if the United States did not tighten security on its satellite communication links and other space systems.[73]

As the new Bush administration was gaining its sea legs and working on the preparation of a new strategic vision, therefore, much attention had been focused on the issue of whether to deploy a national missile defense system. The issue was contentious, if for no reason other than the high cost of such a system, which would either require a substantial increase in the defense budget or the transfer of funds from defense programs more favored by others. And, there was another reason—predictable opposition from Russia and China and increased friction with European allies.

The subject of a terrorist threat to the U.S. homeland was under discussion during the early months of the new administration, but most effort was directed at threats considered much more likely to become imminent. Intelligence agencies had detected little threat activity of significance and the idea of an asymmetric threat to the United States itself was still considered by the Defense Intelligence Agency to be "more a theoretical concept."[74]

The situation changed suddenly in late spring 2001. Various pieces of information suggested that operatives of a group known as al Qaeda were planning some kind of attack on U.S. interests. The attack on the USS *Cole* a few months earlier in Yemen and other available information led analysts to believe that any attack would be made against U.S. military forces overseas. As a consequence, the threat condition for military forces in the Persian Gulf was increased, some forces were moved, travelers' alerts and warnings of possible terrorist activity were issued by the State Department, and the first of three warnings was issued to all domestic law enforcement agencies. Little public note was made by the Bush administration of these actions. According to one account, National Security Advisor Condoleezza Rice thought that the Clinton administration "had made a major mistake after the [1998] embassy bombings by saying we're going to war on terrorism and then not doing it." This opinion was shared by George Tenet, director of the CIA and a holdover from the Clinton administration.[75] The Bush administration preferred to say nothing and to deal with the problem "by putting together a plan."[76]

In August another domestic warning was issued. A meeting of the Principals Committee, the government's most senior group of national security officials, was scheduled for 4 September. The purpose of the meeting would be to consider a counterterrorism plan that had been under discussion for several months at lower levels of the government and to reach decision on a proposed new national security presidential directive (NSPD), which would establish the president's policy.[77] Lower-ranking officials had agreed that the objective should not be to "roll back" al Qaeda, but to eliminate it.[78]

While defense analysts and senior policy makers continued work on the strategic review and the Principals Committee wrestled with the question of what specific action to take against al Qaeda, most Americans were going about the business of their daily lives secure in the knowledge that our country was not at war and that we are the most powerful nation on the planet. Surrounded by two oceans and two friendly and militarily weak neighbors, there was sufficient reason to believe that short of an attack of intercontinental ballistic or cruise missiles, no foreign nation could threaten our cities or institutions. Absorbed in their work and the routine of daily life, Americans did not know that nineteen young men from the Middle East were at work on more somber business.

Most of the young men were from Saudi Arabia, but at various times in the recent past they had lived in Arizona, California, Massachusetts, and New Jersey. They were educated and leading middle-class lives. Some had gone out of their way to live openly and to blend into their surroundings. They were polite, but they kept to themselves. For the first few months of the year, some of the men had lived in Florida before moving to Laurel, Maryland, and Newark, New Jersey, in August and early September. Others moved frequently from one cheap inconspicuous dwelling to another while honing the recently learned skills that were required to fly aircraft and to use the GPS-3 global positioning system. Some studied the security procedures at airports in Newark, Boston, Portland, Maine, and at Dulles International just outside of Washington, D.C. The men used aliases and false identification as they moved about the country. A few were on a U.S. government watch list of suspected terrorists.

Using normal means, including Internet Web sites, all the men became ticketed passengers on commercial aircraft scheduled to fly from the east to the west coast. Early on the morning of Tuesday, 11 September, five of the men boarded American Airlines Flight 11 in Boston. The Boeing 767 was bound for Los Angeles. The plane took off at 7:45 AM. Thirteen minutes later, United Airlines Flight 175 left Boston, also bound for Los Angeles. That flight carried five more of the young men. At 8:01 AM United's Flight 93 departed Newark for San Francisco, carrying four of the men. Nine minutes later, the remaining five men departed Washington's Dulles International Airport aboard American's Flight 77, which was bound for Los Angeles.

At the Pentagon, the twenty-three thousand military and civilian personnel who worked there had been at their desks or walking briskly through the building's seventeen and a half miles of corridors for some time. The building is seldom quiet; it is from there that the president and secretary of defense exercise worldwide command of the nation's armed forces. At any given moment, at several places around the troubled world, actions are occurring that require the attention of watch officers. Early mornings, however, are usually particularly busy. Part of it is culture. Many lieutenant colonel and commander action officers prefer to start work as early as 6:30 AM to allow time to be prepared for the first order of the day's business with more senior officers. A 1992 publication commemorating the first fifty years of the Pentagon described it as three in one: a building, an institution, and a symbol. Characterizing it—along with the White House and the Capitol—as one of the three buildings housing institutions of the U.S. government that have come to be regarded as national monuments, Alfred Goldberg spoke with what later seemed to be prophetic words when he declared "the Pentagon above all is a metaphor of American power and influence with all the good and bad images such a symbol suggests."[79]

Since shortly after nine o'clock, many Pentagon occupants had been glued to television monitors. News of the plane crashes at New York's World Trade Towers had swept like wildfire through the offices and conference rooms. Most watched in disbelief. What they were watching was unthinkable. Several people had already concluded from the second crash that terrorists were at work. The question was: Where next? At 9:43 AM, the answer became tragically clear. The United States was again at war, this time, in a new kind of war, in a much different world.

2

Locust Years

Security against foreign danger is one of the primitive objects
of civil society. It is an avowed and essential
object of the American Union.

—James Madison, *The Federalist*, No. 41, 1787

Former Secretary of Defense Caspar Weinberger observed that history "cannot . . . be a tidy account of several well-behaved crises and episodes each of
which has a beginning, middle and an end. The best way to think of them is as
a series of overlapping concentric circles, continuously revolving and each
requiring constant attention, with a bewildering array of ever-changing events,
as the various bits and pieces of actions that went into and formed each of the
circles, shifted and shimmered in much the same way that a kaleidoscopic pattern is never still, never the same."[1] So it can be said of the history of terrorism. Certainly, it is not a new phenomenon.

Whether or not terrorism is defined as "the deliberate military targeting of civilians as a method of affecting the political behavior of nations and leaders," as Caleb Carr, a student of the tactic, has recently suggested,[2] the phenomenon can be traced back at least as far as the Roman Republic's late third century destruction of Carthage, the famous city of Antiquity and the home of Hannibal, the young military genius who surprised Rome in the Second Punic War. In modern times, terrorism has been practiced by individuals and groups as divergent as the Irish Republican Army, Hitler in his 1940–41 air attacks against the people of London, the Japanese in the rape of much of China before the Pearl Harbor attack, the Black September Terrorists at the 1972 Olympic Games in Munich, and the current defenders of extreme Islam, such as al Qaeda, Hezbollah, and Islamic Jihad.

Acts of terrorism involving Americans occurred at least as early as the late 1960s when terrorist hijackings of international flights were often the center of public attention. By 1979 acts of terror against Americans were becoming commonplace. On 4 November 1979 Iranian students seized the U.S. embassy in Tehran. Fifty-two people were taken hostage and kept in captivity for 444 days. In 1980, 278 terrorist incidents occurred and the number of casualties was climbing. Americans were increasingly becoming targets. In April 1983 the U.S. embassy in Beirut was car bombed. Early in the morning of 23 October 1983 a truck loaded with explosives crashed through the security perimeter of the marine barracks in Beirut, killing 241 and wounding 80. Acts of terror against non-American world leaders were also becoming common. Pope John Paul II was shot in St. Peters Square in 1981. Egyptian president Anwar Sadat was assassinated in Cairo in October 1981. Shlomo Argov, Israel's ambassador to Great Britain, was severely wounded in London in June 1982.

Precedent existed for a government response to the threat of terrorism. After the 1972 seizure of Israeli athletes at the Olympics and the attack of the Japanese Red Army on passengers at the Lod Airport in Israel, President Nixon created the Cabinet Committee to Combat Terrorism, a high-level group to coordinate U.S. counterterrorist efforts.[3] The new wave of terrorist attacks convinced George Schultz, President Reagan's second secretary of state, that some form of offensive action was required. He convened a series of meetings in early 1984 to explore the possible elements of a new counterterrorism policy. Believing that public debate would sharpen the thinking of policy makers, Schultz soon called for a rejection of a purely defensive posture. In a 24 June 1984 speech, he asked, "Can we as a country, can the community of free nations, stand in a purely defensive posture and absorb the blows dealt by terrorists? I think not. From a practical standpoint, a purely passive defense does not provide enough of a deterrent to terrorism and the states that sponsor it. It is time to think long, hard, and seriously about more active means of defense—about defense through appropriate preventive or preemptive actions against terrorists *before* they strike."[4] His call for action fell largely on deaf ears. Even though the disastrous April 1980 attempt by the Carter administration to rescue the hostages held in Iran had focused public attention on the military component of a national policy to counter terrorism,[5] by 1984 the executive branch of the government was still "so fragmented that it was impossible to orchestrate all counterterrorist efforts effectively or even to get agreement that there should be a specific counterterrorist effort."[6]

In the absence of a multinational or even an effective U.S. counterterrorism strategy, the attacks continued. On 12 October 1984 a bomb placed by the Irish Republican Army blew up a large part of a hotel in Brighton where Margaret Thatcher, Britain's prime minister, was staying. Nineteen days later, India's prime minister Indira Ghandhi was assassinated in New Delhi. In December Shiite terrorists hijacked a Kuwaiti airliner and forced it to Tehran. Two U.S. passengers were murdered. On 14 June 1985 terrorists hijacked a TWA flight en route to Rome from the Middle East. Most of the passengers were Americans. A U.S. Navy diver was beaten, shot in the head, and thrown out of the aircraft onto the tarmac during a temporary stop in Beirut. On 7 October 1985 the Italian cruise ship *Achille Lauro*, with four hundred passengers, was seized by Palestinian terrorists as it lay off the port of Alexandria, Egypt. A handicapped U.S. tourist was shot and thrown overboard in his wheelchair. In December twenty people, including five Americans, were killed by simultaneous attacks in the Vienna and Rome airports.

By early 1986 terrorism was registering as the greatest concern of Americans. On 6 March 1986 Vice President George Bush issued the report of the task force on terrorism. Speaking at a press conference that day, he said that "[w]e should reiterate the willingness of our Administration to retaliate and retaliate swiftly when we feel we can punish those who were directly responsible." It was not an idle threat. On 5 April a bomb blast in a West Berlin discotheque wounded fifty to sixty Americans. U.S. intelligence reports clearly placed responsibility on Libya. Nine days later U.S. naval and air forces launched a series of strikes against military facilities in Tripoli. Speaking on national television from the Oval Office, President Reagan characterized Libya's ruler, Col. Muammar Gadhafi, as an enemy of the United States. He concluded his remarks with the words, "[Colonel Gadhafi] counted on America to be passive. He counted wrong. I warned that there should be no place on Earth where terrorists can rest and train and practice their deadly skills. I meant it. I said that we would act with others, if possible, and alone if necessary to ensure that terrorists have no sanctuary anywhere. Tonight we have."[7]

With the U.S. strike against Libya much on their minds, the leaders of the seven leading industrial democracies met in Tokyo three weeks later at their annual conference. A joint declaration was issued; it stated that "[t]errorism has no justification." Terrorism was condemned "in all its forms," including its accomplices and "those, including governments, who sponsor or support it." A second initiative was taken by the United States. As a result of the findings of Bush's task force, President Reagan formalized counterterrorism policy in National Security Decision Directive (NSDD) 207. NSDD-207 assigned responsibility for domestic terrorism to the Federal Bureau of Investigation (FBI). Jurisdiction for international terrorism was assigned to the Department of State.

With the successful conclusion of the Persian Gulf conflict in February 1991 the Bush administration turned again to the deepening crisis in the Soviet Union and the management of what was being described as a "new world order." In the August 1991 statement of its national security objectives, the administration declared that the world was in a period of transition. The nation was being confronted by dangers more ambiguous than those previously faced;

it must be prepared to counter security threats that were "short of armed conflict, including the threat of international terrorism."[8]

National security issues had little or no effect on the 1992 presidential election. Bill Clinton knew this was not his area of strength. His lack of experience did not, however, prevent him from making large promises. According to David Hendrickson, Clinton's "strategy in the game of political poker he played with Bush was to see all bets the incumbent had placed and then raise him."[9] The result was that there was "scarcely an item on the wish-list of contemporary American internationalism—preventing aggression, stopping nuclear proliferation, vigorously promoting human rights and democracy, redressing the humanitarian disasters that normally attend civil wars—where Clinton promised a more modest role."[10]

Soon after assuming the presidency in January 1993 it became clear that Clinton was "quite uninterested in foreign policy, which would include intelligence matters as well."[11] Even the Central Intelligence Agency (CIA) director was unable to meet personally with Clinton and this lack of access became the subject of White House jokes.[12] David Gergen, who worked for several different presidents including Clinton, expressed the view that because of his lack of interest in foreign policy matters, Clinton spent only 25 percent of his time on the subject in the early years of his presidency compared to the 60 to 75 percent of other presidents.[13] In winning the election, Clinton defeated an incumbent who was a combat veteran of World War II. George H. W. Bush's foreign policy credentials were among the best of any individual who had ever held the presidential office. His popularity had skyrocketed after the overwhelming U.S. victory in the Gulf War the year before the election. Clinton also won despite adverse publicity from a letter written as a youth expressing "loathing" for the military, his efforts to dodge the draft, and his participation in demonstrations against the war in Vietnam while he was in Britain on a Rhodes scholarship.

What Clinton *was* interested in was certain promises that he had made in his campaign. In his first meeting with the Joint Chiefs of Staff five days after his inauguration, he said not one word about his plans for the post–Cold War

U.S. relationship with Russia and China, difficulties with Saddam Hussein, emerging terrorists threats, or the conflict in Bosnia. Rather, he said that he was interested in keeping his campaign promise to remove the prohibition against military service by gays.[14] On this issue, he was strongly opposed not only by the senior leaders of the U.S. Armed Forces, but also by influential members of his own party.

Less than four weeks after Clinton's meeting with the Joint Chiefs of Staff, a terrorist bomb was detonated in the parking garage of New York's World Trade Center. The blast killed six people, wounded over one thousand, and caused massive destruction. It was the largest incident handled in the 128-year history of New York City's fire department.[15] It was the first attack by foreign terrorists on U.S. soil. After the attack, Clinton never visited the site. He referred to the attack only once during the regularly scheduled Saturday radio address shortly after the bombing and he urged Americans not to "overreact."[16] In the ensuing two years, he never met with the CIA director to discuss the possibility of another attack.[17]

For the first twenty-four months of his presidency, Clinton predictably focused on domestic matters. The early tenure was marked by several blunders that did not improve his relationship with the leadership of the U.S. Armed Forces. His "early defeats and stumbles and his tendency to back down," said one critic, left the impression "that not only were he and his administration not quite up to the job, but perhaps worse, that under pressure and opposition, he might quickly fold."[18] There were also distractions. On 20 July 1993 the White House's deputy counsel was found dead from a self-inflicted gunshot wound. On 20 January 1994 the U.S. attorney general selected an independent counsel to head a federal investigation into matters relating to Whitewater Development Corp., a company formed by the Clintons in the late 1970s. On 11 February 1994 Paula Jones, a former Arkansas State employee, filed a civil action in the U.S. District Court for the Eastern District of Arkansas, accusing Clinton of making persistent, continuous, and unwanted sexual advances toward her during a business conference prior to the 1992 election. On 26 July 1994 Congress commenced hearings into the Whitewater matter. On 5 August

Kenneth Starr, a former federal judge and U.S. solicitor general, was named the new independent counsel in the investigation of Whitewater-related matters. On 6 December Webster Hubbell, a close friend of the Clintons and a former U.S. associate attorney general in the administration, pled guilty to mail fraud and tax evasion.

Over two years into Clinton's first term, terrorism was still not receiving much attention. In a 2 March 1995 presidential decision directive (PDD), which established intelligence collection priorities, terrorism ranked third behind support for ongoing military operations and analysis of potential enemies in Russia, China, Iraq, and Iran.[19] Terrorism was still perceived by most Americans to be a form of violence that took place in the Middle East, or at least elsewhere. On 20 March 1995 a Japanese "doomsday cult" released the nerve agent sarin into the Tokyo subway system. Suddenly, the threat was brought home to the consciousness of Americans. Political leaders became sensitized to the obvious fact that if such an incident could take place in Tokyo, it could also take place in Los Angeles, New York, or Chicago.[20] Thirty days later terrorism hit home again. On 19 April a truck bomb destroyed the Murrah Federal Building in Oklahoma City, killing 168 people. It was the worst terrorist attack on U.S. soil in the country's history.

On 21 June the White House issued PDD-39, a general policy statement on counterterrorism. While it would later be described by members of the Clinton administration as among the most important policy documents of his presidency, the document only generally described certain policy goals. For example, it stated, "The United States shall reduce its vulnerabilities" and "The United States shall seek to deter terrorism." It did, however, recognize a new form of terrorism, one involving weapons of mass destruction. As a result of the sarin attack in Tokyo, concern about earlier kinds of terrorism such as kidnapping of diplomats, hijacking of commercial aircraft, and protest bombings was being replaced by a new concern for possible terrorist attacks involving nuclear, biological, or chemical materials or weapons. PDD-39 directed the National Security Council (NSC) to "coordinate" interagency terrorism policy issues.

Four months later, in a speech celebrating the fiftieth anniversary of the United Nations, President Clinton suggested to the gathered world leaders a "challenging agenda" of global terrorism, organized crime, drug trafficking, and the smuggling of nuclear weapons. He invited them to join in an international declaration on citizens' security that he said would commit countries to deny sanctuary to terrorists, narcotics traffickers, and other international criminals.[21] The terrorist threat was still being characterized as a criminal matter, to be addressed by declarations, rather than a national security matter requiring action. On 13 November 1995, twenty-two days after the president's UN speech, an explosion occurred at a U.S.–leased office building in Riyadh, Saudi Arabia, from which U.S. soldiers and civilians trained the Saudi Arabian National Guard. Four persons were killed and almost forty were wounded.

The urgency of the terrorist threat and the dangers posed by the proliferation of weapons of mass destruction and their delivery systems were discussed in some detail in an April 1996 publication from the Office of the Secretary of Defense. The preface contained chilling, sobering, words: "The proliferation of these horrific weapons presents a grave and urgent risk to the United States and our citizens, allies and troops abroad. Reducing this risk is an absolute priority of the United States."[22] Two months later, a massive explosion outside of the Khobar Towers, a U.S. Air Force housing complex in Dhahran, Saudi Arabia, killed nineteen people and wounded nearly five hundred.

On 5 August 1996 the rhetoric about the threat continued. In brief remarks at George Washington University, the president claimed that he was pursuing a "concerted national and international strategy on three fronts."[23] The first front identified was the planned opening of law enforcement offices in six countries and an effort to "rally other nations to the fight against terrorism."[24] The second part of the purported strategy was a request for legislation to increase wiretap authority and to require the marking of chemicals that could be used in making bombs "without undermining our civil liberties."[25] The third element was an increase in hand searches and machine screening of luggage at airports and preflight inspections of aircraft.

Despite the rhetoric, little action was taken by the White House to address the growing threat, other than polling by the president's political consultants to assess the possible impact of the issue upon his reelection campaign. Clinton himself remained passive. He may have been distracted again. On 22 March 1996 a federal appeals court panel overseeing the investigation of the independent counsel expanded the Counsel's authority to include the administration's firing of several long-time employees of the White House Travel Office. In May the independent counsel obtained convictions of Jim Guy Tucker, the governor of Arkansas, and James McDougal and Susan McDougal, Clinton's Whitewater partners. On 25 October 1996, only days before the election, the judicial panel granted the independent counsel authority to investigate the White House's improper request for the confidential FBI files on nine hundred Republicans who had served in previous administrations, including the file on former Secretary of State James Baker.[26] "Even as he fretted about whether to sign the welfare reform act and brooded about the FBI, Paula Jones and Whitewater scandals," Dick Morris, one of the president's advisors, later reported, "he seemed curiously uninvolved in the battle against terror."[27]

Action had been taken by Congress. Senators Sam Nunn, Richard Lugar, and Pete Domenici led the enactment of Title XIV of the Fiscal Year 1997 Defense Authorization Act, which became known as the Defense against Weapons of Mass Destruction Act. The legislation was an effort to improve the capabilities of federal, state, and local emergency response agencies to prevent or respond to domestic terrorist incidents. It called for the training and equipping of cities over a four-year period. In response to the legislation, the Department of Defense established the goal of providing training to officials in the largest 120 U.S. metropolitan areas by the end of 1999. Unfortunately, competition for resources suddenly made available for defense against terrorism spawned ninety different programs for the single purpose to which the legislation was directed.[28]

The second Clinton administration began with a new secretary of defense. Former senator William S. Cohen was sworn into office on 24 January 1997. His first task was to complete the next congressionally mandated quadrennial defense review (QDR). In a 19 May news release accompanying the issuance of the QDR report, it was described as "a comprehensive assessment of the nation's defense requirements, based on emerging threats to U.S. security over the next two decades."[29] Little was said in the QDR report, however, about specific actions that were planned to counter asymmetric threats other than "increased focus and funding" and "efforts to enhance intelligence collection capabilities and protect critical infrastructure."[30]

In February 1997 the Federal Emergency Management Agency (FEMA) issued a terrorism incident annex to the federal response policy statement included in PDD-39, which had been issued almost two years earlier. The stated purpose of the annex was to "describe the Federal concept of operations to *implement* PDD 39." FEMA broke the concept into separate elements of "crisis management" and "consequence management." By declaring that crisis management would be predominantly a law enforcement response, the annex stated that federal law assigns: (1) Primary authority to the federal government to prevent and respond to acts of terrorism; state and local governments provide assistance as required, and (2) primary authority to the states to respond to the consequences of terrorism; the federal government provides assistance as required. The annex did not offer any kind of a national strategy on terrorism.

The administration's warnings about the increased danger to the United States, however, continued. In a November 1997 op-ed article, Secretary Cohen declared, "Terrorists groups and even religious cults will seek to wield disproportionate power by acquiring and using those weapons that can produce major casualties."[31] He further stated that the Department of Defense had begun to treat the threat of chemical and biological weapons as a likely and early condition of warfare. "Most ominous among these threats is the movement of the front line of the chemical and biological battlefield from foreign soil to the American homeland."[32]

No one could have predicted the bizarre series of events that would affect the nation's reaction to terrorism in 1998. The year started with the president's involvement in several matters unrelated in any way to matters of national security. In May 1997 the U.S. Supreme Court had unanimously rejected his request that the Paula Jones lawsuit against him be delayed until he left office. In January 1998 his deposition was taken in that case and he was immediately forced to deal with new allegations that he had engaged in a sexual relationship with a young White House intern. On 3 March James McDougal, the president's former Whitewater business partner, died in his prison cell.

Meanwhile, the escalating violence in Kosovo was causing the administration to consider military intervention in the Balkans to stop the actions of Slobodan Milosevic, the president of what remained of Yugoslavia who was fanning the flames of Serb nationalism. The timing could hardly have been worse. Aside from the fact that much of the military leadership did not believe that the conflict in the Balkans was sufficiently connected to important U.S. security interests to warrant intervention, institutional suspicion and dislike of the president complicated the policy equation.

This is not the place to fully analyze the unusual tension that existed between Clinton and most senior military leaders early in his first administration. It should be noted, however, that by 1998, the sixth year of the Clinton presidency, the tension was not primarily the result of the actions he had taken as a young man to evade military service, the blunders he had made early in his first term including his handling of the 1993 incident in Mogadishu, Somalia, involving Task Force Ranger,[33] or even his proclivity to use military force as the first tool of foreign policy rather than the last. No, it was more than that. A great part of the problem was the cultural clash between two totally different value systems. David Halberstam, a journalist and historian who has covered military affairs for more than three decades, described the tension. "[T]he senior military men still did not really trust Clinton and the people around him, and he, in turn, . . . did not trust them. Their purposes were more often than not different, their codes were different, their journeys to the top were different, their Americas were different, and their worlds were different."[34] The differences did not stimulate close consultation on what appeared to be a distant, but increasingly important, threat of terrorism.

In May 1998 PDD-62 was signed by the president. It attempted to clarify the terrorism-related responsibilities of the departments and agencies. Read in conjunction with PDD-39, it made the FBI the lead federal agency for responding to domestic terrorism. The State Department was assigned lead agency responsibility for international terrorist incidents. PDD-62 also created the Office of the National Coordinator for Security, Infrastructure Protection and Counterterrorism. John Roos, the editor of a military journal, later wrote, "on paper, at least," the government's counterterrorism activities were in good order, but in reality, "the NSC's National Coordinator oversees a complex, labyrinthine organization—one that is, in many cases, only loosely strung together by the dedicated efforts of mid-level managers of many stripes."[35]

At approximately 10:30 AM local time on 7 August 1998, powerful explosions rocked the U.S. embassies in the Kenyan capitol of Nairobi and the Tanzanian capitol of Dar es Salaam. Both explosions were the result of bombs detonated near the embassies. Over three hundred African and U.S. citizens lost their lives. Thousands more were seriously injured. On 17 August the president testified before a federal grand jury about his relationship with the White House intern. In a televised address following his testimony, he admitted having had a relationship with the intern that was not appropriate and that he had misled the public and his family about the nature of the relationship. Three days later, military strikes with cruise missiles were carried out against terrorist training facilities in remote regions of Afghanistan and a pharmaceutical plant in northeast Khartoum, Sudan. In a sign of the times, Secretary of Defense Cohen found it necessary to alleviate public suspicion by giving assurance that while the purpose of the attack was limited to the disruption and possibly the destruction of the sites, it had not been made for the purpose of diverting attention away from the president's legal problems. "The only motivation driving this action," the secretary said, "was our absolute obligation to protect the American people from terrorist activities."[36]

For the remainder of the year, the attention of the White House, Congress, and the public was not focused primarily on security matters, but on an evolving story with historic implications. On 9 September the independent counsel submitted his report on the investigation of the relationship between Clinton and the White House intern to the House of Representatives. The report—

with all of its jarring, graphic detail—was released to the public on 11 September. On 8 October the House of Representatives voted to commence an impeachment investigation of the president's conduct. On 13 November the president agreed to pay Paula Jones $850,000 to settle the sexual harassment lawsuit against him. On 16 December the United States and Britain launched four days of air strikes against Iraq. In a televised address, the president said the attacks were carried out because of Iraq's refusal to cooperate with UN weapons inspectors. On 19 December the House of Representatives approved two articles of impeachment against the president. The first article charged that he had given "perjurious, false and misleading testimony to [a federal] grand jury." The second charged that he had obstructed justice in the Paula Jones sexual harassment action. He was the first elected president to be impeached in the nation's history.

As the tumultuous year came to a close, it could at least be said that federal funding for the defense against terrorism had increased in recent years and that various broad organizational programmatic schemes had been proposed or initiated. Unfortunately, the funding and new programs had taken place in the absence of what was later characterized as "the critical analysis and rigorous prioritization needed to establish clear and well-defined requirements" for the efforts.[37]

The problems involved in defending the United States from an attack by either terrorists or rogue states were not respectful of the press of personal problems upon the American president. The independent commission, led by Donald Rumsfeld, concluded in 1998 that the threat of a ballistic missile attack involving a weapon of mass destruction had matured so rapidly that the United States could be subjected to such an attack "with little or no warning."[38] After studying the Clinton administration's policy statements on terrorism and weapons of mass destruction, a private consulting firm concluded that "[a] real strategy has not yet been offered nor have solutions to bureaucratic obstacles."[39] The firm noted two policy initiatives by the administration to establish mechanisms for the coordination of efforts to protect critical infrastructures,[40] but it expressed doubt about "the level of commitment" in the initiatives and uncertainty about how far the changes would extend.[41]

The bureaucratic challenges involved in the preparation of effective home-land security are unquestionably formidable. The need to coordinate policy and actions between the federal departments and agencies, and between the federal government and hundreds of state and local governments—all in the context of ensuring the protection and defense of the U.S. homeland—is with-out precedent. The complexity of the challenge in 1998 was obvious. "Interagency coordination is no small task," the consulting firm said, "even among agencies accustomed to participating in the national security commu-nity. Bring to the mix agencies with little experience in national security activ-ities, states, and territories, and a private sector reluctant to address their own vulnerabilities in a public forum, and the degree of complexity becomes evi-dent. Counterterrorism alone involves the integration of no less than 40 U.S. agencies but is at least recognized as a federal responsibility. Critical infra-structure protection, on the other hand, requires the active participation of the private sector, which owns or operates (under close regulation) nearly all of the relevant assets."[42] The problem had been made worse by overlapping legal jurisdiction, fragmentation of effort, redundancy, an absence of standards, the complexity of the structure of the federal government, and the widely vary-ing resources and expertise of individual departments and agencies at all lev-els of government.

Subsequent to the bombing of the Murrah Federal Building in Oklahoma City, the FBI had been given lead agency responsibility for *crisis management,* defined as predominantly a law enforcement response. FEMA had been given lead agency responsibility for what was called *consequence management,* which included measures to protect public health and safety, restore essential gov-ernment services, and provide emergency relief to government, businesses, and individuals. The Department of Justice later acknowledged, however, that "there is often no clear point in time when resolution of a terrorist incident moves from the crisis to consequence management stage. Indeed, these phases may occur simultaneously or, in some cases, the consequence management phase may actually precede the identification of a terrorist event."[43] Successful preparation for homeland security, therefore, involves several elements. It requires leadership. It requires a comprehensive strategy. It requires effective organization and coordination.

Unfortunately, these elements continued to be missing in 1999. In January a homeland defense working group of the Center for Strategic and International Studies (CSIS) issued a report that addressed the issue of the role of the U.S. Armed Forces in a plan of response to a terrorist attack. It concluded that if such an incident was threatened or actually took place in wartime, the Defense Department would have to take the lead responsibility because only the armed forces would have "the managerial and logistical capabilities to mount the all-out defensive effort called for by the enormity" of such a threat.[44] CSIS further concluded, "Inadequate or insufficiently understood legal authorities for a military role . . . pose significant national security risks," and "today DoD is not prepared for this mission."[45] In April the president of Business Executives for National Security (BENS) was quoted as saying: "What's less heartening is that there doesn't seem to be a clear U.S. policy in place for responding to the new terrorism threat."[46] In an unclassified version of a classified May 1999 report the General Accounting Office (GAO) declared, "Proposed interagency Domestic Guidelines have not been completed or coordinated with all federal agencies with domestic counterterrorism roles. For example, the FBI has not coordinated the proposed Domestic Guidelines with the Department of the Treasury even though it could have a significant role in an actual terrorist incident. Furthermore, approval of proposed interagency International Guidelines has been delayed because the Department of State, the Department of Justice and the FBI have not reached agreement on the level of State participation in highly sensitive missions to arrest suspected terrorists overseas."[47] The GAO also found that despite explicit statutory language that directed FEMA to conduct interagency field exercises to test its consequence management role in the event of a major terrorist attack, no such exercises had been planned.[48]

In July 1999 the congressionally mandated bipartisan Commission to Assess the Organization of the Federal Government to Combat the Proliferation of Weapons of Mass Destruction reported to Congress that the "nation lacks a comprehensive policy and plan to meet the threat posed by the proliferation of weapons of mass destruction."[49] The commission further concluded that the efforts of the government had been "neither effective nor [did they] command an appropriately high policy priority in the Executive Branch of the Government."[50] This conclusion was of more than passing interest because this particular commission was chaired by John M. Deutch, who had served as President Clinton's deputy secretary of defense (1994–95) and as his director of the CIA (1995–96). On 15 September 1999 another bipartisan commission, the U.S. Commission on National Security/21st Century concluded that the United States was not prepared to defend itself against terrorist threats at home.[51]

In the absence of a national strategy or other comprehensive policy guidance from the president, and despite its effort to share with other departments and agencies whatever lessons were learned during coordination meetings and field training exercises,[52] the Department of Defense was left to its own devices in an effort to organize for the defense of the U.S. homeland. The same problem had arisen during the Vietnam conflict when civilian leaders failed to make decisions on basic strategic issues, thus leaving the military commander no choice but "to invent his own strategic concept."[53] On 1 October the Joint Task Force for Civil Support (JTF-CS) was created within the new U.S. Joint Forces Command. The task force focused exclusively on consequence management, that is, on providing troops that had special skills and equipment to support the FBI, FEMA, and other federal agencies during the aftermath of a WMD event. Contrary to the principle of assigning only the most senior and experienced officers to the problems of greatest difficulty, the officer who was appointed to head the task force was a relatively junior general officer. He was given a small staff and his office was established at Fort Monroe, Virginia. His responsibility, however, was substantial. Once military support to civil authorities was authorized, JTF-CS would be deployed to the site of the catastrophe to act as the command and control element for all DoD units ordered to respond.

The matter of military support to civil authorities is discussed further in Chapter 5, but it should be noted here that this initiative was based upon two implicit and false premises. First, that the support required of the armed forces in the event of catastrophic terrorist attacks in the United States would always be limited and it was not necessary to place responsibility for that support in the hands of a more senior officer. Second, it was assumed that a military officer should be in charge of what is, in reality, a high-level federal/state/local political leadership/management challenge. A catastrophic terrorist attack would almost certainly affect people in several states and hundreds of communities. Political and managerial pressures and problems created by the competing demands of state and local officials for military resources and expertise would escalate very quickly and necessarily require the immediate intervention of senior federal officials.

Immediate policy development and civilian oversight of the civil support function, however, was not placed in the hands of the secretary of defense, the deputy secretary of defense, any of the four undersecretaries (two of which were created by the Clinton administration), or even any of the assistant secretaries of defense. Rather, it was assigned to a junior official who was not even a presidential appointee. The assistant to the secretary of defense for civil support position had responsibility for incidents involving a weapon of mass destruction, but the Department of the Army's director of military support continued to be responsible for non-WMD contingencies. The arrangement was soon the subject of criticism because it did "not provide clear lines of authority and responsibility or ensure political accountability."[54]

In one area of policy, the Department of Defense had a clear plan of action, but it failed to perform. In May 1998 a program was unveiled to set up twenty-seven (later increased by Congress) specifically trained National Guard civil support teams that would be capable of responding to nuclear, chemical, and biological weapons attacks in all fifty states. The first ten teams were to be certified as ready to assist civil authorities by April 2000. In February 2001 the Department of Defense's inspector general issued a report that concluded that after three years and the expenditure of $143 million, the National Guard program had been sidetracked by poor training, defective equipment, and design flaws. Thirteen months after the target date, not a single team had received certification or was even fully operational.[55]

The leadership, organizational, and other related problems continued during the last year of the Clinton administration. Whether the distrust between the president and the senior military leadership contributed to the failure to take decisive action regarding the terrorist threat is doubtful, but relations did not improve. The president was acquitted on 12 February 1999 by the Senate of the impeachment charges brought by the House, but the acquittal was due less to a general belief that he was innocent of the charges than a conclusion by some that, despite the conduct that led to the charges, he should not be removed from office. Senator Robert Byrd, for example, a member of Clinton's political party, declared on the floor of the Senate that "the evidence against Mr. Clinton shows that he willfully and knowingly and repeatedly gave false testimony under oath in judicial proceedings."[56] Nevertheless, he voted to acquit.

Many military men and women were offended by the president's dalliance with a young intern in the White House. It was not because they operate under an illusion that the private lives of all civilian leaders are models of faultless conduct. Nor was it because all military people are prudes. Military leaders deal daily with the kind of realism reflected in Rudyard Kipling's poem about the British soldier Tommy Atkins: "[S]ingle men in barracks don't grow into plaster saints."[57] It was because the dalliance took place in the White House, the place from which Lincoln had acted to save the Union, where Roosevelt and Churchill had mapped strategy in World War II, and where Kennedy had faced the Soviets during the Cuban Missile Crisis. It took place in one of the enduring symbols of the presidency, the U.S. government, and the American people.

But even this was not the main reason for the continuing distrust of Clinton by much of the military leadership. The main reason can be summed up in one word: honor. "What the military in its codes valued more than anything else," Halberstam concluded, "was honor."[58] Many expected the language of politicians to be more ambiguous than what they used. But ambiguity is much different from willful, knowing, and repeated "false testimony under oath in judicial proceedings." In the dangerous world in which military people operate, lying is absolutely unacceptable. Lives may be at stake. People in uniform also work in a world of strict accountability. They knew that if they had engaged in the same conduct as their commander-in-chief, they would have been

court-martialed and convicted; their military careers would have been terminated. The lack of trust in Clinton had consequences. Richard Kohn, a scholar
who has written widely on civil-military affairs, concluded that the Clinton
administration's "indifference to military affairs and the decision to take no risks
and expend no political capital in that area produced paralysis."[59]

On 15 December 1999 the bipartisan Advisory Panel to Assess Domestic
Response Capabilities for Terrorism Involving Weapons of Mass Destruction,
also known as the Gilmore Commission, concluded that "valid concern
remains that the United States is still not appropriately organized and prepared to counter and respond to the threat of either mass casualty or [chem-
ical, biological, radiological, and nuclear] terrorism."[60] A full year later and
only one month before Clinton left office, the same commission concluded,
"The United States has no coherent, functional national strategy for combating terrorism."[61] In a report submitted on 7 June 2000, the congressionally established National Commission on Terrorism noted that international
terrorism posed "an increasingly dangerous and difficult threat to America."
An attack with a weapon of mass destruction, the commission asserted, "even
if it succeeds only partially, could profoundly affect the entire nation."[62] The
report concluded, "The government must do more to prepare for such an
event."[63] Even the National Security Council staffer responsible for overseeing the $11 billion counterterrorist programs agreed that the federal efforts
had been fragmented.[64]

Four and half years after the seriousness of the threat had been recognized
and three years after he had declared in an op-ed piece that the threat of terrorist attack with chemical and biological weapons is a likely and early condition of warfare, Secretary of Defense Cohen conceded in a speech at the CSIS
that no comprehensive policy to protect the country existed. "We have yet to
begin the debate on homeland defense," he said, and "if you think about it in
terms of terrorism coming to U.S. soil, the prospects are that you will see multiple attacks that will occur nearly simultaneously."[65] After acknowledging that
the Department of Defense would be asked for assistance in the event of mass
casualties from multiple attacks, he said, "We need to work this out in advance,

so that we don't have the kind of constitutional challenge or confusion taking place in those times of crises."[66]

By any fair standard, the response of the Clinton administration to the recognized threat of terrorism was marked by excessive caution and the absence of presidential leadership. Daniel Benjamin and Steven Simon, two former members of the administration, have attempted to explain and justify the inaction and lack of effective action. They have cited Federal Rule of Criminal Procedure 6E, which generally forbids the release of information presented to federal grand juries; the "failure" of James Woolsey, Clinton's first director of central intelligence; congressional objections to certain steps; bureaucratic stagnation; the conservatism of the armed forces; the lack of money; reluctance to take action that might have "constrained the next President's room for maneuver"; and circumstances that prevented action because it was not "politically feasible.[67] Incredibly, they have argued that presidents are greatly handicapped by the "minimal powers accorded them by the Constitution and established practices of American government," by the "little real power" of the White House, and by the inability to make changes in the executive branch of government. ("Only so much crockery can be broken before there is a news story, an embarrassment, and a public brouhaha no one wanted.")[68] For reasons that are discussed in Chapter 6, it is very likely that Presidents Abraham Lincoln, Theodore Roosevelt, and Franklin D. Roosevelt would be amazed to hear such rationalizations.

Although he later claimed some antiterror accomplishments, Clinton also acknowledged failures.[69] Through his final day in office, "terrorism on the grand scale remained a hypothetical danger."[70] The main reason for inaction was a lack of political will and courage. Clinton preferred to follow public opinion rather than to lead it. Barton Gellman, a journalist who studied the administration's performance, concluded, "Though his government came to believe that the Taliban was inextricably tied to [Osama] bin Laden, Clinton never seriously entertained the use of military force against the Islamic fundamentalist regime."[71] He permitted the al Qaeda sanctuaries in Afghanistan to continue training thousands of new terrorists with impunity. Many world leaders and members of his administration were dismayed. In an interview with the German newspaper *Bild* soon after the 11 September 2001 attacks, Russian president Vladimir Putin recalled his own discussions with the Clinton administration about Osama bin Laden: "They wrung their hands so helplessly and said, 'The Taliban are not turning him over, what can one do?' I remember I was surprised: If they are not turning him over, one has to think and do something."[72]

Clinton's assistant secretary of defense for special operations, recalled, "There was a growing sense over time" that the national leadership should "get off the pot" and decide whether to strike.[73] His assistant secretary of state for South Asian affairs attempted to justify the inaction by declaring that "there was certainly not any ground swell of support to mount a major attack on the Taliban."[74] Clinton's last assistant secretary of state for counterterrorism expressed thoughts undoubtedly shared by many others who served in the administration: "In light of September 11th, we ought to do some soul-searching. That's what I'm doing. But it has to be said that it was the collective judgment of the American people, not just the Clinton Administration, that the impact of terrorism was at a level that was acceptable."[75]

In an essay written in April 1999 Ralph Peters, a military theorist described by the *Pittsburg Post-Gazette* as "arguably the best thinker . . . on international affairs in America today," put the matter this way: "Our problems lie with a generation of leaders who deemed themselves of too much worth to serve in uniform, and who arrived at the pinnacle of power ignorant of what militaries can and cannot do. It is a generation accustomed to easy success, and it cannot understand why bloody-minded foreigners behave so badly. . . . [I]t is a generation sheltered from much of the world's reality. It knows how to win elections, but not how to lead. And leadership is crucial to the effective use of the military. . . . [T]he leader is the most important factor in deciding between victory or defeat. . . . This has not changed since the battle of Jericho, or the fall of Troy."[76]

Napoleon's second maxim of war was that in formulating a plan for a military campaign, it is imperative to foresee everything that the enemy may do, and be prepared with the necessary means to counteract it.[77] A national strategic plan of defense against a major terrorist attack—a truly comprehensive national approach to the establishment of policies, programs, and operations—must necessarily be based on the intelligence estimates of the federal intelligence agencies. Such a plan can be formed effectively only by the federal government. But, and this is an important qualification, while a strategic plan must be more than the sum of the plans of the individual states or the individual federal departments and agencies, however good those individual plans may be, the plan must be developed with the active support and recommendations of the states and local authorities. Policy guidance must identify national objectives, set clear priorities, and identify lines of authority and responsibility with as much precision as possible. The policy guidance must be understood and enthusiastically—or at least aggressively—implemented by the federal, state, and local departments and agencies that must be involved in efforts to prevent an attack or, failing that, respond effectively to it.

In the spring of 1999 I took advantage of a brief professional interlude to work at the National Defense University in Washington, D.C., to study the Clinton administration's approach to the terrorist threat. I was particularly interested in the way the government was being organized to meet the threat. When I began work I suspected that the problems of overlapping jurisdiction, turf fights, and finding effective ways for the armed forces to support federal and state agencies in the counterterrorism effort were very similar to those I had encountered from 1989 to 1993. During that period, I had the privilege of serving as the Department of Defense official responsible for the implementation by the armed forces of President George H. W. Bush's national drug control strategy and additional counterdrug missions assigned to the armed forces by law. Because I had no responsibility for the government's actions in 1999, I was able to take a detached view of matters through the prism of my past experience while I reviewed the conclusions of the several independent commissions studying various aspects of the terrorism threat.

Over several months of research and reflection, it became clear to me that the absence of presidential leadership was the major problem. While Congress has significant national security responsibilities, only the president can provide the clear direction, force, and energy necessary. I began to publicly speak about the problem. In a speech delivered eleven months prior to the 11 September attacks,[78] I asserted that the indispensable element in the preparation of a plan of preparedness is the sustained personal leadership and commitment of the president. Only the president, or at least the vice president working as the representative of the president, can set national priorities, bust through bureaucratic log jams, hold federal departments and agencies accountable, and integrate a government-wide preparation effort. I noted the conclusion of one commission, which stated that any national strategy must have "the direct leadership, guidance, and imprimatur of the President. Only [in] that way can a strategy have a truly national tenor," and express the direction of the nation's chief executive on the most appropriate division of roles, missions, and responsibilities.[79] I argued that the president is the nation's "Captain of the Gate," that a president must never forget the words of Theodore Roosevelt: "A council of war never fights and in a crisis the duty of a leader is to lead and not to take refuge behind the generally timid wisdom of a multitude of councillors."[80]

The constitutional and political history of the United States makes it clear that the first priority of the federal government is the safety of the country. A similar point was made by Winston Churchill in November 1936 in a speech on the floor of the House of Commons. During the course of a defense debate on the rapid growth of Germany's air force, he turned to the government's excuses for delays over the previous three years in embarking upon a rearmament program. "I have heard it said," he declared, "that the Government had no [political] mandate for rearmament until the General Election. Such a doctrine is wholly inadmissible. The responsibility of Ministers for the public safety is absolute and requires no mandate. It is in fact the prime object for which Governments come into existence."[81] In words that seem strikingly appropriate for the vacuous national security policy direction experienced during the two Clinton administrations, Churchill continued: "The Government simply cannot make up their mind, or they cannot get the Prime Minister to make up his mind. So they go on in strange paradox, decided only to be undecided, resolved to be irresolute, adamant for drift, solid for fluidity, all powerful to be impotent. So we go on preparing more months and years—precious, perhaps vital, to the greatness of Britain—for the locusts to eat."[82]

The most candid and damning evaluation of the U.S. government's performance prior to 2001 was one made shortly after the 11 September attacks by Gen. Barry McCaffrey, USA (Ret.), who had served in the White House as Clinton's drug czar. Attacking the nation's "political, economic, media, and military elites" over a period of several years, he declared that "our shortcomings were a lack of leadership and sensible policy judgments. . . . We were collectively incompetent in the face of growing mountains of evidence, indicating that our nation was increasingly at risk of catastrophic losses from terrorist attacks on our citizens."[83] Noting that calls to action were "wittily debated" but not implemented by the U.S. political leadership and that terrorism had been relegated to the status of a law enforcement issue to be investigated after an attack, he soberly concluded, "We should be ashamed of ourselves. We left the American people undefended and thousands have perished needlessly."[84]

3

Counterterrorism Strategy on the Run

[W]hen you see a rattlesnake poised to strike, you do
not wait until he has struck before you crush him.

—President Franklin D. Roosevelt, Radio Address, 11 September 1941

When President George W. Bush spoke to the nation nine days after the
11 September 2001 attacks, Americans were still in shock. Never before had a
surprise act of war against the United States been directed at thousands of innocent civilians. Unlike the circumstances of the attack at Pearl Harbor, where the
Rising Sun on the fuselage of the attacking aircraft clearly identified the aggres-
sor nation, it was not even clear that our country had been attacked by another
nation. President Bush could only say that the evidence gathered to date "all points
to a collection of loosely affiliated terrorist organizations known as al Qaeda."

In the course of my official travel during the administrations of Presidents
Ronald Reagan and George H. W. Bush, I had often reflected upon the fact that

almost every country I visited bore the scars of war from foreign aggression. How blessed America was! In addition to all of the obvious measurements of economic, political, and military strength, which demonstrated our unique good fortune, Americans felt secure from outside threats. We took our security for granted. The wars in which the United States had engaged during the last century and a quarter were always conducted "over there," whether the "over there" was Cuba, France, Korea, Southeast Asia, the Persian Gulf, or some other location. Unlike the people of London, who daily observe the lingering evidence of German bombing in World War II, no such damage scarred our country's buildings.

Now, the United States was again at war. This time, the first casualties were innocents, all going about their routine peaceful pursuits at home. Suddenly, Americans felt very vulnerable. If it could happen once, it could happen again. And, we were unprepared. Commentators had described the president's national security team as one of the most seasoned ever, but the stark fact was that the United States had neither a counterterrorism nor a homeland defense strategy for fighting an enemy it could not yet even identify with certainty. The U.S. Armed Forces had no contingency plans for Afghanistan.[1] Dr. Condoleezza Rice, the president's national security advisor, said simply, "There was nothing on the shelf for this kind of war."[2]

In a briefing a week before the Bush administration assumed office in January 2001, George Tenet, the CIA director, had informed the president-elect and the vice president–elect that Osama bin Laden and al Qaeda were one of the primary threats facing the United States.[3] Subsequent steps were taken by the new administration in the development of a counterterrorism strategy, but other subjects were given higher priority during the first months. This was not unusual. Two former members of President Clinton's national security staff described the start up problems of new presidents: "All new administrations come into office with a short To Do list and need time to think through how they wish to conduct policy on the vast number of issues that played no role in their campaign. They must vet, hire and shepherd through the confirmation process hundreds of appointees, and they need time to figure out how to operate a policy apparatus that has evolved since they were last in power. Most important of all, they need time to adapt the simplifications of campaign slogans and television talking points to the complex realities of a world with which they have been, to varying degrees, out of touch."[4]

Among the more important steps taken was the ongoing work of the Deputies Committee, a group of second-tier officials from departments and agencies that are a part of the National Security Council (NSC). In a 30 April committee meeting, Deputy Secretary of State Richard Armitage focused the internal debate by declaring that the actual destruction of al Qaeda should be the country's first priority in South Asia.[5] By 7 June the working group reached agreement on a policy of phased escalation against al Qaeda that would ultimately result in its elimination. A multiyear and multifaceted policy would be pursued involving diplomatic, economic, intelligence, and law enforcement efforts and—if necessary—military force.[6] Gen. Henry Shelton, USA, who was still serving as chairman of the Joint Chiefs of Staff when the American Airlines flight crashed into the Pentagon, later said that he had been troubled by that formulation of proposed policy. Because al Qaeda was operating in several countries, "to say 'eliminate' is to define defeat for yourself right up front."[7] He believed that reducing the al Qaeda network, degrading it, or rendering it operationally ineffective was a more realistic objective.[8] Still, a specific course of action had at least been tentatively identified. By 10 September 2001 the national security advisor had a national security presidential directive (NSPD), a formal policy statement, ready for the president's review.[9]

On 8 May 2001 Bush asked Vice President Dick Cheney to make an official assessment of the government's ability to respond to a terrorist attack involving a weapon of mass destruction, including a review of current plans for management of the consequences of such an attack. He also asked Cheney to make recommendations for improving homeland security. The same day, the president had also announced a new Office of National Preparedness for Terrorism at the Federal Emergency Management Agency (FEMA). No individual was given overall authority for homeland security, however, and nothing was said about a homeland security strategy.

Irrespective of the status of the government's preparation prior to 11 September, after that date the country was ready for war. On 14 September the Senate unanimously authorized the president to strike against individuals or nations that "planned, authorized, committed or aided the terrorist attacks." A few hours later, the House of Representatives approved a resolution authorizing the president to "use all necessary and appropriate force" against those involved in the attacks. An ABC News/Washington Post poll found that 69 percent of Americans polled were in favor of war even if it proved to be lengthy and involved heavy casualties.[10]

In an interview with John Miller of ABC on 28 May 1998 Osama bin Laden had expressed his contempt of U.S. military power and resolve. "We have seen in the last decade," he said, "the decline of the American government and the weakness of the American soldier, who is ready to wage cold wars and unprepared to fight long ones. This was proven in Beirut when the marines fled after two explosions. It also proves that they can run in less than 24 hours and this was also repeated in Somalia."[11] Apparently, he saw no difference in the value the United States placed on the operations in Somalia and Beirut and that attached to the sanctity of its homeland. It is difficult to imagine a more deadly miscalculation of the American character, especially if it is not constrained by poor leadership.

An ambitious, long-term, and somewhat open-ended U.S. objective in the new war was declared by the president in his 20 September address: "Our war on terror begins with al Qaeda, but . . . it will not end until every terrorist group of global reach has been found, stopped and defeated." Fortunately, the administration's first efforts at a military response were marked by candor and realism. Early suggestions for some form of an early and massive military counterattack would be rejected. The natural public clamor for quick retribution would not determine the nature, the timing, or the duration of U.S. actions. Our military response would involve "far more than instant retaliation and isolated strikes. Americans should not expect one battle, but a lengthy campaign, unlike any other we have ever seen."[12] The goal would be to "starve terrorists of funding, turn them against one another, and drive them from place to place, until there is no refuge or rest."[13] Nations that provided aid or safe haven for terrorists would be considered hostile to the United States. "Every nation, and every region, now has a decision to make," declared the president in words on which critics would later focus. "Either you are with us, or you are with the terrorists."[14] The new kind of conflict was not likely to conclude with the type of clear-cut victory Americans preferred and which had characterized the conclusion of the Persian Gulf War a decade earlier. "I'm sure," Secretary of Defense Donald Rumsfeld observed, "there will not be a signing ceremony on the [USS] *Missouri*."[15]

Good diplomacy and the restraint and discipline exercised by the administration in the first days of the military campaign permitted the development of an innovative and effective initial operational plan while a longer-term counterterrorism strategy was being developed. A delicate balance was being sought regarding the use of force. Whatever law enforcement or other resources of national power might be required in the next phase of the war against worldwide terrorism, military force would be necessary in the first phase to overthrow the Taliban regime and neutralize a country that had long provided a safe haven for terrorists. Military failure was absolutely unacceptable, but it was recognized that excessive or wrongfully applied force risked uniting the many Afghan tribes and militias to fight the United States just as they had united and fought the Soviet Union earlier.[16] Sensitivity to the potential instability of neighboring and nuclear-armed Pakistan and the possible opposition of the Arab world was also required.

During the early spring, the president had expressed impatience with his administration's slow development of a plan for breaking al Qaeda. At a meeting at Camp David four days after the attacks on New York City and Washington, the CIA director made his recommendations of an operational plan to do just that. CIA paramilitary teams would be deployed with small numbers of special operations personnel to aid the Afghan opposition forces on the ground and to assist aircraft in designating bombing targets. U.S. intelligence agencies would collaborate with foreign intelligence and law enforcement agencies to break up al Qaeda cells and to freeze or confiscate its funding. The plan would later be described a plan for a war "fought by others, with the U.S. role both obvious and covert, a combination of brute force, financial muscle and behind-the-scenes finesse."[17] The government's planning process would later be characterized by the deputy national security advisor as makeshift, "Come as you are."[18] On 17 September the plan was approved by the president.

Diplomatic success was achieved almost immediately. Pakistan agreed to stop all support of the Taliban. Russian president Vladimir Putin threw the weight of his nation behind the U.S. effort, as did dozens of other nations. Several countries, including some that were formerly part of the Soviet Union, agreed to provide bases and fly-over authority, necessary for the projection of U.S. military forces to the region.

On 7 October Operation Enduring Freedom commenced with strikes by both land- and carrier-based U.S. aircraft and cruise missiles against Taliban forces, al Qaeda fighters, and fixed assets such as training sites, command-and-control systems, and radar installations. Twelve days later teams of U.S. Special Forces and U.S. Army Rangers were landed. By early November the effectiveness of the air campaign improved significantly. Greater numbers of daily sorties were only one reason. A more important reason was the almost flawless ground-air teamwork, which involved the use of U.S. Special Forces forward air controllers, networked sensors, better fusion of battlefield intelligence systems, joint communications, and improved precision munitions. The sensor-to-shooter time (i.e., the time between the identification of a target and its destruction) was reduced to less than twenty minutes. Approximately 80 percent of the U.S. Navy's strike sorties attacked targets that were unknown to the aircrews when the planes left the carrier.

Potential targets were initially identified by troops on the ground, often with the assistance of CIA operatives or by JSTARS, Boeing 707 aircraft equipped with radar that can pick up a moving vehicle almost two hundred miles away and scan up to nineteen thousand square miles at one time. Predator unmanned aerial vehicles (UAVs)—carrying continuous video, global positioning system (GPS) technology, and laser designators—were often flown in for a closer look. Special forces teams or the Predators were then used to "paint" or designate the targets with laser range finders.[19] Two thousand pound "dumb bombs" retrofitted with electronic "brains" and fins for steering—devices called JDAMs (joint direct attack munitions)—were then programmed with the coordinates of the targets. As each bomb fell, its position in space was calculated with signals from GPS satellites and its vanes activated to guide it to its target. Ninety-three percent of the bombs dropped by naval aircraft were precision guided, a great improvement over the experience in Operation Desert Storm ten years earlier, and 84 percent hit a target.[20]

In late November marine expeditionary units (MEUs) were moved over four hundred miles in CH-53 Super Stallion helicopters, from the assault ship USS *Peleliu* (LHA-5) sailing in the Arabian Sea, to establish a base approximately sixty miles southwest of the Afghan city of Kandahar. By then, the Afghan militia forces opposed to the Taliban were heavily engaged in the fighting and the rout of enemy forces was under way. By 16 November defense officials judged that the Taliban controlled less than a third of the country, compared to 85 percent control only a week earlier.

Over the next few months the military operation against al Qaeda and the Taliban became one of rooting out pockets of the enemy from dug-in positions in the mountains. In December Afghan and Allied forces concentrated on the mountainous complex of caves and tunnels called Tora Bora, some thirty-five miles south of Jalalabad near the Pakistan border. It was believed that much of al Qaeda's remaining strength remained in that area. Within days, large numbers of caves that might have provided sanctuary were closed or destroyed and all resistance had disappeared. By early March 2002 Hamid Karzai, the interim Afghan leader, was calling the Shahikot Valley in eastern Afghanistan "the last isolated base of terrorism"[21] in that country. Operation Anaconda, a ground operation involving more than one thousand U.S. troops and almost that many Afghans, began on 2 March. The operation did not, however, prevent significant numbers of Taliban and al Qaeda fighters from fleeing across the mountainous and porous Afghan-Pakistan border.

By early May Britain's entire fighting strength of 1,700 troops in Afghanistan launched Operation Snipe in an area twenty-five miles from the eastern town of Khost. The al Qaeda forces and the mullahs of the Taliban were no longer fighting from concentrated positions, but were mixing with the civilian population and attacking in small bands from tribal areas inside Pakistan where the Musharraf government in Islamabad could only assert limited authority. Allied forces responded by ceasing large-scale operations like Anaconda and using smaller units to apply "unrelenting pressure."[22] The counterinsurgency operations were more reliant on mobile allied troops with intelligence elements than on air strikes or the participation of Afghan militia forces as the earlier operations had been. British officers expressed the view that the counterinsurgency action could last five years.[23] Still, the success to date could not be denied. One commentator wrote that for the most part, the war in Afghanistan had thus far been a "masterpiece of military creativity and finesse."[24]

Within weeks, operational challenges began to increase and questions were being raised about the tactics used. Predictably, as the weather warmed, al Qaeda and Taliban forces moved to reestablish communications networks. Allied forces responded with "light footprint" raids in which troops would drop into an area unexpectedly, search for al Qaeda or Taliban fighters, and then leave as suddenly as they came. An echo of the conflict in Vietnam could be heard as some Allied officers argued that the raids be replaced or at least supplemented by the construction of several small bases in the Pashtun tribal area from which a more focused effort could be made to capture the "hearts and minds" of the native population.[25] Even where support of the Taliban was not particularly strong, the conservative Islamic tribesmen were deeply suspicious of foreigners, especially non-Muslims. Complicating the overall effort was a decision by Pakistan not to commit more troops to the joint effort and to withdraw needed intelligence and communications specialists. The specialists were sent to Pakistan's eastern border where tension with India was high as a result of a long-standing dispute in Kashmir.

As the first phase of the new multifaceted counterterrorism strategy was being implemented, questions were being raised about what to do next. Former secretary of state Henry Kissinger asserted broadly that the war on terrorism was not "just about hunting down terrorists." It is, he said, above all, about protection of "the extraordinary opportunity that has come about to recast the

international system."[26] Relations with former adversaries could go "beyond liq-
uidating the vestiges of the Cold War" and new roles for the major states.[27]

Within months, this prophecy became almost self-fulfilling. On 13 May
2002 the United States and Russia announced that they had reached agreement
on a new arms-control treaty. President Bush characterized the treaty, which
requires each country to reduce the number of its nuclear warheads by two-
thirds,[28] as one that would "liquidate the legacy of the Cold War."[29] The next
day, NATO and Russia reached formal agreement on the creation of a NATO-
Russia council, through which Russia—the former enemy of NATO—would
become an equal partner of the nineteen NATO nations for the setting of joint
policy on such issues as counterterrorism, the proliferation of weapons of mass
destruction, civilian emergency planning, management of regional crises, military cooperation, and missile defense. The agreement solidified what was characterized as "an almost surreal sense of a major change in Russia's relations with
the West."[30] Russia's president, Vladimir Putin, agreed. "The significance" of the
agreement, he declared, "is difficult to overestimate," noting that only a few
years earlier, the idea of Russian participation in the councils of NATO "would
have been, simply, unthinkable."[31]

A new relationship with India also began to bloom. Throughout most of
the Cold War, India had pursued a policy of nonalignment with either the West
or the Soviet Union, but the latter was its major weapons supplier. Tension
between the United States and India increased in 1998 after the United States
imposed economic sanctions following India's test of nuclear weapons.
Although India was motivated in large part by its desire to obtain modern military technology and the United States to some degree by the potential of India
as a strategic counterweight to China, India's unequivocal support of the
United States after 11 September 2001 resulted in the lifting of the sanctions
and a jump-start in new military cooperation. When Secretary of Defense
Donald Rumsfeld arrived in New Delhi on 12 June 2002 as part of a U.S. effort
to diffuse the crisis between India and Pakistan in Kashmir, he was said to "have
the ear of India's senior political leaders in a way that would have been hard
to imagine for most of the past three decades."[32]

But this did not answer immediate questions. When the Taliban and al Qaeda were no longer an imminent threat in Afghanistan, would it be necessary for U.S. military forces to pacify that country or to engage in nation-building efforts there? What kind of exit strategy should be developed for the removal of U.S. forces? How could the president's broad goal of finding, stopping, and defeating "every terrorist group of global reach" be achieved? Jim Hoagland, a highly regarded syndicated columnist, opined that a viable answer to such questions would be "an evolving, messy combination of outside pressures and rewards and internal changes. Something new in statecraft."[33]

Terrorism had changed in recent years, in several ways. There was now a trend away from involvement in terrorism by nation-states and a trend toward the use of terrorism by stateless actors. Terrorism was also becoming more lethal. Since 1968 only fourteen of the more than ten thousand incidents of international terrorism recorded prior to 11 September 2001 had resulted in one hundred or more fatalities.[34] And, there was a trend away from the use of terrorism to bring attention to a cause(presumably because random violence was becoming counterproductive) toward its use solely for the infliction of death and destruction. Proclaimed religious beliefs and political extremism were creating highly combustible launch pads. "Those convinced that they have the mandate of God to kill their foes," said one analyst, "have fewer moral qualms about mass murder. . . . They have no political agenda to promote. And in the minds of the devout, death in God's cause brings reward in the hereafter."[35]

The geographic reach of terrorists had also expanded greatly. Attacks were now being carried out in one country by groups of terrorists recruited from a second country pursuant to a plan developed in a third. Indeed, the FBI would soon conclude that while the idea of the 11 September attacks came from al Qaeda leaders in Afghanistan, the actual planning was performed in Germany and funding for the operation came through the United Arab Emirates from sources in Afghanistan.[36]

Moreover, the enemy was not a single group of combatants that received immediate direction from a central authority. After being driven from Afghanistan, al Qaeda operatives had dispersed to other countries where they regrouped as semi-independent sleeper cells, each with its own mission. Entering into loose, makeshift alliances with other militant groups in countries like Lebanon,[37] Algeria, and Egypt, the groups were flexible, adaptable, and in no hurry. Their strategy appeared to have two elements. First, continued large-scale attacks were planned on U.S. targets, both in the United States and abroad. Second, small-scale attacks were designed to destabilize and ultimately to undermine secular governments in Islamic countries, all for the purpose of killing Americans and establishing a "Muslim state in the heart of the Islamic world."[38] Many concluded that the main front on which the war on international terrorism had to be fought was the terrorist infrastructure. It had to be destroyed, or at least regularly disrupted. Terrorist safe havens anywhere in the world would have to be penetrated and eliminated.

Paul Pillar, former deputy chief of the CIA's Counterterrorist Center, was of the view that the battlefields of the new war would have to be "behind countless closed doors in scores of foreign countries where individual terrorists and cells and branches of groups do their business of recruiting and raising money and making plans."[39] This part of the war would have financial, law enforcement, intelligence, economic, diplomatic, communications, and domestic security elements. The greatest support needed by the United States in the war would not be military combat units; rather it would be the cooperation of foreign police, intelligence, and internal security services.[40]

Although most forms of terrorism do not require much money, an early target of the second phase of the counterterrorism strategy was bin Laden's financial network. Aside from his personal fortune, at first estimated to be in the range of $300 million, it was known that many wealthy individuals in oil-rich Persian Gulf countries had funneled hundreds of millions to him through the lax and even corrupt banking system in Pakistan and through dummy companies, private charitable organizations, and "humanitarian" groups.[41] Prior to 11 September Treasury Department officials had resisted efforts to go after the financial assets of terrorists on the ground that actions against private organizations would look punitive and elicit lawsuits. On 24 September, however, the president signed an executive order that immediately froze the financial assets of twenty-seven organizations.[42]

A broader effort would have to be made against the financial bases of all transnational terrorists. The reason was obvious. Increasing reliance by terrorists on information age technology and new banking techniques allowed them to move sums of money for terrorist operations across international borders without detection. Stopping the flow of money into terrorist hands would not be easy. "The ability to move vast quantities of wealth rapidly and anonymously across the globe," said one student of the problem, "sometimes combining modern-day wire transfers, faxes, and Internet connections with centuries-old practices, such as the hawala,"[43] as well as "personal connections and a handshake—gives terrorist . . . networks a strategic advantage over many states."[44]

Nevertheless, the effort to eradicate funding sources soon began. On 25 October 2001, only forty-four days after the attacks in New York City and Washington, Congress passed the USA PATRIOT Act of 2001,[45] a sweeping piece of legislation that amended and strengthened several existing money-laundering statutes. The declared purpose of Title III of the act is "to increase significantly the strength of U.S. measures to prevent, detect, and prosecute international money laundering and the financing of terrorism, and to facilitate dissemination of financial information to the intelligence community in connection with efforts to fight international terrorism."[46] To improve law enforcement overseas, the Government entered into several mutual legal assistance treaties (MLATs) to provide for the exchange of financial information and other evidence in criminal prosecutions. The Treasury Department established a foreign terrorist asset tracking center for the purpose of disrupting the ability of terrorists to manipulate money in the international financial system. The Customs Service began to use recently concluded customs mutual assistance agreements (CMAAs) to collect evidence of money laundering, drug trafficking, violations of export control laws, trade fraud, and smuggling. The Customs Service also assumed leadership of an interagency task force referred to as Operation Green Quest that seeks to stop the exploitation by al Qaeda of financial safe havens in places like Hong Kong, Dubai, and Malaysia.

The Treasury Department–led financial campaign met with some early success. A coalition of 161 nations joined the United States in tightening regulations and blocking bank accounts of individuals and organizations suspected of terrorist connections. By February 2002 more than $100 million had been frozen. It soon became apparent, however, that future success would be more difficult to achieve. Evidence had mounted that soon after the United States froze $254 million of Taliban funds following the 1998 attacks on the U.S. embassies in Kenya and Tanzania, al Qaeda operatives began to move money out of bank accounts into untraceable commodities such as gold, diamonds, and other precious stones and metals.[47]

Even while the NSC was soliciting recommendations for the second phase of the unfolding counterterrorism strategy, it was apparent that future battles in the war were unlikely to resemble either the military operations in Afghanistan or the Clinton administration's methodology. Security analysts had complained for years that terrorists were regarded only as criminals to be brought to justice rather than adversaries in combat to be destroyed. That approach was sure to change. But, the next steps were not yet clear. Deputy Secretary of State Armitage stated, "There's no 'one size fits all' strategy."[48]

Slowly and publicly, phase two of the strategy began to emerge. In his address to Congress on 20 September 2001 the president had declared war with "every terrorist group of global reach" and with nations that provide "aid or safe haven to terrorism." On 6 November he declared further that the United States would not wait for terrorists "to gain weapons of mass destruction."[49] On Tuesday 29 January 2002 he delivered his State of the Union Address to Congress. It was much more than a substantive contrast to his first State of the Union Address. It was, in many ways, an announcement of a sharp turn in our country's foreign policy. Some shared the concern expressed by a Washington journalist that it was a step into "uncharted, hazardous territory" that committed the nation to the fighting of "an ill-defined, possibly ill-prepared war against new enemies."[50] Certainly, the address was unequivocal. It had, said another journalist, "the clarity of a church bell on a clear Sunday morning."[51]

The war, the president said, had "two great objectives." First, the United States would "shut down terrorist camps, disrupt terrorist plans, and bring terrorists to justice." He noted that tens of thousands of terrorists were still at large and that terrorist camps still existed in at least a dozen countries. "A terrorist underworld," he said, "operates in remote jungles and deserts, and hides in the centers of large cities." The second "great objective," was to "prevent the terrorists and regimes who seek chemical, biological or nuclear weapons from threatening the United States and the world." In words that would illicit critical comment in subsequent days, the president identified North Korea, Iran, and Iraq as nations that constituted an "axis of evil" because of their efforts to obtain weapons of mass destruction.

The real news in the speech, however, was missed by most of the listening public and even some of the media. He would not, he said, "wait on events, while dangers gather." He would not "stand by, as peril draws closer and closer." The United States of America would not, he declared in a sentence later characterized as the most significant sentence by a U.S. president in almost twenty years,[52] "permit the world's most dangerous regimes to threaten us with the world's most destructive weapons." The speech left little room for doubt that the Bush administration would not wait for other terrorists, other states, or other regimes to strike a first blow. The United States would take *preemptive* action if necessary. And it was prepared to act alone.

As I listened to the president's words, my mind focused on an event that occurred in October 1991. Seven months after the cease-fire had terminated combat operations against Iraq in the Persian Gulf War and even before all U.S. reservists had returned home from the theater of operations, I made a visit to Israel in my capacity as assistant secretary of defense for reserve affairs. The purpose of the visit was to study the mobilization procedures of the Israeli Defense Force. Israeli males serve in Israel's reserve forces until age forty-five; in time of war, most of the population is mobilized. The last senior government official I met before leaving Israel was David Ivry. At the conclusion of our meeting, he gave me a book, inscribed with the words "with friendship, from the Conductor of the 'Opera.'"

Although he would later serve as Israel's ambassador to the United States, in 1991 Ivry, a retired air force major general, was serving as a senior Ministry of Defense civilian official. Ten years earlier, he had been commander of the Israeli air force as a French-built nuclear reactor was rapidly nearing completion at Osirak, Iraq. Saddam Hussein would soon be able to extract plutonium from the spent fuel rods of the reactor and it was estimated that by the mid-1980s at the latest, he would have a nuclear weapon. Three years of diplomatic efforts to persuade France, Brazil, and Italy not to assist Iraq in the completion of the reactor had failed. On 25 April 1980 the Iraqi president had urged his soldiers "to prepare for the liberation of Palestine from the filth of Zionism."[53]

A military attack on the reactor after it was activated would greatly increase the danger of radioactive contamination. The only remaining option was a preemptive attack on the reactor in July or September 1981 before it was activated. The risks of making such an attack were substantial. More than ordinary operational dangers were present. A preemptive attack would inflame world opinion and Israel would be blamed for an unprovoked initiation of hostilities.

On the afternoon of Sunday 7 June 1981 eight multipurpose F-16 aircraft, which Israel had received from the United States, and an escorting group of F-15s took off from Israel for a flight to Iraq. An hour and a half later, the Iraqi reactor was destroyed. The following day, the U.S. State Department issued a statement condemning the air strike, partly because it had been carried out with aircraft the United States had sold to Israel under the foreign military sales program and on the conditions that Israel would use the aircraft "solely to maintain . . . its legitimate self-defense" and that it would "not undertake any acts of aggression against any other state,"[54] and partly because of the attack's "unprecedented character."[55] While the Reagan administration could not overlook the Israeli action, President Reagan rejected demands for stronger sanctions and ordered the suspension of a planned delivery to Israel of additional aircraft. The suspension was later lifted. One can only imagine how Operation Desert Storm would have been affected in 1991 if Saddam Hussein had possessed nuclear weapons.

Much of the editorial reaction to the president's State of the Union Address referred to what was characterized as a new and even radical foreign policy. One columnist stated that the new policy was based on the principles of morality, unilateralism, and preemption.[56] Another said that it rested upon three tenets: "(1) America first. . . . (2) Good is good and bad is bad. . . . (3) If you know where you stand, you can dance."[57] The French foreign minister criticized Bush's new policy as "simplistic," but most Americans understood that the purpose of the war was less about retribution than about preventing another 11 September.

Henry Kissinger provided a conceptual foundation for the new preemption policy. "Until September 11, the United States and its allies withheld military action until after terrorist attacks had, in fact, occurred; constraint was sought via the same principle of deterrence that was applied to weapons of mass destruction in the hands of the major powers—the expectation that rational leaders would avoid action leading to their own destruction. But when such weapons are within reach of countries that have employed them against their neighbors and their own people (as Iraq), or of nations that at times have made systematic assassination part of their policy and where hundreds of thousands have been sacrificed to death by starvation (as North Korea), or of national leaders who have backed virulent terrorist groups and hostage-takers (as Iran) and those whose attacks are made by suicide bombers, these constraints may not operate any longer. . . . [and] preventive action must be considered."[58]

In early June 2002 the president expanded upon his new strategic doctrine. In remarks at the graduation ceremonies of the U.S. Military Academy at West Point, he noted that the United States faces a threat "with no precedent." He said the attacks of 11 September required only "a few hundred thousand dollars in the hands of a few dozen evil and deluded men." Our country would continue to rely upon the Cold War doctrine of deterrence and containment, he said, but "[d]eterrence—the promise of mass retaliation against nations—means nothing against shadowy terrorist networks with no nation or citizens to defend. Containment is not possible when unbalanced dictators with weapons of mass destruction can deliver those weapons on missiles or secretly provide them to terrorist allies."[59] Privately worrying that weapons of mass destruction in the hands of terrorists or a rogue state could result in the deaths of hundreds of thousands of Americans,[60] he asserted, "[I]f we wait for threats to fully materialize, we will have waited too long." He also said, "the war on terror will not be won on the defensive" and that the "only path to safety is the path of action." Summarizing his new policy, he said "We must take the battle to the enemy, disrupt his plans, and confront the worst threats before they emerge."

Within days, the new doctrine of *preemption*—soon to be known also as the doctrine of anticipatory self-defense—was expanded upon. National Security Advisor Condoleezza Rice noted that the most successful preemptive actions in recent history did not involve military strikes. Referring to the 1962 Cuban missile crisis as an example, she pointed out that military advice to launch a direct attack on the Soviet missile sites had been rejected. "They settled on a strategy," she said, "that actually was preemptive, but didn't use military force to do it, and thereby preserved the possibility for the Soviets to back down."[61] Secretary of State Colin Powell observed that several instruments of national power other than military strikes could be employed preemptively, for example, arrests, seizures, diplomatic initiatives, and aggressive financial measures. But, he argued that if military strikes are ordered, they must not be performed in a half-hearted way. "If you have a preemptive option, a target," he said, "you should do it in a way that removes the threat, that is decisive."[62]

The embrace of the concept of preemption was soon characterized as a radical shift from reliance exclusively on the policies of deterrence and containment.[63] Editorial columns pointed out that it is contrary to our nation's historic image of itself and to the tradition that Americans don't shoot first.[64] The doubts of NATO partners about preemption also received attention. The intelligence collection, weapons design, and other problems in effectuating a preemption policy were highlighted. But, while the problems were not to be minimized, an important fact was beyond dispute. A clear, decisive statement of the first phase of the nation's counterterrorism strategy had been made.

In mid-March 2002 the nature of the second phase of the strategy in the war against terror became clearer. Speaking at a ceremony on the South Lawn of the White House on the sixth-month anniversary of the 11 September attacks, the president described the second phase as "a sustained campaign to deny sanctuary to terrorists who would threaten our citizens from anywhere in the world." In a significant expansion of the nation's commitment to a global fight against terrorism, he publicly promised for the first time that the United States was willing to provide training and resources to "governments everywhere" that were working to eradicate terrorism. "We will not send troops to every battle," he said, but our country would "actively prepare other nations for the battle ahead."[65]

In his June speech at West Point, he was more specific. "Along with our friends and allies," he said, "we must oppose proliferation and confront regimes that sponsor terror, as each case requires. Some nations need military training to fight terror and we'll provide it." The expanded commitment did not go unnoticed. The Cato Institute, a conservative think tank, declared that from a war against terrorists with global reach, the war on terrorism had "ballooned" into a global war against terrorism and weapons of mass destruction.[66] A *Washington Post* editorial opined that if the president's stated policies were implemented, they would "make him one of the most aggressive of internationalists among presidents."[67]

There could be no doubt about the government's concern about the continuing threat. In a series of public appearances, Vice President Cheney spoke of terrorist cells operating in "60-odd countries" that were "determined to kill Americans by any means, on any scale, and on our own soil."[68] "The prospects of a future attack against the United States are almost certain," he said on NBC's "Meet the Press" in May. "Not a matter of if, but when." Senator Joseph Lieberman, Cheney's political opponent in the 2000 presidential elections, asserted that the "fanatical forces of Jihad" were attempting to build a "theological Iron Curtain" to divide the Muslim world from the rest of the world.[69] As the president called for patience and courage in what was clearly going to be a long conflict, Cheney called it the "defining struggle of the 21st Century."[70]

The surprise of many commentators in mid-2002 about the direction of counterterrorism policy in the Bush administration was itself surprising. They had not been listening. In its nuclear posture review, which was completed at the end of 2001, the administration had made it clear that any weapons—including nuclear weapons—might now be considered for use to preempt a likely terrorist or state-sponsored attack involving a weapon of mass destruction. The new posture implied "that deterrence is a meaningless concept for suicidal terrorists," and that the Bush team was prepared to carry out preemptive attacks if necessary, to prevent rogue states "from passing on weapons of mass destruction . . . to terror networks."[71] The administration's public pleas for patience and its effort to place on the table any policy that might prevent any further attacks received widespread public approval. In a March 2002 Washington Post/ABC News poll, 90 percent of Americans indicated support of the war in Afghanistan, even though more than 80 percent were of the opinion that "the most difficult part is yet to come."[72]

The implementation of the second phase of the counterterrorism strategy began promptly. The first venue for action was the Philippines. After finding no active terrorist training camps in Somalia and receiving promises of cooperation from Sudan, the first of what would eventually total nearly thirteen hundred troops, including special forces personnel and hundreds of support troops, were sent to the Philippines to train Philippine soldiers and to engage in joint exercise support operations against the Abu Sayyaf, a Muslim extremist movement. The Abu Sayyaf had been holding an American missionary couple and a Philippine nurse hostage for a year. The rebels were notorious for their bombing, kidnapping, and related activities. In the 1990s they had received funds from Osama bin Laden's brother-in-law and Philippine officials feared that the movement could provide a haven for members of al Qaeda. In a November meeting with Philippine president Gloria Macapagal Arroyo, President Bush agreed to provide debt relief and approximately $100 million in military equipment, including an AC-130 gunship, eight Huey helicopters, secure radios, and thirty thousand M-16 rifles.

By January the equipment had been delivered and the operations had begun in Mindanao and neighboring islands. Because of political constraints that the Philippine government placed on the six-month training mission, U.S. advisors were prohibited from a direct combat role. This proved costly. In a fire-fight on 7 June between Philippine troops and the Abu Sayyaf rebels holding the hostages, one of the missionaries and the nurse were killed and the second missionary was wounded.

Nevertheless, the following day the Philippine defense minister urged the United States to extend and expand the joint military exercises. U.S. authorities agreed to permit special forces advisors to accompany small units of Philippine troops on future patrols. By 31 July the bulk of U.S. forces had departed, but agreement had been reached for a follow-on assistance program in the coming year in which U.S. military instructors would train two elite light (90-men) reaction companies and eight regular infantry battalions. Work also continued within the Philippine government to approve a mutual logistics support arrangement (MLSA) with the United States that would permit construction of U.S. storage facilities in the Philippines. The ongoing effort at cooperation had taken on particular importance after a terrorist cell linked to al Qaeda was broken up in the Philippines, Singapore, and Malaysia. The cell purportedly was planning attacks against Western government, commercial, and military targets in Southeast Asia.[73] There were also more subtle reasons for the continuing Philippine interest in U.S. assistance. Requesting anonymity, a Philippine official said that the arrival of U.S. advisors and intelligence equipment made it more difficult for the Abu Sayyaf to learn of troop deployments from corrupt military officers. "Something seems to have changed," he said. "It looks like the U.S. presence has brought in more integrity."[74]

Other early efforts to provide assistance to countries where terrorists groups were active took place in the former Soviet Republic of Georgia and in Yemen. Georgia is an important transit point for oil from the Caspian Sea area. It had been considered a U.S. ally since it won independence in 1991. The twenty-one-month U.S. mission there had two major objectives. First, it provided helicopters and counterterrorist training to four Georgian battalions to prepare them for combat against rebels from the Russian Republic of Chechnya who were seeking refuge in the area of the Pankisi Gorge, a region along the country's mountainous northern border with Russia. Second, it confronted terrorists, with connections to bin Laden, who take sanctuary there. The U.S. aid package of $64 million was also expected to include vehicles, communications equipment, small arms, training and medical equipment, and approximately 180 military advisors.[75]

Aid to Yemen posed a particular problem. Relations with the primitive country had long been colored by its hatred of Israel, strong suspicion of the United States, political instability, and a history of isolation from the modern world. Relations were further strained when President Ali Abdallah Salih was slow to cooperate with U.S. investigators after the October 2000 suicide bomber attack by suspected al Qaeda operatives on the USS *Cole* in the Yemeni port of Aden. Nineteen U.S. sailors were killed.

Offsetting factors were present, however. Since 11 September Yemen had vowed cooperation in the war on terrorism and had energized its help in the investigation. U.S. officials believed that Yemen was a refuge for al Qaeda fighters fleeing Afghanistan after the start of the U.S. military operations there. Officials also believed that al Qaeda and groups associated with it had targeted "western interests in Djibouti, which lies only a few miles across the Red Sea from Yemen."[76] Because suspicions of U.S. motives remained high, the U.S. effort in Yemen was expected to be far more circumspect than in the Philippines or Georgia; it was limited to fewer than one hundred troops who would train Yemenis, help the country build a coast guard to protect its long unprotected coast, and install a computerized surveillance system to monitor air and sea ports.[77]

While the counterterrorism efforts in the Philippines, Georgia, and Yemen were the focus of early attention, less visible work was being performed by U.S. military forces in many other places. A new Joint Task Force Horn of Africa was established in Djibouti and on U.S. Navy ships in the Red Sea. Close to Yemen and near the Bal el Mandeb Strait, an important choke point where the Red Sea meets the Gulf of Aden, the task force was ideally located. It consisted primarily of marines and special operations troops, all under the control of the commanding general of the 2d Marine Division based at Camp Lejeune, North Carolina. The mission of the task force was to prevent al Qaeda and other terrorist networks from finding new sanctuaries in Somalia, Yemen, or elsewhere in the region. A fifty-five-officer planning staff of the U.S. European Command was also closely watching developments in the Balkans, North Africa, Lebanon, Syria, the Caucasus, and parts of sub-Saharan Africa to ensure that none of the areas became havens for terrorists forced out of other countries. Because Congress had recently removed restrictions on direct military assistance to Azerbaijan and Armenia, the U.S. European Command was also evaluating the types of training and equipment that would be most effective in the counterterrorism work in those two countries.

Not all early counterterrorism efforts met with immediate success, however. Despite the possession of evidence that al Qaeda members had fled to Indonesia, and concern that Indonesia may become the next haven for international terrorism, the Bush administration was unable to send forces there. In 1993 the Clinton administration had stopped U.S. weapons sales to Indonesia because of human rights violations there. In 1999 Congress had barred funding for assistance to the Indonesian army after widespread accusations had been made that members of the army had engaged in violence against civilians during East Timor's struggle for independence. The unsteady Indonesian government was also reluctant to permit U.S. entry because of the likely opposition of the country's two hundred million Muslims. Nevertheless, the Bush administration continued to press for a resumption of military assistance, despite the absence of evidence of substantive reform by the Indonesian army. The prospects for success improved in June 2002 after the arrest in Jakarta of a suspected al Qaeda operative. In early August Secretary of State Powell announced in Jakarta that the administration would resume military training in Indonesia as part of a broad program of counterterrorism assistance that would total at least $50 million over the next two years.

Within weeks of the 11 September 2001 attacks, an effort began to tie the war on terrorism to the "war" on drugs. Although the term "narco-terrorism" had not been used by the White House, the Drug Enforcement Administration (DEA) had longed believed in a nexus between the illicit drug trade and terrorism. The DEA's chief of intelligence declared, "State-sponsored terrorism is diminishing. These organizations are looking for funding, and drugs brings one thing: quick return on their investment."[78] Noting that the Revolutionary Armed Forces of Colombia (known by its Spanish acronym, FARC) guerillas had been financed for years by illegal narcotics and that the Taliban had been financed by an opium trade to Europe, Robert Novak asserted that support for terrorists was more likely to come from the poppy seed than from a state sponsor.[79]

One thing was certain. After 11 September large amounts of the nation's resources, which had previously been dedicated to the interdiction of illegal drugs, were being redeployed to the fight against terrorism. A spokesman for the U.S. Coast Guard said that as much as 75 percent of the ships and other assets previously used by the service in the counterdrug effort had been moved to the homeland defense mission and counterterrorism patrols.[80] Some analysts estimated that as little as 10 percent of the manpower previously dedicated to drug interdiction remained in place.[81]

As the senior counterdrug official in the Department of Defense from 1989 to 1993, I was particularly interested in the drug/terrorism issue. In the fiscal year 1989 National Defense Authorization Act, Congress had assigned to DoD significant new responsibilities, including (1) responsibility as the single "lead agency" of the federal government for the detection and monitoring of the aerial and maritime transit of illegal drugs into the United States; (2) planning responsibility for a network that would support the integration of U.S. command, control, communications, and technical intelligence assets dedicated to drug interdiction; and (3) enhanced use of the National Guard for counterdrug work. On 5 September 1989 President George H. W. Bush had issued the first national drug control strategy. Thirteen days later, Secretary of Defense Dick Cheney had designated the detection and countering of the production and trafficking of illegal drugs as a "high priority national security mission."

Over the next few years, I had invested much of my life overseeing both the interdiction operations and U.S. assistance to the Andean Ridge nations of Colombia, Peru, and Bolivia, which were the world's three principal cocaine-producing countries. At that time, Colombia was the major final processor, marketer, and distributor of the drugs. Security assistance in those days included training and support of counterdrug operations, but it was U.S. policy that DoD personnel would not accompany host-nation government personnel on actual field operations.

By spring 1992 I had been able to report to Congress that considerable success had been achieved in Colombia by Colombian counterdrug forces. By striking laboratories, air fields, and transshipment sites, the Colombian government had substantially disrupted the drug cartels. Most of the former leaders of the Medellin cartel were either dead or in jail and the Colombia security forces had seized a record eighty-three metric tons of cocaine in fiscal year 1991.[82] Much had occurred in the drug war and in Colombia since then. As drug-producing areas were closed in other countries, they were rebuilt in Colombia. By 2000 Colombia was providing as much as 90 percent of the cocaine that reached the United States. Moreover, the country's thirty-eight-year-old civil war had spread and intensified; the government's foes had grown more powerful during three years of peace talks.

Three irregular armies were at work in Colombia. The FARC, which began to gain attention in 1964, was a rural-based Marxist insurgency group of approximately eighteen thousand. Another smaller Marxist-oriented rebel group was the National Liberation Army (known by its Spanish acronym, ELN). The United Self Defense Forces of Colombia (known by its Spanish acronym, AUC) was a right-wing paramilitary group of some ten thousand fighters. They were often in combat against the FARC and ELN forces. All three relied upon drug trafficking for financial support. In response to the disturbing developments there, the Clinton administration had convinced Congress to adopt a $1.3 billion aid program called "Plan Colombia." Because of human rights concerns and fear of another quagmire like Vietnam, Congress had capped the number of U.S. military personnel in Colombia at four hundred. It had also prohibited the use of U.S.–provided equipment or training in the war between the government and the insurgency groups.

In February 2002, and for the first time, the Bush administration formally linked the illicit narcotics trade to terrorism. The first public connection appeared in two television commercials that were aired during the Super Bowl.

Nine days later, in announcing an antidrug initiative focused more toward treat-ment of users than on law enforcement, the president stepped into the debate. "Drugs help supply the deadly work of terrorists," he said. "Make no mistake about it: If you're buying illegal drugs in America, it is likely that money is going to end up in the hands of terrorist organizations."[83]

Within weeks another suggestion of a connection became public. An inves-tigation by the staff of the House International Relations Committee concluded in a report, which was disputed by some members of the committee, that mem-bers of the Irish Republican Army had been training FARC guerrillas in urban terrorism. While there was no evidence yet that the FARC had targeted any-one or anything outside of Colombia or that it was connected to al Qaeda, it did appear to have the capability of threatening the stability of the region. The line between lawful counterdrug aid and prohibited counterinsurgency assis-tance had thus become blurred. And, the government of Colombia was fight-ing for its life.[84] In testimony on Capitol Hill, Secretary of State Powell described the fight as a "threat to their survival as a nation."

In subsequent days the administration made its move. In late March Congress was asked to remove all restrictions on U.S. military aide to Colombia. Insisting that it had no intention of involving U.S. troops directly in the Colombian war or exceeding the four-hundred-person cap, the administration proposed that U.S. aid be used in actions by the Colombian government against groups that the United States designates as terrorists. On 18 April the president informed the Colombia president that counterdrug assistance to that country was part of the U.S. campaign against terrorism. On 1 May Attorney General John Ashcroft announced the criminal indictment of the FARC and six of its leaders for the murder of three Americans in 1999. "Just as we fight ter-rorism in the mountains of South Asia," he said, "we will fight terrorism in our own hemisphere."[85] By 30 July federal law enforcement officials had developed a most-wanted list of drug trafficking organizations to compare with the State Department's list of leading terrorist organizations. To the surprise of few, nearly one-third of the groups considered to be major suppliers of illegal drugs were on the list of terrorist organizations. On 2 August President Bush signed documents providing a $29 billion antiterrorism package for Colombia and authorizing previous aid to be used for operations against the FARC, ELN, and AUC.

On 26 May Colombian voters elected Alvaro Uribe Velez as their new president. As a candidate, Uribe Velez had taken a hard line against the guerillas, promising to double the size of Colombia's military and police forces and to create new citizen militias to patrol rural areas where government forces were weak. Receiving an unprecedented 53 percent of the vote in the first round of the election, his mandate was clear. So were the obstacles he faced. On 6 August, the day before his inauguration, the FARC launched a wide-ranging series of terrorist attacks that killed at least sixty people. The following day, even as Uribe Velez was being sworn in as president, mortar shells were fired at the presidential palace next door, killing at least nineteen people and wounding forty.

On 6 May the Bush administration stepped up its diplomatic offensive against state sponsors of terrorism. In a widely reported speech, Under Secretary of State John Bolton named Cuba, Libya, and Syria as "states intent on acquiring weapons of mass destruction." He said that the administration had "broad and deep" evidence that Cuba had "at least a limited offensive biological warfare research and development effort" and that it had "provided dual-use biotechnology to other rogue states."[86] It was the first time that any U.S. government representative had accused Cuba of developing germs for warfare.[87] Asserting that Cuba had "long provided safe haven for terrorists" and was "known to be harboring terrorists from Colombia, Spain, and fugitives from the United States," Bolton also declared that Cuban president Fidel Castro had visited Iran, Syria, and Libya the previous year and had delivered a speech at Tehran University in which he had said, "Iran and Cuba, in cooperation with each other, can bring America to its knees."[88]

Although the speech focused on Cuba, concern was also expressed about the other two nations. Bolton said that since UN sanctions against Libya were lifted in 1999, the government of Muammar Gadhafi had been pursuing nuclear and chemical weapons programs and "may be capable of producing small quantities of biological agents." He said Syria had a stockpile of the nerve agent sarin, that it was "engaged in research and development of the more toxic and persistent nerve agent VX," and that it had the potential means of delivering deadly agents to neighboring countries.[89] He warned that the United States would take whatever action might be necessary to prevent the three nations from delivering such weapons to terrorist networks.[90]

As the first anniversary of the attacks in New York City and Washington, D.C., approached, the Bush administration's counterterrorism strategy in Afghanistan was incurring problems and receiving increasing criticism. Even though the air campaign had been reduced to one of supporting ground troops, mistakes had caused the deaths of several civilians. The extraordinary accuracy of smart bombs was often offset by incorrect target information from local Afghans on the ground. One incident received widespread media coverage. Responding to antiaircraft fire on 1 July, U.S. aircraft attacked a village in southern Afghanistan. Local authorities claimed that forty-eight civilians, celebrating a wedding, were killed. Afghan leaders began demanding some say in how future air raids would be conducted.

A second and related complication involved a new demand by the governors of six southern Afghan provinces that U.S. military commanders seek their permission before launching combat operations in their areas. The warlords' declaration that they intended to form their own "rapid reaction" force and border guard reflected growing political and ethnic tension between the Tajik-dominated central government of Hamid Karzai, the new president, and the Pashtun governors. Media accounts of the incident characterized the declaration as a "direct challenge to the feeble authority of the U.S.-backed central government in Kabul."[91]

Lack of security was also a major problem. In early July Afghanistan's vice president was assassinated. President Karzai was forced to request protection by U.S. military forces. The UN-authorized international security assistance force (ISAF) of 4,650, which included troops from France, Turkey, Germany, and several other nations, was present in the country but it was confined to operations around the capitol of Kabul. Hope that a new Afghan national army of sixty thousand could ensure security and stability was tempered by the fact that it would take some time to build such a force. The first 350 U.S.–trained Afghan soldiers completed a 10-week training program on 23 July, but a lack of resources and Afghan volunteers made the prospects for a rapid building of the national army problematic.

Over the summer months the combat mission in Afghanistan slowly entered a new, more political phase. No longer were large numbers of regular U.S. infantry troops conducting operations in the Shahikot Valley and along the Afghan-Pakistani border. Now small teams of U.S. Special Forces troops were spotting targets for U.S. aircraft and working with Afghan fighters as they had in the first phase of the conflict. In circumstances that were described as "fluid and unpredictable,"[92] the effort to track down remnants of the Taliban and al Qaeda was becoming "primarily a war in the shadows."[93] Units like Task Force 11, a joint special forces unit of several hundred U.S. Navy SEALs (Sea, Air, Land) and U.S. Army Delta Force troops were conducting reconnaissance and raids on Taliban hideouts.[94] The work of the seven thousand member U.S. force was becoming less one of direct combat than of peacekeeping and protection of the central government.

In late August, 2000 U.S. Special Forces, aviation units, paratroops, and civil affairs specialists conducted six air assaults over 150 square kilometers as part of Operation Mountain Sweep, the most aggressive operation since Anaconda in March. A ton of weapons and two caches of Taliban documents were taken, but no contact was made with main units of the Taliban or al Qaeda. A four-day mission, which ended on 11 September 2002, was more successful. In Operation Champion Strike, ground and aviation troops conducted air assault raids into the Paktika Province in southeastern Afghanistan. One high-value target—a high-level financier of al Qaeda and the Taliban—was captured.

A noteworthy development, which mirrored similar developments taking place on U.S. soil as part of the new homeland defense effort, was the increasingly close cooperation between military units and U.S. law enforcement agencies. With the U.S. military success in Afghanistan, al Qaeda shifted east into Pakistan, first into the tribal areas and then to the cities. Intelligence from U.S. reconnaissance units in Afghanistan, satellite surveillance, communications intercepts, and images from unmanned aerial vehicles was being sent by U.S. military units to FBI agents working with local Pakistani police. The law enforcement agents were using the various forms of intelligence to identify specific al Qaeda operatives.

An early success involved the capture of an al Qaeda operative believed to be a field commander; he provided U.S. officials with new intelligence about al Qaeda activities. An even greater success was the capture on 11 September in Karachi of Ramzi Binalshibh, who was believed to have helped plan, coordinate, and provide important financial and logistical support to the terrorists carrying out the attacks in New York City and on the Pentagon. After a three-hour battle, he was transferred to a U.S. military base in Afghanistan. The sharing of information and expertise by the traditionally independent military and law enforcement organizations reflected the FBI's new priority of stopping terrorist attacks, rather than investigating crime, and it was described as "a laboratory for how American power could be used to combat terror."[95]

Critics continued to express concern about a strategic drift,[96] but significant successes were achieved. The Taliban had been removed from power and posed no immediate threat to the new government. Al Qaeda could no longer use Afghanistan as a haven and it was "less able to raise money, cross borders and plot new attacks."[97] President Karzai had been elected in the country's first secret ballot. Security was improving. Donor nations had pledged more than $1 billion for the year. And, thankfully, there was no humanitarian crisis.[98] U.S. officials acknowledged that they were essentially making policy in Afghanistan on the run. "There's no road map for it," Secretary of Defense Rumsfeld informed the Senate Armed Services Committee. "It's not science; it's art."[99]

Hints that a new tack was being considered in the global war on terrorism were first made by the chairman of the Joint Chiefs of Staff on 31 July. In an interview in San Diego, Gen. Richard Myers, USAF, said, "We have to . . . find new sanctuaries where [terrorists] may exist . . . and go after them." The war against terrorism is truly a global one, he said, but it is very different from conventional conflicts "in that you can't put a map in the paper and say 'here's where the front lines are today and here's how they shifted.'"[100] The same day,

Rumsfeld met with the Senate Armed Services Committee. Two days later, he met with Gen. Charles Holland, USAF, the chief of the U.S. Special Operations Command (SOCOM).[101] Shortly thereafter, Pentagon sources said that Rumsfeld had informed the Armed Services Committee of his view that the counterterrorism planning process had been "too rigid and stale" and that he was pushing military leaders to be faster and more creative.[102]

General Holland proposed to do just that. In the first of a series of briefings to Rumsfeld during the first week of August, he set out an aggressive plan that would greatly expand the U.S. Navy's sea interdiction operations. Until then, boardings of suspicious foreign vessels had been restricted to the Persian Gulf and waters off the Pakistani coast. Holland would have SEAL units boarding vessels all over the world if they were suspected of supporting terrorism. He also proposed a series of bilateral agreements with countries around the world in which terrorists were seeking haven or planning on conducting operations. The agreements would permit U.S. special operations teams to act on new intelligence within hours and to attack terrorist cells within each country,[103] all as part of the implementation of President Bush's new policy of preemption.

By September the Bush administration was considering a new command structure as part of a more covert worldwide counterterrorism effort. The idea was to make SOCOM a "supported command" with its own war-planning staff, rather than a "supporting command" that simply provides troops and weapons to the supported combatant commands. This would give SOCOM a measure of independence from the U.S. Central Command so it could focus its relatively limited force of elite troops on the capture of high-profile leaders of al Qaeda such as Ramzi Binalshibh. U.S. Central Command would continue raids on isolated pockets of al Qaeda and Taliban and focus more on contingency planning for a possible war with Iraq.

Even while U.S. military commanders in Afghanistan continued their efforts to capture or kill Taliban and al Qaeda fighters moving back and forth across the Pakistan-Afghanistan border, there were several signs of subtle but significant changes in the tactics used. Sensitive to the tension caused by accidental deaths and injury from combat operations and even the presence of foreign troops on Afghan soil, U.S. forces began to increase the number and type of stability operations. The number of civil affairs teams operating in villages was scheduled to increase from eleven to fifteen and the number of civil affairs personnel from 150 to 350 by November. New emphasis was placed on the construction of schools and roads, the digging of wells, and other forms of humanitarian aid.

Much more significant was the clear, if limited, change in the Bush administration's approach to nation-building in Afghanistan. During the 2000 campaign, Bush had consistently opposed the idea of using U.S. troops for anything other than combat. Even after the decision to go after the Taliban had been made, the White House chief of staff had cautioned the National Security Council, "The President won't want to use troops to rebuild Afghanistan."[104] Nevertheless, in late summer 2002 the United States dropped its opposition to an expansion of the ISAF outside of Kabul. The United States had resisted pressure since January to permit the ISAF to conduct peacekeeping operations in five other Afghan cities on the ground that such a move would interfere with operations against al Qaeda. Now, it supported the move. It also pressed nations that had pledged financial support to the war-torn country to fulfill the pledges, all as part of "a much bigger effort . . . in rebuilding [the] infrastructure of transportation and communications in the country."[105]

Much unfinished business remained in Afghanistan. As the world approached the first anniversary of the attacks that had started the war against terror, twelve thousand coalition troops and eight thousand Americans were still in Afghanistan. They were not coming home soon. In a visit to Bagram air base, the largest allied base in the country, Gen. Tommy Franks was candid. "We have a long ways to go before this is finished."[106] U.S. troops would remain indefinitely, at least for several years, until the country was stabilized and was no longer a safe haven for terrorists.

Both the global counterterrorism strategy and the more limited strategy for Afghanistan had been crafted on the run. The worldwide war on terrorism was far from over. Few officials were willing to predict with certainty what lay immediately ahead.

4

Organizing at Home for a Long War

[O]ur government must be re-organized to deal more effectively with the
new threats. . . . I ask the Congress to [create] a single, permanent
department with an overriding and urgent mission: securing
the homeland of America, and protecting
the American people.

—President George W. Bush, Address to the Nation, 6 June 2002

In many ways the difficulties encountered in the development and implementation of a counterterrorism strategy paled in comparison to those encountered in
the design and implementation of an organization and a strategy for homeland
security. The former effort, at least in its early stages, involved elements of diplomacy and military force almost exclusively, areas in which the president effectively exercised unfettered discretion in his constitutional role as commander-in-
chief. The effort to organize and plan strategy for the anticipated long war

against terrorism at home inevitably involved the clash, sometimes loud, of many competing federal, state, and local interests and viewpoints. In these circumstances, theoretical musings of the ideal organization and strategy have inevitably been tempered by political and bureaucratic realities.

It is helpful to remember that the idea of defending the United States from direct attack is relatively new. According to Dave McIntyre, the idea first arose in its modern context in 1949 when experts completed a review of the potential of biological weapons and reported to the secretary of defense that a need existed for "home defense, involving collaborative efforts of federal, state and private agencies."[1] Apparently, the term "home defense" was not mentioned again prominently until 1997 when the National Defense Panel discussed several emerging threats to the U.S. homeland, including terrorism (especially terrorism involving the use of weapons of mass destruction), commerce in proscribed weapon technologies, the illegal drug trade, and disruption of information systems.[2] As late as June 2000 the term was not even mentioned in the Department of Defense's *Dictionary of Military and Associated Terms*.[3]

The term "homeland defense" was considered to be insufficient to accurately describe all the actions that would have to be taken by multiple levels of government. Six months after the 11 September 2001 attacks, the Joint Chiefs of Staff approved a definition of homeland security: "The preparation for, prevention of, deterrence of, preemption of, defense against, and response to threats and aggression directed towards U.S. territory, sovereignty, domestic population, and infrastructure; as well as crisis management, consequence management, and other domestic civil support."[4] Simpler definitions have also been offered.[5] Homeland defense is now considered by many to be a subset of homeland security and to refer only to actions taken to deter or defend against attack, not to deal with the consequences of one.[6]

Almost immediately after the Bush administration moved into its new quarters in the White House and the first session of the 107th Congress convened, the debate over which federal agency should be given lead responsibility for the development of a homeland security strategy assumed the force of a gale wind. Some argued that Pentagon officials did not want and should not be given responsibility for coordinating the "multi-agency, nationwide effort."[7] A bill was introduced in the House of Representatives to turn FEMA into a new "National Homeland Security Agency." The bill would have transferred the U.S. Coast Guard, the Customs Service, the U.S. Border Patrol, and other offices from the Justice and Commerce Departments to the new agency.[8] It was based on recommendations made the previous month by the Commission on National Security/21st Century. The commission also made several recommendations regarding the Department of Defense, including recommendations that DoD "pay far more attention to [the homeland security] mission in the future" and that "new priorities . . . be set for the U.S. armed forces in light of the threat to the homeland."[9] The bill was immediately opposed by the White House on the ground that more time was needed to study the complex issue.[10] It was quickly recognized that the question of the structure of the decision-making process for homeland security was not merely one of abstract academic inquiry. The structure would likely determine or at least shape the country's homeland security strategy and resulting policies.

On 8 May 2001 President Bush asked Vice President Dick Cheney to make an official assessment of the government's ability to respond to a terrorist attack involving a weapon of mass destruction and to make recommendations for improving homeland security. It was expected that Cheney's recommendations would include a recommendation for organizing the government to meet the threat.

As the weeks passed, most Americans were only vaguely aware, if they were aware at all, that work was under way to create a new homeland security organization. Public speculation tended to focus on the earlier recommendations of three commissions and a Washington-based think tank. The recommendations of the National Commission on Terrorism had been submitted to Congress in June 2000. Focusing more on specific action items that should be part of a "comprehensive [counterterrorism] plan," such as improved intelligence collection and fusion and more aggressive diplomatic efforts, the commission made only modest recommendations for government organization. It was particularly concerned about the absence of a clear line of authority for the preparation of a counterterrorism budget. It thus recommended that the president should require the director of the Office of Management and Budget and the official serving as the national terrorism "coordinator" to "agree on all budget guidance to the agencies, including the response to initial budget submissions"; "both officials should be involved" in presenting the counterterrorism budget appeals of the agencies to the president.[11]

A series of working groups at the Center for Strategic and International Studies (CSIS) recommended that the vice president be made responsible "for most aspects of homeland defense" and that a national emergency planning council be established with representation from all federal departments and agencies, the states, and even private corporations.[12] As chairman of the council, the vice president would be supported by a staff headed by a national "coordinator." The director of FEMA and the coordinator would be confirmed by the Senate and the FEMA director would report to the vice president through the coordinator.

On 15 December 2000 the Advisory Panel to Assess Domestic Response Capabilities for Terrorism Involving Weapons of Mass Destruction, known as the Gilmore Commission, concluded that the United States had no "functional, coherent national strategy for domestic preparedness against terrorism." The organization of the federal government's programs for combating terrorism was "fragmented, uncoordinated, and politically unaccountable."[13] Asserting that at the federal level "no entity has the authority even to direct the coordination of relevant Federal [counterterrorism] efforts," the Gilmore Commission recommended the establishment of a national office for combating terrorism in the executive office of the president. The office would be established by statute. It would "not be an operational entity," but it would "oversee terrorism-related intelligence activities" and "exercise program and budget authority over federal efforts to combat terrorism."[14] In exercising the latter authority, a certification/decertification process would be used. If an agency's budget was determined to not be in compliance with the national strategy, the agency would either revise it or appeal to the president to resolve the dispute.

Only days after the Bush administration assumed office, yet another commission weighed into the ongoing organizational debate. In its third and final report, the U.S. Commission on National Security/21st Century, also known as the Hart-Rudman Commission, concluded that "significant changes must be made in the structures and processes of the U.S. national security apparatus."[15] The fourteen commissioners unanimously recommended that the United States make securing the national homeland its first priority. To this end, a new, independent national homeland security agency (NHSA) should be created with responsibility for "planning, coordinating, and integrating various U.S. government activities involved in homeland security."[16] The new agency would be built upon FEMA, it would include the U.S. Coast Guard, the Customs Service, and the U.S. Border Patrol, and it would consolidate certain offices of the Department of Commerce and the FBI. It would also assume responsibility for "overseeing the protection of the nation's critical infrastructure, including information technology."[17] The director of the NHSA would have cabinet status and be a statutory advisor to the National Security Council.

Perhaps the most interesting of the Hart-Rudman Commission's many recommendations were those regarding the Department of Defense. Declaring that "[i]n the new era sharp distinctions between 'foreign' and 'domestic' no longer apply," the commission said that it did not "equate security with 'defense.'" Noting that the "potentially catastrophic nature of homeland attacks necessitates our being prepared to use the extensive resources" of DoD, the commission argued that the Defense Department "needs to pay far more attention to this mission in the future."[18] It made three specific recommendations. First, a new office of assistant secretary of defense for homeland security should be created "to oversee DoD activities in this domain and to ensure that the necessary resources are made available." Second, new priorities should be set for the U.S. Armed Forces "in light of the threat to the homeland." Third, the National Guard should be assigned the mission of homeland security as a *primary* mission "as the U.S. Constitution itself ordains."

All the recommendations from the several commissions and other interested parties were under consideration as the summer of 2001 was coming to a close. On 11 September the time for deliberation ended. "In one horrible moment," said Tony Cordesman, a military and Middle East expert at the CSIS, "the need for Homeland Defense has gone from being a theoretical risk to a grim reality."[19]

The joint session of Congress on the evening of 20 September 2001 will long be remembered. Tony Blair, the British prime minister, sat in the gallery along with First Lady Laura Bush and Lisa Beamer, the young widow of one of the gallant passengers on United Airlines Flight 93 who had died in the crash in western Pennsylvania after he and other passengers prevented the plane from reaching Washington, D.C. Most Americans were glued to their television sets. It was an emotional time for the country. A collective sigh could almost be heard as President Bush reflected on the sound of our national anthem as it was recently played "at Buckingham Palace, on the streets of Paris, and at Berlin's Brandenburg Gate."

On the floor of the House chamber and in homes, hospitals, precinct houses, fire stations, public offices, military barracks, and airports all over the nation, people waited for some reassurance. Everyone wanted to hear that the government was taking steps to protect them. "Our nation has been put on notice," the president said solemnly. "We're not immune from attack. We will take defensive measures against terrorism to protect Americans." Noting that dozens of federal departments and agencies, as well as state and local governments, have responsibilities affecting homeland security and that their efforts must be "coordinated at the highest level," he announced the creation of the Office of Homeland Security. Its director, who would serve in a cabinet-level position, would report directly to him. After introducing Tom Ridge, Pennsylvania's governor and a decorated veteran of Vietnam, as his choice to lead the homeland security effort, the president defined Ridge's mission in simple terms: "He will lead, oversee and coordinate a comprehensive national strategy to safeguard our country against terrorism, and respond to any attacks that may come."[20]

Initial reaction to the announcement was generally supportive, but cautious. Previous efforts by both Democrat and Republican presidents to create "high-level liaisons, such as anti-drug czars," had met with mixed success.[21] Representative William M. "Mac" Thornberry, the member of Congress who had earlier introduced legislation to create a separate national homeland security agency, called the president's action an "important first step."[22]

But, members of the Senate Intelligence Committee introduced legislation to make Ridge's position permanent and to provide his office with its own budget authority. The chairman of the Senate Government Affairs Committee urged the creation of a new cabinet department that would give Ridge "both budget and direct-line authority."[23] Addressing the question of how much authority should be given to Ridge, Dave McIntyre, the deputy director of a public service research organization, declared that "for more than a decade the 'Drug Czar' has languished in the nether land of political impotence, able to see the problem and able to see the resources available and required to attack the problem, but unable to direct their efficient and effective use."[24]

Conflicting priorities are always a problem. Bill Bennett, the first drug czar under President George H. W. Bush,[25] once came to the Pentagon to seek a change in the allocation of counterdrug resources by DoD. I was present at the meeting with Bennett; Bennett's deputy John Walters; Secretary of Defense Dick Cheney; and Gen. Colin Powell, the chairman of the Joint Chiefs of Staff. Since I was responsible for all DoD counterdrug programs and the supporting budget, I was asked by Cheney whether he should agree to Bennett's request. Reluctantly, I said no. I had solid reasons for the position I took, but they were reasons that flowed from the perspective of the Department of Defense and the many worldwide missions that were then assigned to DoD rather than from the perspective of the drug czar. When Powell concurred with my opinion, Cheney promptly declined Bennett's request. Although I believe that the correct decision was made, the drug czar's lack of direct authority over resources left a large impression.

In late September 2001 additional organizational details were announced by the White House. Vice President Cheney had been working on the homeland security issue since early May. He was tentatively planning to recommend to the president that a White House office on homeland security be established, but a final recommendation was not expected until later.[26] After the 11 September attacks, Cheney reportedly "rushed ahead with a recommendation";

it was made on 19 September.[27] It contained few specifics, so it was likely that most details were hammered out after the president's 20 September address.

A new Homeland Security Council would be established with powers comparable to those exercised by the National Security Council. The new council's membership would include the attorney general; the secretaries of defense, treasury, health and human services, and agriculture; and the directors of the FBI and FEMA. It would be supported by a staff of approximately one hundred people, many on loan from other agencies. Because it would be created by executive order, rather than by statute like the NSC, it would be "empowered by its proximity to the President rather than by actual legal authority."[28] Significantly, and because Governor Ridge would not have to be confirmed by the Senate, there would be no congressional oversight of the work of the new council.

On 8 October 2001 President Bush signed Executive Order 13228 and the new director of the Homeland Security Council took the oath of office. At the same time, Gen. Wayne Downing, USA (Ret.), the former commander-in-chief of the U.S. Special Operations Command, joined the National Security Council staff as the president's deputy national security advisor for combating terrorism. Downing replaced Richard Clarke, who assumed responsibility as the special advisor to the president for cyberspace security.

In the days that followed, endless questions were raised about the authority of the new director of homeland security. Would he have access to intelligence information from the CIA and FBI? What authority would he have over the budgets of the federal law enforcement, disaster recovery, and intelligence bureaucracies? Which, if any, federal agencies would be put under his direct control? What were his priorities? How would he force cooperation among the forty-six agencies that had some counterterrorist jurisdiction? The consensus seemed to be that Ridge would have to carve out and shape his role by dint of personality and use of his access to the president. At first and even second glance, the task appeared very formidable. Reporter Ann Gerhart characterized it as keeping Americans safe "in a gloriously unrestricted nation of more than 2,800 power plants, 190,000 miles of natural-gas pipelines, nearly 600,000 bridges, 463 sky scrapers, 20,000 miles of border and 285,000,000 people."[29] She could have added that eighteen million cargo containers enter the country each year, anyone can hide a weapon of mass destruction, and thousands of trucks cross the Canadian and Mexican borders each day.[30] Ridge did not underestimate his job. He compared it to three historic national efforts: the victory in World War II, the step of an American on the moon, and the construction of the transcontinental railroad.[31]

While Tom Ridge was struggling to get his arms around a job of enormous scope and complexity and to control or at least influence the allocation of resources to it, the Department of Defense was simultaneously fighting the hot counterterrorism war against hidden al Qaeda and Taliban fighters in Afghanistan and attempting to determine how it could contribute to homeland security. There were several immediate problems. Since the attack on the USS *Cole* in October 2000, military officials had expressed concern about the security of the nation's 580 military installations, 61 of which were overseas or outside of U.S. territorial borders. The concern became greater after the General Accounting Office concluded that eleven major bases in the United States had "numerous potential vulnerabilities."[32]

Within hours after the attacks on 11 September the U.S. Armed Forces had mobilized to defend all U.S. territory in a way not even seen during World War II. Army National Guard personnel were activated to provide security at airports, dams, power plants, border checkpoints, and other critical places. Air National Guard personnel in fighter aircraft flew combat air patrols over the nation's capital and its largest city. Ships armed with surface-to-air missiles patrolled both coasts. U.S. Coast Guard cutters inspected commercial and recreational vessels. Soldiers stood guard on many street corners. Difficult decisions could no longer be delayed. Now it was time to turn to hard business, to both the long-term protection of the homeland and the transformation of the country's armed forces into a force capable of fighting the conflicts of the future. The first question to be addressed on the issue of homeland security and the armed forces was a familiar one. In light of the 20 September presidential guidance, what were the most appropriate roles and missions for the nation's military? Within twenty days after the terrorist attacks, part of the answer became clear.

As required by law, on 1 October 2001 the secretary of defense submitted to Congress the quadrennial defense review report for 2001. While the seventy-one-page document was criticized as only a "thematic" paper that contained few specifics on how the armed forces would be changed, it was useful for several purposes. First, the QDR report declared that the "highest priority" of the U.S. military was now to defend the nation from all enemies. To that end, sufficient military forces would be maintained to "protect the U.S. domestic population, its territory, and its critical defense-related infrastructure against attacks emanating from outside U.S. borders."[33] Although seemingly self-evident, a clear statement of priorities was needed. New emphasis was placed on "the unique operational demands associated with the defense of the United States," and those efforts would be DoD's "primary mission."[34] The QDR report rejected the idea that the Department of Defense has the sole responsibility for homeland security, but it candidly recognized that "DoD must institutionalize definitions of homeland security, homeland defense, and civil support and address command relationships and responsibilities within the Defense Department" so that it can "identify and assign homeland security roles and missions, as well as examine resource implications."[35]

Second, the new defense strategy outlined in the QDR report added a necessary element of certainty to the armed forces planning process. It shifted the basis of defense planning "from a 'threat-based' model that [has] dominated the thinking in the past, to a 'capabilities-based' model for the future."[36] Leaving aside the jargon, the QDR report modified the requirement that the armed forces must be structured and resourced to fight and win two major regional conflicts (presumably against Iraq and North Korea) almost simultaneously. The new capabilities-based model focused "more on how an adversary might fight rather than specifically whom the adversary might be or where a war might occur."[37] Under the new standard, the armed forces would have to be prepared to win one major war decisively. In essence, the armed forces would have to be capable of occupying an adversary's capitol if necessary and, at the same time, be able to swiftly defeat another adversary in a second theater of conflict. The new global war on terrorism was considered to be one of the conflicts.[38]

Finally, the QDR report placed greater emphasis on intelligence collection and special operations to combat terrorist threats before they reach U.S. shores. And, contrary to many expectations,[39] the QDR report recommended retention of the current force structure for both the active and reserve components.[40]

Work to "address command relationships and responsibilities" began immediately. Unlike the circumstances I encountered in 1989 when I was given overall responsibility for the implementation of all counterdrug missions assigned to the armed forces and specific responsibility for the coordination of all counterdrug policy matters, no senior civilian official had been given similar authority within DoD for homeland security. This problem was quickly, if temporarily, fixed. In early October the secretary of the army was named as the interim homeland security coordinator while Pentagon officials decided whether to establish a new assistant secretary of defense position or another senior civilian position dedicated exclusively to the task of coordinating policy, planning, and resources for homeland security.[41]

The question of where to place primary operational authority and responsibility for homeland security took longer to address. In the aftermath of the 11 September attacks, the North American Aerospace Defense Command (NORAD) in Colorado Springs, Colorado, was responsible for the combat air patrol, but the U.S. Joint Forces Command in Norfolk, Virginia, had control of approximately 80 percent of the active military forces in the continental United States, as well as responsibility for military assistance to civil authorities. Evidence indicated that the absence of a clear line of operational authority made the military response to the attacks "more *ad hoc* and more difficult."[42]

Over the next several months, the entire "unified command plan" of the U.S. Armed Forces came under close scrutiny. Defense officials expressed concern about the current structure, which divided the world into five regional unified combatant commands (and four others assigned "functional" missions).[43] The military commander-in-chief (CINC) of each regional command had broad authority to plan and conduct military operations within his geographical area. This structure seemed inadequate for a global campaign against terrorism. Predictably, other officials were suspicious of any effort to establish a counterterrorism CINC with global responsibilities because they feared that the move would result in turf fights between the occupant of that position and the regional CINCs. The idea of a new CINC responsible for defending the continental United States was sufficiently radical to raise many questions. The matter of the most appropriate military organizational structure for the defense of the country's soil was not a mere issue of management or communications flow. The issue had heat. It was influenced by the terrible command relationship between the secretary of defense and the chiefs of the individual services, on the one hand, and a particular CINC, on the other hand, that had existed during the recent Balkan conflict.

The point of departure for any consideration of the matter was the Goldwater-Nichols Defense Reorganization Act of 1986. Passed by Congress over the strenuous objection of Secretary of Defense Caspar Weinberger and most of the service chiefs, the legislation centralized authority on the Joint Chiefs of Staff in the person of the chairman. The chairman was designated the principal military advisor to the secretary of defense and the president. During my service at the Pentagon from 1987–93, I had watched with fascination how two chairmen had exercised the power. With the new law going into effect during his term of office, Adm. William J. Crowe Jr. was a transition chairman. He had exercised his new power quietly and gently. Gen. Colin Powell, who relieved Crowe, placed a much firmer hand on the wheel. "I was not," Powell said much later, "the pipeline for the composite opinions of the Chiefs. I was speaking for myself to the Secretary and the President."[44]

As part of an effort to streamline the chain of command and improve the quality of joint combat operations, the Goldwater-Nichols legislation had also strengthened substantially the power and prestige of the regional CINCs. The individual service chiefs were thus stripped of much authority and left with the task of providing trained manpower and resources to the CINCs. The impact of the change was great. "In the past," observed David Halberstam, "the job as the head of a service—Army Chief of Staff or Chief of Naval Operations—had been the ultimate reward for a successful career. But, Goldwater-Nichols changed that."[45]

The issue of command relationships also has other complexities. Statutory power and political power are different things. Admiral Crowe noted that "no matter what legislation Congress passes," and "no matter how much authority he has, the Chairman needs the Chiefs' expertise and support."[46] There is also what one recent CINC has called the "natural tension between Service Chiefs, who are responsible for a longer-term view, and the regional commanders responsible for the immediate response to crises."[47]

There are also many more subtle elements involved in the sharing of power. When an armed conflict starts, power tends to move to the commander in the field because he is the one on the spot and because Washington officials do not want to be "portrayed as not having given a commander what he needed to do the job."[48] Les Aspin, President Clinton's first secretary of defense, was forced to resign in part because of his failure to provide equipment requested on the scene in Somalia in the fall of 1993. What has been described as the "normal, occasionally edgy relationship between a CINC and the Secretary of Defense,"[49] can also become adversarial as a result of policy differences and personality conflicts. This is clearly what happened in the Balkan conflict in 1999 when the hostility between Secretary of Defense Bill Cohen and Gen. Wesley Clark, the NATO commander, resulted in early termination of the latter's tenure. Clark later described high-level command relationships: "In modern war, there is no sharp dividing line between the matters that diplomats and politicians handle and the activities of the senior military. Consequently, there is a rough-and-tumble, push-and-shove quality within the chain of command which is seldom understood outside the inner circles. Commanders' backgrounds, competence and motivations are often questioned. Decisions are second-guessed, or reviewed before execution. Authorities are withheld. Subordinates are encouraged to give their own opinions, often at variance with the official command view. High command is no place for those who need consensus."[50]

The complexity of a new command for homeland security to which all these elements would contribute would be exacerbated by the unique nature of the job. Whatever difficulties the regional CINCs would face, they would not have to deal on a regular basis with domestic political pressure from fifty states, thousands of local communities, and over forty federal agencies.[51] They would not be subject to continuous close scrutiny by local media in the United States, as well as the national media. They would not have to deal daily with the fear of millions of Americans from attack by terrorists. A new CINC would immediately have to deal with many questions. What forces should now be given specific homeland security missions? What are the missions that must be performed? What should be the responsibility of the Army and Air National Guard? Should the National Guard be deployed under Title 32 of the *U.S. Code*, which governs deployments for state missions, or Title 10, under which the National Guard may be activated for federal missions? Should the states or the federal government pay the costs for the use of the National Guard? What support would civil authorities need in widely varying sets of circumstances?

On 17 April 2002 defense officials announced the establishment of a new U.S. Northern Command (NORTHCOM) that would commence operations on 1 October. Based at Peterson Air Force Base in Colorado, NORTHCOM would be responsible for homeland security. Its area of responsibility (AOR) would include the United States, Canada, Mexico, parts of the Caribbean, and the contiguous waters in the Atlantic and Pacific Oceans. Secretary of Defense Rumsfeld said that the new command would be "responsible for land, aerospace and sea defenses of the United States,"[52] and would provide support to civil authorities, not only in response to terrorist or other attacks, but also for natural disasters. The four star commander of NORTHCOM would also serve as the head of the North American Aerospace Defense Command, a U.S.–Canada command. The responsibilities of all but two of the unified combatant commands would be changed to strengthen the homeland security authority of NORTHCOM.[53] The secretary of defense and the chairman of the Joint Chiefs of Staff characterized the changes as the most sweeping set of changes since the unified command plan was formed in 1946.

In September, only days before the new command became operational, a tentative modus operandi had been established. "My view," Gen. Ralph Eberhart, USAF, the designated commander of NORTHCOM, said, "is [that] in almost every case, we are going to be in *support* of another agency."[54] Plans called for military authorities to follow a four-step process in evaluating a possible response to a terrorist incident or even a natural disaster. Four questions would be asked. What happened? Who's in charge? "What might Northern Command have to offer" in terms of federal military forces? "How should [NORTHCOM] organize . . . to make the best use of those forces?"[55] Plans were also under way for training exercises involving both civilian agencies and military forces. "This should not be a sandlot pickup game," Eberhart said. "We need to be prepared to react, but we need to work harder on the front end of that game," by sharing intelligence with local and regional law enforcement agencies that could deter future attacks.[56]

In the months following the appointment of Tom Ridge as the president's homeland security advisor, the many problems of organizing the nation for the battle against terrorism at home became increasingly apparent. One source of frustration was the difference in the method of operation of the combatants. "Most of what the United States brings to the fight," wrote critic David Wood, are federal agencies that are "stovepipe" or top-down hierarchies with strong leadership at the top that were "designed 50 years ago to harness a massive industrial and military power to struggle against the Soviet Union."[57] The contrast with loosely organized, "floating networks of temporary cells" of terrorists acting "independently, stealthily and unpredictably"[58] was stark. Many believed the answer lay in developing an ability to get "inside" the terrorists' decision loop.[59] The question was, how?

A second problem was founded in both institutional and party politics. In March 2002 the Democrat-controlled Senate invited Ridge to appear at a hearing for testimony on the president's proposed budget for homeland security. Given the significance of the issue and the unquestioned power of Congress to appropriate or withhold funding for it, few doubted the attendant need for congressional oversight. Because Ridge was a personal advisor to the president and did not occupy a position requiring confirmation by the Senate, the White House took the position that he was not required to appear and should not. Immediate objections were voiced by Democrats about excessive secretiveness. In an effort to compromise, Ridge met formally and privately with a House appropriations subcommittee. Senator Robert Byrd, the chairman of the Senate Appropriations Committee, publicly rejected that approach.

As March turned to April doubt began to spread in some quarters not only about Ridge's authority, but also his ability. It was self-evident that he could not ask the president for help every time he had a problem with a federal department or agency. Because he lacked statutory authority, he conceded that he could not succeed unless he was able to obtain consensus for his plans from agency officials. Consensus did not come easily. The attorney general was given the authority to assign the level of risk associated with particular threats under a color-coded terrorism alert system that was developed by Ridge's staff; this incident was reported as a bureaucratic defeat for Ridge. What was described as an "even more humiliating defeat" involved border security. After Ridge proposed the consolidation of federal agencies that had concurrent jurisdiction over border security, officials of those agencies scuttled the idea—at least for the time being. Asserting that he was rapidly losing his credibility, the *Economist* predicted that because Ridge had been "beaten in so many turf wars . . . he [would] soon be looking for office space in Baltimore."[60]

While a considerable part of the difficulty was structural in nature, much of it also lay in the fact that almost ten months after the 11 September attacks, no homeland security strategy was in place. In the absence of a clear strategy outlining short-term and long-term priorities, it was difficult to criticize agency heads acting within the authority of existing law. It was also difficult to evaluate budgetary recommendations. A member of the House Select Intelligence Committee's Terrorism and Homeland Security Subcommittee declared, "There is a 2003 budget request for homeland security of $37.7 billion, but no strategy to explain whether this is the right amount or the right priorities for federal spending. . . . Our homeland security efforts to date have been ad hoc."[61] Such comments about organization and strategy were heard at the White

House. Within days, new developments on these issues propelled the national debate in different directions.

In a televised address to the nation on the evening of 6 June 2002, President Bush reversed his earlier action and proposed a new homeland security organizational scheme, a step that he had been urged to take for months. Explaining what even critics would later describe as a bold initiative, the president called for the creation of a permanent cabinet-level Department of Homeland Security. "After September the 11th, we needed to move quickly," he said, "and so I appointed Tom Ridge as my Homeland Security Advisor. As Governor Ridge has worked with all levels of government to prepare a national strategy, and as we have learned more about the plans and capabilities of the terrorist network, we have concluded that our Government must be reorganized to deal more effectively with the new threats of the 21st century. So tonight, I ask the Congress to join me in creating a single, permanent department with an overriding and urgent mission: securing the homeland of America."[62]

Put together in a six-week period by a handful of White House aides working in conditions of extreme secrecy, the proposal called for what was characterized as "the most significant transformation of the U.S. Government" since passage of the National Security Act of 1947 created the Department of Defense and the Central Intelligence Agency.[63] As envisioned by the White House, the new department would consolidate twenty-two federal agencies into a new department with almost 170,000 employees and a budget of almost $38 billion. The far-reaching plan would establish four divisions within the new department: (1) border and transportation security, (2) emergency preparedness and response, (3) chemical, biological, radiological, and nuclear countermeasures, and (4) information analysis and infrastructure protection. The U.S. Coast Guard, FEMA, the Customs Service, the Immigration and Naturalization Service, the Secret Service, the U.S. Border Patrol, and several other organizations would be consolidated and placed in the new department.

Immediately, problems associated with the creation of a new organization of such size and complexity became the subject of daily discourse. Jeffrey

Sonnenfeld, the associate dean of the Yale School of Management, asserted that while the attempt had to be made, "[i]t has about a 20% chance of working."[64] James Champy, an expert on large corporate mergers, declared that no company would attempt a change on the scale of the proposed department and that it would be five years before the department would have even modest efficiency.[65] Worries were expressed about how the affected agencies would keep up with their non–national security responsibilities. The difficulty of creating a coherent corporate culture out of so many disparate organizational cultures was noted by almost all commentators.

One of the greatest obstacles would involve people. In only half jest, Siobhan Gorman, a journalist who writes on government matters, declared that the head of the new department would have to be a larger-than-life figure.[66] Unlike mergers in the private sector where the surviving chief executive officer (CEO) often assumes dictatorial authority, the political leader of the new department would necessarily share power with other elements within the executive branch and both houses of Congress. There were eighty-eight separate committees and subcommittees in the House and Senate that had some homeland security oversight authority.[67] It would also be difficult to find senior leaders for the department who had experience in all of the operational areas to be placed under their control. In the absence of such experience, they would be dependent upon subordinates. That is a recipe for "a holding company," said Frank Dobbin, a Princeton University expert in organizational behavior, "not a department."[68] Moreover, data from the private sector indicated that in most mergers, productivity drops by 50 percent in the first four to eight months because of the preoccupation of employees with their uncertain future.[69] Yet another factor would compound the predictable complications. Within the next five years, half of the federal workforce, including those who would be placed in the new department, might be eligible to retire.[70] The effect of such a loss in skills, experience, and institutional knowledge could have devastating effects.

Politics would inevitably be involved in all aspects of the consideration by Congress of the president's proposal. However, only five days after the proposal

was made, the leaders of both parties set a goal of establishing the new department by the first anniversary of the 11 September attacks. In order to reach that
goal, legislative priorities were rearranged. Despite the belief of many members
that shortcomings in the performance of the FBI and CIA required a reorganization of the intelligence community, that difficult task was postponed.

Ten days after the terrorist attacks in New York and Washington, D.C., David
Walker, the comptroller general and the chief of the General Accounting Office
(GAO), the investigative arm of Congress, testified before the Senate Committee
on Governmental Affairs. The subject of the hearing was the urgent need for a
strategy for homeland security. "Crafting a strategy for homeland security," he
said, "involves reducing the risk where possible, assessing the nation's vulnerabilities, and identifying the critical infrastructure most in need of protection."[71]
To be comprehensive, "the strategy should include steps to use intelligence assets
or other means to identify attackers and prevent attacks before they occur, harden
potential targets to minimize the danger from an attack, and effectively manage
the consequences of an incident."[72] Without such a strategy, he added, "efforts
may be fragmented and cause confusion, duplication of effort, and ineffective
alignment of resources with strategic goals."[73]

Consensus had been building in several quarters that an important first step
in developing such a strategy would be a national threat and risk assessment,
"a decision-making tool that [would help] to define threats, to evaluate the
associated risk, and to link requirements to program investments."[74] In short,
because of the wide range of the nation's vulnerabilities, it was necessary to
establish policy and spending priorities. In calling for an annual threat assessment, a Center for Strategic and International Studies report argued that such
an assessment would provide federal planners with an analytical structure for
planning.[75] The GAO asserted that it could provide "a framework for action
and facilitate multidisciplinary and multi-organizational participation in planning, developing, and implementing" homeland security programs.[76]

Defense against terrorist threats, however, involves much more than the
efforts of the federal government, even though most Americans have traditionally thought of national defense as the exclusive responsibility of the

federal government. One GAO official said, "National preparedness is a complex mission that involves a broad range of functions performed throughout government, including national defense, law enforcement, transportation, food safety and public health, information technology, and emergency management, to mention only a few. While only the Federal government is empowered to wage war and regulate interstate commerce, state and local governments have historically assumed primary responsibility for managing emergencies through police, fire-fighting, and emergency medical personnel."[77] Still, broad concern existed about the state of federal preparedness. Coordination and fragmentation problems stemming largely from a lack of accountability within the federal government for terrorism-related programs and activities remained. Several departments and agencies had previously been assigned leadership and coordination functions but no single leader had been placed in charge.

It was in this environment that President Bush presented the government's first blueprint to protect the nation against terrorists at a Rose Garden ceremony on the afternoon of 17 July 2002. The seventy-six-page *National Strategy for Homeland Security*, produced after eight months of work, candidly acknowledged that securing the American homeland is a challenge of "monumental scale and complexity."[78] It also admitted that "it is not practical or possible to eliminate all risks," and that there will always be "some level of risk that cannot be mitigated without the use of unacceptably large expenditures."[79]

Three strategic objectives of homeland security were identified: prevention of terrorist attacks within the United States; reduction of the country's vulnerability to terrorism; and minimization of the damage and recovery from attacks that do occur. The national strategy would require a national effort, involving not only the eighty-seven thousand overlapping jurisdictions of the federal, state, and local governments, but also the private sector—the owner of 85 percent of the nation's infrastructure—and an "informed and proactive citizenry." Homeland security functions were aligned into six critical mission areas: (1) intelligence and warning, (2) border and transportation security, (3) domestic counterterrorism, (4) protection of critical infrastructure and key assets, (5) defense against catastrophic threats, and (6) emergency preparedness and response.

Very little was said expressly in the strategy document about specific homeland security responsibilities for the armed forces. It contemplated only "military support to civil authorities" in the form of "providing technical support and assistance to law enforcement; assisting in the restoration of law and order; and assisting in consequence management."[80] The only lead role assigned to the Department of Defense was a vague one of "defending the people and the territory of our country" in certain undefined "extraordinary circumstances."[81] As discussed in Chapter 6, one proposal characterized as a major federal initiative immediately raised cries of alarm in some quarters. "The threat of catastrophic terrorism," the document said, "requires a thorough review of the laws permitting the military to act within the United States in order to determine whether domestic preparedness and response efforts would benefit from greater involvement of military personnel and, if so, how."[82]

In subsequent weeks, civilian defense officials had little or nothing to add. It seemed clear that no separate Department of Defense homeland security policy was being formulated. Initiatives were being left primarily to the yet to be established Department of Homeland Security or at least to the operational planning of NORTHCOM, which would come into effect 1 October. When asked about DoD's plans to aggressively train first responders, the local emergency personnel who would be first on the scene of another terrorist attack, the secretary of defense's special assistant for homeland security, Peter Verga, said only that DoD was waiting for guidance from the new department.[83]

Generally, the new strategy was well received. Like most strategies, it was long on describing the "many different goals that need to be met, the programs that need to be implemented, and responsibilities that need to be fulfilled."[84] Despite a statement in its conclusion, however, that "[t]he principal purpose of a strategy . . . is to set priorities,"[85] it did little to establish spending priorities for homeland security. James Lindsay, a domestic security expert at the Brookings Institute, said that the National Strategy for Home Security listed "everything the

Government wants to do, but without any clear priority for doing it."[86] The setting of priorities would inevitably require a cost-benefit analysis for every desired program, for as journalist Sebastian Mallaby noted, "some kinds of homeland defense are cheap relative to the devastation they could avert" and some homeland security investments might bring other benefits as well, such as an improved public health system.[87] Further recommendations for the allocation of tax dollars to homeland security programs awaited the president's submission of his proposed budget for fiscal year 2004 to the new Congress that would assume office in January 2003. Many in Congress remained hopeful that the budget would be based on a comprehensive threat and risk assessment.

On 26 July 2002, after considerable partisan debate and by a 295–132 vote, the House of Representatives approved the creation of a new Department of Homeland Security. The bill had moved through the House with surprising speed despite fears that it would be delayed by special interest groups opposed to specific provisions or committee chairmen resisting a loss of committee jurisdiction over important agencies of the federal government, or that the non-terrorism responsibilities of agencies to be included in the new department would be given short shrift by department officials in their zeal to concentrate on homeland security. Part of the reason was that members of the House were anxious to complete action prior to Congress's election-year August recess. Desire also existed to pass the legislation prior to the first anniversary of the terrorist attacks.

In the Senate, however, roadblocks were encountered. Senator Robert Byrd of West Virginia and others were considering procedures to delay the bill because of a belief that lawmakers were going too fast and "racing to meet artificial deadlines."[88] Concerned that the president's proposal had been "barreling through Congress like a Mack truck, threatening to run over anyone who dares to stand in its way," Byrd said that he supported creation of the new department in a stage-by-stage approval process over a one-year transition period.[89]

The real point of disagreement, however, was the question of whether the president should be given authority to remove employees in the new department from civil service protection and labor unions for reasons of national security. The bill passed by the House gave the president power to exclude Department of Homeland Security employees from labor-management contracts in individual cases if he determined that the contracts would substantially impair the department's ability to maintain security. The White House wanted the secretary of the new department to be able to design a personnel system that would make it easier to hire, reward, discipline, and move employees. Senator Fred Thompson, who supported the idea, called many of the agencies to be included in the new department "dysfunctional" and said that the situation could only be repaired by giving the new secretary greater flexibility. "We can't apply the same type management that we've had in the past to this new department," he said. "The stakes are too great."[90]

Certainly, the dispute involved elements of institutional politics. The president declared that he would veto legislation "that limits or weakens the President's well-established authorities."[91] Senate Majority Leader Tom Daschle indicated that he would not compromise; he accused Bush of "a power grab of unprecedented magnitude."[92] Behind the surface of the dispute lay politics of a different sort, control of Congress. "By providing Democrats with both money and troops on the ground," said one newspaper, "unions serve as the party's single most important political ally, and lawmakers are loath to cross them just weeks before critical elections."[93]

As unlikely as compromise appeared on the first anniversary of the terrorist attacks, the impasse in Congress was only the first of the anticipated organizational hurdles. The management of the new department was going to be a "massive undertaking," the comptroller general said. The agencies that would be merged in the department "have different personnel systems. They have different cultures. They have different information systems. They have different information management systems. They have different locations."[94]

As work proceeded, government leaders continued to seek what President George Washington had referred to 206 years earlier, namely, "a government of as much vigor as is consistent with the perfect security of liberty."[95] They were also reflecting upon the political changes since 11 September. "[B]y its creation," said one commentator, "a Homeland Security Department would stand as a monument to how much the terrorist hijackings transformed America, not least its Government and politics. Liberals are resigned to more funds for defense, . . . conservatives to some government growth, and both to curbs on privacy."[96]

5

The Threat and the Bureaucratic Maze

[T]he covert threat straddles the divide between national security, law
enforcement, and emergency management, allowing the
Department of Defense to dodge responsibility.

—Richard A. Falkenrath, Robert D. Newman, and Bradley A. Thayer,
America's Achilles' Heel, 2001

It has been asserted with some exaggeration that many Americans believed that
"prior to September 11, Washington's singular preoccupation when it came to
protecting the U.S. homeland was national missile defense."[1] Part of the preoccupation was due to missile technology advances made by rogue states such
as North Korea. Much, however, was due to a reluctance of Americans to
believe that terrorists might actually attempt to attack us at home as well as
an unjustified overconfidence in our country's defenses against more primitive
delivery systems. In testimony before the House Armed Services Committee

in June 1993, for example, the acting director of the Pentagon's ballistic missile defense organization declared that "we have mechanisms in place to detect and counter things like bombs in suitcases, bombs in airline terminals, and bombs in ships of various kinds. These things can be tracked and looked at, and there are ways to counter them. I can't think of anything except a strategic missile today that we don't have a countermeasure in-hand for."[2] In a sweeping statement in November 1996 President Clinton formally certified to Congress that "the United States has the capability to prevent the illegal importation of nuclear, biological, and chemical weapons into the United States and its possessions."[3]

Another contributing factor was what appeared to be a relatively successful de facto policy that had evolved over several years. Its objective was the reduction of terrorist attacks to a manageable level. This was not unlike the Israeli approach to terrorism. In describing Israel's effort to reduce terrorist attacks "to a level that can be lived with," one senior Israeli official has compared the effort to a situation between a doctor and patient. There is no permanent solution to the medical problem. If the patient is left untreated, he will die in three months after suffering great pain. No reasonable patient, so the story goes, would reject a treatment that would greatly reduce the pain and extend his life expectancy to ten years, merely because the doctor could offer no permanent solution to the problem.

Conceding that "what seems self-evident at Harvard [University] often has little to do with Washington's political realities," Richard Falkenrath, Robert Newman, and Bradley Thayer's 2001 America's Achilles' Heel asserted that another of the reasons why U.S. defense policy prior to 11 September 2001 emphasized missile defense was that "the covert [nuclear, biological, and chemical] threat straddles the divide between national security, law enforcement, and emergency management, allowing the Department of Defense to dodge responsibility."[4] No one would dispute that homeland security includes these and other elements. Informed defense policy students would also agree that as the tempo of U.S. military operations increased and the size of the U.S. Armed Forces and the defense budget decreased in the years following the end of the Cold War, military planners were not seeking new missions that might be performed by other arms of government.

To suggest that the Department of Defense dodged responsibility, however, is to assume that only the Pentagon is responsible for the nation's security at home. This was not the case before 11 September and it most certainly is not now. The complicated and often confusing bureaucratic maze that homeland security entails may be simply illustrated by noting certain facts. The Tenth Amendment to the Constitution reserves to the states and to the people all power that is not delegated to the federal government. There are more than eighty-seven thousand different and often overlapping federal, state, and local governmental jurisdictions within the United States.[5] Moreover, the vast majority of the nation's critical infrastructure is owned by the private sector.

The effective integration of agencies of government with widely varying functions is a continuous, major challenge. Homeland security is immeasurably more complex because its first objective is the disruption of terrorist networks and the absolute prevention of clandestine attacks, especially attacks involving weapons of mass destruction. Second, structures must be in place to successfully mitigate the consequences of any such attack that actually occurs.

Most of the focus since 11 September on the nature of the threats the United States faces has been on weapons of mass destruction, and, more specifically, nuclear, biological, and chemical (NBC) weapons. This is not surprising. The knowledge, technology, and materials required to construct such weapons are spreading. President Bush, in the July 2002 *National Strategy for Homeland Security* report by the Office of Homeland Security, declared, "If our enemies acquire these weapons, they are likely to try to use them."[6] These three types of weapons "share three terrible characteristics. The first is immense lethality; a single weapon can kill thousands of people. The second is portability, which allows them to be easily delivered against civilian populations and unprepared military forces. . . . [T]he third is accessibility, which means they may fall into hostile hands, despite the best efforts at prevention."[7]

The emerging threats to a free and open nation with so many vulnerabilities, however, are more diffuse. Even in the absence of mass human casualties, there could be mass disruptions of critical infrastructure, including the delivery of water and power, the functioning of data systems that support endless commercial activities, the functioning of transportation systems, and the continuity of government. Fear and the feeling of helplessness could also make people change their normal patterns of conduct in ways that reduce the quality of their lives significantly. Still, because the effects of a WMD/NBC attack could be catastrophic,[8] defense planning must give these weapons very high priority.

The conventional wisdom is that the threat of a terrorist attack using a suitcase-sized nuclear device is not great, but it is real. Terrorists could steal or purchase such a weapon. To produce one, it would be necessary for a terrorist group to acquire twenty-five kilograms of highly enriched uranium or eight kilograms of plutonium, a real, although limited, possibility given numerous unconfirmed reports of the sale or theft of fissionable materials from the arsenal of the former Soviet Union. It is estimated that within the radius of a few miles of a nuclear blast, at least one hundred thousand people would die instantly. Many thousands more would die later from radiation poisoning aftereffects.

Of greater concern than a nuclear bomb is a "dirty" bomb, simply because it is likely to be more available to terrorists. A dirty bomb is a conventional weapon loaded with radiological garbage, anything from bars of radioactive cobalt that are used to irradiate food to isotopes that are used by radiology clinics. On 3 May 2002 the U.S. Nuclear Regulatory Commission reported that since 1996 in the United States alone, businesses and medical facilities had lost track of nearly fifteen hundred pieces of equipment with radioactive parts that could be used in a dirty bomb.[9] The following month, the Justice Department announced that it had interrupted a plan by al Qaeda to detonate a dirty bomb in the United States by the arrest of a man identified as Abdullah al-Muhajir, a thirty-one-year-old former Chicago gang member named Jose Padilla, who had converted to Islam.[10] A recent report that "only a small fraction of the millions of commercial radioactive sources used globally, perhaps several tens of thousands, pose inherently high security risks"[11] is hardly reassuring.

An even greater danger may be the possibility of an attack on one of the nation's 103 nuclear power reactors,[12] a nuclear weapons storage depot, or some other nuclear facility. Any such attack could cause massive radiation leaks. Al Qaeda's long-standing interest in acquiring a nuclear capability is well documented,[13] but eight months after the 11 September attacks, the Bush administration had not produced a clear strategy for achieving the president's previously stated goal of constricting "the supply of nuclear materials and the means to deliver them."[14]

Chemical weapons have relatively less lethality than nuclear or biological weapons. They are difficult to use effectively because unpredictable winds, temperature, and other climatic factors can dissipate toxic mists. For this and other reasons, many experts believe that the greatest chemical threat is the possibility of terrorist attacks on chemical refineries and other plants. The range of potential targets is huge. One expert informed Congress that approximately 850,000 U.S. facilities, many of which are located in or near major urban areas, use hazardous or extremely hazardous chemicals.[15] An analysis by the Environmental Protection Agency has concluded that 123 plants in the United States maintain amounts of toxic chemicals that, if released, could form vapor clouds endangering in excess of one million people.[16] More than 700 facilities have chemicals that could endanger as many as 100,000 people; approximately 3,015 chemical facilities could put at least 10,000 people at risk.[17] The absence of any federal security standards for chemical facilities stimulated debate in Congress in late 2002 on the issue of whether new legislation should require chemical companies to comply with mandatory government measures or with standards drawn by the American Chemistry Council, the industry's trade association.[18]

Until the attacks of 11 September and the anthrax scare that began with the death of a Florida man a few weeks later, national security policy makers were divided on whether the threat of bioterrorism was theoretical or real. Most major military powers had developed biological weapons at some time during the twentieth century, but moral repugnance and skepticism about their military value prevented countries from using the weapons against each other.[19]

The United States and almost 150 other countries signed the Biological and Toxin Weapons Convention of 1972, which banned the production, stockpiling, and use of bacteriological weapons, but it was not until 1997 that the first systematic survey of biological agents was published.[20]

By the beginning of the twenty-first century, however, the diffusion of relevant "dual-use" technologies was causing many to refer to biological agents as the "poor man's atomic bomb."[21] Almost any country with a pharmaceutical industry can produce biological weapons. "The danger of mass bioterrorism," two experts have noted, "lies precisely in its murderous flexibility. Dozens of biological agents, from plague to salmonella, are available to the determined bioterrorist. . . . Less than 300 grams of dry anthrax, carried into the country as a harmless-looking brownish powder and poured into the ventilating system of a shopping mall, a public building or a traffic tunnel, could fell thousands. A . . . lone individual willing to be infected, could become the carrier of a disease whose effects don't become obvious until days or weeks after first contact is made."[22] A June 2001 war game exercise, which modeled the effects of a smallpox attack on three U.S. cities, reportedly concluded that within two months one million people would have died and twice as many would have been infected.[23]

In many ways the United States was less prepared for bioterrorism in September 2001 than it was for the conventional attacks on the World Trade Center Towers and the Pentagon. An October 1999 General Accounting Office (GAO) report had identified shortages of vaccines and medicines, lax security, and storage facilities filled with expired drugs. A January 2001 report by the Centers for Disease Control and Prevention (CDC) in Atlanta declared that the public health infrastructure was "not adequate to detect and respond to a bioterrorist event."[24] Even though it is the only facility in the United States where medical research is conducted to develop vaccines that can offer protection against biological weapons, the budget and staff of the U.S. Army Medical Research Institute of Infectious Diseases at Fort Detrick, Maryland, was reduced by almost one-third over the 1990s.[25]

The federal government's role and the lack of preparedness has been the subject of particular criticism. "Dozens of federal entities have been fiercely

competing for the missions and money associated with the unconventional terrorism response," said Amy Smithson, a chemical and biological warfare expert
at a national security think tank. She characterized the situation as "an unfor-
tunate circumstance that has resulted in redundant capabilities, wasteful spending and, at the local level, confusion as to which agency would spearhead the
federal component of a response."[26] Jurisdictional issues are also a continuing
problem. Normally, state governors have jurisdiction over public health emergencies. A serious biological attack, however, would almost certainly have
effects that cross state boundaries. The federal secretary of health and human
services has authority to declare a national public health emergency, impose a
quarantine, and require inoculation or treatment, but doubts about the ability
to effectively enforce such authority remains.[27]

On 12 June 2002 President Bush declared, "Biological weapons are potentially the most dangerous weapons in the world" as he signed into law the
Public Health Security and Bioterrorism Response Act of 2002.[28] A start-up
program, its tentative first step toward biodefense was designed to provide new
authority to track biological materials, strengthen communications networks
linking health care providers with public health authorities, strengthen the ability of the health care system to expedite medical treatments, and develop
improved medicines. The act requires the establishment of a national disaster
medical system. It is to be "a coordinated effort" by the Department of Defense,
FEMA, the Department of Health and Human Services, and the Department
of Veteran's Affairs "working in collaboration with the States and other appropriate public or private entities" to respond to "the needs of victims of a public health emergency."[29]

The Department of Defense also expanded a biosurveillance program
called the Electronic Surveillance System for the Early Notification of
Community-based Epidemics (ESSENCE). Initiated in 2000 as a pilot program
to monitor the health of members of the armed forces, their families, and military retirees living in the Washington, D.C., area, the expanded program now
includes outpatient information from 313 army, navy, air force, and coast guard
medical facilities located throughout the world. Graphs of fresh medical data

are compared to historical data to detect unusual spikes in the number of people being treated for disorders that might signal the start of an epidemic.[30]

In addition to threats of attacks by terrorists using weapons of mass destruction as a tactic (i.e., as a means of attack), the threat of attacks on the many sectors of the nation's critical infrastructure is also increasing.[31] The attacks could involve the physical components of the critical infrastructure or the electronic and computer networks that link the sectors and their constituent parts.[32] The former include such things as 460,000 miles of pipelines, endless numbers of electrical power lines, treatment plants, reservoirs, 152,000 miles of rail, bridges, and 361 ports with more than 3,700 terminals through which cargo and passengers pass. Cyberattacks through the use of Internet hacking and computer viruses can be launched from great distances and are difficult to detect. Even routine failures can cause major problems. In January 2000 the computer network of the National Security Agency (NSA) was disabled for three days. At least two additional power-supply breakdowns have occurred since then.[33] Interruptions of NSA's monitoring of telephone and e-mail traffic could reduce its ability to detect preparations for a future attack. A successful attack on the critical infrastructure could literally undermine the nation's security, the economy, and even our way of life.[34] Even months after the 11 September attacks, the government did not have a system to analyze and synthesize apparently unrelated events to determine whether a coordinated attack had been made on our critical infrastructure.

The Bush administration's July 2002 *National Strategy for Homeland Security* document was "based on the principles of shared responsibility and partnership with the Congress, state and local governments, the private sector, and the American people."[35] It recognized that "traditions of federalism and limited government require that organizations outside the federal government take the lead" in certain operational areas.[36] It asserted that cooperation must occur "both horizontally (within each level of government) and vertically (among various levels of government)."[37] It broadly declared that "the challenge is to develop complimentary systems that avoid duplication and ensure essential requirements are met."[38] The difficulty, of course, is in the detailed planning and effective execution of policies to implement the goals of the national strategy to prevent future terrorist attacks, reduce our vulnerability to attacks, minimize the damage, and recover from any attacks that may occur.

Unfortunately, the national strategy document did not answer many important questions for the six critical mission areas it defined. In the chapter on intelligence and warning, for example, it noted that actionable intelligence is essential for preventing acts of terrorism, but it provided little guidance on how the warning information from various sources would be integrated and how and to whom it would be distributed. In the chapter on emergency preparedness and response, it recognized that "at least five different plans . . . [currently] govern the federal government's response" to various types of disasters; that even the best prepared states and localities "do not possess adequate resources to respond to the full-range of terrorist threats we face"; and that we need "a comprehensive national system to bring together and command all necessary response assets quickly and effectively."[39] However, in discussing the question of what military support would be provided to civil authorities, either in preparation for potential attacks or pursuant to an actual terrorist threat or attack, the national strategy document said only that such support "*may* take the form of providing technical support and assistance to law enforcement; assisting in the restoration of law and order; loaning specialized equipment; and assisting in consequent management."[40]

Three broad sets of circumstances were identified in which the Department of Defense would be involved in improving security at home. In undefined "extraordinary circumstances," the Pentagon would "take the lead in defending the people and territory of our country" by conducting military missions "such as combat air patrols or maritime defense operations."[41] The absence of any definitional guide for such circumstances was apparent from the declaration that "[p]lans for such contingencies will continue to be coordinated, *as appropriate,* with the National Security Council, Homeland Security Council, and other federal departments and agencies."[42] A second circumstance in which the Department of Defense would be involved in improving security at home would be during emergencies, "such as responding to an attack or to forest fires, floods, tornadoes, or other catastrophes."[43] Finally, the national strategy document declared that the Department of Defense would take part in what was described as "limited scope" missions, for example, by providing security at special athletic or similar events.[44]

By necessity, a government's strategy, or more appropriately, its war policy or grand strategy, is usually stated in broad terms. Since the purpose is to gain the object of war, a strategy has to be adapted to conditions that will almost certainly change as a conflict progresses.[45] Nonetheless, a much more explicit definition of military missions in defense of the nation's homeland was clearly needed. It became apparent after the 11 September attacks that, in some circumstances, only the armed forces will have the capability to respond to the threat of or an actual terrorist attack. Plans, preparations, and training for such circumstances needed to commence immediately. Surprisingly, for months civilian defense officials appeared content to wait, either for direction from the White House or for future recommendations on the issue from the commander of the new U.S. Northern Command, which would not even officially become an active combatant command until 1 October 2002.

For years it has been easy to imagine the kind of chaos that could result from a terrorist attack with a weapon that could affect dozens of communities in several states. Local police, emergency medical technicians, firemen, hospitals, and other first responders would probably be quickly overwhelmed. Widespread panic might bring public and private transportation almost to a halt and slow or prevent organized evacuation. The governors of adjoining states might have opposing views on such matters as whether or not to quarantine common highways or who has priority on badly needed resources in the region. Critical National Guard units might be unavailable because they have been federalized for duty elsewhere in the worldwide war on terror. Jurisdictional issues, such as which governmental body has overriding authority to take certain actions, would arise immediately. Even constitutional questions, such as the power of the states versus the power of the federal government, the extent of the federal government's authority to use federal troops, and privacy issues, would be likely to need prompt resolution. Coordination of the efforts of the many federal agencies involved and coordination between those agencies and the corresponding state and local agencies would almost certainly prove to be difficult. It would be critically important for everyone involved in a response effort to understand clearly how authority and responsibility was divided, that is, who was in charge of what at each stage of the response and what resources are available from what sources.

Several months after the 11 September attacks, most of the individual states lacked effective plans to either thwart or respond to terrorism. A lack of experience, limited resources, a reluctance to create new levels of bureaucracy, and the lack of guidance from the federal government were contributing factors. There were other reasons. "Underlining it all," said one analyst, were "continued problems with turf, responsibility, control and a basic tension between the imperative to centralize the Nation's response system and the need to ensure flexibility in choosing the tools and tactics that are most appropriate for a given jurisdiction."[46]

Plans to ensure the continuity of the central institution of the federal government were not progressing much faster. It was self-evident that if an attack was made on Congress at a critical time, for example, during a State of Union Address, the entire legislative branch of the government could be lost. Two former speakers of the House of Representatives declared, "[I]t is impossible for [the Congress] to govern through a crisis with a protracted delay in assembling a legislative quorum."[47] And yet, civilian officials at the U.S. Capitol did not have an emergency response plan that was even suitable to handle the fall 2001 anthrax crisis.[48]

The military response to the events of 11 September suggested that the armed forces were reasonably well prepared to perform air defense, port security, and other conventional military operations as part of the national homeland security effort. The main stumbling block appeared to be a rapidly increasing demand for counterterrorism and other information. The *National Strategy for Homeland Security's* introductory paragraph to the chapter on information sharing and systems broadly declared, "Information contributes to every aspect of homeland security." It is "a vital foundation for the homeland security effort."

Also, "*Every* government official performing *every* homeland security mission depends upon information and information technology."[49] The need to share information is obvious. More than twenty-five terrorist lists are maintained by dozens of Defense Department, intelligence, and law enforcement agencies. The lists are not integrated and are not shared.[50]

Two fundamental problems were cited as the reasons why an efficient government-wide information system was lacking. "First, government acquisition of information systems [had] not been routinely coordinated. Over time, hundreds of new systems [had been] acquired to address specific agency requirements. Agencies had not pursued compatibility across the federal government or with state and local entities. Organizations [had] evolved into islands of technology—distinct networks that obstruct[ed] efficient elaboration."[51] The U.S. Navy's $16 billion plan to interconnect all navy and U.S. Marine Corps systems on a new network (the Navy–Marine Corp Intranet) provided a good example of the problem. Because navy officials could not even determine how many systems the navy owned, Congress threatened to stop funding for the new network. In late July 2002 navy officials reported that they were "stunned to find that 20 percent of the computer programs they *could* account for were going unused," even though payments for their maintenance had continued.[52] Much communications equipment used by local first responders was outdated or incompatible with federal equipment. Some police departments were still operating with 1970s-era analog radios. A new model emergency response system, complete with modern interoperable communications equipment, was urgently needed.[53]

The second problem took the form of "legal and cultural barriers [that often prevented] agencies from exchanging and integrating information."[54] Companies and other private sector organizations were understandably reluctant to share proprietary or other information that might reduce their profit margin or increase their liability. Military and intelligence organizations were understandably reluctant to share classified or even unclassified but sensitive information, especially if its release might disclose its source or the method by which it was obtained. Building upon existing information-sharing architectures, such as those that permitted the North American Aerospace Defense Command to exchange data with the Federal Aviation Administration, military officials were soon working to develop a new classification system. The objective was a system that shifted the existing presumption against the requesting party (information released only on a need-to-know basis) to a presumption against the possessor of the information (information released on a need-to-share basis).[55] Meanwhile, defense officials were preparing for the transfer of the national communications system to the new Department of Homeland Security. The communications system is a consortium of private industry telecommunications companies that provides communications during a national emergency. DoD served as the executive agent for the system.

While officials at the Pentagon were concentrating on many aspects of homeland security, a greater level of effort was required to achieve the readiness necessary to provide effective support to civil authorities. The armed forces have long maintained certain specialized personnel and capabilities that either do not exist at the state or local level or are inadequate. Their equipment and expertise might be critical to local needs after a large-scale terrorist attack. Among others, these assets include military police, engineers, medical personnel, air transportation assets, communications equipment, command and control units, and weapons of mass destruction civil support teams.

The mere existence of such specialized capabilities, however, is meaningless in the absence of specific plans to use specific military units in specific types of circumstances. Such plans were impossible before the preparation and dissemination of the *National Strategy for Homeland Security* and the distribution of the promised $3.5 billion in federal aid for state and local security programs. It was imperative, however, that early and rigorous assessments be made by all federal agencies and by the states and local jurisdictions to determine what capabilities were likely to be needed from military authorities. Only then could priorities be established and steps taken to make the necessary capabilities available. Only then could the states and local communities gain a measure of certainty about what resources they could expect to receive from the Department of Defense.

Many questions also remained about the future role of the new U.S. Northern Command. Exactly how much authority would the commander of NORTHCOM have?[56] Would NORTHCOM have under its sole and direct control specially trained, rapid-response units that could be immediately transported to a scene of a terrorist attack? What would be the specific operational responsibilities and working relationship between NORTHCOM, the U.S. Joint Forces Command, and the Joint Force Headquarters Homeland Security (JFHQ-HLS) in Norfolk, Virginia?[57] What would be the relationship between NORTHCOM and the National Guard? For what kinds of potential homeland security technologies should DoD be given the lead in development? What are the specific information sharing/fusion requirements for the armed forces and other federal and state agencies? What military resources are needed for a professional homeland security education program for government policy makers and senior and mid-level management?[58] What would be NORTHCOM's relationship with state governors and local officials with respect to the training that would be essential for any effective military support operation and who would pay for the training? Successful civil support operations will require effective communication and unity of effort at all the relevant levels of government. Peter Peering, terrorism coordinator for the city of Indianapolis, spoke for many when he called for close personal relationships among relevant decision makers. "The NFL's most successful quarterbacks don't meet their receivers for the first time in the huddle."[59]

The answers to these and other critical questions were dependent upon future developments, advance knowledge of which was almost as difficult to obtain as had been advance knowledge of the attacks that triggered the complex homeland defense policy-making process.

6

Posse Comitatus and Military Force

Perhaps no group in the nation has been truer [to the tradition of civilian control of military power] than the military men themselves. Unlike the soldiers of many other nations, they have been content to perform their military duties in defense of the nation in every period of need and to perform those duties well without attempting to usurp power which is not theirs under our system of constitutional government.

—Justice Hugo Black, *Reid v. Colvert*, 10 June 1957

The mere utterance of the term *posse comitatus* is often sufficient to alert the nerve endings of civil libertarians and military purists. Many civil libertarians fear that the use of the armed forces for missions that relate in any way to law enforcement or non–war-fighting activities will undermine civilian control of the military and perhaps infringe upon individual freedoms. Many military purists fear a dilution of combat readiness.

What is *posse comitatus?* How does it relate to the security of our nation's homeland? The term itself, Latin for "power of the county," has its genesis in English common law. Each shire (county) had some form of constabulary ("shire-reeve," eventually, "sheriff") who had the duty to maintain order. *Posse comitatus* referred to all men in the county over the age of fifteen who were required to respond to a sheriff's call for assistance in preventing civil disorder.[1]

The concept became the focus of attention in the United States at the end of the Reconstruction era. Subsequent to the Civil War and until 1877, the former Confederacy states remained subject to military rule. Federal troops were used to help enforce the law, including revenue laws, suppression of illegal whiskey production,[2] and supervision of elections. The Posse Comitatus Act of 1878 was intended to "reinstate regular civil authority in the South, and to confine the role of the military to that which had been viewed to be appropriate before the Civil War."[3]

The current text of the statute is quite simple. Section 1385 of Title 10 of the *U.S. Code* makes it a federal crime (punishable by fine and imprisonment) "except in cases and under circumstances expressly authorized by the Constitution or Act of Congress" to willfully use "any part of the Army or the Air Force as a posse comitatus or otherwise to execute the laws." The statute has been interpreted by the courts to apply to all branches of the U.S. Armed Forces.[4] By regulation, the Department of Defense has extended its application to the U.S. Navy and the U.S. Marine Corps.[5] The statute may be characterized as embodying the long-established U.S. tradition and principle that law enforcement is a civilian function. In recent decades, however, it has consistently been misunderstood and misinterpreted.

The early American opposition to the maintenance of "standing armies"[6] has been well documented. Even the U.S. Supreme Court noted that two conflicting themes were developed at the Constitutional Convention in 1787. "On the one hand," the Court said in a 1990 opinion, "there was a widespread fear that a national standing Army posed an intolerable threat to individual liberty and to the sovereignty of the separate States, while on the other hand, there was recognition of the danger of relying on inadequately trained soldiers as the primary means of providing for the common defense."[7] The concern of civil libertarians in recent decades has been less a fear that a Caesar would rise from domestic employment of the armed forces, than fear that civilian control of the military will be undermined, the line between civil law enforcement and the use of military force will become blurred, civil liberties or even the democratic process will be threatened, or civil officials may abuse the use of military force. Indeed, it is routinely argued that such developments have already taken place through the use, as mandated by law, of the armed forces in counterdrug activities.

Except for agencies like the FBI, whose jurisdiction is limited to violations of federal law, the United States has never had a national police force. Law enforcement is civilian in character and most of it takes place at the state, county, or city level. It is self-evident that the training of local police for the prevention of crime and for the collection of evidence to assist the prosecution of it in courts of law—with attendant regard for the individual rights of those being prosecuted—is much different from the training received by those units of the armed forces that must be prepared to use deadly force.

Almost a quarter of a century ago, Allan Millett, a respected U.S. military historian, asserted that the purpose of civilian control of the military is "to ensure that defense policy and the agencies of defense policy are subordinated to other national traditions, values, customs, governmental policy, and economic and social institutions."[8] As a general proposition, that is undoubtedly true. But, does the use of the armed forces for any purpose other than combat in foreign lands inevitably prevent defense policy and the armed forces from being subordinated to civilian leadership? Are the armed forces currently engaged, or have they been engaged since 11 September 2001 in law enforcement or related activities that have not been expressly authorized by the U.S. Constitution or acts of Congress?

For many military professionals, the central issue is not necessarily about the lawfulness of the use of individual soldiers and military units for purposes not related directly to engagement in or preparation for armed combat; rather the issue is about the wisdom of such use. It has been noted in scholarly journals that in recent years Americans and their representatives in Congress have come to see the military "as a panacea for domestic problems."[9] The obvious exaggeration does not hide an element of truth. Certainly, since the Persian Gulf War of 1990–91 opinion polls have consistently reflected greater public confidence in the U.S. Armed Forces than in almost any other U.S. institution.

It is also true that since the end of the Cold War, the armed forces have been used in a range of "operations other than war" that was unimaginable during the Cold War. The fact that most of the operations took place outside of the continental United States does not minimize the fact that recent presidents have used the armed forces in unprecedented ways. In the fifteen years between the U.S. exit from Vietnam and the end of the Cold War, armed forces personnel were sent on only twenty missions overseas. During the decade of the 1990s, however, they were sent on a unprecedented forty-eight overseas missions.[10] The percentage of U.S. military personnel deployed away from their home station at any one time in 1995 was twice what it was in 1991, the year the Gulf War commenced.[11]

At a time when the size of the U.S. Armed Forces is substantially less than it was at the conclusion of the Cold War, when the National Commission on Terrorism has concluded "when a catastrophe is beyond the capabilities of local, state and other federal agencies . . . the President may want to designate DoD as a *lead* federal agency,"[12] when the U.S. Armed Forces are routinely proposed for missions that do not fit within the traditional parameters for the use of military force, or when a proposed use does not relate directly to what is perceived as a *vital* national security interest, military professionals become very skeptical. This should not be surprising. It has only been thirty years since the end of the Vietnam War, which, in the words of one professional, "took the lives of fifty-eight thousand Americans and well over one million Vietnamese[,] . . . nearly wreck[ed] the American economy[,] . . . divided American society[,] . . . inflicted on the United States one of the greatest political traumas since the Civil War[, and] led Americans to question the integrity of their government as never before."[13] Many of today's most senior officers fought in that conflict.

It has only been forty years since Gen. Douglas MacArthur's famous speech. On 12 May 1962 MacArthur returned to West Point for the last time. After reviewing the corps of cadets at a dress parade, lunching with them, and receiving the Sylvanus Thayer Medal, the highest honor of the U.S. Military Academy, he responded with his "Duty, Honor, Country" address. His remarks about the duty of the professional warrior have been remembered by more than one generation of officers. "[T]hrough all this welter of change and development," he intoned, "your mission remains fixed, determined, inviolable—it is to win our wars. Everything else in your professional career is but a corollary to this vital dedication. All other public purposes, all other public projects, all other public needs, great or small, will find others for their accomplishment; but you are the ones who are trained to fight; yours is the profession of arms."[14]

The first question addressed in this chapter, therefore, is whether the actual or contemplated uses of the armed forces for homeland security are lawful. If they are, the next questions are obvious. Will such use in fact undermine civilian control of the military, violate some other principle in a way that is unacceptable, or affect those "who are trained to fight" in ways the nation cannot afford?

Even a brief review of the relevant provisions of the U.S. Constitution and the several decisions of the U.S. Supreme Court, which either interpret the provisions or otherwise define the limits of the president's authority, leads to the conclusion that the commander-in-chief of the armed forces is lawfully entitled to exercise whatever authority is necessary to deal with the requirements of a particular national emergency, including a terrorist attack on one or more of the individual states. This includes the authority to employ the armed forces in any way that may be necessary. The preamble to the U.S. Constitution specifically declares that one of its objects is to "provide for the common defense." Article 2, which defines the executive power of the federal government, expressly states, "The President shall be Commander in Chief of the Army and Navy of the United States, and of the Militia of the several States, when called into the actual Service of the United States."[15] It also requires the president to "take Care that the Laws be faithfully executed."[16]

The U.S. Constitution did, of course, establish a system of shared, not separate, powers in national security policy making. Thus, Congress also has considerable power over matters that may relate to homeland security. In addition to the power to provide for the common defense, declare war, raise and support armies, and provide and maintain a navy, Article 1 gives to Congress the power "to provide for calling forth the Militia to execute the Laws of the Union, suppress Insurrections and repel Invasions,"[17] and to "make all Laws which [are] necessary and proper for carrying into Execution" its powers and "all other Powers" vested by the constitution in the government or in any department or officer of the government.[18] Article 4 requires the United States to "guarantee to every State in this Union a Republican Form of Government," and "to protect each of them against *Invasion;* and on application of the Legislature, or of the Executive (when the Legislature cannot be convened) against *domestic Violence.*"[19]

The war-making power is of particular importance and interest. It has long been accepted that a president may, without authorization by Congress, use military force abroad when such use is in defense of an attack. Edwin Corwin, a distinguished constitutional scholar, however, posed the question of whether the president is confined to "acts of defense." He has asked more broadly whether the distinction between such acts and "acts of war" is a sustainable one.[20] The issue arose early in the life of the nation. In 1801 President Thomas Jefferson expressed the view that unless and until Congress formally declared war, U.S. warships had the rights only of self-defense against the ships of the Bashaw of Tripoli. Alexander Hamilton ridiculed that view and asserted that the plain meaning of the U.S. Constitution was:

> that it is the peculiar and exclusive province of Congress, *when the nation is at peace* to change the state into a state of war, whether from calculations of policy or from provocations, or injuries received; in other words, it belongs to Congress only, *to go to war.* But when a foreign nation declares, or openly and avoidably makes war upon the United States, they are then by the very fact *already at war,* and any declaration on the part of Congress is nugatory; it is at least unnecessary.[21]

It has thus been recognized and reaffirmed in recent years that in a government of checks and balances, of shared power and responsibility, "[t]he Constitution places the President and the Congress in dynamic tension. They both cooperate and compete in the making of national policy. National security is no exception."[22] Nevertheless, "as Chief Executive and Commander in Chief, and with broad authority in the area of foreign affairs, it is the *President* who is empowered to act for the nation and protect its interests."[23]

The very nature of modern terrorism may also require further scrutiny of the long accepted view that the president's power in domestic matters is much less than his power to conduct foreign affairs under Article 2. In 1936 the Supreme Court had occasion to address the question of the president's *foreign* powers. It recognized that in the "vast *external realm,* with its important, complicated, delicate and manifold problems," the president has "a degree of discretion and freedom from statutory restriction which would not be admissible were domestic affairs alone involved. Moreover," said the Court, "he, not Congress, has the better opportunity of knowing the conditions which prevail in foreign countries, and especially is this true in time of war."[24]

Warfare in the first years of the twenty-first century, as we have tragically learned, does not always fit the traditional model of an armed conflict exclusively between nations in the "external realm." It could also be a conflict between a nation and a small group acting outside of state control. Terrorists now have the capacity to inflict more casualties and greater damage upon the United States than any adversary in any of our previous wars. In responding to the domestic consequences of a catastrophic terrorist attack upon the nation, it is unlikely any president would act contrary to congressional direction, but it might be necessary and lawful.

Curiously, Jefferson understood such dilemmas. Writing to John Colvin the year after he left the presidency, Jefferson said, "[A] strict observation of the written laws is doubtless one of the highest duties of a good officer, but it is not the highest. The law of necessity, of self-preservation, of saving our country when in danger, are of higher obligation. To lose our country by a scrupulous adherence to written law would be to lose the law itself, with life, liberty, property . . . thus, *sacrificing the end to the means.*"[25]

A much more likely circumstance would be one in which a president finds it necessary to act where there is no relevant legislation that expresses the intent of Congress on the matter. In a 1952 case, Supreme Court Justice Robert Jackson observed that in such a situation, there may be "a zone of twilight" where the relative constitutional power of the president and Congress is not clear and that "any actual test of power is likely to depend on the imperatives of events and contemporary imponderables rather than abstract theories of law."[26]

One of the consistent themes that emerges from a review of relevant judicial opinions is that the kinds of emergencies that might require immediate presidential action, including the use of armed forces, cannot be predicted with any degree of confidence. Writing in the *Federalist Papers* before the U.S. Constitution was ratified, Alexander Hamilton—generally considered to be one of the strongest advocates of executive energy—anticipated the difficulty.

> [I]t is impossible to foresee or define the extent and variety of national exigencies, and the correspondent extent and variety of the means which may be necessary to satisfy them. The circumstances that endanger the safety of nations are infinite, and for this reason no constitutional shackles can wisely be imposed on the power to which the care of it is committed. This power ought to be co-extensive with all the possible combinations of such circumstances; and ought to be under the direction of the same councils, which are appointed to preside over the common defense.[27]

This principle was sustained in similar language by the Supreme Court in the 1851 case of *Mitchell v. Harmony*. The issue was whether an officer of the army lawfully took possession of certain private property during the Mexican War of 1845. Writing for the Court, Chief Justice Roger B. Taney recognized that there are occasions in which the conduct complained of could be exercised. He qualified the power of the government, however, by declaring, "[T]he danger must be immediate and impending; or the necessity urgent for the public service, such as will not admit of delay and where the action of the civil authority would be too late in providing the means in which the occasion calls for."[28] Significantly, he added, "It is impossible to define the particular circumstances of danger or necessity in which this power may be lawfully exercised. Every case must depend on its own circumstances."[29]

Twenty years later, the Supreme Court again considered the question. Once again, the circumstances involved the conduct of military officers. In *United States v. Russell*, the Court declared that it had "no doubt . . . that the power of the Government is ample to supply for the moment the public wants in that way to the extent of the immediate public exigency."[30] The Court added, however, "[I]t is the emergency . . . that gives the right, and it is clear that the emergency must be shown to exist" before the otherwise unlawful conduct can occur.[31]

Perhaps the best known and most illustrative examples of a president's inherent constitutional authority to take whatever action may be necessary in the resolution of crises are the several emergency measures taken by President Abraham Lincoln during the Civil War. The unilateral measures included the ordering of a forty-thousand-man increase in the regular army and navy, a blockade of the ports of the states that seceded, an order that $2 million be paid out of the federal treasury, a pledging of the credit of the United States for $250 million, suspension of the writ of habeas corpus, suppression of newspaper publication, the political reorganization of occupied southern states, and even the issuance of the Emancipation Proclamation. All of the actions were taken without congressional authority.[32]

In his message to Congress of 4 July 1861 Lincoln said that the actions he had taken were required because of public necessity and popular demand.[33] On another occasion, he addressed the constitutionality of his actions by asking whether it was possible to lose the nation and yet preserve the constitution. "By general law life and limb must be protected," he argued, "yet often a limb must be amputated to save a life; but a life is never wisely given to save a limb."[34] Congress agreed and promptly passed legislation approving most of the actions "as if they had been done under the previous express authority and direction of the Congress."

An emergency measure that became the subject of adjudication by the U.S. Supreme Court was the blockade of the southern ports. In the *Prize Cases*,[35] the Court left no doubt of the president's authority. "If a war be made by invasion of a foreign nation, the President is not only authorized but bound to resist force, by force. He does not initiate the war, but is bound to accept the challenge without waiting for any special legislative authority. And whether the hostile party be a foreign invader, or States organized in rebellion, it is nonetheless a war."[36]

President Theodore Roosevelt had no doubt about how such a situation should be handled. "I declined to adopt the view," he said in his autobiography, "that what was imperatively necessary for the Nation could not be done by the President unless he could find some specific authorization to do it. My belief was that it was not only his right but his duty to do anything that the needs of the Nation demanded unless such action was forbidden by the Constitution or by the laws."[37]

In World War II, President Franklin D. Roosevelt said much the same thing when he demanded that Congress repeal a provision of the Price Control Act. He indicated that if Congress did not act "it will leave me with an inescapable responsibility to the people of this country to see to it that the war effort is no longer imperiled by threat of economic chaos."[38] In the event that Congress failed to "act adequately," he said, "I shall accept the responsibility, and I will act."[39] President Bush appears to hold the same view. "I will not wait on events while dangers gather," he told Congress in his January 2002 State of the Union Address. "I will not stand by, as peril draws closer and closer."

With the caveat that it will be critically important to work out in advance several policy and operational questions—for example, how responsibility will be divided between the armed forces, federal agencies, and state and local police and other organizations; the chain-of-command (*who's in charge here?*) issues; what rules-of-engagement on the use of force will apply in various sets of circumstances—it may fairly be said that the question of legal authority is settled. The president has clear constitutional authority in the event of a catastrophic terrorist attack—at least on a temporary basis—to use military force and resources in any way necessary.

In addition to his constitutional authority, the president may also act pursuant to the express authority of Congress.[40] Although it is a statute of longstanding, the Posse Comitatus Act is, of course, only a legislative enactment.

It may be amended or even abrogated. In the weeks following the 11 September attacks, senior members of the Senate Armed Services Committee expressly suggested this possibility. "There comes a time," Senator John Warner of Virginia said, "when we've got to re-examine the old laws of the 1800s in light of this extraordinary series of challenges that we're faced with today."[41] Senator Pat Roberts of Kansas agreed. He understood the need to limit domestic military actions, he said, but he added that terrorist threats might mean the rules have to be changed. "It does get very challenging, but if you get into crises management, you have to rely on the resources you have."[42]

Such comments received little public attention until 16 July 2002 when President Bush unveiled his long-awaited *National Strategy for Homeland Security*. It mentioned only three sets of circumstances in which military personnel might be used: (1) to prevent attacks by performance of combat air patrol and maritime defense missions; (2) in response to attacks; and (3) in "limited scope" support missions led by other agencies of government, such as the security work at the recent Winter Olympics in Salt Lake City. Two sentences in the seventy-six-page document triggered what one major city newspaper said would be "the next big debate in American society," one that would be "one of the most unsettling debates of our time."[43]

> Federal law prohibits military personnel from enforcing the law within the United States except as expressly authorized by the Constitution or an Act of Congress. The threat of catastrophic terrorism requires a thorough review of the laws permitting the military to act within the United States in order to determine whether domestic preparedness and response efforts would benefit from greater involvement of military personnel and, if so, how.[44]

Immediate reaction to the proposal, which was not for *change* in the law but rather for a *review* of it, cut across party and philosophical lines. "This is a place," said David Shribman, a researcher at a conservative think tank, "where the liberals meet the libertarians."[45] Senator Joseph R. Biden, a Delaware Democrat, went further than the president's proposal when he declared that the Posse

Comitatus Act "has to be amended."[46] Under the current law, Biden said, soldiers with special knowledge of weapons of mass destruction who discovered a terrorist weapon in the United States would "not be able to exercise the same power a police officer would in dealing with that situation."[47] Senator Joseph Lieberman of Connecticut agreed that a change in the Posse Comitatus Act is "definitely worth considering," stating that he had been "an advocate of the military having a more active role in homeland defense."[48] They were joined by Republican Senator Fred Thompson of Tennessee, who expressed the view that military personnel could be useful for such missions as "surveillance along the thousands of miles of borders that are very difficult for law enforcement to deal with."[49]

Skepticism or outright objection to the president's proposal was voiced by many others. Senator Carl Levin, a Democrat from Michigan, said, "We've done very well by separating the military from law enforcement. There would be a heavy burden for those who want to change" the statute.[50] The legislative counsel for the American Civil Liberties Union made the sweeping assertion that "the military represents a blunt instrument unconcerned with our domestic civil liberties."[51] The "tension between freedom and order," said one newspaper, "is no longer sterile."[52] The senior editor at the Cato Institute[53] asserted that the president's proposal was a dangerous idea because the army is "a blunt instrument: effective for destroying enemy troops en masse, but ill-suited to the fight on the home front, which requires subtler investigative and preventative skills."[54]

Interestingly, an immediate and almost visceral objection to the proposal on apparent federalism grounds was not made by a consortium of state governors or local mayors, but by the executive director of the National Guard Association of the United States (NGAUS).[55] He argued that elements of the federal government should not be inserted into a state role. The real objection of NGAUS seemed to rest more on grounds of self-interest. "The value and purpose [translate to read "resources and power"] of the Guard," he said, "should be preserved in this equation. The more you make federal forces available, . . . the less dependence you have on the Guard."[56]

The split of opinion was perhaps best illustrated by reactions within the White House and the defense establishment itself. Within days of the release of the strategy that he and his Office of Homeland Security staff had prepared, Tom Ridge was quoted as saying that any expansion of the military's role would go "against our instincts as a country,"[57] that it is "very unlikely" that a change in the *posse comitatus* legislation would be made,[58] and that he personally believes that military personnel should not have authority to arrest U.S. citizens.[59]

As recently as May 2001 Defense Secretary Donald Rumsfeld had said that the DoD would not seek any changes in the law.[60] It was widely believed that because the U.S. Armed Forces were already overextended, Rumsfeld was against any change in the statute. When the strategy proposal became public, an anonymous senior Defense Department official declared, "This was their initiative, not ours."[61] Only days after the strategy document was published, Rumsfeld maintained that he had "not seen any reasons why [he] would propose any changes."[62] The designated commander-in-chief of the new U.S. Northern Command, however, strongly supported the proposal. "My view," Gen. Ralph Eberhart, USAF, said, "has been that Posse Comitatus will constantly be under review as we mature this command, as we do our exercises, as we interact with FEMA, FBI, and those lead federal agencies out there."[63] The law should be reviewed on a regular basis "if we think it ties our hands in protecting the American people."[64] He was already thinking of how new military technology might be employed in homeland defense, referring specifically to remote-controlled surveillance blimps operating at seventy thousand feet and Predator unmanned aerial vehicles (UAVs) that could patrol U.S. coastlines.[65]

The debate that had been renewed with the issuance of the president's *National Strategy for Homeland Security* was focused on the possible domestic use of the regular armed forces or National Guard personnel activated and operating as federal troops under provisions of Title 10 of the *U.S. Code*. The use of the National Guard for domestic purposes pursuant to Title 32 of the *U.S. Code* is not covered by the Posse Comitatus Act.[66] Thus, until the president calls the Army or Air National Guard of a state into federal service, the governor of the state has great discretion in the employment of it within the state to respond to an emergency. Because any use of the regular armed forces—or the National Guard after it has been called to federal service—will be effectuated only

through the civilian secretary of defense acting at the direction of the nationally elected president and its use must be funded by the elected members of
Congress, it is difficult to see any significant risk to what the Supreme Court
has called "this Nation's tradition of keeping military power subservient to civilian authority."[67]

As the preceding discussion demonstrates, issues of the *lawfulness* of the use
of the armed forces for domestic purposes are related to but separate from questions about the *wisdom* of such use. Often, opposition to the use is based on the
"myth" that military personnel and equipment may only be used in "the most
extraordinary situations."[68] The misconceptions about the Posse Comitatus Act
are so widespread that John Brinkerhoff, a former defense official, concluded,
"[T]he misinterpretation of the . . . Act has become an urban myth that is
widely believed without substantiation" and "much of what has been said and
written about the . . . Act is just plain nonsense."[69]

While some misconceptions are believed in good faith, even if they are
wrong, there is reason in many cases to suspect that the opposition to the use of
military resources for domestic purposes is less one of misunderstanding the law
than of an attempt to use the law as a shield against policies or proposed uses that
are not favored. "Some cynics" hold the opinion that "the Department of Defense
and the military services support the erroneous application of Posse Comitatus
because they do not want to get involved in domestic emergencies."[70] It is difficult to gauge the degree to which this opinion is accurate, but reservations about
the use of military resources, even for something as critical as homeland security,
are often expressed in terms that raise the *posse comitatus* issue.

This was my experience through the first years of the administration of
George H. W. Bush. Congress had passed legislation that gave the Department
of Defense specific new counterdrug responsibilities with respect to the support
of civilian law enforcement agencies.[71] As part of the president's national drug
control strategy the detection and countering of the production and trafficking
of illegal drugs had been established as a "high priority national security mission"
of the DoD. The sensitivity of some military leaders to a possible violation of the
Posse Comitatus Act, however, was extreme. The presumption seemed to be that
any support of a law enforcement agency was suspect.

Leaving aside the question of the wisdom of all such policies, I took the position that government officials should both presume the lawfulness of the policies established by Congress and the president and energetically seek to implement them. Only a few weeks after the drug control strategy was issued, I expressed this view to Congress. "The Department of Defense is not," I asserted, "a law enforcement agency. . . . There is, however, much that we can do without usurping a police role."[72] Each proposed military counterdrug operation was carefully scrutinized in advance by civilian officials to ensure its lawfulness. Each operation was structured to enhance combat readiness by using the existing military occupational specialty (MOS) skills of the personnel involved. As a result, and because Congress was providing additional funding to pay for the operations, the *posse comitatus* concerns began to disappear.

More recently, the same kind of questions have been raised about the use of the armed forces for homeland security. Shortly after he was given temporary responsibility for the coordination of DoD's homeland security efforts, for example, Secretary of the Army Thomas White declared broadly that "as a general matter of policy we want to avoid the use of federal troops in police activities."[73] On another occasion, a defense official declared, "Our tradition has been to say that we don't enforce civil laws, we're not cops. Add to that the fact that the war against terrorism overseas is consuming a lot of resources, and we're even more reluctant to deplete them with homeland missions."[74]

Such caution, if expressed in good faith, is not bad. Indeed, it can serve as a healthy check on the tendency of too many officials to quickly reach for the sword on an ad hoc basis in the absence of a clearly defined strategy or policy. It must be remembered that the decisions to use military force or even benign military resources in particular circumstances are political decisions. The decisions must be principled if matters involving truly important security interests are to be separated from the unimportant, if long-established legal traditions are to be maintained, and if the squandering of valuable military capabilities and resources is to be avoided.

Complicating the debate on a possible amendment to the Posse Comitatus Act was a natural tendency of individuals to cast their arguments in the most extreme and exaggerated form. No one seriously suggested that army tank units replace the patrolling cars of county sheriffs or that U.S. Navy SEALs interrogate suspected terrorists in U.S. cities. No one proposed that the National Guard be replaced or relegated to insignificant duties within several states. The president merely proposed a review of the statute to ensure that a law drafted shortly after the Civil War does not prevent the use today of unique military resources in a world that is much different than what existed when Rutherford B. Hayes was president. It would be folly to exclude from use any national asset when the army surgeon general has estimated that a well-planned terrorist attack against a single chemical facility near a densely populated area could kill or injure as many as 2.4 million people.[75]

A recent study concluded, "[T]he policies underlying the [Posse Comitatus Act] are of great significance, but limited application. Even when the [Act] applies, it preserves a broad field of lawful activities to the military apart from the exercise of police powers, including activities in support of law enforcement."[76] It remains to be seen whether the public servants who are responsible and accountable for the nation's security conclude that even more domestic security activities should at least be authorized for military personnel, even if the new authority is not immediately exercised.

By coincidence, at the same time that U.S. military forces were working side by side with U.S. allies in the global war against terrorism, a related matter, the establishment of the International Criminal Court (ICC), became the subject of strong disagreement with many of the same allies. The perceived need to establish an international criminal court to prosecute crimes such as genocide was recognized by the United Nations as early as December 1948. For years, the idea languished because of the inability of the members to obtain consensus on the definition of aggression. In 1989 the UN General Assembly commenced a new effort to establish such a court and give it jurisdiction that would include drug trafficking cases. In 1993 the armed conflict in the former Yugoslavia began and reports of ethnic cleaning and other atrocities led the UN Security Council to establish the ad hoc International Tribunal for the Former Yugoslavia.

Believing for several reasons that there were too many deficiencies in ad hoc tribunals and that a permanent court was necessary,[77] the UN General Assembly decided to convene a United Nations Diplomatic Conference of Plenipotentiaries on the Establishment of an International Criminal Court. The conference was subsequently held in Rome 15–17 June 1998 with representatives from 160 countries attending. The purpose of the conference was to finalize a draft statute or treaty (the "Rome Statute") that, when ratified, would establish such a court.

The idea of an established system to bring perpetrators of war crimes to justice was widely lauded. UN Secretary General Kofi Annan expressed the views of many when he observed, "[M]any thought . . . that the horrors of the Second World War—the camps, the cruelty, the exterminations, the Holocaust—could never happen again. And yet they have. In Cambodia, in Bosnia and Herzegovina, and Rwanda. Our time—this decade even—has shown us that man's capacity for evil knows no limits. Genocide . . . is now a word of our time, too, a heinous reality that calls for a historic response."

Although the United States supported the objective of the Rome Statute, many considered it seriously flawed. Even though he stated that the treaty was so flawed that he would not forward it to the Senate for advice and consent to ratification or recommend that his successor forward the treaty to the Senate, President Clinton signed the treaty on 31 December 2000, only hours before the cutoff date and less than three weeks before George W. Bush assumed the presidency. He apparently hoped that the signing of the treaty would give the United States an opportunity to repair the flaws.

By its terms, the Rome Statute provided that it would enter into force on a date following the date on which the sixtieth country submitted its instrument of ratification to the UN. On 11 April 2002 a group of ten countries ratified the treaty in a ceremony at UN headquarters, bringing the total number of signatories to sixty-six. The treaty establishing the ICC became effective on 1 July 2002. The ICC tribunal is now based at The Hague, Netherlands.

The Bush administration made no secret of its strong objection to several provisions of the treaty. The general opposition was based on a fear that members of the U.S. Armed Forces might be unfairly prosecuted as they faithfully carried out authorized operations around the world in support of U.S. national security objectives, including counterterrorism and other missions related to homeland security. It was undeniable, as one commentator pointed out, that

"America in its unchallenged preeminence has responsibility unlike any other nation now or ever."[78] When the sixtieth country signed the treaty, the United States had approximately 220,000 troops deployed overseas.

The United States also had several related technical objections.[79] First, the Rome Statute purports to vest the ICC with universal jurisdiction,[80] that is, with the power to assert jurisdiction over any individual for alleged crimes committed anywhere and to demand extradition of the accused from a third country even if the accused's country is not a party to the treaty. Second, a risk of arbitrary or politically motivated prosecutions exists. The prosecutor is empowered to commence investigations of possible violations of international law at the request of a single state that is a party to the treaty and, with the agreement of a panel of only three of the eighteen judges, can bring a formal indictment against any suspected individual anywhere in the world. Third, the ICC is not subject to the kinds of checks and balances to which U.S. courts are subject. The unelected judges are under no obligation to comply with the provisions of the U.S. Constitution or to follow the expressed will of Americans on any of the political issues that may come before it. The prosecutor is not accountable to either the UN Security Council, of which the United States is a permanent member, or to any elected body.

The fourth technical objection flowed from treaty provisions that permit the ICC to reject the decision of a sovereign state not to prosecute and a decision by a court of a sovereign state not to convict. A fifth objection was that the treaty permits signatory countries to "opt out" of crimes that may be added to the statute later. The effect of that provision is to exempt citizens of signatory countries from the ICC's jurisdiction over the new crimes, but not citizens of states that did not ratify the treaty. The final objection was based on the fact that concepts like "war crimes" and "aggression" are not defined in the treaty. "The problem is not just that the ICC is 'above the law' but also that there is not much clear and pertinent law to be above."[81]

Few principles are more clear under the U.S. concept of due process of law than the principle that an individual may not be charged with a crime when the governing statute is so vague that it prevents a fair understanding of what conduct is proscribed. U.S. objections, however, were not based on abstract legal concepts; rather, they were based on the hard realities of modern warfare.

An example of current realities was described in an editorial appearing four days after the celebration of the ratification of the Rome Statute by the sixtieth country. "[T]he principles of 'discrimination' and 'proportionality'" the author noted, "require that one distinguish between military and civilian targets, and avoid undue civilian harm. In World War II, bridges, ports, oil depots, refineries, and electrical plants were considered valid targets because they contributed to the war effort."[82] But, after the NATO air campaign in Kosovo, "Yugoslavia sued in the World Court charging that NATO's attack on infrastructure unduly burdened civilians and was illegal."[83]

Henry Kissinger, who was awarded the Nobel Peace Prize for his role in resolving an armed conflict, expressed his skepticism of the concept of universal jurisdiction. "Most Americans would be amazed to learn that the [International Criminal Tribunal for the Former Yugoslavia] (ICTY), created at American behest in 1993 to deal with Balkan war criminals, asserts a right to investigate America's political and military leaders for allegedly criminal conduct—and for the indefinite future, since no statute of limitations applies."[84] His statement turned out to be surprisingly prescient. In July 2002 the Croatian World Congress sent a letter to the ICTY demanding that a criminal investigation be made to determine whether charges should be made against U.S. leaders for supporting a 1995 military offensive by Croatia that recaptured territory then held by rebel Serbian forces. The U.S. leaders to be investigated included Clinton, his two former national security advisors, and two former ambassadors.[85] It is not surprising, therefore, "that Washington is reluctant to have its war fighting methods controlled by law professors and foreign magistrates appointed to a new International Criminal Court."[86]

On 6 May 2002, and despite the fact that it is "emphatically committed to international accountability for war crimes, genocide, and crimes against humanity,"[87] the United States formally notified the UN that it did not intend to become a party to the Rome Statute. In a prepared statement, Secretary of Defense Rumsfeld stated the government's position. "We want to make clear," he said, "that the United States rejects the purported jurisdictional claims of the ICC—and the United States will regard as illegitimate any attempt by the court, or state parties to the treaty, to assert the ICC's jurisdiction over American citizens."[88] He then explained the reasons for the government's position. "[T]he ICC provisions claim the authority to detain and try American citizens—U.S. soldiers, sailors, airmen and Marines, as well as current and future officials—even though the United States has not given its consent to be bound by the treaty. When the ICC treaty enters into force, . . . U.S. citizens will be exposed to the risk of prosecution by a court that is unaccountable to the American people, and that has no obligation to respect the constitutional rights of our citizens."[89]

The implications of these developments for the global war on terrorism were significant. "Clearly the existence of an International Criminal Court," Rumsfeld noted, "will necessarily complicate U.S. military cooperation with countries that are parties to the ICC treaty—because those countries may now incur a treaty obligation to hand over U.S. nationals to the court, even over U.S. objections."[90] By placing U.S. military personnel at risk of politicized prosecutions, he concluded, "the ICC could well create a powerful disincentive for U.S. military engagement in the world."[91]

Predictably, reaction to the U.S. decision from human rights organizations was one of outrage. The U.S. action was also criticized in the media of some allies as "highly unusual and perhaps unprecedented."[92] The BBC News solemnly declared, "[T]his decision serves as further proof of a unilateralist approach to foreign policy and puts [President Bush] at odds with allies, including Canada and the European Union, which support the ICC."[93] The State Department did not disagree. "What we've learnt from the war on terror," the U.S. ambassador-at-large for war crimes issues responded, "is that rather than creating an international mechanism to deal with these issues it is better to organize an international mandate that authorizes states to use their unilateral tools to tackle the problem we have."[94]

Within days of its formal rejection of the Rome Treaty, the Bush administration commenced a diplomatic offensive aimed at the protection of the 712 U.S. personnel currently participating in fifteen UN peacekeeping operations around the world. The first U.S. move was an effort to amend a UN Security Council resolution extending the peacekeeping mission to East Timor. The proposed amendment would have exempted all UN troops serving in that country from prosecution from any international tribunal. The responsibility for prosecution of war crimes or other, related activity would be left to the governments of the alleged offenders. Noting that military forces serving with the UN have long enjoyed diplomatic immunity from countries to which they are deployed, U.S. officials explained that they avoided limiting the proposed amendment to Americans in the hope of obtaining broader support for it. The amendment was withdrawn in the face of strong opposition from Britain and France, but John Negroponte, the U.S. ambassador to the UN, declared, "[W]e put down a marker last week. We . . .want to make it clear that when we participate in peacekeeping missions, . . . we intend to seek some kind of exception to international criminal court jurisdiction."[95]

The effort in East Timor was merely the first step of a broader U.S. effort to establish a legal precedent that could be applied to all UN peacekeeping operations or to otherwise obtain immunity from prosecution by the ICC of Americans serving in such missions. Rumsfeld had hinted at the effort in his 6 May statement. "Fortunately, there may be mechanisms within the treaty by which we can work bilaterally with friends and allies, to the extent they are willing, to prevent the jurisdiction of the treaty and thus avoid complications in our military operation."[96] One long-term option would involve the renegotiation of bilateral treaties with hundreds of countries to obtain the protection sought.

As the date for the formal establishment of the ICC came and went, the strength of the U.S. opposition to it became increasingly apparent. In mid-June the Senate approved a measure that authorized the president to use force to rescue any American held by that court. The Bush administration introduced a draft resolution in the UN Security Council that would exclude all military and civilian personnel involved in UN peacekeeping, humanitarian, and other missions from the ICC's jurisdiction. On 30 June the United States vetoed a six-month extension of the UN peacekeeping mission in Bosnia, citing concern that the several thousand U.S. personnel participating in the mission could be subject to a politicized prosecution by a prosecutor answerable to no one. The United States also ordered the withdrawal of three U.S. military observers of the UN mission in East Timor. In his first public comments on the matter after the veto of the mission in Bosnia, the president declared, "We'll try to work out the impasse, but the one thing we're not going to do is sign on to this International Criminal Court."

European leaders strenuously objected to the U.S. position, but two indisputable facts made the U.S. action inevitable. First, the terms of the Rome Treaty. They were even criticized starkly by at least one European newspaper.[97] Second, U.S. military strategy is based on the ability to project force anywhere in the world. As the most powerful democratic nation, the United States is called on more than any other country to perform a wide range of international missions. The members of its armed forces are necessarily more vulnerable to a politicized prosecution than military personnel from other nations. The choice open to the weaker and less willing nations was clear: If they desired the protection of U.S. military force, they must find a way to meet the U.S. objection to the ICC. Senator Robert Bennett of Utah spoke for many of his colleagues when he described his own reservations about the ICC. "I do not reject the International Criminal Court because I want Americans to dismiss the importance of international law," he said. "After all, the United Nations, which heavily influences the development of international law, was an American idea and is located on American soil and has been supported by American appropriations. Most United Nations functions around the world involve American troops." But, he added, the "specter of an American president called before an international tribunal for actions as straightforward as President Clinton's were [in the former Yugoslavia] is a specter I do not want to see repeated."[98]

After vetoing a six-month extension of the UN peacekeeping mission in Bosnia, and amid European concerns that a withdrawal of U.S. troops would jeopardize stability in the Balkans, U.S. negotiators agreed to a series of short extensions of the mission while negotiations on the ICC continued. The action was necessary because the negotiators failed to obtain the nine votes required in the fifteen-member UN Security Council to pass a U.S.–sponsored resolution that would have empowered the council to indefinitely postpone prosecutions of individuals from countries that have not ratified the ICC treaty.

After several days of highly contentious negotiations, the UN Security Council voted 15–0 on 12 July to accept a new U.S.–sponsored resolution, which did not provide the permanent immunity originally sought but did provide a one-year exemption from ICC prosecution for nationals of countries that have not ratified the Rome Statute. The resolution also states the council's "intention" to order further one-year exemptions "for as long as may be necessary." Each additional exemption will require a formal vote of the council.

The U.S. compromise was quickly characterized as a "setback for pro-defense hard-liners" like Vice President Cheney and Defense Secretary Rumsfeld and a victory for Secretary of State Powell and National Security Advisor Condoleezza Rice.[99] Some members of Congress were also unhappy with the new U.S. position. Ambassador John Negroponte, however, defended the action as a "first step" and said that the United States intended to seek a renewal of the exemption each year.[100] An administration spokesman said that efforts would also be made to negotiate bilateral agreements with as many nations as possible to prevent countries from extraditing any American who might be indicted by the ICC.[101] The effort started promptly. On 1 August Romania became the first country to agree to provide immunity from the ICC to U.S. peacekeepers operating on its territory. Israel, Tajikistan, and East Timor soon followed.

In antiterrorism legislation signed by the president the same week, Congress gave the White House powerful new tools. One provision authorizes the president to withdraw military aid—including training, assistance in the financing of weapons and equipment purchases, and military education—from nations that refuse to agree not to extradite Americans to the ICC for trial. Another provision of the new law authorizes the president to free Americans—by any "necessary and appropriate means," including military force—who may come within the custody of the new court. Members of NATO and certain other major U.S. allies, for example, Japan, Australia, Egypt, and South Korea, are exempted from the military aid prohibition. There was every reason to believe that the president was prepared to exercise his new authority. In remarks to soldiers of the U.S. Army's 10th Mountain Division, he said, "Every person who serves under the American flag will answer to his or her own superiors and to military law, not to the rulings of an unaccountable international criminal court."[102]

In the opening passages of his important study of civil-military relations, Professor Samuel P. Huntington asserts that the military institutions of any society are shaped by two forces: "a functional imperative stemming from the threats to the society's security and a societal imperative arising from the social forces, ideologies, and institutions dominant within the society. Military institutions which reflect only social values may be incapable of performing effectively their military function. On the other hand, it may be impossible to contain within society military institutions shaped purely by functional imperatives."[103] The threat to the United States from global networks of terrorists, using weapons with huge destructive power, is real and imminent. The functional imperative is clear. The skills, experience, capabilities, and resources of the U.S. Armed Forces must be fully available to aid in the prevention of terrorist attacks, or, in the event that further attacks do occur, to aid in the response to them.

The societal imperative is also clear. The use of the armed forces within the United States must, to every extent reasonably possible, be consistent with long-standing legal traditions and social norms. Only in the most extreme circumstances should the president exercise all the powers available to him under the U.S. Constitution. If it is necessary to use those powers, however, the president should not hesitate to do so.

In these morning hours of the twenty-first century, Americans must understand that even though the range and strength of our country's armed forces, the stability of our economy, the pace of our technological and scientific advances, and the attractiveness of our culture are helping us to enjoy what has been recently characterized as "a preeminence unrivaled by even the greatest empires of the past,"[104] our pursuit of a global war against terrorism carries several risks. One of the risks is the increasing international acceptance of the doctrine of universal jurisdiction, as exemplified in the new International Criminal Court. It may be that in time, the Rome Statute will be modified in ways that make it consistent with U.S. constitutional history and practice. Until then, even if we temporarily offend allies whose support our nation may need in the global war on terrorism, the United States must continue to aggressively shield all Americans fighting terrorism around the world from the purported reach of international institutions to which our country is not a party.

7

Mobilizing the Citizen Warriors

[T]he mobilization of Reserve and Guard troops . . . is a strong symbol
of this nation's resolve. . . . [T]he troops who will be called up
understand better than most that freedom has a cost,
and that we're willing to bear that cost.

—President George W. Bush, 17 September 2001

In July 1990, the month before Saddam Hussein triggered the Persian Gulf War
with his invasion of Kuwait, few National Guard personnel or reservists were
following foreign developments with anything more than routine interest. After
all, the nation was at peace and no known threat loomed over the horizon. It
was not yet certain that the Cold War was over, but the possibility of an armed
conflict involving the United States appeared remote.

The possibility of a mobilization of reserve forces for any crisis that might
occur appeared even more remote.[1] After all, it was an undisputed fact that

since the conflict in Vietnam, not a single reservist had been involuntarily activated for an armed conflict. Even though volunteer National Guard personnel and reservists had served in limited numbers in Grenada in 1983 and in Operation Just Cause in Panama in 1989–90, most military leaders believed that the nation's civilian leadership was simply unwilling to accept the political risks thought to be associated with a reserve call-up.

In addition to the interruption of the professional careers and private lives of those affected, it was thought that a mobilization could adversely impact the dynamics of a conflict. Many remembered President Lyndon Johnson's rejection of the advice of military leaders to call-up the reserves during the war in Vietnam. Political advisors to the president had argued that a mobilization of reservists would be perceived almost the same as a declaration of war and that it would greatly increase the chances of a full-scale conflict.[2] The ingrained idea that reservists were not available to military leaders was reflected in official documents. In its 1990 total force report, for example, the U.S. Navy had highlighted the issue:

> The limited availability of Selected Reserve personnel is the biggest obstacle that must be overcome in using Naval Reserve assets to support contingencies short of mobilization. The equipment is there; it is combat ready. The problem is to be able to call-up Reservists to man it.
>
> While there are a broad range of statutory options available to involuntarily recall Selected Reservists, both the domestic and international implications tied to these actions have severely restricted their use. This reluctance to initiate a Reserve call-up places the Navy in a dilemma. Congressional direction and fiscal constraints require that we place equipment and personnel assets in the Reserve component. However, in crisis situations, ready access to those assets is denied.[3]

For months, a contentious debate had been under way within the Pentagon about the force structure and force mix of active and reserve units and personnel that would be required in the future by a military strategy that was changing with the end of the Cold War. A particular force structure that was referred to as the "base force" had been recommended to President George H. W. Bush.[4] It was expected that on 2 August he would announce the broad outline of his plan to restructure the U.S. Armed Forces. That plan would call for an active, professional force that was 25 percent smaller than the existing force. The remarks prepared for the president implied a similar or even larger cut in the reserve components: "The need to be prepared for a massive, short-term mobilization has diminished. We can now adjust the size, structure, and readiness of our Reserve forces."[5]

When Iraq moved on Kuwait, the debate stopped. On 22 August 1990 the president signed Executive Order 12727. It authorized the secretary of defense and the secretary of transportation (with respect to the U.S. Coast Guard when the latter was not operating as a service in the Department of the Navy) "to order to active duty units and individual members not assigned to units, of the Selected Reserve." The number of reservists activated would depend on operational requirements.

One year later, the battle in the Persian Gulf for the liberation of Kuwait and the defense of Saudi Arabia was over and more than 90 percent of the National Guard personnel and reservists mobilized for Operations Desert Shield and Desert Storm were released from active duty. When combat operations ceased on 28 February 1991 a total of 202,337 selected reservists and 20,277 members of the individual ready reserve had been activated.[6] Approximately 106,000 National Guard personnel and reservists had served in the Kuwait theater of operations; 72 died in the conflict. The numbers included thousands of volunteers. National Guard personnel and reservists had performed vital combat, combat support, and combat service support missions. Their performance had been impressive.[7] In an address to a joint session of Congress, President Bush recognized their service: "This victory belongs . . . to the regulars, to the Reserves, to the National Guard. This victory belongs to the finest fighting force this Nation has ever known in its history."[8]

Soon after the Clinton administration assumed office in 1993 it became apparent to reservists that no issue remained of whether they would be activated in the future. It was now a question of how much. The new administration intended to use reservists in historically unprecedented ways. In the summer of 1994 Secretary of Defense William J. Perry advocated involuntary call-ups of reservists for prolonged peacekeeping and humanitarian operations.[9] A few weeks later, at a time when a majority of Congress saw no important U.S. security interest in Haiti and polling data indicated that almost three-fourths of Americans opposed a U.S. invasion of that small country, President Clinton authorized the involuntary activation of reservists for that specific purpose.

The same summer, Pentagon officials announced plans for reservists to repair housing, restore the environment, build a pier for fishing vessels in an economically depressed fishing community, dig wells, and survey the safety of dams, airport runways, and other parts of the domestic infrastructure components.[10] In a speech remarkable for its presumption that reservists should be used for matters not involving national security, one government official called for reservists to be involved in "defending America at home" by attacking "low literacy levels, high unemployment rates, increasing numbers of high school dropouts, unavailability of health care, rising crime, and drug abuse."[11] The idea that reservists should be involuntarily activated only in time of war or emergency was dismissed as a "Cold War relic."[12] When viewed in the context of the tragic events of 11 September 2001 this is an embarrassing reminder of the tendency of some civilian officials to unthinkingly misuse military assets. The pace of peacetime operations in the 1990s was already causing friction in many reserve families and resentment among civilian employers. The chief of the U.S. Air Force Reserve candidly admitted that reserve leaders had not fully explained "how close we are to the breaking point."[13]

In 1995 "peacetime engagement" was added to the list of missions included in the formal statement of the national military strategy. The Commission on Roles and Missions of the Armed Forces, whose chairman was shortly thereafter appointed deputy secretary of defense, recommended that extensive use of reservists be made in such peacetime engagement operations as law enforcement and the "constabulary training of foreign personnel."[14] In a communication to Congress regarding the commission's report, the secretary of defense

agreed that whenever possible, "operations other than war" should be performed by reservists.[15]

The National Defense Panel's December 1997 report stated, "[T]he Army
National Guard may need to downsize and reorganize to reestablish its relevance
in the post-Cold War world," but it also declared that reserve and National Guard
units would play an increasing role in a variety of worldwide operations by
"relieving active units and reducing the operational and personnel tempos of fre-
quent and lengthy deployments."[16] That latter prophecy proved accurate. By
1999 reservists were being activated at a rate thirteen times greater than the rate
at which they had been activated during the Cold War.[17] At the same time, the
total number of reservists had decreased to 876,000 from the 1.8 million who
were serving ten years earlier.[18] The increased tempo of operations and reduced
numbers were harming for both recruiting and retention.

This development was an unanticipated and questionable extension of the
Pentagon's total force policy. Originally designed to place greater reliance upon
the reserve components for budgetary reasons, the policy had been initiated
on 21 August 1970 by Secretary of Defense Melvin Laird.[19] Four years later,
the highly regarded army chief of staff, Gen. Creighton Abrams, began to
implement the policy by integrating the army's active and reserve components
in an unprecedented way. As the vice chief of staff during the buildup in
Vietnam, Abrams had seen firsthand the problems that resulted from President
Johnson's refusal to mobilize reservists. According to his biographer, Abrams
deliberately built into the army's sixteen-division structure a reliance upon
reserves that ensured that no president would be able to send the army to war
in the future without mobilizing its reserve forces.[20] The assumption implied
in Abrams' action was that increased reliance on reserve forces would act to
restrain presidents from pursuing ill-advised military adventures without public support, especially when no important national security interest was
involved. The reliance would also ensure that sufficient military strength was
used to bring success in any armed conflict.

For the next two decades, most reservists believed that they would not be
used as a cheap source of manpower. They expected to be pulled from their

private lives and professional or other employment obligations only for matters that involved vital national interests. By 1997 this premise was no longer
correct. I was one of many to note that the continued improper use of reservists
would "result eventually and predictably in significant declines in combat readiness and the quality of Reserve units."[21] I proposed a solution to the problem.

> Government officials must . . . understand that if the American people have not been
> persuaded to pay for an Active [regular] force structure large enough to carry out
> the number of "operations other than war" desired by a particular administration,
> the solution should not inevitably include involuntary activations of Reservists.
> Rather, the number and scope of such operations should be reduced. In the alter-
> native, more courageous and effective advocacy and leadership should be under-
> taken by political leaders so that Americans understand why the operations are in
> their best interest. Stated differently, if an activist foreign policy that requires fre-
> quent call-ups of Reservists is to be pursued, strong and effective political leader-
> ship, especially presidential leadership, is essential.[22]

Twenty-five days after his inauguration, President George W. Bush expressed his opposition to the "over-deployments" of U.S. military forces in
recent years. Speaking at the headquarters of West Virginia's National Guard,
he declared that he intended to "be careful about troop deployment—judicious
use of our troops."[23] It was welcome news to most of the reserve forces. Located
in almost five thousand cities and towns, reserve forces constitute a part of the
country's armed forces. Any deployment of significant military force inevitably
affects large numbers of reservists and local communities.

The selected reserve elements of the Army National Guard and U.S. Army
Reserve constitute 54 percent of the entire U.S. Army.[24] Many of the army's
capabilities in greatest demand reside in its reserve components, including civil
affairs (97 percent), medical brigades (85 percent), engineering battalions
(70 percent), military police battalions (66 percent), and psychological operations units (81 percent). The reserve components of the air force comprise 34
percent of the total U.S. Air Force.[25] As in the army, many of the most critical
capabilities reside in the Air National Guard and U.S. Air Force Reserve,

including tactical airlift (64 percent), aerial refueling and strategic tankers (55 percent), the strategic interceptor force (100 percent), tactical air support (38 percent), and strategic airlift (27 percent).

The U.S. Naval Reserve and U.S. Marine Corps Reserve constitute a smaller part of the U.S. Navy and U.S. Marine Corps. Each makes up 19 percent of its respective service. However, the contributions of the reserve components are critical in specific areas of capability. The naval reserve, for example, provides 100 percent of the navy's mobile inshore undersea warfare units, 93 percent of its cargo handling battalions, 100 percent of its logistic support squadrons, 40 percent of its fleet hospitals, and 60 percent of its mobile construction battalions. The marine corps reserve provides 100 percent of the corps' civil affairs capability, 33 percent of its intelligence units, 25 percent of its headquarters and service battalions, 25 percent of its communications battalions, and 25 percent of its supply battalions.

As the Bush administration took its first steps in response to the president's call for "a new architecture of American defense for decades to come," considerable thought was being given by the nation's citizen warriors to the question of where they would fit on the blueprint. To what degree would the recommendations of the 1996 quadrennial defense review report or the 1997 National Defense Panel be accepted? It appeared that administration officials agreed with the defense panel's conclusion that "[o]ne of the salient features of U.S. security in 2010–20 will be a much larger role for homeland defense." In a 1999 campaign speech, presidential candidate George W. Bush had declared that "homeland defense has become an urgent duty." But what did this mean for the reserve components?

The issue became of particular interest when the U.S. Commission on National Security/21st Century released its Phase III report in early 2001. "While it is appropriate for the National Guard to play the lead military role in managing the consequences of a WMD attack," the report declared, "its capabilities to do so are uneven." It recommended "that the National Guard be given homeland security as a *primary mission*" and that it "should be reorganized, trained and equipped to undertake that mission."[26] As a result of a recent series of seminar war games sponsored jointly by the Pentagon's Office of Net Assessment, National Guard leaders were already attempting to determine what unique capabilities the service could contribute to the performance of a homeland defense mission.[27]

On 10 September 2001 these types of issues were of interest primarily to civilian officials in the Pentagon and the uniformed leaders of the reserve components. The average reservist was thinking about more routine matters. That would soon change.

In a meeting of the National Security Council on the day following the attacks on the World Trade Center and the Pentagon, President Bush declared that the nation was now involved in "a different kind of war than our nation has ever fought," and that the United States would use all of its resources.[28] Reliance upon the reserve components was immediate. Within hours, Air National Guard personnel in F-15s and F-16s were flying combat air patrols over New York and Washington, D.C., as part of Operation Noble Eagle. Others on fifteen-minute alert status were waiting at twenty-six bases around the country in case they were needed to fly protective patrols over other cities. Reserve port security, medical services, and engineering support personnel were also already at work.

Three days after the attacks, the president declared a national emergency and authorized a partial mobilization of thousands of reservists.[29] In remarks at the Pentagon on 17 September he characterized the mobilization as "a strong symbol of this nation's resolve." Noting the sacrifice that would be made by those mobilized and by their families, he declared, "[T]he troops that will be called-up understand better than most that freedom has a cost, and that we're willing to bear that cost."[30]

The same day, the president also announced an entirely new mission for the National Guard. Until more permanent improvements could be made, National Guard personnel working in a state status and under the control of their respective governors pursuant to Title 32 of the *U.S. Code*, would be used to provide additional security at the nation's 429 commercial airports. "One of the great goals of this nation's war," the president said, was to "restore public confidence in the airline industry."[31] The initial estimates were that about four thousand National Guard troops would be required for up to six months. By early

November, however, seven thousand National Guard troops were working at airports. With the holiday travel season approaching, it was necessary for the president to authorize a total of more than nine thousand. In March 2002 approximately six thousand were still performing duties at airports. In a phased withdrawal, the last troops did not leave the airports until the end of May.

Because of the urgent and widespread need for large numbers of military police (MP), most of National Guard personnel assigned to airports were not MPs, but infantryman, engineers, and cannoneers. It was necessary for the Federal Aviation Administration to provide one to four days of training in the operation of x-ray scanners and metal detectors, the safe handling of dangerous items, surveillance, and incident management and conflict resolution. Except for Oregon, where officials decided that members of that state's National Guard would carry no weapons, most of the National Guard personnel assigned to airports were armed with either standard M16A2 rifles or M9 9-mm pistols.

The month after the attacks, reservists were providing security at nuclear power plants, bridges, water reservoirs, and the company that is the sole provider of the military's anthrax vaccine, as well as providing force protection at federal buildings, military installations, and other security-sensitive spots across the country. In November one hundred National Guard personnel from the District of Columbia were assigned to provide security at the U.S. Capitol. More than four thousand reservists were sent to Salt Lake City to provide security at the Winter Olympics. Units were selected for specific homeland security tasks by assessing both their readiness condition and whether they were scheduled for deployment soon on another assigned mission such as peacekeeping.

The demands of the many new missions had an immediate impact. The chief of the U.S. Army Reserve expressed the view that the new homeland security mission could change the face of the army's reserve components forever. "It's quite clear that we are not going to look in the future like we look today," he said. "We are going to have to change the way we organize."[32] The director of the Army National Guard also predicted a variety of changes. "My priority," he said, "is to align the Guard with the missions before us."[33] One change would involve the conversion of some of the

National Guard's armor and other combat units to units that have greater capability for response to domestic crises. Another change would involve renewed emphasis on certain military occupational specialties (MOSs) that would be most critical in future terrorist attacks, for example, chemical/biological response, military police, almost everything in the medical field, transportation, and communications.

Over the next several weeks, the demands on reservists continued to increase. By the middle of November more than fifty-five thousand reservists had been called to duty. While soldiers in battle dress uniforms (BDUs) were most visible to the public, all reserve components were contributing. With its activation of sailors with skills in intelligence, port security, construction engineering, and health care, for example, the U.S. Naval Reserve was at one point second only to the U.S. Air Reserve components in the number of part-time personnel called to active duty.

With the continuing mobilization and the assignment to reservists of a broad range of missions, attention returned to the National Guard civil support teams. The Weapons of Mass Destruction–Civil Support Team Program was established in 1998 to train Army and Air National Guard volunteers to assist civilian authorities in responding to nuclear, biological, and chemical attacks. The teams were to be trained to deploy rapidly to assist local first responders in determining the nature of an attack, provide medical and technical advice, and pave the way for the identification and arrival of follow-on state and federal military response units. Each unit had two major pieces of equipment: a mobile analytical laboratory and a mobile communications facility.

The first ten of the twenty-two-member teams were scheduled to be certified as ready by April 2000. However, the tenth team was not certified until 17 October 2001.[34] The DoD inspector general's report called the management of the program ineffective and said that it failed to provide adequate guidance, training, and equipment for the first ten teams.[35] A later report by the General Accounting Office (GAO), the investigative arm of Congress, concluded that the teams had continuing problems regarding their readiness, doctrine, role, and their ability to respond quickly to a terrorist attack.[36]

The civil support teams faced several challenges in addition to those associated with defective equipment. Team members were required to complete eighteen months of training in techniques that would permit them to survive and operate in areas contaminated by nuclear, biological, or chemical weapons. Opportunities for promotion within a team are limited and commercial companies are eager to hire those who completed the expensive training. These factors and a standard tour length of only three years made it difficult to achieve consistently good team performance.[37]

Despite the problems, on 13 October 2001 the army chief of staff directed the National Guard bureau to speed up the certification of the next seventeen teams. Their certification was announced on 28 January 2002. In the Defense Authorization Act for FY 2003, which did not become law until November 2002, Congress authorized a total of fifty-five teams, two for California and one for each other state and territory.

In December 2001 a federal agency request was made for yet another form of National Guard assistance. The request soon raised several contentious issues. The subject? The security of U.S. borders. The memory of the 1999 arrest of Ahmed Ressam was fresh in the minds of most officials responsible for border security. He was arrested as he was attempting to enter the state of Washington from Canada in a car filled with explosives. Ressam—a suspected associate of Osama bin Laden—had been convicted in Los Angeles of smuggling, conspiracy to engage in terrorism, and other charges stemming from what investigators described as a plot to bomb the Los Angeles International Airport during the 2000 millennium celebrations.

The porous and loosely guarded U.S. border with Canada is 5,500 miles long. It has 157 official border crossings. In 2001, 100 million people entered the United States through the Canadian border. The same year, 314 million people entered the United States across the two-thousand-mile border with Mexico, which has thirty-three border crossings. Canadian intelligence officials estimated that approximately fifty terrorist groups had operatives in Canada, including al Qaeda, the Irish Republican Army, and Hamas. Slightly more than three hundred U.S. immigration agents were assigned to the northern U.S. border.

Concerned about border security during the twelve to eighteen months it would take to obtain permanent funding and to train the new border agents recently authorized by Congress,[38] U.S. Attorney General John Ashcroft proposed an emergency plan to strengthen border security. Under the plan, National Guard troops would assist federal Customs Service agents, Immigration and Naturalization Service agents, and the U.S. Border Patrol by searching vehicles and containers, flying surveillance aircraft, providing perimeter security, performing intelligence work, managing traffic, and processing people designed to enter the country. The first National Guard troops would be sent to a dozen border states in which the ports of entry of most concern were located. The Departments of Justice and Treasury would reimburse the Defense Department for the cost of the troops.

The first point of contention was the chain of command. Members of the Joint Chiefs of Staff at first opposed the idea of placing the approximately seventeen hundred National Guard troops under the control of civilian agencies.[39] This was surprising because military personnel had been effectively supporting federal law enforcement agencies in counterdrug operations since at least 1989. The issue disappeared after the Secretary of Defense Rumsfeld agreed to the control of the troops by the agencies.

The next controversial issue was the recurring one of *posse comitatus*. Critics of the plan to use troops at the borders were quick to refer to the 1997 incident on the Texas border with Mexico in which a Mexican goatherd was killed by a marine who was involved in a counterdrug operation in support of civil authorities. They expressed concern that the troops would be involved in law enforcement in violation of the Posse Comitatus Act. They also voiced the argument that the border work would prevent the National Guard troops from training for their primary missions, presumably missions to be performed outside the United States, as if all "primary" missions of the individual National Guard troops were now of more importance to the nation than its defense at home.

The major issue, however, resulted from the dual federal-state status of the National Guard, from the fact that each individual in the National Guard serves two masters.[40] When the president asked the nation's governors to provide

National Guard units at airports, the troops served under state control even though they received federal funding. There were advantages to this procedure. Federalization of the troops would have placed greater restrictions on their use. State officials had greater say in which units and personnel were mobilized. According to one adjutant general, state control also permitted National Guard troops to be deployed to airports near their home, thereby improving morale and reducing travel and lodging expenses.[41]

There were also disadvantages associated with the procedure. The standards of training and operating at airports varied widely among states. There were also complaints that National Guard troops working in a state (or Title 32 of the U.S. Code) status did not enjoy the same civil and financial protections as National Guard troops who were federalized pursuant to Title 10. Because state laws differ, there was particular concern about reemployment rights.[42] Officials at the Pentagon decided to federalize the National Guard troops assigned to border security duty. On the surface, the decision seemed straightforward. The agencies requesting assistance were federal agencies and the security of the nation's international borders is a responsibility of the federal government.

Placing the troops under federal control, however, did raise complications. The troops were barred by the Posse Comitatus Act from searching individuals or making arrests. This seemed like a minor limitation because the National Guard troops would be working in tandem with federal agents who were so authorized. But, National Guard leaders soon objected to the federalization on several other grounds, much preferring that the Pentagon foot the bill for the border security mission, but leave control of the troops in the hands of state officials. This approach, they argued, would place what they characterized as essentially a law enforcement mission in the hands of state leaders who are better qualified to understand regional and local concerns. The commander of California's National Guard even accused the Pentagon of deliberately delaying the deployment of National Guard troops to the Canadian border. In an interview, he said that the delays would not have occurred if the troops had been under state control.[43]

The issue became more heated in February after the Department of Defense signed memoranda of agreement (MOAs) with the Justice and

Treasury Departments that set forth the terms of service by the National Guard. The other departments agreed to provide force protection for the National Guard personnel and the DoD agreed that they would not be armed. An officer at the Pentagon said that weapons were not required for the tasks the National Guard troops had been asked to perform.[44] Since troops previously engaged in drug interdiction operations had been permitted to carry firearms, the real reason was probably more related to sensitivity to foreign policy concerns. A DoD spokesman said, "[W]e didn't want to give the impression we were militarizing the border."[45]

In a remarkable demonstration of their dual status, political independence, and their own perception of their political power, a letter in the form of a resolution was sent to the president on 25 February 2002 from fifty adjutants general, the senior National Guard leaders in the states.[46] They attacked the DoD decision to federalize the National Guard personnel. "Post-September 11 security measures and inadequate federal staffing at U.S. border ports of entry," they said, "are limiting the flow of persons, goods and commerce at our land borders, causing continuing and serious damage to the American economy." Relief at the nation's borders, they asserted "has already been delayed for more than 4 months by DoD's refusal to accept Title 32 National Guard assistance and by DoD's insistence on federalizing the National Guard," to include creating "a new and costly federal command and control system for such federalized forces."[47]

Various arguments were advanced for placing the National Guard personnel under state control. First, the federalization of the troops would "eliminate any role for the Governor in this homeland security mission" and establish "an unwise and unacceptable precedent."[48] In support of this argument, it was asserted that federally funded Title 32 state duty has been used "for more than 12 years for National Guard counterdrug support . . . under individual Governors' Counterdrug Plans."[49] Second, the stationing of "federal military forces at the United States' borders . . . would be an action that is unprecedented in modern history."[50] Third, the federalization of the National Guard would "immediately degrade the wartime readiness of each unit from which soldiers are mobilized."[51] Finally, federalization of the National Guard would, "according to most legal experts, violate the Posse Comitatus Act."[52]

Unfortunately, the merits of the case that could have been advanced by the adjutants general were weakened not only by the strident tone of the resolution, but also by their arguments. A decision by the president and secretary of defense, especially in a time of armed conflict and possibly imminent danger to the nation, must not be characterized as "unacceptable" by uniformed officers. The example of the counterdrug plans of the governors was also poor. In fact, it had long been the practice that each governor's counterdrug plan had to be approved by the Department of Defense and the Justice Department before funds could be released to pay for the implementation of the plan.[53] The argument that the stationing of federal troops at the borders is "unprecedented" was hardly persuasive because almost everything about the war on terrorism is unprecedented. Although some "legal experts" may have been consulted, it is difficult to see in retrospect how the Posse Comitatus Act would be violated by federal troops acting not as federal law enforcement officers, but in support of them.

The letter to the president also lambasted the DoD agreement that the National Guard personnel would not be armed. The agreement, the adjutants general said, requires "junior enlisted personnel to perform law enforcement duties without any officer supervision and require[s] them to perform potentially dangerous security duties unarmed and without appropriate means of self-defense or self-protection." Noting that civilian employees of the federal government "who perform the same tasks are required to be armed," the letter charged that the DoD decision placed "the young men and women of the states' military forces in grave and imminent danger."[54] On 22 March the National Guard leaders received political reinforcements. A letter from fifty-eight U.S. senators asked the president to overturn the DoD decision. The decision was not reversed, but it was modified. In June it was announced that over two hundred "selected" members of the National Guard assisting U.S. Customs Service agents at remote border crossings would be trained and permitted to carry sidearms until the border security mission ended on 30 September.

Disputes between the states and the Department of Defense are not uncommon. In the months preceding the 1990–91 Persian Gulf War, Governor Rudy Perpich of Minnesota and Governor Michael Dukakis of Massachusetts filed suit in federal court, challenging the right of the president to order members of the National Guard to active duty for purposes of training outside the United States during peacetime and without either the consent of the governor or the declaration of a national emergency. They were specifically opposed to the training of their states' National Guard in Central America. The case eventually reached the U.S. Supreme Court. Because I had spent much of my professional life in courtroom advocacy and was the senior official in the government directly responsible for the National Guard, the U.S. solicitor general requested my assistance in the preparation of the government's brief. The solicitor general presented the case in oral argument on 27 March 1990. In its 11 June 1990 opinion, a unanimous Supreme Court held that since "several constitutional provisions commit matters of foreign policy and military affairs to the exclusive control of the National Government," the legislation that gave the president the authority to issue the orders in question was constitutionally valid.[55]

Another example of the tension created by the dual nature of the National Guard is the litigation that occurred between the state of Wyoming and two of its most senior National Guard officers. In the spring of 1998, the Wyoming legislature amended state law to require that the occupants of the state's two assistant adjutants general position—one of which commands the state's Army National Guard while the other commands the state's Air National Guard—be residents of the state. After the Wyoming attorney general issued an opinion concluding that the Wyoming constitution also prevents nonresidents from holding the positions, the two incumbents, both of whom were residents of Colorado and had served in the Wyoming National Guard for well over a decade, were removed from their positions. They filed suit in a U.S. district court, which ruled in their favor. The case was appealed. In an unanimous opinion on 3 July 2002 a three-judge panel of a U.S. court of appeals ruled that the residency restriction violates the privileges and immunities clause of the U.S. Constitution.[56] The court noted at some length the National Guard's dual role as both a state and a federal entity, but declared that "virtually all state control . . . is subject to federal regulation, and the National Guard is a component of the national defense forces at all times whether called-up to federal service or not."[57] Because service in a state unit of the National Guard "bear[s] on the vitality of the Nation as a single entity," the court said, service in the Wyoming National Guard is a privilege protected by the privileges and immunities clause.[58]

For students of the American colonial experience, the fight over the federalization of the National Guard troops assigned to duty at the borders is a strong reminder that the issue faced by Gen. George Washington in 1775 is still present 215 years after the drafting of the U.S. Constitution. Assuming command of the new Continental Army on 3 July 1775, Washington attempted to infuse a new spirit into his untested troops with these words:

> The Continental Congress having now taken all the Troops of the several Colonies . . . into their Pay and Service. They are now the Troops of the United Provinces of North America; and it is hoped that all Distinctions of Colonies will be laid aside; so that one and the same Spirit may animate the whole, and the only Contest be, who shall render, on this great and trying occasion, the most essential service to the Great and common cause in which we are all engaged.[59]

At the six-month anniversary of the tragic events of 11 September 2001 our nation's citizen warriors were face to face with the many uncertainties of an open-ended war on terrorism. Unlike the Persian Gulf War of 1990–91 in which a single enemy in one area was the focus of an intense and relatively short U.S. military effort, the prolonged worldwide nature of the new low-level conflict presented different problems. Some were obvious. First, it was difficult to identify and to locate the new enemy. Second, it was not at all clear how long the new conflict might last.

The consequences of these facts were significant. The civilian occupations of a large number of reservists are concentrated in law enforcement, emergency response, and other public service agencies. In Los Angeles in the summer of

2001, for example, 652 officers and civilian employees of the Los Angeles Police Department were reservists, as were 236 deputies from the Los Angeles County Sheriff's Department.[60] And, the new element of fear for safety at home had suddenly changed the opinion of many for the use of U.S. troops elsewhere. "If we have an attack on the U.S.," said one defense analyst, "we're going to need those people here—not walking children to school in Bosnia."[61] A member of the Senate Armed Services Committee expressed the same opinion. "My major concern is capacity. How much can you spare for homeland security?"[62]

By early January 2002 more than sixty-seven thousand reservists had been mobilized. Combat air patrol aircraft had flown thirteen thousand sorties over U.S. cities. Stop-loss policies suspending the voluntary separations and retirements of reservists had been initiated by all of the military services for certain specialty and career fields such as military police, civil affairs, and psychological operations. The president had recently signed new legislation into law that authorized the services to increase manning levels by 2 percent. On 13 March the Pentagon announced that 80,576 reservists from fifty states, the District of Columbia, and Puerto Rico had been activated. The number did not include the National Guard personnel—about nine thousand at the peak—who had been activated in a state status for airport-security duties.

Military leaders began to express concern about the exhaustive pace of the efforts required to continue the fighting in Afghanistan, to support counter-terrorist and other operations in other parts of the world, and to protect the United States. "They're tired, sir," the commander-in-chief of the U.S. Joint Forces Command informed Congress in endorsing proposals to increase the size of the armed forces. "We are busier than we have ever been."[63] The commander-in-chief of the U.S. Central Command said that he might ask mobilized reservists who were serving in his area of responsibility to voluntarily remain on active duty after their mobilization orders expired because they were so important.[64] In the jargon of force planners, the army chief of staff continued to advance his argument that the army was "too small for [its] mission profile."[65] Secretary of Defense Rumsfeld was particularly anxious to have reservists relieved of security duties at the nation's airports and along the borders. "They are civilian functions," he said, "and they ought to be performed over any sustained period of time by civilians. . . . We train our people to be warfighters."[66]

The financial, personal, and professional hardships faced by activated reservists were ameliorated somewhat by two developments that affected all of the reserve components: the Uniformed Services Employment and Reemployment Rights Act (USERRA) and an improved family support system.

When reservists were mobilized for the Persian Gulf War in 1990 many new lessons were learned. Reservists had never been mobilized since the nation had adopted an all-volunteer force following the conflict in Vietnam. Because they considered mobilization unlikely, many reservists had failed to take prudent measures to protect their families in the event they were activated. The military services had not established effective family support programs for activated reservists. Most employers had no policies in place regarding employees who were suddenly taken from the workplace. Mississippi Congressman Gene Taylor, who was then a freshman representative and later chaired the House National Guard and Reserve Components Caucus, recalled that in 1990 "the employers and the families, they were aghast. When they got called-up, it was no longer some far-and-away war. It became everybody's war."[67]

Since 1940 federal law had provided reemployment rights to reservists. In 1946 the Supreme Court had sustained the law in an opinion that declared, "he who was called to the colors was not to be penalized on his return by reason of his absence from his civilian job."[68] Many avenues had remained open for subtle pressure by employers, however. Slow promotions, infrequent pay raises, and poor assignments were not uncommon.

A vigorous effort to improve the employment protection of reservists and to more effectively communicate to employers the increasing importance of reservists was commenced in the Pentagon in early 1988. By the time of Operations Desert Shield and Desert Storm, much had been done. A February 1991 survey determined that employers in the Baltimore-Washington, Chicago, Houston, Minneapolis–St. Paul, and Milwaukee areas had generally exceeded the requirements of the law during the Persian Gulf War. During the absence of their reservists-employees almost a third of the companies surveyed had elected to pay the employees an amount that, when added to their military pay, equaled their regular civilian income.[69] Twelve percent of the employers said they were paying their reservists-employees their full civilian salaries for periods of time ranging from one month to the entire length of mobilized service. Ten months after the Persian Gulf War ended, another survey found that 95 percent of the respondents were aware that an employee could not be denied a promotion because of the obligations of reserve service.[70]

Problems remained, however. Two U.S. courts of appeal had recently interpreted the current law in a way that required the application of a reasonableness test to a reservist's request for leave to comply with reserve service obligations. The test required consideration of the burden that would be placed on the civilian employer. That situation had to be changed. When the war tocsin sounds and citizen warriors are called to the colors, military commanders cannot afford to wait for a judicial balancing of the nation's needs against those of a private employer.[71]

Because I was serving in a government position that permitted me to help in the effectuation of change, I did. After considerable effort, new legislation to clarify and to improve the law and to prevent the application of a reasonableness test was submitted to Congress in February 1991. On 13 October 1994 USERRA became law.[72] Among other things, the legislation requires all employers to reinstate reservists when they return from active duty with the same status, seniority, retirement benefits, and compensation that were in place at the time of activation. It also requires employers to continue paying health insurance premiums for thirty days after a reservist-employee is mobilized. Today, it is common for corporate policies to continue health insurance for the dependents of activated reservists and to provide the difference between military and civilian pay for up to twelve months. Some large employers even offer the differential pay for as much as five years.

Many small companies and companies in economically depressed industries, however, simply cannot afford to continue to provide such benefits. Many companies cannot even afford the loss of their reservists-employees for any period longer than the predictable annual training time. In the months following

President Bush's September 2001 mobilization order, these and similar problems appeared to have an adverse impact on the relationship between reservists and their civilian employers. A survey by the GAO concluded that the relationship was in clear need of improvement.[73] The Pentagon's Office of Employer Support of the Guard and Reserve was receiving increasing numbers of complaints.

Fortunately, the family support systems of each of the reserve components had improved markedly since the end of Operation Desert Storm. More than 50 percent of the U.S. Armed Forces personnel are married. Defense officials now understand fully the importance of family support to military readiness. Still, obtaining adequate medical coverage for families is a continuing problem for mobilized reservists, many of whom do not live near military installations. The problem is sufficiently serious that several proposals were offered in Congress in 2002 to address the issue. The geographical disbursement of reserve families and the isolation of many of them from military installations will always make effective support a challenge, but several new tools have been developed.[74] Reservists now had three remaining questions. How long would the current tempo of operations be continued? What were the prospects for an armed conflict with Iraq, which would likely require a larger mobilization? What long-term homeland security responsibilities would be assigned to reservists?

During July 2002 Congress was rushing toward its election year August recess. An intense and ultimately unsuccessful effort was under way to complete work on legislation creating the new Department of Homeland Security so that the law could be enacted by 11 September to commemorate the one-year anniversary of the terrorist attacks in New York City and Washington, D.C. In the western part of the country, National Guard personnel and reservists from several states were fighting massive forest fires. More than eighty-two thousand National Guard troops and reservists were still performing homeland security and related duties, the largest homeland defense effort since President Woodrow Wilson mobilized the entire National Guard in 1916 after Pancho Villa raided Columbus, New Mexico, and killed thirty people.[75] Civilian officials at the Pentagon were scrambling to meet short-term operational requirements without increasing the number of Americans in uniform, either through the mobilization of more reservists, or increases in the end strength, that is, the total number, of active personnel.

After a relatively quiet August the nation paused to recognize the first anniversary of the attacks on the World Trade Center and the Pentagon. On the morning of 11 September senior Department of Defense officials presided over ceremonies at the Pentagon and later at Arlington National Cemetery. The same day a Pentagon news release announced that 74,120 National Guard personnel and reservists were on active duty. One-fourth of the roughly eight thousand U.S. troops in Afghanistan were reservists. In the year since the war on terrorism began, approximately 130,000 reservists had been activated. Many of those still on active duty faced a prolonged absence from their families, additional missed civilian career opportunities, and continued reductions in income. The Pentagon had recently decided to retain almost fifteen thousand air force reservists and Air National Guard personnel on active duty. And, there was strong reason to believe that a much larger mobilization and prolonged activation was a certainty if hostilities were to be commenced against Iraq. Crew members of air force transport and refueling aircraft would be needed even before the war commenced. It was also likely that large numbers of reservists would be needed early for the protection of critical domestic infrastructure and landmarks against possible backlash terrorist attacks.[76]

It was public knowledge that the Bush administration was planning a complex and lengthy military occupation of Iraq if U.S. forces removed Saddam Hussein's regime. The task of administering and rebuilding the fractious country of twenty-three million inhabitants and overseeing the first steps to political reform was expected to be dangerous, difficult, and costly.[77] The policing of a conquered area the size of California, the restoration of court and police systems and other parts of the domestic infrastructure, and related postwar recovery efforts would require large numbers of military police and civil affairs specialists, most of whom were reservists.[78] Government officials could be forgiven for focusing attention and energy on immediate and difficult problems. The danger of additional terrorist attacks was significant and the nation had endless vulnerabilities. A war against Iraq was still considered likely, if not imminent.

The longer-term issues involving the nation's citizen warriors, however, cried out for attention. New thinking was required to ensure that the future balance between active and reserve forces meets the nation's new security needs. Perhaps reservists with unique or critical skills and experience need to be organized, trained, and compensated differently than other reservists. Perhaps the civilian employers of some reservists need to be compensated for their disproportionate contributions to the nation's security. Perhaps military personnel with high-demand skills should only serve in the active force. Perhaps new planning principles need to be established and enforced so that manpower, equipment, and other resources are allocated to the active and reserve forces not on the basis of political pressure, tradition, or long-standing practice, but solely on the basis of need, demonstrated capability to perform specific missions and operational tasks, and cost.

Long-term answers about the future use of the reserve components for homeland security and other missions were in short supply. Difficult questions had only recently been asked. The Pentagon's 30 September 2001 quadrennial defense review report had stated a need "to size U.S. military forces not only for the most demanding near-term warfighting tasks, but also for a plausible set of other near-term contingencies."[79] The QDR report, however, had offered no solutions and spoke only vaguely of the future development of a "strategic human resources plan" that would "examine the balance of personnel and work among the Active, Reserve and civilian work places."[80] The secretary of defense's August 2002 annual report to the president and Congress declared that the reserve components "are an integral part of the defense strategy and day-to-day operations of the U.S. military," but it offered no view of the future, saying only that an ongoing review of "the Active and Reserve mix, organization, priority missions, and associated resources" was under way.[81] The review had been directed almost a year earlier by the QDR report.[82]

In a 9 September 2002 speech, David Chu, the under secretary of defense for personnel and readiness, raised the question of whether reserve units should be a mirror of the active force or draw on the special qualities of the reserve components, but he proposed no answer. He also declared that the reserve components "can play a much larger role" in homeland defense, but he conceded that "what that role will be and who will be asked to do what is one of the critical issues in front of us."[83] Some of the possible answers to these and related issues were suggested in April 2003 when the Department of Defense submitted to Congress a series of proposed legislative changes. One of the proposed changes would authorize each of the military departments, with the consent of the relevant governors in the case of the National Guard, to involuntarily activate reservists with critical military occupational skills for up to ninety days of training.[84]

While editorial columns and talk shows continued to devote attention to the contentious White House instruction to lawyers at the Defense and Justice Departments to review the Posse Comitatus Act and any other laws that might restrict the ability of regular military personnel to perform homeland security duties,[85] many outside the Pentagon had specific ideas about the role of reserve forces in homeland security. Members of the U.S. Commission on National Security/21st Century continued to urge the recommendations made in the commission's 15 February 2001 report. Declaring that the National Guard "should redistribute resources currently allocated predominately to preparing for conventional wars overseas to provide greater support to civil authorities in preparing for and responding to disasters, especially emergencies involving weapons of mass destruction,"[86] the commission proposed five courses of action. First, the National Guard should "[p]articipate and initiate, where necessary, state, local, and regional planning for responding to a WMD incident." Second, it should "[t]rain and help organize local first responders." Third, it should "[m]aintain up-to-date inventories of military resources and equipment available in the area on short notice." Fourth, it should "[p]lan for rapid interstate support and reinforcement." Finally, it should "[d]evelop an overseas capability for international humanitarian assistance and disaster relief."[87]

A Homeland Security Task Force, formed by a leading conservative research and educational institute, also declared that the top priority for improving military antiterrorism operations to defend the homeland was to enhance "the capabilities of National Guard and Reserve units to respond to terrorist events. This means freeing some of these units from having to provide combat support and combat service support for the active forces by adding more active duty personnel to current force levels."[88] A liberal think tank agreed: "The Guard's deep knowledge of emergency response systems, crisis management needs and law enforcement concerns makes it ideally suited to take the lead on homeland security."[89] Another independent commission soon recommended that "certain [N]ational Guard units be trained for and assigned homeland security missions as their *exclusive* missions," federal funding be provided to the states through the secretary of defense for the civil support training of National Guard personnel, and a "regionally organized system for providing National Guard military assistance to civil authorities . . . be developed."[90]

Senator Joe Lieberman, a member of the Senate Armed Services Committee and former Democrat vice presidential candidate, shared these views. After observing that "[m]ost of today's Guard remains structured, trained, and equipped to augment and reinforce active-duty troops," he asserted that "in the age of terrorism, we also need more talented hands on deck right here, right now."[91] Echoing the recommendation of the commission, he proposed giving the National Guard lead agency responsibility in homeland security and requiring it to oversee training for state and local law enforcement and emergency personnel.[92] He further proposed that the National Guard be included in the new Department of Homeland Security.[93] "No part of our military," he declared in a speech in Washington, "is better suited to aid in providing for the common defense of the homeland than the National Guard."[94]

Many reserve leaders were less than enthusiastic about these ideas. Some feared a loss of prestige if the primary federal mission of the National Guard was something other than warfighting on foreign soil.[95] Others feared a loss of federal funding or less control of the National Guard by state governors.[96] An internal DoD study recommended that reserve component units not be assigned any exclusive homeland security missions; rather the reserve component forces should be "dual missioned" for both wartime and domestic support missions.[97] Despite the opposition, however, a clear need existed to fashion new doctrinal concepts for how all reservists, including National Guard personnel, would be trained and employed in the future for what everyone agreed would be a wider range of threats than had confronted previous generations, in a conflict that might continue for years.

Once again, the issue was one of balance. How could the nation obtain the most for its security needs from the reserve components without making reserve service so burdensome as to drive the best reservists—who are all volunteers—from the armed forces? What kind of change is necessary to transform the reserve components from a Cold War structure to one fully capable of supporting a military response to the most likely future threats? How fast can the change take place?[98] How can reservists continue to assume the role of soldier without laying aside the role of citizen? Much depends on striking the correct balance to these and many related questions.

Small signs of future change could be detected. On 8 September 2002 the U.S. Army announced an Army National Guard Restructure Initiative (ARNGRI) that will restructure several National Guard combat formations. New mobile, light brigades using wheeled platforms rather than tracked armored vehicles will be created as units within multifunctional diversions designed to perform homeland security as well as other missions. The brigades will be capable of protecting critical infrastructure, such as nuclear power facilities or major bridges, or patrolling the border. A new year-long personnel study by the army was also going to evaluate the wisdom of forward-deploying National Guard and reserve units to Europe and South Korea to perform missions currently performed by permanently stationed active soldiers.

Still, much work remained. As late as a year after the terrorist attacks and twenty months after the Bush administration took office, Congress had not yet confirmed an assistant secretary of defense for reserve affairs, the Pentagon's senior reserve forces official.

8

American Due Process and the Laws of War

Matters intimately related to foreign policy and national security are rarely proper subjects for judicial intervention. . . . It is "obvious and unarguable" that no government interest is more compelling than the security of the Nation.

—U.S. Supreme Court, *Haig v. Agee,* 1981

The date was 25 June 2002. The setting was the Lewis F. Powell Jr. United States Courthouse in Richmond, Virginia. A three-judge panel of the U.S. Court of Appeals for the Fourth Circuit was hearing oral argument in *Yaser Esam Hamdi v. Donald Rumsfeld, et. al.,* a high-profile constitutional drama that had all of the earmarks of a case that would eventually reach the U.S. Supreme Court. Because two of the judges lived in another state within the circuit, the proceeding was being conducted by teleconference. The arguments of the lawyers and the questions and comments of the judges were being piped through speakers into the courthouse so they could be heard by reporters and others gathered there.

The presiding judge was Chief Judge J. Harvie Wilkinson III, a 1984 appointee of President Reagan. The remaining members of the panel were Judge William Byrd Traxler Jr., a 1998 appointee of President Clinton, and Judge William Walter Wilkins Jr., appointed to the circuit court by President Reagan in 1986. Counsel for the government was a deputy U.S. solicitor general, a fact of some significance.[1] An assistant federal public defender was representing the appellee and subject of the case, Yaser Esam Hamdi, the twenty-one-year-old son of Saudi parents. Hamdi was born in Louisiana and reared in Saudi Arabia. He was now the subject of considerable national attention.

After his capture with a Taliban unit and while armed with an AK-47 assault rifle in a combat area in Afghanistan in November 2001, the U.S. government declared Hamdi to be an "enemy combatant" and sent him to a detention facility on the U.S. naval base in Guantanamo Bay, Cuba, for interrogation.[2] When it was learned that he was born in the United States and may not have renounced his citizenship, he was moved to a naval brig in Norfolk, Virginia, on 5 April for additional interrogation. No charges were filed against him. On 11 June a U.S. district court judge in Norfolk had granted the public defender's request to engage in unmonitored discussions with Hamdi and to have unrestricted access to him. The government promptly filed an emergency motion with the court of appeals seeking a stay and a reversal of the district court's order. The issue before the court of appeals was whether the public defender could provide legal representation to Hamdi. The broader question was whether Hamdi could continue to be detained for the purpose of gathering intelligence and as an enemy combatant in accordance with the laws and customs of war and whether he could be denied the right of an attorney for representation in the U.S. court system.

The case was not of interest solely to law school professors and historians. No, this case was receiving much broader attention. It was the latest and most important judicial proceeding to date in the ongoing national effort to strike a proper balance between the traditional protection of civil liberties in the United States and the national security imperatives presented by the new war against terrorism.

In a brief filed with the court prior to the oral argument, the government had argued that the U.S. Armed Forces, pursuant to the direction of the president, have exclusive authority to designate a person an "enemy combatant." Citing the 1942 decision of the U.S. Supreme Court in *Ex Parte Quirin*,[3] the government asserted, "Not only do courts lack the expertise to evaluate military tactics, but they will often be without knowledge of the facts or standards upon which military decisions are based."[4]

The ninety-minute oral argument was spirited. The questions from the bench were sharp. Expressing strong skepticism about the breadth of the government's argument and about its implication for the doctrine for separation of powers,[5] Chief Judge Wilkinson observed that in the conflict in Afghanistan, it is "difficult to determine who is a combatant and who is a villager. One seems to melt into the other." He asked the government's lawyer, "You are saying [that] the judiciary has no right to inquire at all into someone's status as an enemy combatant?"[6]

Although expressed in nonconfrontational language, the government's position remained firm: It could not successfully prosecute a worldwide armed conflict if such fundamental matters of military judgment as the capture and interrogation of battlefield combatants were second-guessed by lawyers in civilian courts far removed from the scene. While the court could "evaluate the legal consequences" of the president's determination of enemy combatant status, it could not substitute its judgment for that of the president. Interference by the courts would reduce or eliminate the military's ability to obtain intelligence about possible future terrorist attacks because the introduction of additional parties into the intelligence-gathering process, especially defense lawyers who urged the detainees to claim constitutional protection against self-incrimination, could break the "atmosphere of trust" the government was attempting to establish.[7] It might even result in the transmittal of information from a captured combatant to potential terrorists through the detainee's attorney.

The court's questioning of the public defender was also pointed. "What is unconstitutional about the Government detaining that person and getting from that individual all the intelligence that might later save American lives?" Judge Wilkinson asked.[8] Was the public defender really arguing that the government could not even detain a citizen "who has taken up arms against America?" When the lawyer asserted that the issue of the district court's appointment of legal counsel for Hamdi was separate from the issue of the lawfulness of his detention, the judge expressed doubt. "If counsel is appointed," he said, "we are deciding . . . that someone who may well be an enemy combatant has a right to counsel, No. 1. That's a major issue. I don't know how counsel can be separated from access or indeed from the other rights in the criminal justice system. I don't know how you can appoint counsel without throwing into jeopardy the Government's intelligence-gathering operation."[9]

The court's unanimous ruling was rendered the following day. It did not receive as much public attention as another judicial decision made on the same day. A panel of the U.S. Court of Appeals for the Ninth Circuit issued an opinion in San Francisco declaring that the Pledge of Allegiance is unconstitutional because it contains the words "under God." The decision of the Fourth Circuit, however, was studied closely by many. Without reaching the questions of whether Hamdi could be detained indefinitely or whether he could be represented in the courts in the future by a lawyer representing his father, who had only recently filed a petition for habeas corpus as Hamdi's "next friend,"[10] the court ruled that the public defender had not demonstrated that he had a significant relationship with Hamdi, thereby failing "to satisfy an important jurisdictional pre-requisite for next friend standing."[11] In short, the public defender could not meet with Hamdi or represent him in court and the district court did not have subject matter jurisdiction of the case. The case was ordered to be dismissed. Most eyes now turned to the new and separate petition filed by Hamdi's father. Some eyes, however, were already beginning to turn to the Supreme Court.

Within hours of the 11 September 2001 attacks, a fundamental reassessment began of the approach to terrorism by federal law enforcement agencies. For years, terrorism had been treated primarily as a criminal problem. Fearful that military responses would only invite retaliation, the Clinton administration preferred to seek convictions in court as part of an effort to depoliticize and deligitimize terrorism in the eyes of the world.[12] Now, criminal convictions were no longer the first target of criminal investigations. In testimony before the House Committee of the Judiciary on 24 September, the U.S. attorney general declared that the fight against terrorism was now "the highest priority of the Department of Justice." The fight "is not merely or primarily" a criminal justice endeavor. "We cannot wait for terrorists to strike to begin investigations and to take action," he said. "The death tolls are too high, the consequences too great. We must *prevent* first—we must *prosecute* second."[13]

To implement the new policy, new tools were necessary. Law enforcement tools created decades earlier, said the attorney general, "were crafted for rotary telephone—not e-mail, the Internet, mobile communications and voicemail."[14] To prevent future terrorists attacks, he argued, new legislation was needed to update the pen register and trace laws, clarifying how they applied to the Internet and e-mail.[15] Law enforcement and national security agencies must be permitted to share wiretap and grand jury information without a court order. A federal court judge should be authorized to issue a single order that would apply to "all providers in the communications chain, including those outside the region" where the judge's court was located. The Immigration and Naturalization Service needed increased authority to detain or deport suspected alien terrorists. Criminal liability for money laundering needed to be expanded. Law enforcement agencies need to be able to seize, rather than just freeze, the assets of terrorists.[16]

The Bush administration's proposal moved with alacrity through Congress. On 3 October the House Judiciary Committee approved its version of the legislation by a vote of 36 to 0. By 12 October both the House and the Senate had approved separate bills containing provisions that had been sought for years by prosecutors; they had been previously rejected as too intrusive and possibly unconstitutional. On 25 October a compromise bill was approved by the Senate by a vote of 98 to 1. It had already been approved by the House by a vote of 356 to 66.[17] It was signed into law by President Bush the next day.

The line between war and law enforcement was now becoming less bright than it had been in the simpler times prior to 11 September. An important new defense in the war against terrorism was now available. It did not involve gas masks, vaccines, or bomb shelters, but information—intelligence and surveillance information to prevent future attacks.

A key provision of the new law was an amendment to the Foreign Intelligence Surveillance Act (FISA) of 1978. Previously, FISA had authorized the FBI to conduct wiretaps and searches that would otherwise be unconstitutional only if the object was the collection of intelligence, not evidence for use in a criminal prosecution. To guard against government abuse, the attorney general had previously been required to certify to a special court that the primary purpose of a requested FISA wiretap was to monitor a specific individual suspected of being a terrorist or spy. An authorizing order from the special court in advance of the wiretap was required. The Bush administration proposal to change the required wording of a certification so that it only needed to state that the surveillance of a particular suspected person was "a purpose" had been rejected, but a new standard of "a significant purpose" was now included. For the first time, the CIA was authorized not only to influence domestic FBI surveillance operations, but also to have access to information collected by federal grand juries and through criminal wiretaps.

Civil libertarians expressed great concern about both the content of the new legislation and the speed with which it was passed, but normally sympathetic members of Congress were making few apologies for their action. Senator Patrick Leahy, for example, a Democrat from Vermont and the chairman of the Senate Judiciary Committee, said that the terrorist crisis requires aggressive action.[18] Nevertheless, a sunset provision was included that will cause the FISA amendment and other enhanced surveillance features to expire on 31 December 2005 unless they are reenacted.

Within hours after the 11 September attacks, public suggestions were being made that the president should create military tribunals to deal with captured terrorism suspects. Charles Cooper, a former senior official of the Justice Department, argued that "A tribunal is a civilized response that lies between just killing the perpetrators and giving them the full panoply of rights afforded to U.S. citizens in U.S. courts. Civil courts would not be an appropriate forum for those prosecuting war against our country."[19] This was not the first time that military tribunals had been suggested for the trial of suspected terrorists. Five years earlier, in the context of the 1993 bombing of New York City's World Trade Center and the bombing of the Murrah Federal Building in Oklahoma City, a similar suggestion had been made in a fifty-six-page article in a law journal.[20] The suggestion was now being accepted.

On 13 November the president issued a military order with far-reaching consequences. Having determined that "an extraordinary emergency exists for national defense purposes" and that the emergency constituted "an urgent and compelling government interest," the order directed the secretary of defense to establish one or more military commissions for the trial of persons subject to the order who are charged with violations of "the laws of wars and other applicable laws."[21] The individuals subject to the order were to include noncitizens who were members of al Qaeda, anyone who had threatened or attempted to cause harm to the United States,[22] or persons who had knowingly harbored someone who had threatened or attempted to cause such harm.

Concluding that it was not practicable to apply in the military commissions the same principles of law and rules of evidence that apply in the federal civilian courts, the president spelled out some of the principles and rules that would apply. Each trial was to be "full and fair," but the military commissions would sit as triers of both law and fact. There would be no juries. Proffered evidence would not have to meet the strict requirements of the rules of evidence used in federal criminal trials. Rather, evidence would be admitted if it would "have probative value to a reasonable person." Presumably, this could include hearsay evidence. A conviction could be obtained and a sentence determined—including a sentence of life imprisonment or death—if two-thirds of the members of each commission concurred. Unanimity would not be required. Although the record of each trial could be reviewed by the president or the secretary of defense for final decision, there would be no appeals to a higher judicial body.

The use of military tribunals in the United States is not unprecedented.

Indeed, they have a long history. The first, and one of the best known, involved the indispensable American, George Washington. In November 1778 Major Jean André, a charismatic, young officer in the British army, was appointed deputy adjutant general on the staff of Sir Henry Clinton, the new British commander-in-chief. Clinton delegated to André the coordination of British intelligence activities. On the night of 21 September 1780 André came ashore from a British sloop anchored in the Hudson River to meet with Benedict Arnold, the American major general who commanded the strategic American fortification at West Point. Arnold divulged information to André that would permit the British to swiftly capture the post. Because his ship had found it necessary to move downriver, André was unable to return to it after the meeting. He crossed over land through American territory wearing an American uniform. He was captured by American militiamen shortly thereafter and incriminating papers were found in his boot. With courage and candor, André admitted both his identity and his role in the plot during a trial by a military tribunal. On 29 September he was found guilty of being behind American lines "under a feigned name and in a disguised habit."

André had manners and an advanced education that set him apart from his contemporaries. His personal qualifications were so attractive that even Washington admitted that he was a "man of first abilities."[23] After his conviction, he so charmed Alexander Hamilton and other young officers on Washington's staff that they pleaded with Washington to make an exception to the law of war by sparing his life. Washington refused. On 1 October he signed an order directing that André be hanged at noon the following day. "With drums beating, the handsome young Major was escorted to the gallows, where he died with a gallantry that sent tears flowing down the cheeks of every witness."[24] He was thirty-one years old.

André's case is of little value as precedent for the present because the trial was conducted seven years before the U.S. Constitution was drafted. Some historians therefore believe the first documented U.S. military tribunal was established during the Mexican War (1846–48) when Gen. Winfield Scott convened councils of war. The lawfulness of military commissions, however, was not fully tested until the Civil War period. In 1863 the Union Army issued General Order 100. The order declared that under the common law of war military commissions were permitted to prosecute "cases which do not come within the Rules and Articles of war, or the jurisdiction conferred by statute on court-martials."[25] The same year, in the case of *Ex Parte Vallandigham*,[26] the U.S. Supreme Court recognized and by implication accepted the distinction between military commissions and courts-martial. Two years later, military tribunals were used for the trial of civilians charged with conspiring to aid the Confederacy by acting in concert to assassinate President Lincoln. Some of the convicted conspirators were hanged. A military tribunal was also used by the Union for the trial of a Confederate officer accused of committing war crimes at the infamous Confederate prison at Andersonville, Georgia.

In 1866 the Supreme Court again considered the jurisdiction of military commissions. Lambdin P. Milligan, a U.S. citizen and a civilian, was sentenced to death by an army court in Indiana for allegedly disloyal activities. He sought his release in an appeal to the federal circuit court pursuant to the 1863 Habeas Corpus Act. The circuit court was divided on the question of whether civilian courts had jurisdiction over appeals from military tribunals. In *Ex Parte Milligan*,[27] the Supreme Court held that "no usage of war could sanction a military trial . . . for any offense . . . of a citizen in civil life [who is not] connected with the military service" where the civil courts and government remained open and operational.[28]

Many Americans living today remember the work of the international tribunals immediately following World War II. In Nuremberg, Germany, an international tribunal indicted twenty-four men and six organizations for "waging an aggressive war."[29] Separate international tribunals were conducted in Tokyo and Manila for Japanese accused of war crimes.[30] Senator Robert A. Taft of Ohio, the chief spokesman for Republicans in Washington and a likely candidate for his party's 1948 presidential nomination, spoke out forcefully against the "Victors' Justice" aspects of the Nuremberg Trials, despite their popular support across the country. In a 6 October 1946 speech delivered only days before the execution of the Nazi leaders, he declared that the trials violated "the fundamental principle of American law that a man cannot be tried under an *ex poste facto* statute."[31] His principled stand later made him the subject of a profile in courage in a Pulitzer Prize–winning book by John F. Kennedy.[32]

Although less well known today, the military tribunal that has more relevance to President Bush's order is the one that was the subject of the Supreme Court's opinion in *Ex Parte Quirin*,[33] a case decided during World War II. The facts of the case were generally undisputed. After receiving training in the use of explosives at a school near Berlin and instructions from the German high command to destroy war industries and war facilities in the United States, eight German saboteurs traveled to the United States aboard two German U-boats. Three of the agents landed on Long Island, New York, under cover of darkness in June 1942. They carried with them various explosives and related devices. After landing, they buried their German marine infantry uniforms and proceeded to New York City in civilian dress. The remaining four agents landed in Florida. They also carried explosives and related devices. After burying all articles of military dress, they proceeded to various points in the United States. All were taken into custody by the FBI.

On 2 July 1942 President Franklin D. Roosevelt appointed a military commission for the purpose of trying the prisoners for offenses against the law of war and the Articles of War.[34] He also prescribed regulations for the trial procedure and for the review of any judgment or sentence of the commission. The military commission found all the belligerents guilty and sentenced them to death. The defendants then filed petitions for writs of habeas corpus,[35] claiming that the commission lacked jurisdiction and that the tribunal had unconstitutionally denied to them rights specified in article 3 and the Fifth and Sixth Amendments to the U.S. Constitution, namely, the right not to be held for the crimes charged in the absence of an indictment by a grand jury, the right to trial by jury, and the right to a public trial where the alleged crimes were committed.

Even though all state and federal courts in the states in which the Germans were arrested were open and functioning normally, the U.S. Supreme Court unanimously sustained the jurisdiction of the commission. *Ex Parte Milligan* did not apply, the Court concluded, because Milligan had been a nonbelligerent not subject to the law of war. "[T]he detention and trial of [the German agents]—ordered by the President in the declared exercise of his powers as Commander in Chief of the Army in time of war and of grave public danger— are not to be set aside by the courts without the *clear conviction* that they are in conflict with the Constitution or laws of Congress." The Court held that there was no conflict with any statute; Congress had explicitly recognized "the 'military commission' appointed by military command as an appropriate tribunal for the trial and punishment of offenses against the law of war not ordinarily tried by court-martial."[36] "An important incident to the conduct of war," the Court added, "is the adoption of measures by the military command not only to repel and defeat the enemy, but to seize and subject to disciplinary measures those enemies who in their attempt to thwart or impede our military effort have violated the law of war."[37]

The next question the Supreme Court considered was whether the trial by military commission was in conflict with the U.S. Constitution. The Court elected not to discuss with exactness the jurisdictional boundaries of military commissions. "[W]e have no occasion now to define with meticulous care the ultimate boundaries of the jurisdiction of military tribunals to try persons according to the law of war."[38] But, the Court had no trouble sustaining the jurisdiction of that particular commission in the circumstances of the case before it. "By universal agreement and practice the law of war draws a distinction between . . . those who are lawful and unlawful combatants. Lawful combatants are subject to capture and detention as prisoners of war by opposing military forces. Unlawful combatants are likewise subject to capture and detention, but in addition they are subject to trial and punishment by military tribunals for acts which render their belligerency unlawful."[39]

A spy or an enemy combatant "who without uniform comes secretly through the lines for the purpose of waging war by destruction of life or property," the Court said, "are familiar examples of belligerents who are generally deemed not to be entitled to the status of prisoners of war, but to be offenders against the law of war subject to trial and punishment by military tribunals."[40] The "particular acts" of the Germans, therefore, constituted an offense against the law of war that the U.S. Constitution authorized to be tried by military commission.[41] The Court rejected the constitutional claims. "We conclude that the Fifth and Sixth Amendments did not restrict whatever authority was conferred by the Constitution to try offenses against the law of war by military commission, and that petitioners, charged with such an offense not required to be tried by jury at common law, were lawfully placed on trial by the Commission without a jury."[42]

Finally, the Court rejected the claim of one of the petitioners that he was entitled to constitutional protections because of his purported U.S. citizenship. "Citizens who associate themselves with the military arm of [an] enemy government," the Court said, "and with [its] aid, guidance and direction enter this country bent on hostile acts are enemy belligerents within the meaning of the Hague Convention and the law of war."[43]

Several other cases that have come before the Supreme Court have tested other aspects of the jurisdiction of U.S. military tribunals and the law that governs them.[44] Two points about those cases are significant. First, the jurisdiction of military commissions generally rests upon one of two bases: crimes committed during a military occupation or violations of the law of war. Second, the Supreme Court has never ruled that a defendant charged with a violation of the law of war has no constitutional rights whatsoever in a trial by military commission. The Court has only rejected the constitutional claims made in the cases that have thus far come before it.

Predictably, the announcement of President Bush's order directing the establishment of military commissions ignited a vigorous public debate. Civil libertarians immediately expressed a wide range of objections, even asserting that the order recalled the comment attributed to the French premier Georges Clemenceau about the late nineteenth-century Dreyfus Affair.[45] He reportedly said, "[M]ilitary justice is to justice as military music is to music." One U.S. senator worried that the president was "shredding our Constitution." A nationally syndicated columnist called the military commissions "Star

Chamber tribunals."[46] A *New York Times* lead editorial called the president's order a "Travesty of Justice." President Clinton's deputy attorney general, now a Harvard law professor, said that the order reflected "real contempt for the justice system." Unnamed legal experts were quoted as saying that the military tribunals would undermine the country's ability to criticize the human rights records of other countries. Some European countries threatened to refuse requests by the United States for the extradition of suspected terrorists because of their opposition both to the use of military tribunals and the U.S. use of capital punishment.[47]

Most of the criticism of the president's order centered around four perceived flaws. First, critics claimed that the armed conflict with al Qaeda, the Taliban, and other terrorist groups of global reach was not a war because Congress had not formally declared it to be so. They argued that the resolution passed by Congress only authorized the president to "use all necessary and appropriate force against those nations, organizations, or persons [involved in the September 11 attacks] . . . to prevent any future [such] acts of international terrorism against the United States." Second, critics charged that because the order contained no definition of "international terrorism," it invited "arbitrary and potentially discriminatory decisions" about who to charge for trial by military tribunal.[48] Third, the order was criticized as too broad because it could be applied not just to terrorist leaders captured overseas, but to "any ordinary, lawful resident alien" who may have once knowingly harbored a current or former member of al Qaeda or who might be believed to have aided or abetted acts in preparation of terrorism.[49] Finally, concern was expressed because the jurisdiction of the military tribunals would not be limited to the trial of alleged violations of the law of war. The tribunals would also have jurisdiction over alleged violations of other applicable laws.

The criticism was predictable, but so was the immediate response of the Bush administration and its supporters. One nationally syndicated columnist criticized the critics. "[S]ome professional hysterics such as *New York Times* editorialists, have reacted with the theatricality of antebellum southern belles suffering the vapors over a breech of etiquette."[50] Attorney General John Ashcroft made his point in the form of a rhetorical question during an interview with CNN. "Can you imagine the spectacle of capturing a soldier-terrorist in Afghanistan, bringing them back with a publicly paid, high profile, flamboyant defense lawyer on television, making it the Osama Network, sending signals to the terrorists around the country?"[51]

Alberto Gonzales, the White House counsel to the president, pointed out several procedural advantages of military commissions. "They spare American jurors, judges and courts the grave risks associated with terrorist trials," he said. It was public knowledge that the federal judge who presided over the trial of those charged with the 1993 attack on the World Trade Center remained under twenty-four-hour protection by U.S. marshals.[52] "They allow the government to use classified information as evidence without compromising intelligence or military efforts," Gonzales said. "They can dispense justice swiftly, close to where our forces may be fighting, without years of pre-trial proceedings or post-trial appeals." And, he noted, the order preserved judicial review in civilian courts because a defendant could challenge the jurisdiction of the tribunal in a particular case through a habeas corpus proceeding.[53] Senator Orrin Hatch, the ranking minority member of the Senate Judiciary Committee, said that military tribunals made perfect sense. "Who would want to serve on a jury that is trying Osama Bin Laden?" he asked during a congressional hearing. "[W]ho would want to stay in an hotel where jurors are being sequestered?"[54]

The absence of a declaration of war by Congress was dismissed as inconsequential. In testimony before the Senate, Deputy Secretary of Defense Paul Wolfowitz declared emphatically, "The September 11 attacks were acts of war. The people who planned and carried out those attacks are not common criminals; they are foreign aggressors, vicious enemies whose goal was and remains to kill as many innocent Americans as possible." In reference to the armed conflict in Afghanistan, he declared, "This is not a law enforcement action; it is war. We seek to destroy or defeat our terrorist enemies."[55] George Terwilliger, a deputy attorney general under President George H. W. Bush, concurred. In a paper prepared separately, he asserted that the "new paradigm of warfare has blurred the previously more-or-less clear line between national defense and law enforcement." He stated, "National defense is changing to encompass a broader range of threats than [those] historically posed by a warring nation-state."[56] The reality and the recognition "that non-state and clandestinely state-sponsored groups now have the ability and willingness to employ means of mass destruction has dictated . . . that states no longer have a monopoly on war. Therefore, it has become appropriate to use war powers against foreign terrorist organizations."[57]

The fairness of military tribunals was argued with evidence that the conviction rates in the military tribunals in Germany and Japan after World War II were lower than the felony conviction rate in U.S. federal courts in 2000.[58] Media concern about the secrecy of military tribunals was dismissed with the observation that the media have a built-in conflict of interest in assessing the issue. Concern about a possible lack of speedy justice for defendants was rebutted by the facts that the first World Trade Center trial in 1993–94 took six months, a second lasted four months in 1997, and a third trial took eight months in 1995.[59]

Several defenders of the president's order made the point that the proposed tribunals would be used more as facets of military operations than of the judicial system.[60] The tribunals would not be just about punishment, a law school dean pointed out. They would be "extensions of the military campaign" to prevent future attacks. The president had been expressly given authority by Congress to prevent future attacks.[61] This was certainly the view at the Pentagon. "[W]e are at war with an enemy that has flagrantly violated the rules of war," Wolfowitz declared. "And they intend to attack us again." We must, he said, "defend this country from them. Military tribunals are one of many instruments we may use to do so."[62]

Perhaps the most telling arguments in defense of military tribunals were made by a leading liberal professor of constitutional law who also voiced many objections to the president's order and a conservative appellate judge. "In wartime," Harvard professor Laurence H. Tribe asserted, "'due process of law,' both linguistically and historically, permits trying unlawful combatants for violation of the laws of war, without a jury or many of the other safe-guards of the Bill of Rights—provided the trials are conducted by tribunals impartial enough to render fair verdicts, and provided each accused may hear the case against him and receives a fair opportunity to contest it through competent counsel."[63] Tribe had no doubt that the nation was at war. "[T]argeting Americans for murder throughout the world, is more than mere crime. It is war, and the Constitution cannot prevent its treatment as such."[64] The historical concept that it is more desirable to let one hundred guilty men go free than to wrongfully imprison one innocent "describes a calculus," he said, "that our Constitution—which is no suicide pact—does not impose on government when the 100 who are freed belong to terrorist cells that slaughter innocent civilians, and may well have access to chemical, biological, or nuclear weapons."[65]

Judge Richard A. Posner of the U.S. Court of Appeals for the Seventh Circuit was even more direct. Noting that such critical terms as "due process of law" and "unreasonable" searches and arrests are not defined in the U.S. Constitution and have only been given meaning by judges in the process of weighing the competing interests of public safety and liberty, he asserted that in the current circumstances "it stands to reason that our civil liberties will be curtailed."[66] They "should be curtailed," he said, "to the extent that the benefits in greater security outweigh the costs in reduced liberty." Even legality "must sometimes be sacrificed for other values. We are a nation under law, but first we are a nation." The law is not absolute, he declared further, "and the slogan '*Fiat institia ruat caelum*' ('Let justice be done though the heavens fall') is dangerous nonsense. The law is a human creation rather than a divine gift, a tool of government rather than a mandarin mystery. It is an instrument for promoting social welfare, and as the conditions essential to that welfare change, so must it change."[67]

As weeks passed, Pentagon lawyers worked on the crafting of the procedural rules that would govern trials by the military commissions. To minimize future criticism, eminent outside lawyers and senior officials from previous administrations were consulted, including President Carter's attorney general and President Clinton's White House counsel. One advisor said that the test used in evaluating each rule was whether it would be considered fair if it was applied by an enemy to an American prisoner.[68]

In late March 2002 a sixteen-page set of rules was unveiled by Secretary of Defense Rumsfeld. To the surprise of many, the rules met many of the previously expressed objections. Even though they had not participated in the work, the chairmen of both the Senate and House Judiciary Committees promptly expressed pleasure at the final product. Suspects tried before a military commission would be entitled to a presumption of innocence. They would be assigned military lawyers at government expense, or they could retain civilian lawyers at their own expense. The standard of proof for a finding of guilty would be the "beyond a reasonable doubt" standard that is applied to criminal cases in civilian courts. A unanimous verdict would be required before the death penalty could be imposed. The media would be permitted to attend proceedings except when classified information was under consideration. Each commission would have three to seven military officers as members. At least one of the members would be a judge advocate who would serve as presiding officer. Suspects who are convicted would be permitted to seek a review of their case by a three-member review panel of military officers, one of whom must have had prior experience as a judge. Eleven months later, the White House approved a set of "crimes and elements" rules that defined the scope of the tribunals' jurisdiction, that is, the crimes that can be prosecuted before them.[69]

In a development tinged with considerable irony, however, some government officials began to conclude that there might be little use for the commissions because they were planned only for the trial of senior al Qaeda and Taliban operatives. As the number of prisoners increased, it was speculated that they would fall into four general categories: those who would be released after it was determined that no charges would be filed against them; those who would be repatriated to their own countries for trial; those who would be tried before a military commission; and those who would be detained for questioning without charge.[70] For several months most of the enemy fighters captured were "low-ranking foot soldiers."[71] As more senior terrorists were captured and the prospect of trials before military commissions increased, many observers were concluding that future determinations of success or failure of the commission process would be made in the court of public opinion and upon the basis of a simple standard: were they "full and fair"?.

Even as the debate over military commissions seemed to be waning, another issue became the focus of international attention. To what extent were captured al Qaeda and Taliban fighters entitled to rights guaranteed to prisoners of war by the laws of war? The heat that surrounded this issue was almost equal to that which engulfed the issue of the tribunals.

Soon after the first fifty prisoners were transferred from Afghanistan to the U.S. naval base at Guantanamo Bay in January 2002 some European governments and human rights organizations began demanding that the prisoners be designated as prisoners of war. The United States is a signatory of the Third Geneva Convention; under the supremacy clause of the U.S. Constitution the convention rules have the force of domestic law.[72] The Third Geneva Convention states that prisoners of war must be treated humanely. When questioned prisoners are bound to give only their "surname, first names and rank, date of birth, and army, regimental, personal or serial number" or equivalent information.[73] While they readily agreed to treat the prisoners as though the Geneva Conventions standards applied to them, U.S. officials referred to them only as "unlawful combatants" or "unlawful detainees." The captives were not given the status of prisoners of war. President Bush put the matter this way, "They just won't be afforded Prisoner of War status. These are killers. These are terrorists. They know no countries. And the only thing they know about countries is when they find a country that's been weak . . . they want to occupy it like a parasite."[74]

By taking that position, the Bush administration appeared to be sailing into unchartered waters, at least with respect to the members of the Taliban, because the nature of the new war on terrorism was unprecedented. The laws of war draw a fundamental distinction between lawful and unlawful combatants. In order to be considered *lawful* combatants, members of an armed force must generally meet four criteria: (1) being part of a fighting force that adheres to an organized command structure so that the commander can be held responsible for the actions of his subordinates, (2) wearing uniforms or other distinctive emblems or insignia recognizable at a distance (so a party can avoid unnecessary casualties among innocent civilians without fear of counterattack by disguised combatants), (3) carrying arms openly, and (4) conducting operations in accordance with the laws and customs of war.[75] Even if the other conditions could be met, it was undeniable that al Qaeda had deliberately attacked civilians in violation of the laws of war and had otherwise fought without a uniform or distinguishing insignia. Clearly, the Pentagon's first priority was to obtain intelligence about possible future attacks, global terrorism generally, and the al Qaeda network. That could hardly be done if the interrogation of the detainees was limited to name, rank, and serial number. A second priority was to hold the detainees as long as they posed a threat or were dangerous. Prisoners of war are entitled to repatriation to their countries when hostilities end, whenever that might be.

Three weeks after deciding that the Geneva Conventions would not be applied to al Qaeda and Taliban captives, the president modified his policy. Sensitive to the concerns of both the State and the Defense Departments that ignoring the conventions might place captured U.S. troops at risk in the future, he declared that the accords would be applied to captives who had fought for Afghanistan's Taliban regime, but not to al Qaeda combatants. The rationale of the new policy was that Afghanistan was a party to the conventions, even if the United States had not recognized the Taliban as the legitimate government of the country. Al Qaeda, on the other hand, was nothing more than an international terrorist organization that had not signed the global accords.

On 12 July 2002 the next chapter unfolded in the continuing story of Yaser Esam Hamdi. Having dismissed a petition for habeus corpus filed on his behalf by the federal public defender on the ground that the public defender had no standing to appear as Hamdi's next friend, the U.S. court of appeals now addressed a similar petition filed by Hamdi's father as next friend. At issue was an 11 June order of the lower court that had directed the government to allow the public defender unmonitored access to Hamdi without the presence of military personnel or listening or recording devices.

It was again the government's contention that Hamdi was an enemy combatant, that the government had exclusive authority to designate him an enemy combatant, that he could be detained at least as long as the duration of the hostilities, and that "enemy combatants who are captured and detained on the battlefield in a foreign land" have "no general right under the laws and customs of war, or the Constitution . . . to meet with counsel concerning their detention, much less to meet with counsel in private, without military authorities present."[76] The public defender contended that no evidence had been submitted to support the designation of Hamdi as an enemy combatant. He further argued that unlike aliens located outside the United States, Hamdi was a U.S. citizen and, as such, was entitled to constitutional protections, including unmonitored access to counsel.[77]

The court of appeals rejected the government's request to dismiss the petition in its entirety on the ground that to do so would be to embrace the government's "sweeping declaration" that "with no meaningful judicial review, any American citizen alleged to be an enemy combatant could be detained indefinitely without charges or counsel on the government's say-so."[78] Without formally reaching the merits of the arguments presented, the court remanded the case to the district court for determinations of fact and disposition of "the many serious questions raised." It did so, however, with less than subtle suggestions to the lower court about how it should rule.

Noting that the district court's 11 June order arose "in the context of foreign relations and national security, where a court's deference to the political branches of our national government is considerable," the court of appeals declared that the deference "extends to military designations of individuals as enemy combatants in times of active hostilities, as well as through their detention after capture on the field of battle." The federal courts "have many strengths," said the court, "but the conduct of combat operations has been left to others." In its view, "The executive is best prepared to exercise the military judgment attending the capture of alleged combatants."[79] Any judicial inquiry into Hamdi's status as an enemy combatant must, said the court, "reflect a recognition that government has no more profound responsibility than the protection of Americans, both military and civilian, against additional unprovoked attack."[80] Moreover, any inquiry "must not present a risk of saddling military decision-making with a panoply of encumbrances associated with civil litigation." If alleged combatants were permitted to call U.S. commanders to account in federal courtrooms, it would "stand the warmaking powers of Articles I and II [of the Constitution] on their heads."[81]

The judicial contest continued in subsequent weeks. A two-page declaration was filed by a Department of Defense official,[82] setting forth the factual basis for the military judgment that Hamdi was an "unlawful combatant." On 16 August the district court ruled that the declaration was insufficient and ordered the government to submit for judicial review sensitive primary source materials upon which the declaration was based. The lower court judge made no attempt to hide his view of the desirable outcome of the case, describing the situation as "the first in American jurisprudence where an American citizen has been held incommunicado and subjected to an indefinite detention in the continental United States without charges, without any findings by a military tribunal, and without access to a lawyer."[83] Five days later, he authorized the government to seek an interlocutory appeal of the ruling.[84]

As a growing number of Americans awaited the next development in the case, it was characterized as "the classic paradox of a free society conducting war, an enterprise whose very essence is extinguishing with extreme prejudice—without charges, without lawyers, without appeal—the most fundamental rights of enemy combatants (life, for starters)."[85] Many felt the central issue rested less upon an informed analysis of law than of practical common sense. "What kind of logic gives the military the power to kill enemy combatants, . . . but not capture and detain them?"[86] Most of the attention in the case turned again to the court of appeals. The last chapter in Mr. Hamdi's story was not yet written (see Postscript).

On 11 September 2002, exactly one year from the date of the terrorist attacks on New York City and Washington, Ramzi Bin al-Shibh, a major al

Qaeda operative, was captured in Karachi, Pakistan, after a shoot-out. Bin al-Shibh was believed to have played an important role in planning and carrying out the attacks. On 16 September he was transferred to U.S. custody by Pakistani officials and flown out of the country to an undisclosed location. While U.S. officials were most interested in interrogating him for information about al Qaeda's operations and possible future attacks, speculation arose that he was "a perfect candidate for trial by an American military tribunal."[87] He is not a U.S. citizen; he was captured on foreign soil; and he posed a security risk. But, to date, not a single person captured in the new war on terror had faced such a tribunal. However desirable it might be to try Bin al-Shibh, it was almost certain that for the foreseeable future he would probably continue to be detained as an unlawful combatant.

The fact that no military tribunal had even been established did not prevent Bush administration critics from expressing fear that the balance between security and liberty had shifted too far to security. Others disagreed, arguing that the generation that attained adulthood during the social upheaval of the 1960s and 1970s was far too sensitive to perceived slights to civil liberties and that in any event, in the absence of a military draft, a tax increase to pay for the war against terror, gas rationing, or any other traditional form of sacrifice during war, a relatively slight reduction in liberty was a small price to pay for security. The legal counsel for the Office of Homeland Security rejected the idea of balancing liberty and security as a "false choice." In his view, there is no "zero-sum" game. Security and liberty are not only compatible, but mutually supporting, even if the government's powers must be broader now, but still within the law, than in peacetime.[88] U.S. Supreme Court justice Stephen Breyer declared in a speech that disagreements "about government restrictions, security threats, civil liberties, do not mean that disaster is upon us, but that the democratic process is at work."[89]

Most Americans seemed to feel that the Bush administration had the balance about right. Jeffrey Rosen, a law professor at George Washington University, wrote that he had been struck "by how restrained America's legal response appears when contrasted with that of our European allies."[90] Although they had not been directly attacked, he noted that "the countries of the

European Union [had] passed anti-terrorism measures during the past year that [were] far more sweeping than anything adopted in the United States."[91]

With each passing day and each new development in the capture and interrogation of those engaged in armed conflict with the United States, it seemed increasingly likely that it would ultimately be necessary for the U.S. Supreme Court to determine the extent to which enemy combatants are entitled to constitutional protections, as well as the proper balance between the broader concerns of civil liberties and national security, between freedom and order. There was substantial reason, however, to believe that those determinations would not be made until the war against terrorism reached a much lower level of intensity and importance. Much of the reason was supplied by no less of an authority than the chief justice of the United States.

In one of those historical events that can only be explained by attributing highly unusual prescience to the person involved, a book by Chief Justice William H. Rehnquist was published in 1998 on the subject of civil liberties in wartime.[92] He also spoke publicly on the subject only eighteen months before the terrorist attacks on the World Trade Center and the Pentagon. Focusing on Lincoln's 4 July 1861 address to a special session of Congress in which the Civil War president asked rhetorically whether "all the laws but one [are] to go unexecuted, and the government itself go to pieces lest that one be violated?" Rehnquist referred to "the debate that inevitably surrounds issues of civil liberties in war time. If the country itself is in mortal danger, must we enforce every provision safeguarding individual liberties even though to do so will endanger the very government which is created by the Constitution?"[93] The answer, Rehnquist said, may be found in the old maxim of Roman law— *Inter Arma Silent Leges*, which loosely translated means that in time of war, the laws are silent.

Accepting as fact "that judges are loath to strike down wartime measures while the war is going on" and that "the human factor inevitably enters into even the most careful judicial decision," Rehnquist declared that in any civilized society "the most important task is achieving a proper balance between freedom and order. In wartime, reason and history both suggest that this balance shifts to some degree in favor of order—in favor of the government's ability to deal with conditions that threaten the national well-being."[94] While Americans would not wish for a literal application of the full sweep of the maxim *Inter Arma Silent Leges*, he added, "perhaps we can accept the proposition that though the laws are not silent in wartime, they speak with a muted voice."[95] To lawyers and judges, "this may seem a thoroughly undesirable state of affairs, but in the greater scheme of things it may be best for all concerned."[96]

Meanwhile, comfort could be taken from the developments to date. Professor Rosen characterized the situation this way: "[A] year after 9/11, it's worth engaging in a cautious celebration of the resilience of our constitutional checks and balances. So far, in the face of great stress, the system has worked relatively well."[97] And, he added, "Of all of the lessons about America's strength that have emerged since the attacks, this is one of the most reassuring."[98]

9

Iraq—Again!

There are countries which . . . develop weapons of mass destruction,
countries run by people who poison their own people. . . .
[W]e owe it to our children to deal with these threats.

—President George W. Bush, 7 August 2002

Whatever the level of threat to U.S. security posed by Iran and North
Korea—two of the three nations constituting President Bush's "axis of evil"—
there was a growing belief in the spring of 2002 that Iraq posed the most
immediate threat. Within a month after the 11 September 2001 attacks, it
was reported that Iraq possessed "a workable nuclear weapon design" and had
everything needed to build one except the fissile material; that it was "self-
sufficient in biological weaponry"; that it was suspected of holding "at least
157 aerial bombs and 25 missile warheads filled with germ agents and retains
spraying equipment to deliver them by helicopter"; and that it might retain

small stocks of chemical agents, "including the highly destructive nerve agent VX."[1] Since 1998 allied intelligence officials had known that Iraq had modified several Czech-made L-29 trainer jets to convert the aircraft into unmanned vehicles that were fitted with spray nozzles and wing-mounted tanks. The aircraft were capable of carrying up to eighty gallons of liquid anthrax.[2] Some intelligence reports indicated that the threat from Iraq was not imminent, but two Iraqi defectors gave chilling accounts of Saddam Hussein's clandestine efforts—in underground bunkers and mobile germ laboratories—to develop weapons of mass destruction since UN weapons inspectors were forced out three years earlier.[3] One defector, the former managing director of an Iraqi construction company, purportedly had personal knowledge of more than thirty secret biological weapons laboratories inside Iraq. One was reported to be under the Saddam Hussein Hospital in central Baghdad. Others were purportedly located at a presidential complex, in a residential district of Baghdad, and elsewhere.[4]

In late July 2002 Secretary of Defense Rumsfeld declared unequivocally that Iraq had chemical and biological weapons and "an enormous appetite for nuclear weapons."[5] A former leader of Iraq's nuclear weapon program, now a U.S. resident, declared that in addition to the processing of its own yellowcake uranium, Iraq was also processing 1.3 tons of low-enriched material purchased from Brazil.[6] In early September a report of the London-based International Institute for Strategic Studies concluded that Iraq could produce one or more nuclear weapons within months of acquiring sufficient fissile material.

Saddam Hussein was apparently financing the development of the weapons in at least two ways. First, he was using funds from the UN-authorized sale of oil—funds that were supposed to be used only for the purchase of food, medicine, and other humanitarian needs of the Iraqi people. An 18 September 2002 report by the nonprofit Coalition for International Justice concluded that Saddam would make as much as $2.5 billion in 2002 from the UN program through kickbacks and smuggling operations, including more than $1 billion from the illegal sale of oil to Syria.[7] Second, it was believed that he was unlawfully using equipment that was supposed to be used solely for the manufacture of pharmaceuticals.

A "regime change" in Baghdad had been official policy of the U.S. government since 31 October 1998 when President Clinton signed into law the Iraq Liberation Act of 1998. In Section 2 of the act, Congress made several findings: (1) on 22 September 1980 Iraq had invaded Iran, starting an eight year war in which Iraq employed chemical weapons against Iranian troops, and (2) on 16 March 1988 Iraq had used chemical weapons against Kurdish civilians in the town of Halabja, killing an estimated five thousand Kurds. Unstated in the legislation was how dangerously close Saddam Hussein had come to the use of chemical or biological agents against U.S. troops in the Persian Gulf War of 1990–91. In August 1995 shortly after Hussein Kamel Hassan Majeed, the former director of Iraq's weapons of mass destruction program, defected to Jordan, Iraqi officials admitted to the United Nations that Iraq had loaded three types of deadly nerve agents into roughly two hundred bombs and missile warheads in December 1990. The bombs and warheads were then distributed to air bases and a missile site. Iraqi officials also admitted that in August 1990—the month it invaded Kuwait—the country had begun a crash program aimed at producing a nuclear weapon within a year.[8]

Certain facts supporting military action against Iraq were undisputed. To effectuate a ceasefire in Operation Desert Storm in February 1991, a UN Security Council resolution had declared the "suspension" (not the termination) of offensive operations, thereby leaving intact the original authorization to use force. Iraq subsequently accepted the ceasefire conditions specified in UN Security Council Resolution 687, which required the country to "disclose fully and permit the dismantlement of its weapons of mass destruction programs and submit to long-term monitoring and verification of [the] dismantlement."[9] Since March 1996 Iraq systematically sought to deny weapons inspectors from the UN Special Commission on Iraq (UNSCOM) access to key facilities and documents. It also "persisted in a pattern of deception and concealment regarding the history of its weapons of mass destruction programs." Since 5 August 1998 Iraq had ceased all cooperation with UNSCOM.[10]

As a result, the Iraq Liberation Act contained a provision that expressed the sense of Congress regarding U.S. policy toward Iraq: "It should be the policy of the United States to support efforts to remove the regime headed by Saddam Hussein from power in Iraq and to promote the emergence of a democratic government to replace that regime."[11]

By the spring of 2002 U.S. policy makers believed that the previous decade's containment policy, consisting of "no-fly" zones in the northern and southern areas of the country, economic sanctions, and occasional bombings of Iraq's air defense system, had simply not worked and would not succeed in the long run. The central question was how to bring about a change in the regime, or at least how to eliminate Iraq's weapons of mass destruction.

Over the next several months discussion of the issue focused on at least five theoretical options with many variations. First, an internal coup d'etat by the Iraqi armed forces would be ideal. The chances of a coup, however, were considered to be remote at best. Several had been attempted in the past and all had met with disaster. A 1996 CIA-inspired attempt was compromised early by Iraqi government infiltrators. Unknown numbers of suspected participants were executed. No one doubted Saddam Hussein's ruthlessness or the historical effectiveness of his purges.[12] It was reported that CIA director George Tenet gave this option only a 15 percent chance of success.[13]

A second theoretical option was a "Gulf War" option that would involve as many as 250,000 troops, include armor units, and take advantage of other weapons far more accurate and lethal than those used in the 1990–91 Gulf War. Most of the attack would be mounted from Qatar, Turkey, and Kuwait. This "heavy" option was attractive because it would guarantee Iraq's defeat. It was certain, however, that Saddam Hussein would not again permit the massing over several months of the logistical base needed for such a force. It was considered likely that the force would be the target of a chemical or biological attack during the build-up.

A third option might involve a surprise attack with between fifty and eighty thousand troops that could be moved into the region slowly and clandestinely, either aboard ship or under the guise of routine troop rotations or major exercises. The objective would be to quickly seize cities in the south so they could be used as bases for a nationwide mutiny of the Iraqi troops before an assault began on Baghdad.[14]

A fourth possibility under early discussion was referred to as an "inside-out" or "intermediate" option. It would involve a sudden strike at headquarters and command and control sites, especially those in Baghdad, with mobile strike forces that would include helicopter assault units, paratroops, light infantry, special forces, and marine expeditionary units. The attacks would be preceded and supported by intense air attacks. This option would be designed to "decapitate" Iraq's military control capability and cause a collapse of the remaining forces.[15] The idea would be to bypass entrenched forces in outlying areas and attack Baghdad so quickly that Saddam would not have time to hide large numbers of troops around Baghdad or in other cities.

The last or "light" option, openly discussed and debated, would involve a proxy war by Iraqi opposition forces aided by the kind of special forces and air attacks that proved to be successful in the early stages of the operations in Afghanistan a few months earlier. This option carried significant risks. The seven major groups of the Iraqi opposition, including Shi'ite Muslims in the south and Kurds in the north, were divided politically, religiously, and even ethnically. Also, they lacked a leader who commanded broad support. They were suspicious of U.S. promises of assistance, because the United States had failed to help in earlier revolts.

For months debate raged within and outside of government circles on the necessity and the prospects for success of a U.S.–led military solution. In early 2002 Henry Kissinger opined that before the overthrow of Saddam Hussein was seriously considered, three prerequisites should be met. First, the military operational plan had to be "quick and decisive." Second, "prior agreement on the kind of governing entity that would replace him" must be reached. Third, "the support or acquiescence of key countries needed for implementation of the military plan" was necessary.[16] By the summer of 2002 none of the criteria had been met. In May Gen. Barry McCaffrey, USA (Ret.), a veteran of Operation Desert Storm and President Clinton's drug czar, predicted that the United States would invade Iraq in early 2003 with three Kuwait-based divisions if other efforts to oust Saddam proved unsuccessful. "This will be a turning point in military history," he told a San Antonio audience. "We've never taken military action in anticipation of a threat to the American people. But, at the end of the day . . . we will deduce that it will be unacceptable to face an Iraq sometime between five and ten years out that possesses 30 nuclear weapons."[17]

Former British prime minister Margaret Thatcher brought to the debate the same fortitude and rhetoric that she had used in the days following the 1990 Iraqi invasion of Kuwait when she had advised President George Bush that it was "no time to go wobbly."[18] Asserting that the proliferation of weapons of mass destruction had "fundamentally changed the world in which we and our children will live" and that it is "the greatest challenge of our times," she argued that Saddam must be removed; we "should not try now to predetermine the final outcome" for a post-Saddam Iraq.[19] "In great strategic questions," she said, "it is possible to be too clever. We need to concentrate on what we can achieve with the instruments at hand, and then press ahead boldly with the task before us."[20]

While there was little doubt that the United States could defeat Iraq if the full force of U.S. military capabilities was used, the potential difficulties were not taken lightly. Unlike the circumstances that existed during the Persian Gulf War of 1990–91, the United States could not count on the active support of Arab allies this time or even access to bases in the Persian Gulf. Only weeks after Vice President Cheney toured the region in an unsuccessful attempt to gather support for taking the war on terrorism to Iraq, Arab leaders at an Arab League summit meeting declared that they rejected any idea of "attacking Iraq or threatening the security and safety of any Arab state." They would consider such an attack "a threat to the national security of all Arab states."[21]

Four months later the Saudi Arabian foreign minister publicly reiterated his government's refusal to permit the United States to use Saudi territory as a staging area for an invasion of Iraq.[22] A state-controlled Egyptian newspaper said that invasion plans were a "mad whim."[23] Jordan's King Abdullah warned that action against Iraq could precipitate an "Armageddon" in the Middle East.[24] Turkey, a NATO ally whose support would be important for any major military operation in neighboring Iraq, also expressed opposition to U.S. military intervention. It was assumed that such comments were directed at least in part to local audiences, but many countries were obviously fearful of the instability that might erupt in their respective countries if they were to once again support the United States in a war against a Muslim nation.[25]

European and UN Security Council support for an attack on Iraq was not much stronger initially, and support weakened through the summer months. Most European leaders preferred to pressure Saddam Hussein to accept UN weapons inspectors again, rather than to even talk of war. Rumsfeld warned other NATO ministers that the West did not have the luxury of waiting for "absolute proof" of terrorist threats. He said that traditional definitions of collective defense must be reexamined. NATO must be prepared to take preemptive action against terrorists. NATO's secretary general responded that "[w]e are a defensive alliance and we remain a defensive alliance. We don't go out looking for problems to solve."[26] German chancellor Gerhard Schroeder launched an uphill reelection campaign with a declaration that his government would not provide troops or money for an invasion. In a tone that soon severely strained his relations with Bush, he said, "We're not available for adventures and the time of checkbook diplomacy is over once and for all."[27] Officials of the fifteen-nation European Union argued that the United States should resolve the long-standing Israeli-Palestinian conflict before taking action against Iraq. France announced that it would not support U.S. efforts to change the regime in Iraq without a clear mandate from the United Nations. Most European nations would not even give firm guarantees that they would increase defense spending to modernize their military equipment, even though they spend an average of only 1.8 percent of their gross domestic product on defense, barely half what the United States spends.[28]

By late summer 2002 opposition to military action against Iraq was increasing even in Britain, the Bush administration's strongest European supporter. Prime Minister Tony Blair reportedly told President Bush privately that Britain would support a U.S. attack if Saddam refused to accept renewed UN weapons inspections,[29] but left-wing members of his ruling Labor Party were openly

critical. People with defense credentials also expressed great concern. Gen. Sir
Michael Rose, the former chief of the British Special Air Service (SAS) and of
UN forces in Bosnia, said there were "huge political and military risks associ-
ated with launching large scale ground forces into Iraq."[30] Field Marshal Lord
Bramall, a former chief of the defense staff, warned in a letter to a London
newspaper that an invasion of Iraq would pour "petrol rather than water" on
the flames and provide al Qaeda with more recruits.[31] Sir Michael Quinlan, a
senior defense official under Prime Minister Thatcher wrote in the *Financial
Times* that "a UK [United Kingdom] Government decision to participate in a
U.S.-led assault could provoke more severe domestic division than Britain has
seen since the Suez crisis."[32] It became increasingly apparent that most
European political leaders did not share the American view of the world. Many
divergent reasons were given.[33]

At home, various difficulties were cited by those with strong reservations
about a military operation against Iraq. Perceived difficulties included the substantial reduction in the size of the U.S. Armed Forces during the preceding
decade, the depletion of munitions during the operations in Afghanistan, the
absence of persuasive evidence tying Saddam to al Qaeda and the resulting
absence of the simple moral clarity that had marked the previous response to
11 September 2001, the lack of broad international support, the potential for
a large number of casualties, the risk that an attack on Iraq might lead to further terrorist attacks on the United States,[34] and the risk of further alienation
of the global community of Muslims, already enraged by the recent Israeli
attacks into Palestinian-controlled areas of the West Bank. Many concerns were
also expressed that a regime change would require a long-term and costly commitment to the country.[35] There was also predictable opposition from some
members of the former Clinton administration.[36]

The risk of chemical or biological warfare in an action against Iraq was also
considered by many to be greater than in 1991. Even though Iraq had not used
such weapons, a U.S. military campaign aimed at a regime change would be
much different from the campaign to eject Iraq from Kuwait. It was difficult for
many to imagine that Saddam Hussein would exercise similar restraint if he

thought that the only alternative was death or capture by U.S. forces. In addition to the casualties that could be expected in the event of a chemical attack, there were associated problems. U.S. chemical suits are heavy, bulky, and hot. They reduce a soldier's ability to move, especially in close quarters. Also, the shorter days of winter would extend the advantage the United States has operating in darkness, thus making it increasingly unlikely that any new armed conflict would be initiated before November. Operational planners are always reluctant to commence hostilities in the desert in the summer.

Reportedly, President Bush was advised in early May that at least 200,000 troops would be required for an operation against Iraq. It was unknown whether the figure assumed a "quick and decisive" victory or if it took into account the possibility "of becoming bogged down in bloody block-by-block urban warfare in Baghdad."[37] A classified computer-simulated war game exercise suggested that the United States could mount such an operation and still meet current global commitments, but it also highlighted shortages in equipment for surveillance, intelligence collection, refueling and transport aircraft, command control, and communications.[38]

After being informed that Pentagon planners needed three to five months to position sufficient forces for an invasion of Iraq, and requesting congressional funding of the development of a missile that could penetrate hardened and deeply buried underground targets in Iraq,[39] President Bush concluded that various options to remove Saddam Hussein from power should be attempted before a military assault was authorized. He thus signed a highly classified intelligence finding that authorized certain actions relating to Saddam's ouster.[40] That order was subsequently broadened, but the CIA director expressed the opinion that a CIA effort alone, in the absence of complimentary military, diplomatic, and economic action, had no more than a 20 percent chance of success.

There was, in fact, some diplomatic success. Since January 2001 the Bush administration had sought revisions in the eleven-year-old sanctions policy to ease the delivery of nonmilitary items into Iraq while preventing the importation of items that had military applications. On 14 May 2002 the UN Security Council unanimously adopted a new sanctions policy against Iraq. Sanctions against nonmilitary items would be lifted. Sanctions against military items would remain in place until UN weapons inspectors were permitted back into Iraq and they had verified that Iraq was complying with the obligations it agreed to after its defeat in the Persian Gulf War including, specifically, its agreement to dismantle all programs to develop weapons of mass destruction. The new policy stopped efforts by other nations to end sanctions altogether. It was hoped that the new policy would also deter criticism that the economic measures were only harming ordinary Iraqis rather than Saddam Hussein.

Through the summer debate over whether to attack Iraq, and the planning for such an attack, continued. Much debate took place within the administration. Media attention was focused particularly on the acknowledged disagreement between "moderate" State Department policy makers, led by Colin Powell and supported by several prominent former members of the George Bush administration, and the more conservative "hawks" at the Defense Department, led by Donald Rumsfeld and supported by Vice President Cheney. The removal of Saddam was not an issue in the internal debate. Rather, the value of international support and the steps required to obtain it were the focus of attention. After Cheney dismissed the idea of additional weapons inspections in Iraq when he said they would "provide no assurance whatsoever," Powell continued to argue that as a first step UN inspectors should attempt to return to Iraq.[41]

For months some civilian officials and analysts had been expressing greater public confidence about the outcome of a large-scale military operation in Iraq than the uniformed officials who would be directly responsible for planning, resourcing, and conducting it.[42] A 24 May national newspaper article reported that the Joint Chiefs of Staff were seeking to delay action until 2003;[43] this was promptly interpreted as evidence by some of strong disagreement between political leaders and military professionals. It was even reported that a small group of civilian officials in the Pentagon were excluding military leaders from the planning for such an operation if they were thought to be reluctant or too unimaginative.[44] A "senior administration official" was quoted as saying that ultimately, "the military has limited influence in this administration."[45] Senior military officers were reportedly concerned about "the casual march to war" being pursued by civilian hawks in the administration. One hawk reportedly replied that the decision to take on Saddam Hussein boils down to a question of how much risk the U.S. government is willing to take and "that's a political judgment that these guys aren't competent to make."[46]

At least some of the internal debate was the result of cultural and personal differences between several important civilian and military officials. One unnamed civilian political appointee complained about the perceived reluctance of military leaders to go to war: "The system has created a military that is a professional bureaucracy. Once you make one star, they start sending you to charm school."[47] Rumsfeld reportedly believed that the Pentagon war-planning process was too ponderous and that too many military leaders were risk averse. Some civilian officials felt that many general and flag officers "have won more academic degrees than combat decorations" and that they are "far more savvy about writing budgets and buying weapons systems than any quick-study political appointee could hope to be."[48]

Some senior civilian officials were simply disliked; they were seen as disorganized, indecisive, and confused.[49] Supporters of a more cautious approach to a conflict with Iraq also noted repeatedly that most of the civilians in the administration who were most aggressive on the question of Iraq had never served in the U.S. Armed Forces, much less subjected themselves to the dangers of combat. Reporters noted that Powell and Deputy Secretary of State Rich Armitage were Vietnam veterans and that Powell was the only former chairman of the Joint Chiefs of Staff to serve as secretary of state other than George Marshall.[50] Retired four-star U.S. Marine Corps general Tony Zinni, the former commander-in-chief of the U.S. Central Command and a recent White House point man on the Israeli-Palestinian crisis, observed, "It might be interesting to wonder why all of the generals see it the same way, and all those [who] never fired a shot in anger [and] are really hellbent to go to war see it a different way."[51] Senator Chuck Hagel of Nebraska, a Vietnam veteran, was even more blunt. "It is interesting to me," he said, "that many of those who want to rush this country into war and think it would be so quick and easy don't know anything about war. They come at it from an intellectual perspective versus having sat in jungles or foxholes and watched their friends get their heads blown off."[52]

Curiously, during this very public debate, a new book on the relationship between military leaders and political leaders in time of war appeared in bookstores across the country. Its author, Eliot Cohen, was a current member of the Defense Policy Board, an advisory body within the Office of the Secretary of Defense. Rejecting "the notion that generals once given a mission should have near total discretion in its execution," he argued that "civilian intervention in military matters [is] a matter of prudence, not principle." The "great war statesmen" were great precisely because they asked hard questions of their generals and, when in extremis, dictated military action.[53] In a separate article, Cohen conceded that there is "a large moral difference between those who served and those who deliberately evaded the draft." But, he argued, "military careers spent in hierarchical, rule-bound, tightly controlled organizations are not necessarily the best preparation for accurately judging the fluid world of politics at home and abroad." Being a veteran "is no guarantee of strategic wisdom."[54] The self-evident truth of the proposition did not, however, address the danger of initiating a complex armed conflict without strong agreement or at least cooperation between political and military leaders.

As the policy debate intensified in Washington, D.C., and other capitals, Saddam Hussein was not sitting still. Recognizing that it was to his clear advantage to avoid an armed conflict with the United States, he began a diplomatic peace offensive in March 2002. It was aimed particularly at countries in the Persian Gulf area that might provide basing for any U.S. military strike. He took his most significant step at an Arab summit in Beirut. In exchange for its recognition of the border with Kuwait, its discussion of missing Kuwaiti prisoners, and its agreement to talk about the return of Kuwait's national archives stolen during the 1990–91 Persian Gulf conflict, Iraq obtained a declaration from the other Arab states that called for "respecting Iraq's independence, sovereignty, security, territorial integrity, and regional safety."[55] Subsequently, Iraq signed new economic agreements with Saudi Arabia, Egypt, and Turkey. It also tried to capitalize on antiwar sentiment in Britain.[56]

Two other political steps were also visible. The first involved the continuing Palestinian-Israeli crisis. Although it had long been believed by U.S. intelligence agencies that Saddam had established a practice of paying $25 thousand to the families of Palestinian suicide bombers, Saddam increased his public rhetoric about Palestinian-Israeli crisis. His efforts had some effect. Several respected U.S. foreign policy analysts expressed the view that any attack on Iraq in the near term would be premature. They felt that it should be postponed until the tension in the West Bank and Gaza was relieved. For example, Brent Scowcroft, the chairman of the president's Foreign Intelligence Advisory Board and the former national security advisor to the president's father, warned on CBS's *Face the Nation* that a U.S. invasion of Iraq "could turn the whole region into a cauldron and, thus, destroy the war on terrorism."[57]

Iraq's second political action involved the United Nations. Since the end of the 1990–91 Gulf War, Iraq had gained considerable sympathy at the UN over its complaints that the economic sanctions imposed by the UN Security Council had only caused suffering among the Iraqi people. Saddam now engaged in a new effort to maintain the status quo and purchase time by appearing to be cooperating with the UN on the question of weapons inspections. Negotiations were opened with UN Secretary General Kofi Annan on the terms under which UN inspectors might be allowed back in the country.

In a more ominous development, it appeared that Saddam had adopted a war-fighting strategy that was as shrewd as it was predictable. U.S. intelligence officials obtained evidence that he planned to avoid the open desert fighting that had been so disastrous for his forces in 1991. Instead, it was believed that he planned to mass his troops in major cities to increase U.S. casualties and to make it very difficult for the United States to attack targets that would cause major civilian casualties.[58] Potential military targets were spread all over Baghdad, a city of almost five million people. One intelligence analysis concluded, "[T]here is little doubt that Saddam Hussein, his sons and other key leaders will attempt to bury themselves in secure facilities surrounded by 'innocent civilians' to avoid being liquidated at long range by U.S. PGMs [precision guided missiles] or readily snatched by U.S. SOFs [special operations forces]."[59]

Another major force was also stirring during the summer of 2002: the U.S. Congress. Sensitive to the president's soaring popularity in the months immediately after 11 September 2001, Congress had generally been content to endorse all U.S. military action to date. There was little doubt that the action had been authorized by Senate Joint Resolution 23, passed after the attacks on the World Trade Center and the Pentagon. An invasion and regime change in Iraq was, however, another matter.

For months, several administration officials argued that no new legal authority was necessary for an attack on Iraq because Saddam's refusal to permit inspection of his weapons programs was in violation of the terms of the UN Security Council resolutions that had ended the Gulf War. In early 1991 Congress had passed Public Law 102-1; it authorized the president to use the U.S. Armed Forces to enforce the UN Security Council resolutions, both to force Iraq out of Kuwait and "to restore international peace and security in the area." Some argued that peace and security had not been restored to the area.[60] Some advisors also believed that Bush had inherent presidential authority to "make" war, while Congress had only the power to "declare" war. As early as June, however, several congressional leaders began to raise the issue of congressional approval.[61] By July resolutions had been introduced in Congress that would require the president to seek congressional approval. At the end of July, while hearings were being conducted by the Senate Foreign Relations Committee, administration officials assured congressional leaders that no attack would be made before the November elections.

The irony of the situation did not escape political veterans of the 1990–91 war against Iraq. A vigorous debate had taken place within the administration of President George H. W. Bush on the question of whether to seek formal congressional approval before commencing hostilities. Secretary of Defense Dick Cheney, a former senior member of the House of Representatives, had opposed the idea on the ground that the repercussions of a negative vote were too dangerous to risk. Eventually, approval was sought and after increasingly rare debates on the floors of the Senate and House, a resolution approving the use of force had been approved by the Senate in a vote of 52 to 47 and by the House in a vote of 250 to 183.

Now, congressional approval was necessary at least as much for political reasons as for reasons of law. While there was agreement that the United States would prevail in a military conflict, the cost of victory in blood and treasure, the broad lack of foreign support, and obvious differences within the administration made congressional support attractive. Without such support at the beginning, the degree of support in the aftermath and in the rebuilding of Iraq might be questionable. Although current polls reflected domestic support for a war against Iraq,[62] should military operations encounter unexpected difficulty or the number of casualties be perceived as unacceptable, U.S. policy in the area could be ruined.

George Will, an incisive critic of the U.S. political system, put the matter this way:

> Today the justifiable, but undeniably radical, policy of preemptive war compels Congress to play a dramatically different role. What is underway is without precedent in U.S. history. It is a methodical and semi-public preparation for a massive military operation to achieve an aim frequently proclaimed at the highest levels of government. The aim is to compel a change of regime in a nation that is intensely and increasingly menacing as it strains to achieve the capacity for attacking American interests. . . . [P]recedent in international law is no substitute for congressional authorization. . . . Furthermore, it would be mere lawyerly cleverness—the opposite of wisdom—to argue that a full-blown war is sanctioned by the congressional resolution authorizing enforcement of U.N. sanctions against Iraq. . . . War of the sort being contemplated is not the sort of plunge into uncertainty that a prudent president wants to embark upon alone, even if the Constitution permitted that.[63]

While congressional approval was almost assured, one development would help immeasurably with both domestic and international support: a *casus belli.* An obvious one would be the failure of the UN effort to persuade Iraq to permit unfettered inspection of its weapons facilities. Another would be the undisputed discovery of weapons of mass destruction within Iraq. Yet another would be stronger evidence of a connection between Iraq and al Qaeda. A fourth possibility, a direct threat by Iraq against the United States, was considered very unlikely. Whatever else he did, Saddam Hussein was not going to give the United States an easy excuse to attack.

As the nation observed and passed the first anniversary of the 11 September attacks, the Bush administration continued to grope for a way to eliminate the danger from Iraq. The answer had to be decisive and not contrary to constitutional and international norms. The United States was clearly entering "an autumn of grave decisions" on the issue.[64] Bowing to increasing bipartisan political pressure, the president promised to obtain additional authorization from Congress before taking military action. The White House announced that, in fact, no serious consideration had ever been given to suggestions to avoid consultation with Congress despite the solid legal arguments that express authorization from Congress was unnecessary.

Meanwhile, the continuing national debate began to focus on the objectives of military action and the burden and standards of proof that should be met before hostilities commenced. Critics in Congress requested specific evidence about the threat posed by Iraq. Other critics complained of the largely circumstantial evidence regarding Iraq's weapons of mass destruction and the absence of a "smoking gun" connection between Iraq and al Qaeda.[65] Yet others pointed to the lack of clear proof that Saddam's acquisition of nuclear weapons was imminent or that Iraq was a "clear and present danger" to the United States.[66] Former president Jimmy Carter declared, "[T]here is no *current* danger to the United States from Baghdad."[67] Even potentially supportive European allies expressed uneasiness about the use of military force to effectuate a regime change as opposed to the elimination of weapons of mass destruction, ignoring the fact that the latter was unlikely to be achieved without the former.

Supporters of immediate action asserted that the stakes were far too critical to confuse a decision to go to war with the processes of a judicial proceeding and that, in any event, if a burden of proof was relevant at all, it rested on those who believed that the disarmament of Iraq could be achieved without a regime change. "With America's political culture increasingly colored by the legal culture, . . . there is a growing tendency to treat foreign policy crises as episodes of 'Law & Order,' crises to be discussed in television-courtroom patois, such as 'smoking gun.'"[68]

Two former secretaries of state argued that legal authorization for military action was already clear. "The war with Hussein never ended," Alexander Haig said. "Whatever the merits of announcing a preemptive military strategy or an objective of regime change, we need neither of these to justify action against Iraq. Iraq's agreement that international inspectors would confirm the destruction of its weapons of mass terror was essential to ending the Gulf War. Hussein has grossly violated these provisions since 1998."[69] Calling resolution of the issue "a defining moment in international affairs," George Schultz argued that self-defense is a valid basis for preemptive action and that the danger was immediate. "Some argue that to act now might trigger Hussein's use of his worst weapons. Such self-imposed blackmail presumes easier judgments when he is even better equipped than now. Time is his ally, not ours."[70]

Acknowledging that the precise status of Iraq's arsenal of chemical, biological, and nuclear weapons was unclear, Vice President Cheney and Secretary of Defense Rumsfeld continued to aggressively push the case for action. Clearly, the administration was at least concerned about Saddam's demonstrated brutality and intentions, as it was about evidence—of the quality that would permit its admission in a court of law—of his current capabilities. It was also recognized that his mere possession of nuclear weapons could radically change the balance of power in the Middle East. "The argument comes down to this," Cheney said in a late August speech in Nashville. "Yes, Saddam is as dangerous as we say he is, we just need to let him get stronger before we do anything about it." In a speech to Korean War veterans in San Antonio, he said, "The risks of inaction are greater than the risks of action." In an appearance on the CBS News program *Face the Nation,* Rumsfeld referred to the attacks a year earlier: "Imagine a September 11 with weapons of mass destruction, it's not 3,000; it's tens of thousands of innocent men, women and children."

Dr. Condoleezza Rice, the president's national security advisor, struck the same note. Speaking on CNN's *Late Edition,* she said, "[T]here will always be some uncertainty about how quickly" Iraq could produce a nuclear weapon. But, she added, "We don't want the smoking gun to be a mushroom cloud."[71] The Pentagon informed members of Congress that Iraq's biological weapons were even more of an immediate threat than its nuclear threat.[72] Perhaps the best articulation of the grounds for the use of force was voiced by George Will: "The uniquely virulent constellation of four factors—[Saddam] Hussein's character, the terrorists' proclamation of war against the United States, the various intersections of Iraqi policy with the culture and apparatus of terrorism, and the technologies of mass destruction developed in the last 57 years—constitute a new kind of *casus belli*."[73]

The president's determination to take some form of action remained fixed. On 7 August he spoke to the students at Madison Central High School in Madison, Mississippi. "There are countries which . . . develop weapons of mass destruction, countries run by people who poison their own people." The threats, he said, are real. "[W]e owe it to our children to deal with these threats." On 4 September he informed congressional leaders in a meeting at the White House that "doing nothing . . . is not an option."

The circumstances were unavoidably reminiscent of those that Britain faced in the fall of 1938. Writing later, Winston Churchill set down "some principles of morals and action":

> The Sermon on the Mount is the last word in Christian ethics. Everyone respects the Quakers. Still, it is not on these terms that Ministers assume their responsibilities of guiding states. Their duty is first so to deal with other nations as to avoid strife and war and to eschew aggression in all its forms, whether for nationalistic or ideological objects. But the safety of the State, the lives and freedom of their own fellow countrymen, to whom they owe their position, make it right and imperative in the last resort, or when a final and definite conviction has been reached, that the use of force should not be excluded. If the circumstances are such as to warrant it, force may be used. And if this be so, it should be used under the conditions which are most favorable. There is no merit in putting off a war for a year if, when it comes, is a far worse war or one much harder to win.[74]

In a speech to the UN General Assembly on the first anniversary of the attacks on the World Trade Center and the Pentagon, Secretary General Kofi

Annan warned against independent military action by the United States. The terrorist attacks of 11 September 2001 "were not an isolated event," he said. "They were an extreme example of a global scourge, which requires a broad, sustained and global response. " He added that even though all states retain the inherent right of self-defense under Article 51 of the UN Charter, "there is no substitute for the unique legitimacy provided by the United Nations."[75] He urged continued efforts to convince Iraq's leaders to accept UN weapons inspectors as "the indispensable first steps towards assuring the world that all Iraq's weapons of mass destruction have indeed been eliminated."[76]

On the morning of 12 September 2002 President Bush gave the international community what it wanted. In a greatly anticipated speech to the UN General Assembly the day after a series of solemn ceremonies marking the anniversary of the attacks, he described a series of steps to be taken "[i]f the Iraqi regime wishes peace." The first required Iraq to "immediately and unconditionally foreswear, disclose and remove or destroy all weapons of mass destruction, long-range missiles and all related material." The United States would work with the UN Security Council "for the necessary resolutions," he said, "but the purposes of the United States should not be doubted. The Security Council resolutions will be enforced, the just demands of peace and security will be met, or action will be unavoidable."

The United States was now committed. Intense diplomacy would still be required, because at least two members of the UN Security Council were threatening to veto any resolution that authorized an immediate use of force. An intense political effort would also be required to obtain a broadly supported authorization from Congress before the November elections. Few were willing to predict with certainty what lay over the horizon. But, a course had been charted. It remained to be seen whether unpredictable winds would knock the ship of state off its course.

While public attention was directed at the noisy and ongoing domestic and international debate, there were several signs of quiet steps being taken by the U.S. Armed Forces to prepare the potential battlefield. Tanks and artillery sufficient to equip a twenty-five-thousand-troop division were moved from warehouses in Qatar into Kuwait, near its border with Iraq. Munitions were moved from the United States to Qatar and to Diego Garcia, a British island base in the Indian Ocean that is about thirty-four hundred miles from Baghdad. The Pentagon asked Britain to approve the construction on Diego Garcia of special shelters for as many as six B-2 bombers. The U.S. Air Force began to improve airfields in Bahrain, Oman, the United Arab Emirates, and Kuwait and to increase production of the satellite-guidance kits that are used to make precision munitions from dumb bombs. The U.S. Navy accelerated the training and maintenance schedules for three aircraft carrier battle groups on the U.S. west coast, including the carriers *Nimitz, Carl Vinson,* and *Constellation.* The U.S. Transportation Command ordered twenty ships in the ready reserve force to hire full crews and to conduct drills at sea. The Military Sealift Command chartered three ships from the commercial market for trips to unspecified ports in the Middle East. The U.S. Central Command made plans to send six hundred headquarters personnel from its base in Tampa to a new base in Qatar. The Pentagon resumed the anthrax inoculation of certain troops.

Ongoing operations in the Persian Gulf were also modified. U.S. and British aircraft patrolling the no-flight zones in northern and southern Iraq began bombing major Iraqi air defense sites. Rumsfeld asserted that the change in tactics was made to protect allied aircraft from the almost daily Iraqi antiaircraft fire. Iraqi command and control sites were hit; they were linked by new (since the Gulf War) Chinese-made fiberoptic networks for the control of surface-to-air missiles. But, a collateral objective was obvious. Destruction of the air defenses would permit access into Iraq of helicopters carrying U.S. Special Forces troops responsible for locating Iraq's mobile Scud missiles. It was no coincidence that at the same time that air operations in the Persian Gulf were changing, the United States was conducting a major helicopter attack exercise in Poland. The exercise pitted the most modern U.S. gunship, the AH-64D Apache Longbow, against surface-to-air missile systems similar to the type used by Iraq.

After receiving several briefings from Gen. Tommy B. Franks, the commander of military forces in the Persian Gulf region, on a broad concept of operations, President Bush requested specific military options in August. Only days before the first anniversary of the terrorist attacks in New York and

Washington, he had a war plan in hand. There was much speculation about its details, but the goal of a swift and decisive campaign was widely shared by current and former war planners. "Our largest concern is that we do not allow time to become our enemy," one officer said.[77] If fighting should bog down for as long as two or three months, warned a former planner, it would be time to brace for "protracted and costly fighting, the further mobilization of radical Islam in the region, and the ensuing collapse of one or more U.S.-allied governments in Egypt, Saudi Arabia or Pakistan."[78]

For the first time, plans for a post-Saddam Iraq were starting to receive the attention they deserved. Although various working groups of the Future of Iraq Project, a State Department–directed effort to study public finance, political structure, legal, economic, and other anticipated problems had been under way for some time, little preparation by the Pentagon for the aftermath had occurred. That was now changing. A senior-level, interagency task force, referred to as the Executive Steering Group, was now coordinating planned postwar reconstruction initiatives. It was becoming accepted that despite the Pentagon's reluctance, U.S. forces would have to remain in Iraq for at least a couple of years[79] for a stabilization and peacekeeping mission and that the occupying force would be sizable.[80]

The exact nature, scope, and length of a U.S. military role in Iraq after Saddam would depend on future circumstances that could not be predicted with certainty. Ensuring public order and providing security and stability would clearly be a core mission as would be the location and destruction of weapons of mass destruction, the distribution of humanitarian aid, and getting the oil fields back to full production to support the economy. Western-style democracy and shared power would be new concepts in Iraq. How long would it be before power could be passed from an initial period of postwar U.S. military or international rule to a new, permanent Iraqi government? Whatever the answer, it was likely that the political reform of Iraq would require a longer-term commitment by the United States than government officials desired or had previously planned for. U.S. troops would have to be the point of the spear in the commitment.

The armed forces now awaited the president's decision. Even Americans who had not supported him in the presidential election had admired the discipline, simplicity, directness, moral clarity, and vigor with which he had exercised leadership thus far in the new kind of war against terrorism. Even his predecessor had grudgingly conceded that "when people are insecure, they'd rather have somebody who's strong and wrong than somebody who's weak and right."[81]

The stakes in Iraq, however, were much different from those in Afghanistan. The risks much greater. "Leadership," John Keegan, a highly respected scholar, has written, "is, like priesthood, statesmanship, even genius, a matter of externals almost as much as internalities."[82] A theatrical impulse is essential to the strong leader. "In no exceptional human being will it be stronger than in the man who must carry forward others to the risk of their lives." The leader of men in warfare, he has argued, "can show himself to his followers only through a mask, a mask that he must make for himself, but a mask made in such form as will mark him to men of his time and place as the leader they want and need."[83]

Despite the plans and national effort to date to defend the nation's homeland, despite operational success in Afghanistan, despite the use of a mask and conduct that had resulted thus far in broad public approval of his performance in office, the success or failure of a new war in Iraq would likely determine whether George W. Bush was the leader Americans wanted and needed in the new war against global terrorism. No group of Americans had more at risk in the determination of the question than the men and women in military uniform.

10

Building for Tomorrow

They intend to strike the homeland again.

—George Tenet, Director of the
Central Intelligence Agency, 17 October 2002

In a statement only slightly tinged with hyperbole, Michael Mandelbaum has asserted, "It is a truth universally acknowledged that the central feature of the world at the outset of the twenty-first century is the enormous power of the United States."[1] The principal use for this power, he argues, is to defend, maintain, and expand peace, democracy, and free markets.[2] In 2002 the Department of Defense was in full agreement. The first sentence of the first chapter of its August 2002 *Annual Report to the President and the Congress* declared, "America's goals are to promote peace, sustain freedom, and encourage prosperity."[3]

The broadly stated goals are not new. What is new are the means adopted by the Bush administration in the weeks and months after the 11 September

2001 terrorist attacks to achieve the goals. The attacks changed much more than the Pentagon's previous war planning assumptions. Michael Hirsh, a former foreign editor of *Newsweek*, has asserted that the policy and ideological principles that President Bush carried with him into the White House, "which condemned Clinton as a serial intervener and sought to withdraw from U.S. overcommitments to peacekeeping, nation-building, and mediation," are "in direct conflict with the reality [the president] was handed on September 11."[4] It can at least be said that the new reality has affected the nation's strategic imperatives in ways that were not foreseen prior to 11 September 2001.

On 17 September 2002, one year and six days after the terrorist attacks, the president issued a state paper of major importance. The thirty-one-page document, titled *The National Security Strategy of the United States of America*, was immediately characterized as "the most dramatic and far-reaching change in national security policy in a half-century."[5] It contained adaptations from several speeches the president had made since the 11 September attacks. A senior administration official said the *National Security Strategy* contained three strategic priorities: (1) to "lead the world" against terrorists and "aggressive regimes seeking weapons of mass destruction"; (2) to preserve the peace by "fostering good relations among the world's great powers"; and (3) to extend the benefits of liberty and prosperity through the spread of American values and tangible rewards for good governance.[6] The priorities were based on what were called traditional U.S. principles: "[W]e do not use our strength to press for unilateral advantage. We seek instead to create a balance of power that favors human freedom."[7]

The drama and far-reaching change, however, was found in the formal substitution of the Cold War strategy of deterrence and containment for a concept more appropriate "to the capabilities and objectives of today's adversaries."[8] "Traditional concepts of deterrence," the president declared, "will not work against a terrorist enemy whose avowed tactics are wanton destruction and the targeting of innocents."[9] The concept of "imminent threat" would be adopted and applied, if the risk of attack is great enough. To forestall or prevent hostile attacks involving weapons of mass destruction, "the United States will, if necessary," the president said, "act preemptively."[10] Americans are now "threatened less by conquering states than we are by failing ones," the president continued. "Today, the distinction between domestic and foreign affairs is diminishing" and "we are menaced less by fleets and armies than by catastrophic technologies in the hands of the embittered few."[11]

John Keegan later referred to the new threat in these words: "The emergence of fundamentalist terrorism promises to undermine Clausewitz for good. The terrorists are not an army, nor a people, nor a state. They present none of the targets which a traditional military establishment is trained to place under attack. They have no apparent geographical base, . . . they are not an arm of any government, they do not belong to any identifiable ethnic group."[12] He asked, "How do you defeat an enemy who does not mind dying?"[13] The new *National Security Strategy* attempted to answer the question. To meet the new threat, the president said, Americans "must build and maintain our defenses beyond challenge."[14] Because the "military's highest priority is to defend the United States," the U.S. Armed Forces and the Department of Defense would have to be *transformed* "to ensure our ability to conduct rapid and precise operations to achieve decisive results."[15]

The new strategy did not receive universal praise. One analyst observed almost with nostalgia that "[t]he common characteristic of the whole 20th century was the readiness of the United States to respond to attacks to its security and its reluctance to initiate conflict or issue ultimatums to anyone. When aggressors pushed forward, we pushed back—hence Korea, Vietnam and the Persian Gulf War. But we did not start fights ourselves."[16] A critic of the new strategy worried about the danger of unintended consequences, opining, "Preemptive military action would require the Administration to draw early conclusions about a rival nation's capabilities and intent, placing a premium on accurate intelligence and judgment. It would necessitate a clear public case to avoid sharpening the perception that the United States plays by its own rules in foreign affairs."[17] Another analyst observed that in implementing the new doctrine, U.S. military forces would have to strike with precision because the danger of retaliation would be great. "You don't get a second chance."[18]

At least partially because the principal tenets of the *National Security Strategy* had been laid out in speeches by the president over several months, Congress was relatively quiet on the subject of preemption immediately following its publication. West Virginia Democrat Senator Robert Byrd, however, was not. A ferocious defender of congressional prerogatives, he made a broad request of law school professors all over the country for their opinions on the question of whether the president has constitutional power to act preemptively. Some lawyers even suggested that the new doctrine was really threat *prevention*—an illegitimate use of force that focuses primarily on a state's capacity rather than on its intent to attack or not—not preemption.[19]

Predictably, most European countries were openly critical and suspicious of any U.S. strategy to go it alone without international approval in advance.[20] The British edition of the *Financial Times* led its 7 October 2002 front page with the headline "War To Oust Saddam 'Illegal.'" Government lawyers advised Prime Minister Tony Blair that military action not authorized by the UN Security Council would be contrary to Article 2 of the UN Charter and thus violate international law. "Popular opinion in Europe," said one journalist, "wants America not just to take its case to the U.N.—it wants America to obey the U.N.'s ruling."[21] The European Union's external affairs minister argued that more emphasis should be placed by the United States on the purported root causes of terrorism, such as poverty and lack of freedom.[22] Another European official claimed that people on the European continent were so unhappy with the U.S. position that "President Bush would not be able to walk the streets of Berlin shaking hands right now, or the streets of Madrid."[23]

In the United States, the debate was less frantic and much more realistic. While the limits of the preemption doctrine were yet to be publicly identified,[24] government officials made it clear that it did not imply that the United States would suddenly launch military strikes whenever the country was threatened.[25] Some turned to precedent, quoting Elihu Root, a former secretary of state, secretary of war, senator, president of the American Society of International Law, and recipient of the Nobel Peace Prize for 1912. Root referred to "the right to every sovereign state to protect itself by preventing a condition of affairs in which it will be too late to protect itself."[26]

Short shrift was given initially to suggestions to focus solely or even primarily on the underlying root causes of terrorism, at least in the short term. It was likely that most Americans would have agreed with former secretary of state George Schultz's comments about acts of terrorism in the early 1980s. "If we got ourselves in the frame of mind that these terrorist acts could be justified and legitimized—and that somehow *we* were to blame—then we would have lost the battle. . . . Do poverty and injustice cause terrorism? We should work for social betterment but not legitimize terrorism in the meantime. Does political oppression cause terrorism? We should work for human rights and diplomatic solutions to conflicts."[27] Even a critic of the Bush administration argued that the new doctrine of preemption did not violate international law.[28] In any event, "no international treaty can override the constitutional duty of the President and Congress to protect the American people from nuclear threats, whether imminent or not-so-imminent."[29]

Whatever operational success could be attributed to the military component of the *National Security Strategy*, however, there was reason to believe that more work was necessary to achieve political objectives. Fareed Zakaria, the editor of *Newsweek International*, conceded that the war on terror has had an effect. "The destruction of al Qaeda's base camps in Afghanistan, the detention of suspects around the world, the scrutiny of bank accounts—all this has made mass terror more difficult. But," he added, "while the Bush Administration has a coherent military strategy in place, it does not have a similar political one."[30] Citing recent political gains by Muslim fundamentalists, the growing anti-Americanism in the Middle East, and other facts, he concluded, "In the war against terror, we are doing well militarily. But it will account for little without an effective political strategy. Otherwise, we will kill fundamentalists but feed fundamentalism."[31]

Such views were shared and were soon expressed by influential members of the president's party in Congress. "Military action will be necessary to deal with serious and immediate threats to our national security," said Senator Richard Lugar, the soon-to-be chairman of the Senate Foreign Relations Committee in early 2003, "but the war on terrorism will not be won through attrition—particularly because military action will often breed more terrorists."[32] To win the war, he added, "the United States must assign to economic and diplomatic capabilities the same strategic priority we assign to military capabilities."[33]

In ideal circumstances, the new national security strategy, including both its political and its military components, what Liddell Hart would have called the "Grand Strategy,"[34] would have been announced earlier. It would have been followed by development of a war-fighting strategy against worldwide terrorism and a homeland security strategy. Only then would the implementation phase have begun, including the creation of a Department of Homeland Security and the restructuring of the U.S. Armed Forces. The initial reaction to the deadly, irrational terrorist enemy, however, did not take place in ideal circumstances.

As the nation prepared to commemorate the first anniversary of the terrorist attacks, it was important to take stock of the work in progress, to evaluate the effectiveness to date of the military effort in three critical and related areas: the global war on terrorism, homeland security, and transformation of the armed forces to fight terrorism and other likely threats of the future. Only after an evaluation of the plans, operations, executive actions, and organizational realignment taken to date could future plans be made with confidence. Most Americans shared three simple and almost inevitable conclusions about the past year: much had been accomplished, there was much more to do, and the danger of additional terrorist attacks was significant.

On 29 January 2002 the president had identified two objectives in the war on terrorism. First, the terrorist camps in Afghanistan would be closed, terrorist plans would be disrupted, and the terrorists would be brought to justice. Second, threats to the United States and the world by terrorists and regimes that seek to use chemical, biological, or nuclear weapons would be prevented. Progress was apparent in relation to both objectives. In testimony before the Senate Armed Services Committee on 31 July 2002 Defense Secretary Donald Rumsfeld proudly noted that only a year earlier, Afghanistan was a pariah state, the Taliban regime was in power, and the country was a sanctuary for "thousands of foreign terrorists who had free range to train, plan, organize, finance attacks on innocent civilians across the globe."[35] Now, he said, and as the result of the low to mid-intensity military operations, "the Taliban has been driven from power, al Qaeda is on the run, Afghanistan is no longer a base for terror-ist operations or a breeding ground for radical Islamic militancy."[36] These were significant achievements, for as terrorism expert Brian Jenkins said, "If al Qaeda can be kept on the run, the numbers it can train will decline. And declining numbers eventually will result in a corresponding qualitative decline in terror-ist operations."[37] Rumsfeld also noted, with justifiable satisfaction, that a new president and a new cabinet had assumed office in Afghanistan and that a new Afghan national army was being trained.

Unstated, but equally significant, was the leap in intelligence that had been made possible by the interrogation of captured enemy combatants, as well as the seizure of documents and even computer equipment. In remarks at the Pentagon commemorating the events of 11 September 2001 President Bush noted that the United States had also "captured more than 2,000 terrorists" and that "a larger number of killers have met their end in combat." Seven months earlier, syndi-cated columnist Charles Krauthammer had evaluated developments in Afghan-istan in words that, although undoubtedly appreciated by many, were at least premature. He asserted that the United States had been on a well-deserved "hol-iday from history" during the 1990s. "For 50 years (December 1941 to December 1991)," he said, "America had lived locked in titanic, existential struggle with fas-cism, Nazism and communism. We won, but half a century of mobilization can be psychologically exhausting. We needed a rest." Then, he added, after 11 September, "we brandished steel." The demonstrated resolve of Americans "forged a new America."[38]

Perhaps the best indicator of the military success enjoyed to date in achiev-ing the first objective was what had not occurred. While it was impossible to accurately determine what additional attacks might have been made on U.S. soil without the military counterterrorism and homeland security efforts, it was fact that no additional attacks had occurred. Even the terrorist operations attributed to al Qaeda overseas—in Afghanistan, Pakistan, and Tunisia—had not been significant.[39]

The success, however, had to be balanced against hard realities. At the 31 July Senate Armed Services Committee hearing, Gen. Tommy Franks, the commander of the U.S. Central Command, tempered the undisputed operational accomplishments with a strong note of caution about the future.[40] "Al Qaeda's senior leadership is in disarray," he conceded, but "al Qaeda has not lost its will to conceive, to plan, to execute terrorist operations worldwide." A report only ten days later stated that al Qaeda had established two main bases in Pakistan, that it was preparing for a massive strike against the new Afghan government, and that it was attempting to acquire surface-to-air missiles capable of hitting U.S. B-52 bombers.[41] On 5 September 2002 a powerful car bomb exploded in Kabul, killing at least a dozen people. Three hours later, Afghan president Hamid Karzai narrowly escaped an assassination attempt in Kandahar.

General Franks also disabused those who thought that a sixty-thousand-man Afghan army could be trained overnight to provide stability in the country. He noted that only thirteen thousand soldiers would be trained by the end of 2003. When he was asked when his mission in Afghanistan would be finished, he could not provide an answer. During a tour of the region four weeks later, he said that the seven to eight thousand U.S. troops would remain in Afghanistan indefinitely. By early September even Pentagon officials who had vigorously opposed all previous suggestions that U.S. troops engage in peacekeeping or nation-building activities in Afghanistan were endorsing expansion of the international security assistance force there and hinting at a broader and larger U.S. commitment.

There were many other reasons to believe that the war was far from over. The whereabouts of Osama bin Laden; Ayman al-Zawahiri, al Qaeda's other senior leader; and Mullah Mohammed Omar, the leader of the Taliban, were still unknown. A draft report by a UN group responsible for the monitoring of international controls on terrorist groups, concluded that al Qaeda had not yet encountered significant difficulty in funding its operations. Only $10 million of identified terrorist assets had been frozen since the beginning of the year. The Treasury Department denounced the report as "incomplete," but European prosecutors believed that most of al Qaeda's wealth had been converted to gold or diamonds and was thus beyond the reach of bank officials.[42]

The month following the anniversary of the attacks in New York City and Washington, D.C., harsh new evidence showed that the war on terrorism was far from over. On 6 October an explosives-laden boat rammed a French oil tanker in Yemen, killing a member of the crew and releasing more than ninety thousand barrels of oil into the Gulf of Aden. Yemen's interior minister said that the bombing was a deliberate act of terror. On 16 October terrorist bombs exploded in two nightclubs packed with partygoers on the Indonesian Island of Bali, killing 190 people. The next day, two terrorist bombs in a shopping district on the southern coast of Mindanao, Philippine Islands, killed 6 and wounded 150.

On 16 October the State Department announced that in the 3–5 October meetings in North Korea, officials of that country's government admitted that for years, and in clear violation of their agreement with the United States, they had pursued a secret program designed to produce enriched uranium for use in nuclear weapons.[43] Fate had now intervened in events in a bizarre fashion. Exactly forty years earlier to the day, a meeting had taken place at the White House to discuss the results of a 14 October 1962 reconnaissance mission over Cuba by a U-2 aircraft. Photographs from the mission had produced the first verified evidence of the existence of Soviet offensive medium-range ballistic missiles in Cuba. President Kennedy had opened the meeting by asking Secretary of State Dean Rusk for his views. "Mr. President," Rusk had replied, "this is a . . . serious development. It's one that we, all of us, had not really believed the Soviets could . . . carry this far. . . . I do think we have to set in motion a chain of events that will eliminate this base."[44] Within days, U.S. intelligence officials concluded that Pakistan, an important new ally in the fight against terrorism, had been a major supplier of equipment critical to North Korea's nuclear program. On the basis of his review of intelligence estimates, Rumsfeld said that he believed that North Korea already had a small number of usable weapons.[45] Former secretary of state James Baker said that there were credible reports that Pyongyang might be "no more than a year away from mass producing up to six a year."[46]

The extent and ominous nature of the continuing terrorist threat became public within days. The director of the Defense Threat Reduction Agency declared, "[W]e can expect to see [weapons of mass destruction] in the United States territory."[47] Rumsfeld conceded that "[a]s we put pressure on and close a door here, [the terrorists will] push and find a door somewhere else."[48] An independent task force concluded, "A year after September 11, 2002, America remains dangerously unprepared to prevent and respond to a catastrophic attack on U.S. soil. In all likelihood, the next attack will result in even greater casualties and widespread disruption to American lives and the economy."[49]

The day after the State Department announcement of developments in North Korea, the director of the Central Intelligence Agency testified before a congressional panel. His testimony was chilling. "The threat environment we find ourselves in today," George Tenet said, "is as bad as it was last summer, the summer before 9/11. It is serious. They have reconstituted. They are coming after us. . . . They intend to strike the homeland again."[50]

The experience of the armed forces during the first several months of the global war on terrorism had already affected the thinking of defense planners about the future. Many policy and operating principles and guidelines had been learned or re-learned and political and military leaders declared their desire to apply them in future crises and conflicts.

The first public articulation of the Defense Department's evolving new thinking about the circumstances in which military force should be used and the elements that will most effectively ensure success appeared in the secretary of defense's August 2002 *Annual Report to the President and the Congress*. The report declared that the conflict in Afghanistan did not present a model for future military campaigns, but certain lessons could be drawn "from recent events and . . . applied to the future."[51] A few weeks later, the Pentagon released the text of a memorandum originally written by Rumsfeld in March 2001. Revised as recently as the weekend of 12 October 2002, it was titled *Guidelines to Be Considered when Committing Forces*. The guidelines were not offered as official policy, but as a "checklist" that was "worth considering." Nevertheless, they clearly reflected Rumsfeld's views and were immediately characterized as both an echo and a refinement of "military thinking set down in past years by Caspar

Weinberger" and a "significant departure" from that thinking.[52] Official policy or not, the annual report and the guidelines offered considerable insight into the likely outcome of future decisions on the use of military force overseas in the new kind of war.

The annual report first declared that "wars in the 21st century will increasingly require use of all elements of national power—economic, diplomatic, financial, law enforcement, and intelligence, as well as both overt and covert military operations." The defense of the United States requires prevention and may require preemption. The war must be taken to the enemy.[53] The guidelines said the first question to be asked will be: "Is the proposed [military] action truly necessary?" Significantly, the risk of a *vital* national interest might no longer be necessary. "If U.S. lives are to be put at risk, whatever is proposed to be done must [only] be in the U.S. national interest."[54]

The second question to be asked, according to the guidelines, was: "Is the proposed action achievable?" According to the memorandum, the answer to this question depends on the answers to several subsidiary issues, for example, whether the mission is "something the U.S. is capable of accomplishing"; whether it has "clear, well-considered and well-understood goals as to the purpose of the engagement and what would constitute success"; whether the command structure is clear; whether the U.S. will be joined by a "coalition of the willing"; and whether coalition partners are committed to contribute to "whatever might be needed to achieve the agreed goals."[55]

The third question suggested by Rumsfeld is: "Is it worth it?" Are all coalition partners willing to risk lives and to absolutely commit all necessary resources? Is the U.S. leadership "willing to invest the political capital to marshal support to sustain the effort—without any strategic pauses that give the enemy breathing room—for whatever period of time may be required?" Also, what are the implications for the United States in other parts of the world "if we prevail, if we fail, or if we decide not to act?"[56]

If there is to be action, decisive action must be taken early, "during the pre-crisis period, to try to alter the behavior of others and to prevent the conflict." The force used should be that "necessary to prevail, plus some."[57] Nothing should be ruled out in advance. The ability of U.S. forces "to communicate and operate seamlessly on the battlefield will be critical," but it must be remembered that "the new and the high-tech have not totally replaced the old and conventional." Military operations must also be linked directly with humanitarian assistance, radio broadcasts, rewards, and other efforts "to help the local population and rally them to the U.S. cause." Also, "[a]rbitrary deadlines as to when the U.S. will disengage" should not be set. The enemy "must understand that the United States will use every means at its disposal to defeat him."[58]

Finally, Rumsfeld's guidelines declared that the U.S. leadership must be "brutally honest with itself, the Congress, the public and coalition partners. We must not make the effort sound even marginally easier or less costly than it could become." If a risk of casualties exists, that fact should be acknowledged at the outset. Government officials should "promise less, or no more, than we are sure we can deliver," and Americans "must know that—good news or bad—their leader will tell it straight."[59]

It did not take long for some of the ideas expressed in the annual report and the guidelines to be applied. On 12 October 2002, two days before the *New York Times* gave front page coverage to his new guidelines, Rumsfeld announced in an interview that he had ordered the regional CINCs (now referred to in the Pentagon as "combatant commanders") to rewrite all existing war plans to ensure that full use will be made of better intelligence, precision weapons, and speedier deployment. Because new precision weapons offer much greater lethality than those used as recently as the 1990–91 Persian Gulf War, Rumsfeld asserted that fewer troops and fewer munitions would now be required for the same mission, thus permitting faster mobilization and deployment and fewer ships to carry munitions to a war zone.[60] Rumsfeld's comments were supported by Gen. Peter Pace, USMC, the vice chairman of the Joint Chiefs of Staff, who declared that fewer troops arriving at a crisis point in a faster time might present greater concentrated power than a larger force arriving later. "If you can deliver five divisions anywhere in the world in 90 days, might you have the same impact," he asked rhetorically, "by getting three divisions there in 30 days?"[61]

At face value, the arguments postulated had a great deal of logic. It was unarguable that they needed to be fully considered and tested. There were, however, other factors to consider, as critics promptly pointed out. It was a question of how much risk was acceptable. A concern for potentially high casualties might still require overwhelming numerical superiority to ensure success in a difficult mission. Large numbers can also demonstrate U.S. resolve. Skepticism about the actual speed of the deployment could also be forgiven. During the Cold War, the war plans for a conflict with the Soviet Union and the Warsaw Pact called for the United States to deliver ten divisions of ground troops to Europe within ten days. Many senior defense officials at the time did not believe that was possible.

A review of the effectiveness of military planning and action in the transformation of the armed forces for future threats, including terrorist threats to the nation's homeland, was more daunting than an evaluation of the conflict in Afghanistan. Insufficient time had passed to be able to take much of a long view. Individual effort was not an issue. Americans in uniform and their civilian counterparts in federal and state agencies were straining all over the world to meet the rapidly increasing security demands. Aggressive attitude and superhuman effort, however, cannot always compensate for time and resource limitations.

While public attention was focused on Afghanistan, the United States had, in fact, engaged in significant military operations around the globe. Because it had not been fully anticipated, the war on terrorism was continuing to require a substantial investment of time by national security officials. Geopolitical priorities were changing and under constant review. Intense planning was under way for the anticipated war against Iraq. Efforts to transform the U.S. Armed Forces, a steep mountain to climb in the best of circumstances, were inevitably relegated to whatever time was available to the most senior officials.

Concern also existed in many quarters about the effect the global war on terrorism was having on the U.S. economy. The economy was struggling. It was unclear how much of a drain the war, including a possible invasion of Iraq, worldwide implementation of the new doctrine of preemption, and all other security efforts would be. Would the open-ended war on terrorism require a major mobilization of the nation and large-scale transfers of resources from the civilian to the military sector? Would the Bush administration incur the risk of trying to have both guns and butter? Observing that "history is full of examples of governments that greatly underestimate the cost of fighting wars," a *Business Week* article stated that more spending on security might drain the economy, hold down private investment and consumer spending, and force "draconian choices that will destabilize domestic political peace."[62]

It was generally accepted that the armed forces would be assigned unprecedented homeland security responsibilities in the future. Policy decisions on the precise nature and extent of those responsibilities had still not been made. Believing that the armed forces should concentrate on overseas security missions that can only be performed with U.S. military power, military leaders were still very reluctant to assume responsibility for any domestic task that could conceivably be performed by some other department or agency of government. So strongly was this view held that defense officials added a new term to the Department of Defense lexicon: "homeland defense." Defined as the "protection of U.S. territory, domestic population, and critical defense infrastructure against external threats and aggression,"[63] the term was intended to distinguish between combat operations, which were still perceived to be the primary mission of the armed forces, from domestic military requirements, generally referred to as "civil support."[64]

As a matter of defense policy, Rumsfeld remained unwilling to commit military personnel or material resources beyond the three sets of broadly stated circumstances set forth in the *National Strategy for Homeland Security*,[65] even though the president had declared that the "U.S. Government has no more important mission than protecting the homeland from future terrorist attacks."[66] The Department of Defense's 2001 QDR report had declared that the defense of the United States would be DoD's primary mission.[67] In fact, more than a year after the 11 September attacks, the department still distinguished between warfighting on foreign territory and warfighting at home; it still gave the former a much higher priority than military support to civil authorities.[68]

Recognizing that important and generally salutary measures had been taken by the federal government and the states in the months after the 11 September attacks to respond to the risk of catastrophic terrorism, an independent task force nevertheless expressed concern that the nation's leaders were beginning to forget President Bush's declaration that the war on terrorism had to be fought at home, as well as on foreign soil. The task force recommended strongly that homeland security priorities "should be pursued with the same sense of urgency and national purpose as our overseas exertions."[69] On this score, the Department of Defense was receiving mixed reviews.

In their book on large-scale organizational change, Christopher Laszlo and Jean-Francois Laugel wrote,

> In the realm of physics, it is now widely accepted that Newtonian laws, while relevant to the trajectory of mechanical objects in steady state environments, are not able to explain the so-called Brownian motion of electrons or the air flow of a jet engine through space. The new twentieth century science of Einstein, Hawking, Prigogine, Thom, and others came to incorporate phenomena such as relativity, uncertainty, instability, and chaos. Yet in management circles, the predominant schools of thought remain anchored in nineteenth century theory and practice.[70]

They believe the only successful way for large organizations to adapt to chaos and complexity is to strive for "perpetual transformation." They use the term *transformation* to mean a process of altering context. "The alteration reinvents the [organization]. It is like the transformation of a chrysalis into a butterfly. A butterfly is not a new and improved pupa: it has fundamentally changed its existence. Transformation alters the essential nature and context of [an organization]. In the process it allows an organization to create something that is not possible in its present reality."[71]

The war on terrorism has increased the need to think about national security in this kind of untraditional way. "For far too long," T. Irene Sanders, executive director of the Washington Center for Complexity and Public Policy, has observed, "[O]ur military and intelligence establishments have simply analyzed the past in order to anticipate the future—relying on what's commonly called a linear way of thinking."[72] In her view, "Linear thinkers tend to rely on past experience to travel from Point A to Point B. Non-linear thinkers tend to look for changes since the last time they made the trip."[73] While it is not possible to predict the future with certainty, she believes that use of the mathematical science of chaos theory and the science of complexity will permit defense planners to identify small changes, new conditions, subtle shifts, and changing patterns that are beginning to influence the future. This will permit "the development of forces and capabilities that can adapt quickly to new challenges and unexpected circumstances," a critical ability in a conflict against loosely connected terrorist cells that have a high degree of adaptability and derive protection by "operating in the shadows, blending into the societies they intend to attack,"[74] rather than using size and strength to fight conventional armed conflicts. In an early evaluation of the Bush administration's progress in transforming the armed forces, John Roos, the editor of *Armed Forces Journal*, summarized the challenge in simple terms. After it commenced efforts to "inject a healthy dose of commercial business savvy into how the U.S. military conducts the business of defense . . . along came bin Laden, a quick rewrite of the Quadrennial Defense Review, and a new priority number-one."[75]

Evidence of competition between the overseas war against terror and efforts to transform the armed forces and provide security at home was the continuing absence of strategic guidance on transformation and homeland security priorities. Only days after the 11 September terrorist attacks the president had recognized the country's almost limitless vulnerabilities. "We can't chase everything," he said. "Let's prioritize, let's assess risk and then let's figure out the strategy necessary to deal with each risk."[76] A terrorism expert made the same point more recently. "Priorities must be set. Instead of trying to protect every conceivable target against every imaginable form of attack, policymakers must explore strategies that accept a higher level of risk but offer greater strength or resiliency."[77] These views are a modern application of Frederick the Great's well-known aphorism: "Little minds try to defend everything at once, but sensible people look at the main point only; they parry the worst blows and stand a little hurt if thereby they avoid a greater one. If you try to hold everything, you hold nothing." Because it is impossible to eliminate all risks of new terror attacks at home, informed choices needed to be made about how to allocate finite resources, including the men and women in military uniform. Many competent mid-level civilian and military leaders, working under difficult circumstances to improve security at home, were still hampered by outdated organizational structures, legacy information technology systems that could not communicate with other systems, and bureaucratic cultures resistant to change.

In February 2002 President Bush submitted his proposed budget to Congress for fiscal year (FY) 2003. The military part of the budget was the first military budget to reflect the new national security strategic vision. The request recommended a major reordering of domestic spending priorities, including large increases for homeland security. By the time Congress adjourned for the November elections, however, final action on the overall budget for the government was still pending. In October, after the government's new fiscal year had already begun, the president was finally able to sign into law a $355.4 billion defense bill, which increased spending by more than $34 billion dollars over the previous year.

Doubt remained, however, about the priorities of the FY 2003 budget. The enormous efforts of officials at the Office of Management and Budget and the Office of Homeland Security, along with those within the Department of Defense, were still being carried out in the absence of a comprehensive threat and risk assessment that would determine which critical assets and structures required higher or special protection from attack as well as what forces and weapons systems are required in the 2015 time frame and beyond to give the United States the kind of military capabilities required for future security needs. A priority-setting budget was a necessary part of any plan to operationalize the transformation of the armed forces; set specific goals; establish priorities, milestones, and metrics to evaluate performance; and link individual performance to a reward system. According to David Walker, the U.S. comptroller general, an integrated, enterprise-wide approach to homeland security and transformation was still missing, even though defense leaders had taken some recent steps to institutionalize needed changes.[78]

Even the definition of *transformation* was still being debated a year after the terrorist attacks. Did the term refer to a process, or a desired result, or both? The working definition at DoD in September 2002 was "'a sustained, iterative and dynamic process' that: develops and integrates new concepts, processes, technologies, and organizational designs; rebalances capabilities and forces; and seeks to ensure a 'substantial margin of advantage' over potential enemies, while minimizing the chances and consequences of surprise."[79] Transformation is not, according to DoD, "a definitive or unchanging blueprint; a silver bullet; something done to the force all at once; accomplished in a short period of time; or just about systems and platforms."[80] Historical examples of military transformation cited included the transition from mounted knights to massed archers during the 100 Years War, the movement from offensive cavalry to static trench defenses during World War I, and the German concept of blitzkrieg during World War II. A sign that DoD's working definition had not yet gained universal acceptance was the October 2002 definition recommended by the comptroller general.[81]

Even before the United States observed the first anniversary of the terrorist attacks, critics were claiming the death of the transformation effort. "Between his inauguration . . . and the September 11 attacks," said one public policy institute, "Bush's defense transformation died a quiet death. The ' iron triangle' of Congress, the defense industry, and the Pentagon bureaucracy effectively killed the initiative."[82] "After September 11, and the war in Afghanistan," the 11 June 2002 CATO Institute report continued, "President Bush had the opportunity to use his prestige and high public approval ratings, as well as renewed public interest in national security issues, to resuscitate his defense reform agenda. Instead, the president took the easy way out, asking for the largest increase in defense spending since the military build up during the Reagan Administration."[83] Andrew Krepinevich, the director of another Washington think tank and a former member of the staff of Andrew Marshall, the chief of the Pentagon's Office of Net Assessment, was only slightly less critical, but more direct. "They've done a terrific job in identifying the new challenges," he said, "but have fallen down badly in defining what kind of weapons systems and warfighting doctrine they need to meet them."[84]

Within the Pentagon, opinion was also divided. A September evaluation by Rumsfeld's new Office of Force Transformation, aided by two defense contractors, criticized the transformation plans of the individual military services for failing to adequately address interoperability, joint command and control, logistics support, and information operations architecture.[85] The Joint Staff called for a separate assessment and, according to one official, had very different ideas about what transformation means.[86] The differences were not helped by the fact that the Office of Force Transformation technically did not exist because it had no operating charter defining the scope of its authority and responsibility,[87] and because there was no current, overarching, joint operational blueprint to guide the development of service concepts, organization, and technology.[88] A "detailed planning guidance laying out clear transformation goals and the criteria necessary to attain them" was recommended;[89] it appeared to be badly needed.

Early help was promised. A Pentagon official said that the pivotal "crossover point" between traditional program procurement plans and future technologies that might help in the transformation effort was not the FY 2003 budget, which did not resolve the mismatch between defense needs and resources, but rather the FY 2004 budget, which would be recommended by the president in early 2003. That budget was the "one which would begin to give more definition to the priorities for the transformational effort."[90] As 2002 came to a close a senior defense official claimed that the FY 2004 budget would, in fact, shift funds to more futuristic or transformational programs.[91] Others, however, were very critical of the proposed budget. Some warned that in taking many weapons systems out of service, including aircraft and over twenty warships, in order to free up funds for new systems in the future, there would be insufficient numbers of current systems and the new systems would be so expensive that only a few could be afforded, resulting in a procurement "death spiral" in which existing systems grow older and more dangerous to use.[92] Others asserted that the Bush administration's plans did not go far enough, noting that funds would continue to flow to every legacy system that had been up for review. "You had the resistance of the military services to rapid change," said one critic. "You had the relative superficiality of the Bush Administration's transformation vision. Trying to make a major change in defense spending is extremely difficult and there is no political support for it."[93]

No one expected immediate results. To develop a shared culture of reinvention, it would probably be necessary to replace current leaders with what private industry has called "real change leaders," leaders who believe that the future is dependent on change and who have the courage to challenge existing norms,[94] leaders who are not tied to the past by previous success,[95] leaders who believe it is acceptable to increase the risks for the present to achieve greater capability in the future.[96] The effort might also require more increases in defense spending, because without additional resources, transformation and homeland security needs could be funded only by cutting programs that are considered essential by the military services.

Other struggles could be expected at each step. "I do not think there is going to be a single [transformation] decision," Deputy Secretary of Defense Paul Wolfowitz had said a year earlier, "that will not be opposed by someone."[97] He added that it would be unrealistic to think that a major change could be achieved in ten years. "If we could achieve a 15 percent transformation in 10 years," he said, "I would consider that reasonable."[98]

As if Pentagon officials were not already facing major challenges in preparing for a possible war with Iraq, transforming the armed forces, and assuming new responsibilities for homeland security, a complicating factor, which had been pushed to the rear during the first stages of the war on terrorism, began to re-emerge in subsequent months. The subject was the continuing tension in the relationship between civilian and military leaders.

A lengthy 16 October 2002 article in the *Washington Post* outlined what was described as "a pronounced civilian-military divide at the Pentagon under Rumsfeld's leadership," which had risen to the surface "as the Pentagon [planned] for a possible war in the Persian Gulf and for a fiscal 2004 budget that is in danger of being swamped by war costs and long-deferred expenditures on modernization, new weapons, and Rumsfeld's desire to transform the military into a 21st-century force."[99] Some senior officers were reportedly very unhappy with Rumsfeld's exclusionary personal style, as well as some of his goals. They described him as abusive, indecisive, unwilling to delegate, too personally involved in operational planning, "seemingly eager to slap down officers with decades of distinguished service," and trusting only a close, tiny circle of civilian advisors that "is not tolerant of ideas it doesn't already share." The unhappiness was characterized as being "so pervasive that even the three [civilian] service secretaries [were] said to be deeply frustrated by a lack of autonomy and contemplating leaving by the end of the year."[100] *USA Today* reported that military officers and defense analysts said that relations between a defense secretary and the armed forces had not been strained so badly since the tenure of Robert McNamara during the Vietnam War.[101] "It goes back to what the military calls 'command climate,'" one senior officer said. "Does he have a command climate where senior military people can tell him the truth about dangers he is about to walk into?"[102]

Reportedly, Rumsfeld believed that the military establishment, especially the Joint Staff,[103] had become too independent during the eight years of the Clinton administration. He denied that he ignored military advice and was unapologetic about his efforts to assert civilian control of the military. "Someone ought to go back and read the founding fathers and what they had in mind," he said. "It is intended that there be civilian control in this department. That's the design of the system."[104]

Civilian control was certainly important, as were many, if not most of the management and war-fighting reforms that Rumsfeld was trying to impose on the Pentagon. There was reason to believe, however, that whatever the management performance of certain senior civilian leaders, insufficient attention was being paid to old-fashioned leadership. As British field marshal Sir William Slim, the architect of the Allied victory in Burma in World War II, noted, there is a difference between management and leadership. "Leadership is of the spirit," he said, "compounded of personality and vision; its practice is an art. Management is of the mind, more a matter of accurate calculation, of statistics, of methods, timetables and routine; its practice is a science. Managers are necessary; leaders are essential."[105] Similar words were soon spoken by the outgoing army chief of staff.[106]

Aside from difficulties presented by style of management, the issue was larger than the effort to transform the armed forces or even the tensions involved in the planning for possible war with Iraq, which were discussed in Chapter 9. To a great extent, the issue highlighted the need for a recalibration and improvement of the working relationship between the civilian and military leadership in times of both peace and war. Notwithstanding Rumsfeld's aggressive assertion of authority, Richard Kohn, a critic of the civilian-military relationship, has concluded, "[I]n recent years civilian control of the military has weakened." The issue "is not the nightmare of a coup d'état but rather the evidence that the American military has grown in influence to the point of being able to impose its own perspective on policies and decisions."[107] Kohn quoted a senior civilian official as saying that what "weighs heavily . . . everyday" is "the reluctance, indeed refusal, of the political appointees to disagree with the military on any matter, not just operational matters."[108]

A critique of the state of civilian-military relations in the United States is not appropriate here, but it can at least be said that the civilian-military friction in the waning months of 2002 complicated decisions on homeland security, transformation, and even preparations for a possible conflict against Iraq. It may also be noted that if today's armed forces are substantially more professional, more capable, and more indispensable than their predecessors,[109] and if some civilian leaders have in fact actually "abdicated responsibility for strategic management for so long . . . that reclaiming it now will be difficult,"[110] the answer to the problem lies not in inhibiting the full exercise by military leaders of their experience and skills, but in exercising strong civilian leadership as well as strong management. Perhaps the standards by which potential political appointees for the Pentagon are evaluated should also be raised or changed. Too often, administrations of both political parties appoint people to positions of authority in the Pentagon for purely political purposes, instead of upon the basis of merit.[111] It is not obvious that people who have no substantial experience in the heavy competition of the marketplace, in managing complicated organizations and large numbers of people, in assuming responsibility for matters that entail complexity and significant risk, and serving in or at least working with the armed forces, should be given the kind of authority that must be exercised by civilian leaders in the Pentagon.[112]

In the months following the 11 September attacks, various factors limited bold new homeland security initiatives within the Pentagon. The president's new, over-arching *National Security Strategy of the United States of America* publication was not issued until September 2002. The Office of Homeland Security's *National Strategy for Homeland Security* was not issued until July 2002. Despite the president's call in June 2002 for a new Department of Homeland Security, Congress adjourned for the November elections without taking action and defense officials were reluctant to take action that had not been directed or requested. And, of course, the U.S. Armed Forces were already heavily engaged in the global war on terrorism and in preparation for a likely war with Iraq.

There was no presidential appointee in the Pentagon with clearly defined homeland security responsibilities. There was no clear legislative or policy direction on spending and operational priorities for homeland security. The individual military services were, therefore, to a considerable degree, left to their own devices. Available resources were applied to the nation's immediate needs after 11 September, but existing programs and proposed budgets for transformation into the forces of the future now had to be balanced against new demands for improved homeland security, modernization of existing forces, and the probable war in Iraq. Each service revived its plans and assets and commenced studies to determine how it might contribute to the new mission of homeland security in the longer term. In the short term, the military services generally did only what they were directed to do.

Traditionally, U.S. naval forces have been designed almost exclusively to project offensive power. Even though the planning for U.S. naval power had evolved in recent years from the blue-water, war-at-sea focus of the 1980s "maritime strategy" to a broader concept of joint operations, especially in the littoral areas of the world, the navy still thought of "defense" in terms of the protection of individual ships, a task force, and sea lines of communication.

One of the first reactions of the navy to the events of 11 September was to transfer tactical control of thirteen *Cyclone*-class navy coastal patrol ships to the U.S. Coast Guard, the lead agency for maritime homeland security and the organization responsible for the protection of more than 360 ports and 95,000 miles of U.S. coastline.[113] This was seen as a first step in what was described by the chief of naval operations (CNO) as a new effort to "expand partnerships with sister services and agencies to pool resources and talent for maximum effect."[114] Another early step was the realignment of the navy's domestic organizational regions with those of FEMA, a move designed to "promote seamless responses to potentially time-critical events."[115] Early consideration was also given to the use of an embryonic littoral surveillance system and to the idea of designating FFG-7 *Perry*-class frigates scheduled for decommissioning as homeland defense ships.[116] The ships would be assigned to areas close to major harbors not frequented by navy ships.

By 11 September 2002 the navy was analyzing its potential contribution to homeland security in the context of missile defense and "Sea Power 21," the CNO's new vision for the future navy. An important part of Sea Power 21 was "sea shield," described as a concept involving "layered global defensive power based on control of the seas, forward presence, and networked [interagency] intelligence."[117] Designed to extend the security of the country seaward by the early detection, that is, as far away from the homeland as possible, of vessels or aircraft suspected of carrying weapons, the concept would involve the instantaneous use of intelligence information and multisensor cargo inspection equipment. Sea shield would also involve the use of forward-deployed naval forces to destroy cruise missiles and ballistic missiles in the boost or mid-course phase of their flight. Meanwhile, the navy assigned three hundred sailors to work with coast guard personnel in the National Maritime Intelligence Center and made available to civil authorities personnel qualified to assist in emergencies.[118] The main limiting factor for navy initiatives on homeland security was funding, a significant issue for a service that had been cut to just over three hundred ships from a 1989 level of almost six hundred ships and that was purchasing new ships and aircraft at a rate insufficient to sustain even the current force levels.

The first marine corps contribution to the naval forces devoted to homeland security took visible form in an unusual standing unit. In a prescient and forward-looking speech to the National Press Club in October 1997, Gen. Charles C. Krulak, commandant of the U.S. Marine Corps, had identified the battlefield of the asymmetric, chaotic warfare of the future: the cities and urban slums.[119] He noted that the service's new chemical/biological incident response force (CBIRF) was met with great skepticism when it was established. There was no skepticism in October 2001 when the CBIRF responded within two hours to the anthrax contamination of government buildings and post office in the nation's capital area.

The immediate response of the U.S. Air Force to the terrorist attacks was a surge of "air sovereignty" operations. As previously noted, combat air patrols were flown over thirty U.S. cities. The operations involved more than 250 aircraft and approximately 22,000 airmen and maintenance personnel. Almost thirty air force bases around the country placed fighter aircraft on "strip alert," ready to be airborne within fifteen minutes. New concepts for possible longer-term missions were soon being studied. It was considered likely that future homeland security missions would require the full range of the air force's intelligence, surveillance, and reconnaissance capabilities; command, control, and communications assets; and air mobility and medical capabilities.[120] As part of an effort to transform the air force to a capabilities-based force, the air force chief of staff created seven new war-fighting task forces to drive the service's plans, programs, and budgets.[121] Recognizing that the air force could contribute more to homeland security than just continental air defense, he directed a new Homeland Security Task Force to provide support to the air component of the new U.S. Northern Command. Separately, the air force was being urged to place a high priority on the development of capabilities "to detect nuclear weapons and materials at distances that permit an effective military response *before* they can be used."[122]

Even before the 11 September attacks, leading U.S. Army thinkers had begun to confront the question of whether the army had sufficient resources to perform the kinds of homeland security missions that might be assigned to it. Seven general mission areas were identified: (1) land defense (e.g., border control); (2) response to chemical, biological, radiological, nuclear, and high-yield explosive (CBRNE) incidents (training and equipping special units that could support a lead federal agency); (3) national missile defense (contributions to the testing, development, and operation of a land-based system); (4) combating terrorism (in support of domestic law enforcement agencies); (5) protection of critical infrastructure (forces and equipment to prevent or assist in the restoration of telecommunications, electric power, oil and gas, transportation, emergency services, banking and finance, and government operations); (6) information operations (attack of an adversary's systems and protection of the country's own); and (7) military assistance to civil authorities (providing resources in natural or other disaster situations beyond the capabilities of civil authorities).[123]

"History shows," said one analyst, "that frequently only the Army has adequate surge capacity to respond quickly to large-scale disasters" and that disasters on the scale of the one experienced by New York City on 11 September 2001 "would overtax the resources of all but the Nation's largest cities."[124] By one estimate, the resources required to respond to the detonation of a ten-kiloton nuclear device would include "four (light) infantry battalions;[125] five medical companies; three chemical battalions; three engineer construction battalions; three military police companies; four ground transportation battalions; an aviation group; three direct support maintenance battalions; and two general support maintenance battalions."[126] The contribution of even a single medical, chemical, or signal element to a homeland disaster, however, could make larger units incapable of performing missions overseas.

In the months immediately after the 11 September attacks, as discussed in Chapter 7, most of the army's new homeland security tasks were being shouldered by the Army National Guard. The importance and demands of the new mission were stimulating calls for both a new assessment of the most effective future role of the National Guard and increased spending for research and development of new systems needed for the homeland security mission. The capabilities of the army for homeland security, however, had to be balanced against other current and likely demands. By 11 September 2002 it was becoming increasingly apparent that the United States would be involved in Afghanistan for the foreseeable future and in "stability operations," a combination of peacekeeping and nation-building that is required in areas lacking a local government strong enough to stand on its own. "As terrorist groups gravitate toward unstable regions or dysfunctional states for secure bases of operations, U.S. counterterrorism efforts will blend into a host of much broader counterinsurgency and foreign internal defense activities."[127] Estimates of requirements for stability operations in Iraq after the fall of Saddam Hussein were still almost shots in the dark.

Meanwhile, the army was already providing a stabilizing presence in places like Kosovo, Bosnia, and the Sinai. New demands for homeland security also had to be met while the army was simultaneously attempting to transform itself to the lighter, quicker-reacting, more lethal army of the future[128] and filling an immediate "gap between [its] powerful but slow-to-deploy heavy forces and its light rapid-reaction units that lack protection, mobility and lethality once on the battlefield."[129] That was not the only gap. The "delta," or difference between the army's rapidly increasing mission assignments and the resources required to perform them, would stimulate close scrutiny by the next Congress.

Though technically not a part of the Department of Defense,[130] the U.S. Coast Guard was, by almost any other measure, one of the "armed forces" most heavily engaged in homeland security immediately after 11 September 2001. Part of the reason was because the commandant of the coast guard had been personally studying and writing about the matter *prior* to the attacks.[131] Less than 2 percent of the coast guard's personnel and its seagoing and other platforms were involved in providing security to U.S. ports before 11 September. Within two days of the attacks, however, the figure had soared to 60 percent. Shortly after the first aircraft hit the World Trade Center, the coast guard assumed control of all vessel movements in navigable U.S. waters out to three miles from the shore.

Special precautions were taken "in high-risk waterfront facilities and with all bulk oil, gas, and chemical tank vessels."[132] More than one hundred security zones and protection zones around navy ships were established and patrolled. A National Vessel Movement Center was organized and reporting requirements for all ships destined for U.S. ports were improved. Joint U.S. and Canadian coast guard teams began boarding all foreign-flagged vessels entering the St. Lawrence Seaway.[133] Four elite 100-member maritime safety and security (antiterrorism) teams were established for deployment to the busiest ports.

In many ways, and to the extent of its capabilities, the coast guard is the ideal service for the homeland security mission. Long thought of as "a multi-mission, maritime military service,"[134] it has a unique civilian-military character. Its operations are not limited by the Posse Comitatus Act. Not surprisingly, the U.S. Commission on National Security/21st Century concluded, "[I]n many respects, the Coast Guard is a model homeland security agency given its unique blend of law enforcement, regulatory and military authorities that allow it to operate within, across and beyond U.S. borders."[135]

Unfortunately, the agency faces many problems. Many within its ranks favor its humanitarian missions, especially lifesaving, over other missions.[136] Its deep-water fleet "is a hodge-podge of old cutters and refurbished Navy ships," many designed in the 1960s or 1970s.[137] Even before 11 September 2001 it was reducing its missions because of a chronic shortage of resources. The coast guard has a history of few champions in Congress and it has seldom received aggressive leadership from its civilian executives. And, its tasks are stagger-ing. One example is illuminating. Nearly 95 percent of the goods entering the United States come by sea, yet just 2 percent of ship-borne containers are inspected. The coast guard commandant informed the U.S. Senate that inspec-tion and evaluation of "just the 50 busiest of the Nation's 361 ports would take at least a year."[138]

In months following the terrorist attacks, however, the coast guard's prob-lems seemed to have a silver lining. Years of austere budgets "created an extremely nimble, versatile force capable of shifting gears rapidly in response to the crisis du jour."[139] And, to the relief of many, it was transferred to the new

Department of Homeland Security on 25 February 2003. Its thirty-eight thousand members make it the second-largest agency in the new department and the possible recipient of funding almost unimaginable prior to 11 September 2001.

Mental health professionals know that the reactions of people to the anniversary of traumatic events are a normal part of grieving as well as a normal part of the healing and growth process that follows. So it was in the United States of America. In response to a joint resolution of Congress, President Bush proclaimed 11 September 2002, the first anniversary of the attacks, to be Patriot Day. Across the nation, flags were lowered to half-mast. At 8:46 AM, the time that the first airliner crashed into one of the World Trade Center towers, a moment of silence was observed.

Fifty-one minutes later, the time that American Airlines Flight 77 crashed into the west side of the Pentagon, another moment of silence was observed by the thirteen thousand people who had gathered at that crash site. The fire, smoke, rubble, and devastation of the previous year were gone. A remarkable rebuilding project had already been completed, prompting the chairman of the Joint Chiefs of Staff to tell the construction workers involved in the massive effort, "[Y]ou did more than repair our windows and walls; you repaired our souls."[140] The next day a single coffin bearing the unidentifiable remains of the victims of the Pentagon attack was carried by a horse-drawn caisson to Section 64 of Arlington National Cemetery.

Postscript: A Volatile Second Year

It has been said that an immemorial lesson of war is that its true aim "is the mind of the hostile rulers, not the bodies of their troops," and that "the balance between victory and defeat turns on mental impressions and only indirectly on physical blows."[1] On 11 September 2001 America received the most severe physical blow on its homeland since the 7 December 1941 attack on Pearl Harbor that resulted in the nation's entry into World War II. The emotional impact was at least as great. The 1941 attack was on a territorial possession located far from the heartland, beyond the view and personal experience of most Americans. The attacks on the nation's capital and financial center were watched on television by millions of Americans.

The subsequent response to the new, dangerous, and much different kind of war by the sovereign power of the nation, the American people, will undoubtedly be the subject of intense scrutiny by future historians. Whatever other conclusions may be reached, it is certain that the actions taken by the elected representatives over the first two years following the attack will not be faulted for lack of audacity. Nor will there be any doubt that those actions reflected the courage and will of Americans in all parts of the country.

During the second year, however, critical and often discouraging developments seemed to occur with increasing alacrity. After considerable initial success in the worldwide war on terror, America was beginning to realize that the conflict is less a contest of strategies and the material elements of military power than a contest of wills. With each piece of news about difficulties encountered and new threats to the American homeland, political and military officials scrambled to neutralize any adverse mental impressions upon the public at large, or to at least balance them with news of real progress; to explain why the war will be long; and to persuade a notoriously impatient nation that the sacrifices being made are necessary for victory.

On 11 October 2002, and after several days of solemn but spirited debate, the U.S. House of Representatives and the U.S. Senate gave overwhelming approval to a joint resolution that authorized the president to "use the armed forces of the United States as he determines to be necessary and appropriate in order to defend the national security of the United States against the continuing threat posed by Iraq and enforce all relevant United Nations Security Council Resolutions regarding Iraq." The House approved the measure by a vote of 296 to 133. The Senate voted for the resolution 77 to 23.[2] A national newspaper said that the bipartisan vote demonstrated "how dramatically the terrorist attacks on September 11, 2001, have changed U.S. foreign policy and altered views about preemptive military action to disarm hostile regimes."[3] Rep. Richard Gephardt, then the leader of House Democrats and a soon to be presidential candidate said, "The events of that tragic day jolted us to the enduring reality that terrorists not only seek to attack our interests abroad but also to strike us at home."[4] Democrat Sen. Thomas Daschle, then the Senate Majority Leader, spoke for many when he said, "I believe it is important for America to speak with one voice. It is neither a Democratic resolution nor a Republican resolution. It is now a statement of American resolve and values."[5]

In mid-October 2002, and despite his own strong reservations, the opposition of some military personnel, and the purported fear of civil libertarians,

Secretary of Defense Donald Rumsfeld authorized the use of military surveillance equipment and personnel in support of an ongoing law enforcement
effort to capture a sniper who had killed nine people and seriously wounded
two others in the greater Washington, D.C. area during the previous two
weeks. A four-engine turboprop RC-7 surveillance aircraft used for the detection of illegal drug crops in Colombia carried civilian law enforcement officers
in a search for the sniper or his getaway vehicle. The concern of civil libertarians reportedly made defense officials reluctant to offer other capabilities.[6]
There was no report of any concern about the Posse Comitatus Act by either
the families of the victims or the thousands of people who were terrorized by
the random murders.

In late October, news surfaced that the Pentagon had decided to quietly scale
back its operations against international drug trafficking, including the use of
special operations troops and intelligence-gathering equipment, because of
"[t]he changed national security environment, the corresponding shift in the
department's budget and other priorities, and other evolving support requirements."[7] The step was consistent with Rumsfeld's earlier contention that counterdrug missions assigned to the U.S. Armed Forces by law are "nonsense." He
believed that the training of foreign troops and police; the detection, monitoring, and interdiction of drug traffickers attempting to enter the United States
from foreign countries; and all related missions should be performed by civilian agencies.[8] The counterdrug missions had originally been designated a "high
priority national security mission" of the Department of Defense in 1989.[9]

Only days later, U.S. law enforcement officials announced that they had
broken up two major plots to use funds from illegal drug sales to purchase
weapons for terrorists. Attorney General John Ashcroft again asserted a "deadly
nexus between terrorism and drug trafficking."[10] Asa Hutchinson, then the chief
of the Drug Enforcement Administration, declared that "[D]rug traffickers and
terrorists work out of the same jungle; they plan in the same cave and they train
in the same desert."[11] By October 2003, U.S. military and civilian officials were
expressing strong confidence about progress against drug trafficking in

Colombia and about President Alvaro Uribe's prospects of reaching his goal of a 50 percent reduction in the Colombian coca crop by 2005.

Monday, 28 October 2002, was a gloomy, rainy day in Richmond, Virginia. Activity was brisk, however, in the large, dark-paneled courtroom on the second floor of the U.S. courthouse. Members of the media, law students from two universities, and other interested members of the public were moving to the best seats to watch the 2:00 PM oral argument before a three-judge panel of the U.S. Court of Appeals for the Fourth Circuit. If anyone present did not already understand the importance of the case, evidence soon appeared. A few minutes before the hour, a group of men walked in and took their seats either immediately behind the table or in seats reserved for the lawyers representing the government. The group included the White House counsel, the counsel to the vice president, and the general counsel of the Department of Defense.

As expected, the oral argument was vigorous. Once again, much was at stake. Once again, the thrust of the government's argument was that in inquiring into a range of specific details underlying the factual basis for the government's military judgment in wartime that Yaser Esam Hamdi was an "enemy combatant" and could thus be detained without access to legal counsel for the duration of the hostilities that led to his capture, the lower (district) court had disregarded "fundamental separation-of-powers principles." Why? Because "[i]n our constitutional system," the government insisted, "responsibility for waging war is committed to the political branches," who, unlike the judiciary, are accountable to the public.[12] The federal public defender representing Hamdi also assumed a predictable position. First, he argued, "[I]t is for the federal courts, not the Executive Branch, to decide whether Hamdi's imprisonment is consonant with the Constitution."[13] Second, he stated that the Fifth and Fourteenth Amendments to the U.S. Constitution "prohibit the Government from 'depriving' any person of liberty 'without due process of law,' both inside and outside the country."[14]

Ten weeks later, a unanimous court issued it's fifty-four-page opinion. Declaring that "[j]udicial review does not disappear during wartime" and that the "duty of the judicial branch to protect . . . individual freedoms does not simply cease whenever our military forces are committed by the political branches to armed conflict," it nevertheless directed that Hamdi's petition be dismissed.[15] "We are not here dealing with a defendant who has been indicted in the exercise of the executive's *law enforcement* powers," the court said. "We are dealing with the executive's assertion of its power to detain under the *war powers* of Article II [of the Constitution]."[16] Those powers, the court said, afford the president "extraordinarily broad authority . . . and compels courts to assume a deferential posture" in reviewing exercises of the authority.[17] "[S]eparation of powers," the court added, "takes on special significance when the nation itself comes under attack." Because the two political branches of the government have greater war-making expertise and experience and are more accountable to the people, and because it was undisputed that Hamdi was captured "in a zone of active combat in a foreign theater of conflict," no further inquiry into the government's action was necessary.[18] The balance between national security and due process of law had just been recalibrated.

On 9 July 2003, and despite the *Amici Curiae* arguments advanced by 171 law professors and interested organizations in support of Hamdi, the court ruled *en banc* that he was not entitled to a re-hearing of the issue. On 1 October 2003, Hamdi's lawyers exhausted their last procedural option by petitioning the U.S. Supreme Court for a Writ of *Certiorari.*[19]

In October 2002, a long-term plan for the war on terrorism was approved by the Bush Administration and sent to U.S. military commanders. The classified 150-page document, titled *National Military Strategic Plan for the War on Terrorism,* was more a framework of general principles and goals for the commanders than a blueprint for operations. It identified three phases of the war. In the first and current phase, the focus would be on the most dangerous threats, for example, al Qaeda and Hezbollah. In the second phase, increased pressure would be placed on countries that support terrorist activities. The pressure could involve military force as well as diplomatic, financial, and law enforcement actions. In the third phase, military authorities would address the "root causes" of international terrorism, including the economic or political conditions that foster terrorist activities, by efforts to build an antiterrorist environment in which "terrorism . . . like slave-trading, [will be] completely discredited."[20] The third phase is expected to last for decades.

Twenty-one months after the Bush Administration assumed office and thirteen months after the 11 September attacks, Congress confirmed the president's nominee to serve as assistant secretary of defense for reserve affairs. The office had not been filled by a presidential appointee for four and a half years. In November 2002 legislation authorizing a new position of assistant secretary of defense for homeland defense finally became law. Despite the importance of both reservists and special operations in the war on terrorism, however, it was reported that Rumsfeld was considering proposing legislation that would elim-inate the offices of assistant secretary of defense for reserve affairs and assistant secretary of defense for special operations and low intensity conflict.[21] When the proposed Defense Transformation for the 21st Century Act was submit-ted to Congress in April 2003, no such provision was included, but by November 2003 the special operations position had still not been filled.

In mid-term elections on 5 November 2002, Republicans recaptured control of the U.S. Senate and increased the margin of their majority in the House of Representatives by nine to 227–206. It was only the second time in almost a century and a half that the party of an incumbent president gained seats in both the Senate and the House in a first mid-term election. Analysts were divided on the most appropriate interpretation of the returns. Many concluded that the surprising results gave President Bush a political legitimacy that was missing after the heavily litigated election of 2000. There was reason to hope that the closely divided chambers of the 108th Congress, which convened in January 2003, would continue to be able to put aside partisanship for passage of legis-lation important to the nation's security. The hope was fleeting. By October 2003 external criticism of the administration's policy in Iraq and other parts of its counterterrorism strategy by ten announced Democrat candidates for president and Democrat leaders in Congress had reached campaign season strength.

After almost eight weeks of hairsplitting negotiations to meet the demands of France, Russia, and some other nations, the UN Security Council voted unanimously (15–0) on 8 November 2002 to approve Resolution 1441. The vote was a clear diplomatic victory for the United States. The resolution (1) found Iraq "in material breech" of earlier UN resolutions; (2) gave Iraq one "final opportunity" to comply; (3) authorized a tough new round of UN inspections to determine whether Iraq had acted contrary to the Security Council's direction by establishing any program for chemical, biological, or nuclear weapons or ballistic missile systems; and (4) warned Iraq that it would face "serious consequences as a result of its continued violations of its obligations." Even Syria, the only Arab representative on the council and a country that had profited from the unlawful smuggling of Iraqi oil, voted for the resolution. Two weeks after the UN vote, the nineteen members of NATO committed to "take effective action to assist and support" the UN efforts. The first UN inspectors arrived in Iraq on 25 November. Inspections began two days later.

On 7 December Iraq delivered a twelve-thousand-page declaration to the inspectors pursuant to the terms of Resolution 1441. According to Iraqi officials, it contained "currently accurate, full and complete" details of civilian "dual use" facilities and technologies that could be used to make weapons of mass destruction. It also reiterated Iraq's claim that it had no such weapons. Senator Joe Lieberman of Connecticut immediately called the document a "12,000-page, 100-pound lie."[22] In the 1990s Iraq had acknowledged its production of biological and chemical weapons, but inspectors had been unable to verify its claim that the weapons had been destroyed. It remained to be seen whether the most recent denial of the possession of such weapons, the cumulative weight of its deception efforts, a new *casus belli*, or some other factor would present a trigger for a new Gulf War. Meanwhile, the chairman of the Senate Intelligence Committee predicted that one of the ways in which Iraq would respond if attacked by UN or U.S. forces would be by initiating a series of terrorist attacks inside the United States. The day before Christmas, Rumsfeld signed a twenty-plus-page deployment order directing significant numbers of additional combat and logistics forces to the Persian Gulf.

On Veterans Day, 11 November 2002, top national security officials gathered to discuss the creation of a new domestic intelligence agency that would assume intelligence-gathering and analysis responsibilities from the FBI. Concern continued to be felt that the FBI was incapable of effectively crossing the cultural divide between a law enforcement mission of collecting evidence for criminal prosecutions, with strict restrictions on domestic spying on people who are not currently suspects, and a new mission of collecting intelligence to stop the execution of terrorist plans within the United States.[23]

Testifying before a subcommittee of the House Armed Services Committee three days later, the chairman of the Advisory Panel to Access Domestic Response Capabilities for Terrorism Involving Weapons of Mass Destruction called for a new stand-alone national counterterrorism center that would serve as an "all-source fusion and analysis center" for information on terrorist threats, whether the information was collected in the United States or abroad. Conceding that the commission had misgivings about the creation of a new domestic intelligence agency and that it might raise concern about possible infringements on the civil liberties of some Americans, the chairman of the commission, former Virginia governor James Gilmore, said the commission saw no other alternative. "You must get information to where it can do the most good and a simple color-coded warning that says we're in a high level of concern . . . just isn't enough."[24] That night, the FBI issued a warning that al Qaeda might be planning "spectacular" attacks inside the United States that met "several criteria: high symbolic value, mass casualties, severe damage to the U.S. economy and maximum psychological trauma." Nevertheless, because specific information about the time or place of any attack was lacking, the government did not elevate the national color-coded threat indicator.

In recommending the new counterterrorism center, the commission asserted that the government should end the "artificial distinction between foreign and domestic terrorist threats."[25] The challenge, Gilmore said, "is less of technology than of culture." The culture of the several government organizations must be addressed. Leadership must be applied to make them interact and work together more appropriately.[26]

On 1 May 2003 a new Terrorist Threat Integration Center (TTIC) was created. Composed of elements of the FBI, the CIA, the DoD, and the Department of Homeland Security, the joint venture was designed to provide a central location where terrorism intelligence collected both inside the United States and overseas can be fused, coordinated, and analyzed. The TTIC maintains a current database of known and suspected terrorists, which is accessible to both federal and non-federal officials. The head of the TTIC, a federal official, reports to the director of Central Intelligence. Four months later, a Terrorist Screening Center (TSC) was established to provide around-the-clock operational support to consular officers and Homeland Security and FBI agents on the nation's borders. The multi-agency center is administered by the FBI.

On 12 November 2002 the first of several subsequent audio tape recordings that intelligence officials believed contained the voice of Osama bin Laden was broadcast around the Arab world on the al-Jazeera satellite television station. It was the most credible evidence in almost a year that bin Laden was alive. The statement declared that the recent killing of a U.S. marine in Kuwait, the assassination of a U.S. diplomat in Jordan, and the bombing of a French oiler tanker near Yemen were "undertaken by the zealous sons of Islam." The statement also threatened additional terrorist attacks. On 12 February 2003 and 18 October 2003, additional audio messages purportedly made by bin Laden were broadcast on al-Jazeera. The voice in the latter threatened martyrdom (suicide) attacks "inside and outside the United States."[27]

Despite a warning by the U.S. State Department that his execution could result in retaliation against Americans around the world, on 14 November 2002 the State of Virginia executed by lethal injection Mir Aimal Kasi, a Pakistani, who had murdered two people and wounded three outside CIA headquarters in

Langley, Virginia, on 25 January 1993 in what he said was a protest of CIA activities in Muslim nations. Five days later, twenty thousand people packed a soccer stadium in Quetta, Pakistan, for funeral prayers. A Muslim cleric declared, "Aimal Kasi's martyrdom has united Muslims against the United States."

Eight days after the mid-term election in November 2002, and after strong urging by the president, the House of Representatives passed a compromise bill creating a new Department of Homeland Security. The vote was 299 to 121. On 19 November the U.S. Senate followed suit by a vote of 90 to 9. On 25 November, almost fifteen months after the attacks of 11 September 2001, President Bush signed the legislation into law.[28] The president nominated Tom Ridge to be the first secretary of the new department. In a memorandum to federal employees the following day, he declared that the protection of Americans from another terrorist attack was his "highest and most urgent priority as President."

In what portended a possible change in the nation's total force policy, Secretary of Defense Rumsfeld sent a memorandum in early November to the Pentagon comptroller and the director of the office of program analysis and evaluation directing them to identify "critical skills" now resident in the reserve forces that could be transferred to active force units. A few weeks later, he declared that it was "a shame" that large-scale operations could not be mounted without the activation of reservists, who possess many of the critical skills needed. "We intend to see," he said, "that we're no longer organized that way in the future."[29] Citing the "post-9/11 reality" that members of the reserve components will increasingly be assigned homeland-security missions, one Pentagon official declared, "[W]e need a new way to re-balance our overseas interests and our concern for homeland security."[30]

Unfortunately, there was little reason to believe that any significant restructuring of the reserve components would occur anytime soon. On 12 November the deputy secretary of defense implied that there are no flaws in the system.[31] Days later, the assistant secretary of defense for reserve affairs said that a recently completed internal review of reserve component contributions to national defense did not contain any wholesale changes.[32]

Pentagon officials continued to insist that a major restructuring of the reserve components was unnecessary. All that is needed, it was said, is a more efficient process for their use. In his March 2003 testimony before the House Armed Services Committee, David Chu, the under secretary of defense for personnel and readiness, declared that "a key element in transforming our military forces is to ensure efficiency and effectiveness in the use of our part-time reserve forces. There is a need for streamlined personnel management practices."[33] To that end, he said the administration was proposing a "continuum of service paradigm" that would permit reservists who volunteer to serve on active duty each year for more than the traditional thirty-nine days of training duty. Others could serve fewer days.

The proposal did not appear to offer any reassessment of the fundamental question of what conventional and homeland security missions should be assigned to the National Guard and reservists in light of the nation's new security requirements or what active/reserve force mix is necessary to perform those missions.[34] It was anticipated that the specifics of even such limited change would not be proposed until February 2004 and that if approved by Congress it would take the remainder of the decade to put them into effect.[35] It seemed increasingly apparent that if a major restructuring of the reserve components was to occur, it would be necessary for the changes to be recommended by a broadly based group outside of the Pentagon, perhaps a new national commission.

The Foreign Intelligence Surveillance Court of Review is a special federal appeals court created by Congress in 1978 as part of the Foreign Intelligence Surveillance Act (FISA). On 18 November 2002 the court issued a fifty-six-page ruling that the new USA Patriot Act, enacted by Congress only weeks after the 11 September terrorist attacks, removed the wall between counterintelligence and criminal investigations. Previously, government lawyers and counterintelligence agents seeking authority for the use of wiretaps to conduct searches in connection with terrorism and espionage were held to a lower standard of proof (the FISA Standards) than that required in regular criminal proceedings. They could not share with criminal prosecutors any information obtained under FISA Standards. After the USA Patriot Act became law, the Justice Department drafted regulations authorizing the sharing of information. The regulations had been struck down by a lower court that had also been created by the FISA. In reversing the lower court's decision, the Foreign Intelligence Surveillance Court of Review declared, "[W]e think procedures and government showings required under FISA, if they do not meet the minimum Fourth Amendment warrant standards [required in criminal cases], certainly come close. We therefore believe firmly . . . that FISA as amended is constitutional because the surveillances it authorizes are reasonable."[36]

Over the next several months, nearly two hundred cities and three states passed resolutions contending that the Patriot Act unreasonably infringes upon civil liberties. In response, Democrat and Republican lawmakers said that the criticism from both ends of the political spectrum was unmerited. Senator Joseph Biden called the criticism "ill-informed and overblown." Senator Dianne Feinstein declared that there is "substantial uncertainty and perhaps some ignorance about what [the Act] actually does do and how it has been employed."[37]

On 23 December 2002, after they had dismantled monitoring and surveillance equipment, North Korean officials reopened a previously sealed plutonium reprocessing plant. The provocative action was described by the International Atomic Energy Agency (IAEA), a UN entity, as a technically important step to revive a program that experts said could produce nuclear weapons within months. The following day, the North Korean defense minister threatened a "fight to the end" against the United States.[38] Days later, North Korea announced its withdrawal from the nuclear Nonproliferation Treaty and threatened to abandon a 1999 moratorium on the testing of ballistic missiles.

Concern was also increasing over a recent development in Iran, President Bush's third "axis of evil" country. A few days earlier, satellite photography had revealed that what had been believed to be a water irrigation project in the country's northern desert was in fact the construction of a facility for enriching uranium for the production of nuclear weapons. International inspectors subsequently found weapons-grade uranium at two sites in Iran. Both developments were in violation of Iran's obligations under the nuclear Nonproliferation Treaty, which it signed in 1970.

Despite fears expressed by weapons specialists and diplomats that the coincidence of al Qaeda's efforts to obtain nuclear weapons and North Korea's desperate need for hard currency could result in such weapons falling into the possession of the terrorists, the Bush administration reacted cautiously. Asserting that "different circumstances require different strategies" and that the new preemption policy was an option of last resort, it claimed that it would pursue a diplomatic option to resolve the new crisis.[39] Although defense officials expressed confidence that the United States had the military capability to wage and win two nearly simultaneous wars with Iraq and North Korea,[40] there was reason to proceed with caution. A significant portion of South Korea's forty-eight million inhabitants live in or near its capital of Seoul, which is located a relatively short distance from the border with North Korea. A great number of North Korea's long-range artillery pieces, multiple rocket launchers, and surface-to-surface missiles had long been positioned within striking distance of Seoul. Little doubt existed that in the first hours of a short-warning war, North Korea would be able to inflict major damage in the south.[41]

By the fall of 2003, the diplomatic option was being vigorously exercised. Moderating his earlier position in the hope of restarting the six-nation (China, Russia, South Korea, Japan, North Korea, United States) nuclear weapons discussions with North Korea that had taken place briefly in August, President Bush offered new ground rules during a 20 October meeting in Bangkok of the Asia Pacific Economic Cooperation Forum. So long as no formal, bilateral nonaggression treaty was involved and North Korea was taking tangible, verifiable steps to dismantle its nuclear weapons program, he said he would be willing to sign a joint guarantee not to attack the country. After initially dismissing Bush's offer as "laughable" and demonstrating once again its tendency toward provocative action by test firing a surface-to-ship missile into the waters that separate the Korean peninsula from Japan, North Korea agreed in principle to continue the six-party talks.

Meanwhile, the foreign ministers of Germany, France, and Britain flew to Iran to seek a commitment from that country that it would suspend its uranium enrichment operations and accept more stringent inspections by the IAEA in return for European assistance in developing a peaceful nuclear program for the generation of electrical power. The Bush administration signaled that it was not seeking "regime change" in Iran and that it was willing to engage in discussions with Iran about its nuclear program.

On 21 October 2003 Iranian negotiators agreed to temporarily suspend the country's enrichment work, but the length of the suspension was left open and it was not clear whether the agreement would be approved by the Iranian parliament. Only a few days later, Iran declared that despite a U.S. request to do so, it would not turn over 225 suspected members of al Qaeda in Iranian custody, nor would it share intelligence about al Qaeda operatives. It even refused to resume a dialogue until confidence-building measures were undertaken by the United States.

In May 2003 Pentagon officials issued eight-part instructions defining eighteen war crimes and eight other offenses that might be tried by military commissions against alleged terrorists. The appointments of the chief prosecutor and chief defense counsel were also announced. On 26 June Secretary of Defense Rumsfeld delegated to the deputy secretary of defense authority to appoint the members of the commissions and to decide whether there is sufficient evidence to bring particular defendants to trial. A week later President Bush granted military jurisdiction over six individuals detained at the U.S. Navy Base in Guantanamo Bay, Cuba,[42] after determining that "there is reason to believe that each of [the] enemy combatants was a member of al Qaeda or was otherwise involved in terrorism directed against the United States."[43]

In late October the chief prosecutor announced that the commencement of the first of the trials was imminent. Only a few days later, the U.S. Supreme Court issued an order with potentially historic implications by granting the petitions

for writs of *certiorari* by two of the individuals detained in Guantanamo Bay. In
doing so, the court injected itself for the first time into the debate about the role
of the federal courts in the nation's war on terrorism. Without reference to the
merits of any individual case, the court framed the issue before it as "Whether
the United States courts lack jurisdiction to consider challenges to the legality
of the detention of foreign nationals captured abroad in connection with hostilities and incarcerated at the Guantanamo Bay Naval Base, Cuba."[44]

The Supreme Court's decision to consider the threshold issue of jurisdiction surprised government lawyers. The argument of the detainees that
Guantanamo Bay is under the de facto control of the United States had been
rejected by the U.S. Court of Appeals, which had also agreed with the government that the central legal issue was governed by the Supreme Court's 1950
decision in the case of *Johnson v. Eisentrager*.[45] In that case, the court had ruled
that "nonresident" enemy aliens held by U.S. military authorities had no right
to involve the jurisdiction of the civil courts of the United States through a
petition for a writ of habeas corpus. The court had also declared, however, that
an enemy alien within the territorial jurisdiction of a U.S. civil court has qualified access to U.S. courts. It had further assumed a congressionally declared
state of war.

Speculation immediately arose as to the probable basis upon which at least
four members of the Supreme Court had voted to grant the petitions.[46] A decision by the court was expected before it adjourned for its summer 2004 recess.
Speculation also arose as to whether the court would similarly agree to review
the Hamdi case. Whatever ultimate decision might be made in the cases, one
question had apparently already been decided. On the question of the balance
between freedom and order in wartime, the Supreme Court was not going to
"speak with a muted voice."

Despite the opposition of the European Union, on 12 June 2003 the UN
Security Council approved a one-year renewal of a 2002 resolution exempting
U.S. peacekeepers from the jurisdiction of the International Criminal Court.
At the time, thirty-seven countries had entered into individual pacts with the

United States for the same purpose. On 1 July 2003 the Bush administration suspended all military assistance to thirty-five countries that refused to do so. By October seventy nations—approximately one-third of the members of the UN—had signed such a treaty.

Meanwhile—but only after the United States ordered a freeze on funding for NATO buildings in Brussels and threatened to move the alliance headquarters out of the country—the Belgian government agreed to amend its 1993 "universal jurisdiction" statute under which war crimes charges had been filed against President Bush, Britain's Prime Minister Tony Blair, Vice President Dick Cheney, Gen. Tommy Franks, and other officials. New legislation repealing the earlier law was passed by the Belgian parliament on 1 August 2003 and was upheld by the Belgian Supreme Court on 24 September.

In his State of the Union Address on 28 January 2003, President Bush noted that the United States had "called on the United Nations to . . . stand by its demand that Iraq disarm," but that "the course of this nation does not depend on the decisions of others." On 5 February Secretary of State Powell returned to the United Nations to argue that Iraq was still hiding weapons of mass destruction. On 5–6 March, France, Russia, and China announced that they would veto any new UN resolution authorizing the use of force against Iraq.[47] On 19 March the president announced that he had ordered coalition forces to commence military operations to disarm Iraq. In what Vice President Cheney called "one of the most extraordinary military campaigns ever conducted," U.S. forces entered Baghdad twenty-one days later and Saddam Hussein's regime collapsed. On 1 May President Bush declared from the deck of the USS *Abraham Lincoln* (CVN-72) that the major combat phase of the conflict was over. "The Battle of Iraq is one victory in a war on terror that began on September 11th, and still goes on."[48]

Over 125,000 U.S. forces remained in Iraq and more than 300,000 were still in the theater of operations. Declaring that the campaign demonstrated "a new American way of war," Gen. Richard Myers, the chairman of the Joint Chiefs of Staff, observed "[W]e were thoroughly inside the decision loop and capability of the regime."[49] In what he called "this new era of warfare," President Bush asserted that "we are redefining war on our terms."[50]

There was little doubt that the campaign's operational plan was designed to showcase many recently debated theories of military reformers, including Rumsfeld's. It was certain that Operation *Iraqi Freedom*, with its concepts of a "rolling start" (phased) force deployment, extensive use of special operations forces, acceptance of risk to extended and moderately secured supply lines in order to achieve speed of maneuver and advance, "shock and awe" dominance through overwhelming firepower, flexibility in execution, simultaneous air and land assaults, and broad reliance on advanced technology, were already being studied by both friends and potential adversaries of the United States.[51] It was not yet clear, however, what "transforming" principles used in the campaign would inevitably be applicable to future armed conflicts against more capable adversaries in different circumstances.[52]

It was also not clear how long U.S. forces would be required to remain in Iraq for stabilization, support, and reconstruction operations. An administration generally opposed to "nation-building" activities for military forces,[53] now faced a task described by one State Department official as "larger and more complex" than any postwar project since the rebuilding of Japan and Germany more than fifty years earlier. President Bush acknowledged that the United States faced a massive and long-term undertaking in Iraq.[54] By July 2003 criticism of the postwar effort was already becoming widespread.

In May, Sen. Richard Lugar, chairman of the Senate Foreign Relations Committee, had warned that the Bush administration's planning for the post-conflict phase in Iraq was inadequate. In July he expressed the view that the United States would be in Iraq for "at least five years" and that it was necessary for the country to "reorganize our military to be there a long time."[55] In August he said that flawed assumptions about postwar Iraq were undermining the legitimacy of the operation. There was substantial evidence to support that view.

Most of the rapidly increasing criticism centered on analytical failure involving two particular prewar assumptions. First, that Iraq's industrial base and utilities were functioning and that its oil exports would pay for much of the postwar reconstruction. In fact, Iraq's infrastructure was a basket case. Acknowledging that the post-combat phase was not going well and declaring in a televised address on 7 September that Iraq was the "central front" in the war on terrorism, the president announced that he would ask Congress for $87 billion in additional military and reconstruction funding, the largest emergency spending request since the first months of the Second World War. On 3 November Congress approved the spending package.

The second incorrect assumption was that when major combat ended, continued resistance would be minimal and of short duration and that a combination of Iraqi and allied troops and police would perform the necessary—and manpower intensive—peacekeeping, stability, and governmental operations. In fact, most Iraqi troops and policemen melted into the civilian population, and looting, violence, and sabotage rapidly increased. U.S. troops were soon receiving as many as three dozen guerrilla-style attacks each day. U.S. allies were refusing to send enough troops to form a third multinational division that could relieve U.S. troops.[56]

On 28 October 2003 the Pentagon announced that 115 American troops had been killed in combat in Iraq since the day that the president declared that the major combat phase was over, one more than the 114 who were killed during the major combat. After a visit to the country at the request of Rumsfeld, a former deputy secretary of defense under President Clinton expressed fear in a congressional hearing that the Department of Defense was attempting to manage tasks in Iraq for which it had no background and competence and that American willingness to stay the course there was eroding. A bipartisan view that media reports from Iraq were unreasonably negative and ignored the significant progress being made in many areas did not stop the White House from announcing on 6 October that it was asserting greater control over U.S. efforts in Iraq by the creation of an interagency Iraq Stabilization Group to be led by the president's national security advisor.

The strain on the armed forces, especially the army, was obvious. In July, twenty-one of the army's active combat brigades were deployed in Iraq (sixteen), Afghanistan (two), the Balkans (one), and South Korea (two). Three brigades were undergoing modernization and were not deployable. Of the remaining nine brigades that could be rotated to relieve the deployed forces, three were reserved for a possible contingency involving North Korea. The refusal of U.S. allies to send significant numbers of additional troops to the area required the Pentagon to order thousands of National Guard and Army Reserve troops to extend their tours in Iraq to a year and to make plans for the additional activation of several thousand more reservists for the replacement of troops already there. Despite bipartisan support for an increase in the size of the army and in the number of troops in Iraq and calls by key Democrats for a return to a military draft,[57] Rumsfeld fiercely resisted both increases.[58]

Instead, short-term plans were made to replace some of the heavy infantry units with lighter units that were more mobile and thus more capable of engaging rapidly and effectively in low-intensity conflict operations. Longer-term plans to *reduce* U.S. forces in Iraq from 132,000 to 105,000 by May 2004 were announced by Rumsfeld on 6 November 2003. The planned reduction hinged on two early developments, neither of which could be taken for granted. First, a significant improvement in the general security situation in Iraq, a development that could not be assumed in light of the likely effort by the insurgents to increase U.S. casualties during a presidential election year. Second, visible success in the policy of "Iraqification," i.e., the process by which sovereignty and political authority is transferred to the Iraqi people and responsibility for providing security is turned over to newly recruited and newly trained Iraqi army and Iraqi police, civil defense, guards for public facilities, border patrolmen, and other forces.[59]

If the reduction of U.S. forces in Iraq was to be achieved, it would be achieved only by increasing the number and proportional representation of National Guard and reserve troops there and by returning to the country elements of units which had already completed a deployment.[60] On 5 November the Pentagon began alerting some forty-three thousand National Guard and reserve troops, most of whom were in the Army National Guard or Army Reserve. The percentage of Guard and reserve troops in Iraq was expected to increase from 22 percent to 37 percent.

The anticipated mobilization of the additional National Guard and reserve forces was creating widespread concern about the lasting effect upon reserve recruiting and retention. The chief of the Army Reserve was candid. "Numbers tell the story," he said. "Army Reserve soldiers have been deployed 10 times in the past 12 years for operations from Bosnia to Iraq. During the 75 years before that, the Army Reserve had been mobilized just nine times. Since December 1995, we have been in a continuous state of mobilization."[61]

Even the limited goal of efficiency and effectiveness in the use of reservists was elusive. A 21 August 2003 report by the U.S. General Accounting Office concluded that one quarter of the Individual Ready Reserve (more than 300,000 troops) had not been readily available for mobilization; that it had been necessary for the secretary of defense to sign 246 deployment orders to mobilize over 280,000 reservists compared to the less than 10 deployment orders needed to mobilize 220,000 reservists during the 1991 Persian Gulf War; that some reservists had been deployed beyond the dates specified in their orders; and that others had been kept on alert for mobilization for more than a year because the DoD had "lost visibility" of them.

As the nation observed and moved past the second anniversary of the attacks on the World Trade Center and Pentagon, media reports made much of the fact that no weapons of mass destruction had yet been found in Iraq nor had any evidence that Iraq had taken steps after 1998 to produce nuclear weapons. In an interim report released in early October 2003, however, the chief U.S. weapons inspector in Iraq did say that his team had "discovered dozens of WMD-related program activities and significant amounts of equipment that Iraq concealed from the United Nations during the inspections that began in late 2002."[62]

In the minds of most Americans, the absence of actual weapons did not eliminate justification for the war against Iraq since in addition to the moral and political reasons there was undisputed evidence that Saddam Hussein had used chemical weapons in 1988 against thousands of Kurds in his own country and that he had failed to comply with UN Security Council Resolution 1441, which required him to give a complete account of his WMD program.[63] The absence of weapons did, however, raise a question of the future applicability of the new "doctrine" of preemption.

Very few seriously questioned the good faith of the president's decision to go to war in Iraq, but many were now questioning the quality of the intelligence upon which he relied. "If you're going to have a doctrine of preemption," said the senior Democrat on the Senate Intelligence Committee, "then you sure as heck better have pluperfect intelligence."[64] Leaders of the House Intelligence Committee criticized the intelligence community for issuing circumstantial and fragmentary information with too many uncertainties to come to the conclusion that Iraq possessed weapons of mass destruction. Implicitly conceding that Iraq's WMD program posed no immediate threat to the United States, the administration characterized the danger as a gathering storm and asserted that in light of Saddam's clear intentions, officials could not responsibly wait until the evidence of Iraq's possession of such weapons was undisputed.

In the continuing debate about preemption, few people seemed aware of the distinction between treating preemption as an established *doctrine*, and treating it as a policy *option* to be employed only in specific situations. Fewer still realized that it is not a new idea.[65] There was, however, growing recognition of the need to redefine when a particular danger is imminent and to develop workable criteria for national leaders to use in deciding whether to take preemptive action.[66]

Concern also existed that other nations would cite the U.S. example as justification for their own use of preemption.[67] On 7 October 2003 Israel's Prime Minister Ariel Sharon suggested to reporters that in making an attack (4–5 October) in Syria against what was described as a Palestinian terrorist training camp, Israel was adopting the American policy of preemption. On 9 October Russian President Vladimir Putin told journalists that Russia "retains the right to launch a preemptive strike, if this practice continues to be used around the world."[68]

Within days of the fall of Baghdad, the Department of Defense took two additional steps to implement its concept of defense transformation. Responding to earlier criticism, it issued its first *Transformation Planning Guidance*. In addition to stating yet another definition of transformation,[69] the document described

elements of the Pentagon's transformation strategy. The first step was to transform the culture of the Pentagon by "the promotion of individuals who lead
the way in innovation."[70] The second step was to submit to Congress a legislative package of proposed reforms. Among the provisions of the proposed
Defense Transformation for the 21st Century Act of 2003 were several that
would give the secretary of defense new authority to select and retain flag and
general officers who share his view of the department's transformation efforts,
an apparent attempt to replace current leaders with "change leaders."[71]
Unfortunately, the *Transformation Planning Guidance* did not address the many
unanswered homeland security issues.

As the nation reflected upon the two years that had passed since the attacks
in New York and Washington, it was clear that aggressive and, for the most
part, successful worldwide action had been taken by the United States in the
new and different kind of war against terror. In a September 2003 *Progress Report
on the Global War on Terrorism,* the White House expressed justifiable pride in the
facts that in Afghanistan the Taliban had been dismantled and al Qaeda denied
a safe haven; that Saddam Hussein's regime had been defeated; that cooperation in some form was being received from more than 170 nations; that the
Department of Homeland Security had been created; and that the homeland
was "markedly more secure than two years ago."

The upbeat tone of the White House report was deflated to a considerable extent, however, by the more sober tone of a document prepared by
Rumsfeld the following month. In a 16 October 2003 memorandum (titled
"Global War on Terrorism") to two of his closest civilian assistants and the
chairman and vice chairman of the Joint Chiefs of Staff, Rumsfeld asserted that
the nation was having "mixed results with al Qaeda," that "a great many remain
at large," that "we lack metrics to know if we are winning or losing the global
war on terror," and that the United States is "putting relatively little effort into
a long-range plan" to stop the next generation of terrorists.[72] Asserting further
that success would be achieved in Afghanistan and Iraq only after "a long, hard
slog" and that because the DoD has been organized, trained, and equipped to

fight large armies, navies, and air forces it is "not possible to change DoD fast enough to successfully fight the global war on terror," Rumsfeld asked: "Does DoD need to think through new ways to organize, train, equip and focus to deal with the global war on terror?"[73]

Contemporary national surveys were finding that a large majority of Americans were still "concerned or very concerned" about another terrorist attack. It was undisputed that major problems remained, both abroad and at home. In Afghanistan, resurgent Taliban forces were threatening intensified attacks on U.S. and Afghan forces. The occupation and reconstruction of Iraq was proving to be far more complex, dangerous, and expensive than originally anticipated. Al Qaeda cells were working with Saddam Hussein loyalists to make that country the primary target of the jihad cause. It had well-established ties to Iran and it remained a resilient and deadly organization which threatened American interests abroad and maintained an extensive presence in the United States. Within an "arc of instability" in the Islamic world running from Morocco to Indonesia, the danger appeared to be growing. Army Gen. John Abizaid, who had relieved Gen. Tommy Franks as the commander of the U.S. Central Command, informed Congress that "the enemy's ideological base, financial networks and information networks remain strong." "Indeed," he said, "the demographic and economic conditions that breed terrorists may be worsening. And those conditions are heightening the ideological fervor associated with radical Islamic extremism."[74]

At home, major effort had been devoted to the preparation and adoption of broad new homeland security goals, strategies, legislation, and policies, but a June 2003 study by a distinguished Independent Task Force on Emergency Responders concluded that the United States remained dangerously unprepared to deal with a catastrophic attack on American soil.[75] In October the Department of Homeland Security released its initial National Response Plan, but an internal government report released the same month cast serious doubt about the nation's emergency-response capabilities. In evaluating the results of a five-day, $16 million simulated terrorist attack exercise, the largest ever organized, the report said the U.S. response system was weakened by an inability to share vital intelligence information and by confusion about command, control, and the division of responsibilities.[76]

The new Department of Homeland Security was encountering serious problems. One report said that the department was "hobbled by money woes, disorganization, turf battles and unsteady support from the White House."[77] Clearly, much additional work remained to clarify homeland security missions and to establish priorities. In a report prepared only a few months earlier, the GAO had concluded that "[M]uch of the implementation and mechanisms for achieving . . . goals have not been developed, such as establishing meaningful performance measures and clear roles and responsibilities." A results-oriented approach was still needed "to ensure [homeland security] mission accountability and sustainability over time."[78]

In 2002 Congress had agreed. The FY 2003 Defense Authorization Act, which was not signed into law until November 2002, had directed the secretary of defense to submit to Congress a detailed report containing such matters as the DoD's "definition of its homeland security mission, particularly with respect to how it relates to providing military support to civil authorities"; the relationship of the combatant commands, other federal departments and agencies, state and local governments, and the National Guard and federal reserve components "with regard to homeland security"; the "current capability of the Armed Forces to respond" to terrorist attacks employing weapons of mass destruction; discussion of plans "to place new emphasis on the unique operational demands associated with homeland security while ensuring that defense of the United States remains the primary mission of the Department of Defense"; and the "legal impediments to implementing" those activities.[79]

A few weeks later, defense officials had asked the Defense Science Board to form a special task force for a 2003 summer study of these and related issues.[80] The charge to the board summarized the importance of the relationship between homeland security and the Department of Defense: "the DoD has access to many of the systems engineering, technical capabilities, relevant technologies, logistics expertise, and modeling and simulation capabilities needed for effective homeland security. Defense forces are also critically dependent upon various infrastructures operated by DoD or provided by commercial sources and civil utilities to support its force projection war-fighting mission and also provide force protection to forces stationed within the homeland."[81]

In October 2003 the final report of the Science Board's study was completed and a recommendation of the board's task force, which conducted the study, made public. One recommendation received particular attention. Noting that the responsibilities of the Department of Homeland Security and the Department of Defense overlap, and that the DoD goal of deterring, preempting, and preventing terrorist attacks by taking the fight to the sanctuaries of the terrorists should remain a priority, the task force was nevertheless blunt. The secretary of defense "must," it said, give the same emphasis and attention to the countering of transnational threats as is given to major military conflicts. Moreover, the core competencies of the DoD, including its experience in integrating military and civilian efforts for joint warfighting, in operational planning, in training and exercising, in experimentation, and in applying systems analysis techniques should be leveraged and exported to other federal, state, and local agencies. A robust capability to "surge" medical treatment in support of civil authorities was considered necessary, as was an improvement in the coordination between civil authorities and National Guard and other military units located in each state. And, the task force continued, the U.S. Northern Command should be given new authority, specific responsibilities (for example, the operational lead for the protection of the DoD's critical infrastructure and responsibility to develop both an integrated plan for maritime surveillance and a master plan for defense against low altitude air threats), and additional resources.

At what was called a Pentagon Town Meeting in November 2002, a questioner from an audience of Pentagon employees asked about the military's role in homeland security. Rumsfeld asked Gen. Peter Pace, USMC, the vice chairman of the Joint Chiefs of Staff, to answer the question. Pace suggested that the armed forces could fulfill short-term capability gaps until the nation is able to fill the gaps through local law enforcement, but that where the military has a unique capability, it might continue to provide it over the long term.

Rumsfeld followed up Pace's answer by saying that he agreed. His lack of enthusiasm for the homeland security mission, however, was apparent from his subsequent comment, which included nothing about unique capabilities or long-term commitments. "[I]f we're asked to do an *emergency* assignment, like the airports when there's no other capability, . . . it ought to be for a *short* period of time. We ought to get in, do it, and get out, and get back to doing *military* assignments and not essentially *civilian* functions."[82] Additional evidence of his belief that the armed forces should limit their contribution to homeland security to the prosecution of the war on terrorism in foreign lands was his comment at another town hall meeting in March 2003. "We have generally felt," he said, "that the task of defending America was best performed *forward*, by preventing things from threatening our country. It is understandable that some people would look and say 'Well, my goodness, if we have threats right here, shouldn't we keep forces right here to protect against those threats?' and I guess the answer to that is, Isn't it better to deal with those threats elsewhere?"[83]

Therein lies the future challenge. The president has declared that the war against terrorism "is a global enterprise of uncertain duration," and that we will work to defend "the United States, the American people, . . . by identifying and destroying the threat before it reaches our borders."[84] It is undisputed that the prosecution of the war overseas has required the deployment of U.S. forces at an extraordinary pace, a pace that cannot long be sustained. One analyst concluded that a "crisis-ethos" has emerged from the war on terrorism. A "professional military force of limited manpower is being asked to fulfill a national strategic requirement of no less than total world security management—open-ended in terms of historical time, and proactive in terms of combat initiation."[85] In such circumstances, it is imperative that we continuously reassess our worldwide military responsibilities and that we not assign domestic tasks to military personnel, if the tasks can possibly be performed by the civilian institutions of government.

But, the president has also said, "The U.S. government has no more important mission than protecting the homeland from future terrorist attacks."[86] This mission will continue to require major efforts at home, as well as overseas. In addition to the prevention of terrorist attacks, both the *National Security Strategy* and the *National Strategy for Homeland Security* declare the critical importance of consequence management, that is, the minimization of damage and recovery from "attacks that do occur." The objective of emphasizing consequence management is not merely the obvious need to minimize casualties after an attack. It is part of the concentrated effort to *deter* those who possess weapons of mass destruction and to sway those who seek to acquire them by persuading enemies that they cannot attain their desired ends.[87]

It is not sufficient to focus the often unique expertise, experience, and resources of the U.S. Armed Forces solely on the preemption or interdiction of terrorist threats before they reach U.S. shores. Forward defense is an important element of homeland security, but it is only one of the elements. The DoD distinction between homeland "defense" and homeland "security" complicates the problem. Terrorism does not start or stop at our international borders. It is not possible to create a perfect protective envelope around such a large and vibrant nation. It is no more possible to absolutely prevent all terrorist attacks at home than it is to absolutely close our borders to the transit of illegal drugs.

In this new and different kind of war, the traditional line between military and civilian functions is, like the line between foreign and domestic threats, becoming less distinguishable, not because of our preferences, but because of the very nature of the war. The balance between the DoD mission of forward defense and its responsibility to provide critical support at home before and after a terrorism-caused crisis must, therefore, be recalibrated. Effective prevention of additional attacks will depend upon actions taken at home, as well as overseas. Moreover, depending upon the circumstances, it is highly likely, if not certain, that after another major attack, state and local jurisdictions would be overwhelmed. Substantial military assistance in a variety of forms would be needed immediately. The hard decisions to prepare for that possibility must not be postponed.

The U.S. Northern Command currently has few forces permanently assigned to it. Additional military units with specific skills must be dedicated to specific homeland security missions at home. A badly needed realignment of the force structure and the active/reserve force mix must be made. Consistent with the principle that military units fight as they train, the military units assigned homeland security responsibilities must train and exercise with civil authorities at all levels of government. State and local officials need predictability, so they should be given clear information on what military support can and cannot be given in the event of a future attack.

A transformation of the thinking of defense leaders about the homeland security mission is no less urgent than the other aspects of transformation within the Department of Defense. Instead of responding only to direction from the White House, legislative mandates by Congress, or reluctantly to pleas from the Department of Homeland Security, other civil agencies, or state or local officials, defense leaders must actively search for ways in which the unique experience and resources of the armed forces can contribute both to the prevention of additional terrorist attacks at home and the preparation of the nation for the consequences of such attacks.[88]

Budgetary and other resource implications, will, of course, always be important. But, if the new missions require additional resources, the case must be made to the American people for additional resources, whatever the political consequences. If the Pentagon and Congress are in disagreement about whether the source of the new resources should be the closure of unneeded military bases, the cancellation of major weapons systems, the transfer of certain responsibilities from military to civilian personnel, or additional appropriations, the tough choices must be made—and soon. If we do anything less, future historians will wonder in amazement how leaders of the world's wealthiest and most productive nation focused more on temporary budgetary dislocations than on the security of its people.

It has been observed that only twice in U.S. history has the nation fought a global war. The first was World War II, which ranged across six continents. The second is the current war on terrorism.[89] The first year after the United States entered World War II is considered "a pivotal point" in our history.[90] Future Americans are almost certain to say the same thing about the two years that followed the

11 September 2001 attacks. A nation which has long sought to avoid unnecessary foreign entanglements and which fosters a political culture more akin to the mindset of a sprinter than a marathon runner; an administration which came to power with a narrow view of national self-interest and asserting that the use of "the American Armed Forces as the world's '911' will degrade capabilities, bog soldiers down in peacekeeping roles, and fuel concern among other great powers;" the international envy and resentment resulting from the often moralistic tone of U.S. foreign policy and some U.S. foreign policy spokesmen; and the fact that the U.S. is the only remaining superpower—these factors and others have suddenly become secondary to the new reality. For many days to come, the United States of America will be engaged in a war of a different kind, a war against the threat of terrorism, especially the threat of weapons of mass destruction in the hands of terrorists or rogue states.

This new war will require us to think and plan differently. Whatever imperatives existed prior to 11 September 2001 to structure, resource, and use our armed forces in new ways, in ways that protect us from new dangers, are even greater now. We must now stand sentry duty against terrorism at home, as well as overseas. We will need to continually reassess our strategies for fighting the new war, the tasks assigned to the armed forces and the resources given to them, the use of our part-time citizen warriors, and the balance between measures taken for purposes of security and any adverse impact upon our freedom.

The new war will also test our collective resolve, i.e., the minds of the nation's rulers. We have rediscovered the wisdom of Thucydides. War is indeed a stern teacher. In the fall of 2003, public opinion surveys reflected eroding support for the U.S. effort in Iraq.[91] More ominous for the president were polls showing that while a majority of the public still believed that the conflict in Iraq is part of the war on terrorism, only 14 percent agreed with his view that it is the central front of the war. The director of a non-partisan research center said that most Americans believed the "central front" in the war is at home.[92]

Analogies to the war in Vietnam were being made by the antiwar left and many Europeans even though the factual basis for such analogies was essentially nonexistent.[93] After weeks of increasingly sophisticated attacks on innocents and U.S. military personnel alike in the "Sunni Triangle" north and west of Baghdad,[94] the administration took steps to improve military intelligence in the area and to increase the pace of "Iraqification."[95]

Meanwhile, the pressures of time in an election year were being felt. The commander of U.S. forces in Iraq declared that the recent increase in violence there was "not a battle per se . . . because there is no military contest." Rather, he said, "The goal of the enemy is to break the will of the United States of America."[96] A leading newspaper observed that the Saddam loyalists and foreign terrorists behind the insurgent attacks "know they do not have to win in Iraq; they merely have to prevail in Washington."[97] Sen. John McCain asserted that "The time window is three to six months in which we have to succeed."[98] The sounds were familiar. American veterans of Vietnam remembered well that the United States ultimately withdrew from that country because of the psychological effect of the war on the home front, despite an almost unbroken series of victories in the major military engagements there.

It remained to be seen whether the effect upon Americans of the tragedies of 11 September 2001 would make the circumstances of the U.S. effort to stabilize and reconstruct Iraq different from those encountered in Vietnam and whether President Bush and future presidents could fortify the national will for a long, difficult struggle in the broader war on terror. The president's position on Iraq was as unequivocal as his position in the broader conflict. In a Rose Garden news conference on 28 October 2003, he said simply, "We're not leaving."[99] On the eve of a visit to Great Britain, where he was expected to encounter antiwar demonstrations, he expressed both understanding and determination. "I can understand people not liking war . . . . I don't like war. War is the last choice a president should make. . . . And, yet, we are at war. That's what September the 11th taught us. It's a different kind of war. And I intend to, as long as I'm the President, wage that war vigorously to protect the American people."[100]

There was reason to believe, however, that the president's determination was not the key variable in the public's tolerance of the conflict in Iraq. A new study of public opinion concluded that the main factor was the perception of the likelihood of "victory." To that end, one of the authors of the study recommended that the president develop convincing measures of success there and "worry less about persuading the American people he really did the right thing, and more about ensuring that the mission is going to be successful—and persuading the American people of that."[101]

The president's leadership in Iraq and in the broader war was increasingly being viewed as a central issue in the 2004 presidential election. British Prime Minister Tony Blair, the leader of a left-of-center Labor Party who was facing his own political difficulties because of his support of a conservative American president, noted the paradox of the situation. "The oddest thing about the past couple of years since September 11," he said, is that "it is completely muddled up, left and right, in the political spectrum." But, he said, "There is a real, serious, fundamental type of security threat that we face, it is of a different nature . . . [and] it has to be tackled in a different way."[102]

The stakes in both the long term and short term were high. Declaring that the establishment of a new Iraqi government by free elections could take as long as two years, former secretary of state Henry Kissinger worried that "If the American occupation were to wind down into a radicalized or fundamentalist Iraq, what is now a conflict with a segment of Islam could turn into a clash of civilizations."[103] Failure was universally considered by western nations to be unacceptable. Even the French foreign minister, who had strongly opposed U.S. plans to attack Iraq, said that an early U.S. withdrawal "would be catastrophic."[104]

We were unprepared. We took up our new responsibilities with courage, but at times "in clumsy and imperfect fashion."[105] Even in the time of crisis, petty partisanship intruded. Decisions which would have established priorities and given the armed forces and civilian agencies at various levels of government the tools to do the many jobs asked of them were often avoided or postponed. Still, we emerged from the devastation of 11 September 2001 with a plan of action, strong presidential leadership, and a sober understanding of the dangers our nation faces, both at home and around the world. The president called it "a new condition of life." So be it. He also said that we will adjust to it and thrive. So we will. So we must.

Our defense forces in the new war, which has no front lines, will now include firefighters, local police officers, mayors, intelligence analysts, public health and local emergency personnel, and many others. But, the primary custodians of our security in the worldwide war on terrorism and against other threats will continue to be the volunteer men and women in military uniform. On several occasions since 11 September 2001 it has been noted that "the element of shared sacrifice that should be expected in a nation at war is missing,"[106] and that decades have passed since the United States has had a draft, which would make the U.S. Armed Forces reflective of society at large. Those who serve in military uniform today—whether they are active or reserve, and whether they serve overseas or at home to defend us from terrorism—are volunteers. When Congress authorized the use of force in Iraq, not a single one of the 435 members of the House of Representatives and only one of 100 senators had a son or daughter serving in the enlisted ranks of the U.S. Armed Forces. Only three members of the House had children who were officers.[107] Americans in uniform know that few of their fellow countrymen are aware of or understand the extent of the sacrifices that they and their families make daily to ensure our nation's security. Yet, they still volunteer to serve.

The author of this book does not have to look far to see an example of this kind of courage and selfless patriotism. My oldest daughter, the mother of three small children, is a lieutenant commander in the Naval Reserve. Her Naval Academy classmate and husband routinely assumes the entire parental yoke when she is training away from home. The husband of my youngest daughter is an information technology manager. As the year 2003 opened, he was engaged in the work of his regular job, completing a master's degree, and waiting for his promotion to staff sergeant in the Marine Corps Reserve. Already the parents of a three year old and a two year old, he and my daughter were anxiously looking forward to the birth of their third child a few weeks later. Upon short notice on 10 January 2003, their fifth wedding anniversary and only thirty days prior to the date of the anticipated birth, he was mobilized for immediate deployment to the Persian Gulf. Ten weeks later, he was part of the Second Marine Expeditionary Brigade that was engaged in fierce fighting near An Nasiryah, Iraq.

On the walls of the Pentagon's several miles of corridors, the service of America's armed forces in the nation's previous wars are illustrated by a great variety of paintings, photographs, and static displays. For me, the one that best expresses the courage and sacrifices of the volunteer men and women in U.S. military uniform, whether the danger is old and predictable, or new and of a different kind, is a very large painting that dominates the staircase wall directly across from the Office of the Secretary of Defense. The painting depicts a military family at prayer. Below the painting is a short inscription from Isaiah 6:8:

Whom shall I send and whom will go for us? . . .
    Here am I: Send Me.

Notes

Preface

1. Rick Atkinson, *Crusade* (Boston: Houghton Mifflin Company, 1993), 492.

2. Mary Jordan, "800,000 Jam D.C. for Tribute to Troops," *Washington Post*, 9 June 1991, A28; E. J. Dionne Jr., "In Victory, Battle Turns to Parades' Meaning," *Washington Post*, 9 June 1991, A29.

3. Will Durant and Ariel Durant, *The Lessons of History* (New York: Simon and Schuster, 1968), 81; Frederick W. Kagan, "Strategy and Force Structure in an Interwar Period," *Joint Forces Quarterly* (spring/summer 2001): 94.

4. Kagan, "Strategy and Force Structure."

5. Francis Fukuyama, "The End of History?" *National Interest* 16 (summer 1989): 3–18.

6. John Keegan, *War and Our World* (New York: Vintage Books, 2001), 1, 64.

7. John Adams, Letter to Abigail Adams from Paris, 1780, quoted in David McCullough, *John Adams* (New York: Simon and Schuster, 2001), 236–37.

8. Winston S. Churchill, *The World Crisis* (London: Odhams Press Limited, 1938), 33.

9. Robert D. Kaplan, *Warrior Politics* (New York: Random House, 2002), 14–15.

10. George W. Bush, State of the Union Address, *Weekly Compilation of Presidential Documents* 38, 5 (29 January 2002): 133.

11. In his seminal book *Strategy*, B. H. Liddell Hart distinguished between "the sphere of *policy*, or the higher conduct of war, which must necessarily be the responsibility of the government and not of the military leaders it employs as its agents in the

executive control of operations," and *strategy*, which he defined as "the art of distributing and applying military means to fulfill the ends of policy." B. H. Liddell
Hart, *Strategy*, 2d rev. ed. (New York: Meridian, 1991), 319–21. War policy and strategy are, of course, intimately connected.

12. Winston S. Churchill, *The Gathering Storm* (Norwalk, Conn.: Easton Press, 1989), 410.

Chapter 1. The Unthinkable

1. Johanna McGeary, "Odd Man Out," *Time*, 10 September 2001, 24.

2. Condoleezza Rice, "Promoting the National Interest," *Foreign Affairs* (January/
February 2000): 51.

3. Ibid., 47.

4. Eliot A. Cohen, "Defending America in the Twenty-First Century," *Foreign Affairs*
(November/December 2000): 41 (emphasis added).

5. Senator Pat Roberts and Senator Max Cleland, "Seven Principles for Shaping a New
National Strategy," *Armed Forces International* (January 2001): 12.

6. Gen. Anthony C. Zinni, "A Commander's Reflects," *U.S. Naval Institute Proceedings*
(July 2000): 34.

7. George Bush, *National Security Strategy of the United States* (Washington, D.C.: White
House, March 1990), v.

8. Ibid.

9. The debate, its implications, and its results are far too complex to discuss here. It is
fair to say, however, that it pitted senior Pentagon officials, who were skeptical of
the capabilities of certain National Guard and reserve units and who wanted to
reduce the reserve components' portion of the total force mix, against senior members of Congress, most of whom were supportive of National Guard and reserve
forces. For a broader discussion of the 1990 force structure/force mix debate, see
Stephen M. Duncan, *Citizen Warriors: America's National Guard and Reserve Forces and the
Politics of National Security* (Novato, Calif.: Presidio Press, 1997).

10. Ibid., 162–63.

11. The base force was subsequently defined as the mix of forces necessary to execute
President Bush's new military strategy. See Lorna S. Jaffe, *The Development of the Base
Force, 1989–1992* (Washington, D.C.: Joint History Office, Office of the Chairman
of the Joint Chiefs of Staff, July 1993).

12. Les Aspin, Secretary of Defense, *Annual Report to the President and the Congress*
(Washington, D.C.: U.S. Department of Defense, January 1994), 2–3.

13. Ibid., 5.

14. Ibid. The most likely adversaries in planning scenarios for the two regional conflicts
were Iraq and North Korea.

15. The Clinton administration's actual defense budget for fiscal year 1995 and the fiscal years 1995–99 defense program called for only 331 ships by 1999.

16. Aspin, Secretary of Defense, *Annual Report to the President*, 27.

17. Eliot A. Cohen, "Defending America in the Twenty-First Century," 42.

18. *National Defense Authorization Act for Fiscal Year 1997*, 104th Cong, 2d sess., H.R. 3230, sec. 922.

19. The examination was to be of the defense strategy, force structure, force modernization plans, infrastructure, budget plan, and other elements of the defense program and policies with a view toward determining and expressing the defense strategy of the United States and establishing a revised defense program through the year 2005.

20. William S. Cohen, Secretary of Defense, *Report of the Quadrennial Defense Review* (Washington, D.C.: U.S. Department of Defense, May 1997), iv.

21. Ibid., v, 7.

22. A former commander of the Marine Corps Combat Development Command would later observe that in recent years, various terms have been used to describe ways to improve U.S. forces. "In the 1980s, the favorite expression was the 'military reform movement.' After Operation Desert Storm, 'military technical revolution' came into fashion, followed shortly by 'revolution in military affairs.'" Paul K. Van Riper, "Preparing for War Takes Study and Open Debate," *U.S. Naval Institute Proceedings* (November 2002): 2.

23. Douglas A. Macgregor, "Resurrecting Transformation for the Post-Industrial Era," *Defense Horizons*, (Center for Technology and National Security Policy of the National Defense University) (September 2001).

24. David L. Grange, "Transforming Isn't Chanting Slogans," *U.S. Naval Institute Proceedings* (August 2002): 2.

25. Adm. Jay Johnson, Address at the U.S. Naval Institute Annapolis Seminar and 123d Annual Meeting, Annapolis, Md., 23 April 1997.

26. Vice Adm. Arthur K. Cebrowski, "Network-Centric Warfare Its Origin and Future," *U.S. Naval Institute Proceedings* (January 1998): 32. *Speed of command* has been defined as "the process by which a superior information altering of initial conditions, the development of high rates of change, and locking in success while locking out alternative enemy strategies. It recognizes all elements of the operating situation as parts of a complex adaptive ecosystem and achieves profound effect through the impact of closely coupled events." Ibid., 35. *Self-synchronization* has been defined as "the ability of a well-informed [military] force to organize and synchronize complex warfare activities from the bottom up. The organizing principles are unity of effort, clearly articulated commander's intent, and carefully crafted rules of engagement.

Self-Synchronization is enabled by a high-level of knowledge of one's own forces, enemy forces, and all appropriate elements of the operating environment. It overcomes the loss of combat power inherent in top-down command directed synchronization characteristic of more conventional doctrine and converts combat from a step function to a high-speed continuum." Ibid.

27. National Defense Panel, "Transforming Defense: National Security in the 21st Century," *Report of the National Defense Panel* (Arlington, Va.: National Defense Panel, December 1997), ii (emphasis added).

28. Ibid. (emphasis added).

29. Ibid., 11.

30. Ibid.

31. Ibid., 28.

32. Sun-Tzu, Sun Pin, *The Complete Art of War*, translated by Ralph D. Sawyer (Boulder, Colo.: Westview Press, Inc., 1996), 131–32.

33. Donald Kagan, *The Peloponnesian War* (New York: Penguin Group, 2003), 59. Victor Davis Hanson, another respected scholar, has also put the concept of asymmetric warfare in perspective. "The Greeks would tell us that war is like water, and the method that manifests itself is just the pump. And the pumps change, but the water does not. We need to realize that, because we're hearing a lot of cacophony about fourth-generational warfare, asymmetric warfare, postmodern warfare, and postheroic warfare, almost every element of the war on terror we are experiencing now has been seen before. Fred L. Schultz, "Interview: Victor Davis Hanson," *U.S. Naval Institute Proceedings* (March 2003) 98.

34. Karl von Clausewitz, *On War*, edited and translated by Michael Howard and Peter Paret (Norwalk, Conn.: Easton Press, 1991), 198.

35. Hart, *Strategy*, 147.

36. James Pringle, "Viet Victor Casts Self as 'General of Peace,'" *Washington Times*, 20 June 1991, 1.

37. Howard R. Simpson, "A Conversation with General Giap," *Army* (September 1991): 46.

38. See Robert Coram, *Boyd: The Fighter Pilot Who Changed the Art of War* (Boston: Little, Brown and Company, 2002), 328.

39. Ibid., 333–34. The idea is to operate within what Boyd called the Observe-Orient-Decide-Act cycle, or "OODA Loop," a way of getting *inside* the mind and the decision cycle of an adversary. The objective is to compress the time between observing a situation and taking action and then "to select the *least-expected* action rather than what is predicted to be the *most-effective* action" to cause the enemy "to unravel

before the fight." In more recent years, a growing body of research suggests that not only the quickest, but also the most brilliant decisions in complex situations like the battlefield, tend to be instinctive, less dependent upon rational analysis than upon imperfectly informed gut feelings. See, e.g., Thomas A. Stewart, "Think with Your Gut," *Business* 2.0 (November 2002): 99.

40. Coram, *Boyd: Fighter Pilot,* 332, 336.

41. The term and concept found their genesis in an October 1989 article in *Marine Corps Gazette* that addressed the future of warfare. The authors postulated that first-generation warfare was characterized by the close-order formations of line and column in the age of Napoleon. Second-generation warfare took advantage of improvements in firepower to defeat an enemy through attrition. Examples would be the Prussian army, the British and French in World War I, and even U.S. forces in Vietnam where "body count" became a measure of success. Third-generation warfare was seen as a response to increased firepower and was defined by a renewed emphasis on maneuver and creative, decentralized attacks. The German *blitzkrieg* of World War II might be an example. The authors argued that fourth-generation warfare will involve small, highly maneuverable, independent units that do not rely on logistical or other lines of communication; the units will seek to achieve psychological goals, at least as much as physical ones. See William S. Lind, Col. Keith Nightingdale, USA, Capt. John F. Schmitt, USMC, Col. Joseph W. Sutton, USA, and Lt. Col. Gary I. Wilson, USMCR, "The Changing Face of War: Into the Fourth Generation," *Marine Corps Gazette* (October 1989): 22–26.

42. Jason Vest, "Fourth-Generation Warfare," *Atlantic Monthly,* December 2001.

43. Harold A. Gould and Franklin C. Spinney, "Fourth-Generation Warfare Is Here," *Defense Week* (15 October 2001).

44. William S. Cohen, Secretary of Defense, *Report of the Quadrennial Defense Review,* iii.

45. Andrew F. Krepinevich Jr., "Why No Transformation," *Joint Forces Quarterly* (autumn/winter 1999–2000): 101.

46. Ibid.

47. Hans Binnendijk, ed., "Introduction," *Transforming America's Military* (Washington, D.C.: National Defense University Press, 2002), xix.

48. "Rumsfeld Returns to the Fray," MSNBC News, 28 December 2000.

49. Ibid.

50. Frank Carlucci, Robert Hunter, and Zalmay Khalilzad, "A Global Agenda for the U.S. President," *RAND Review* (spring 2001).

51. G. John Ikenberry, quoted in Kurt M. Cambell, "The Last Superpower Ponders Its Next Move," *New York Times,* 10 February 2001, A15. After exploring "just how

dominant the United States is today" in military, economic, and technological power, two other scholars concluded that "what truly distinguishes the current international system is American dominance in all of them simultaneously" and "the United States has no rival in any critical dimension of power." Stephen G. Brooks and William C. Wohlforth, "American Primacy in Perspective," *Foreign Affairs* (July/August 2002): 20–33.

52. Jeffrey W. Legro, quoted in Kurt M. Cambell, "The Last Superpower Ponders Its Next Move," *New York Times*, 10 February 2001, A15.

53. Russ Bennett, "Service's Business Mind-Set Overshadows Navy's Purpose," *Navy Times* (29 January 2001): 54.

54. Ibid.

55. George C. Wilson, "CEO Rumsfeld and His Pentagon, Inc.," *National Journal* (17 March 2001): 812.

56. Donald H. Rumsfeld, Secretary of Defense, Remarks at the Pentagon, Washington, D.C., 10 September 2001.

57. David S. Broder, "A Challenge to Lead," *Washington Post*, 21 January 2001, B7.

58. Vince Crawley, "Bracing for Change: Rumsfeld Promises Sweeping Reviews," *Army Times* (22 January 2001): 8.

59. James Dao and Steven Lee Myers, "Bush Warning on Military Spending Challenges Pentagon," *New York Times*, 5 February 2001, 1.

60. Ibid.

61. Joshua L. Weinstein, "Navy Vision Vital," *Kennebec Journal* (Maine), 6 February 2001, A1.

62. John Dillin, "Pentagon Braces for a Makeover," *Christian Science Monitor*, 12 February 2001, 1.

63. Richard J. Newman, "Tough Choices," *U.S. News and World Report*, 26 February 2001, 18.

64. Thomas E. Ricks, "Pentagon Study May Bring Big Shake-Up," *Washington Post*, 9 February 2001, A1.

65. Bob Woodward, *Bush at War* (New York: Simon and Schuster, 2002), 23.

66. "Dearth of Access to Rumsfeld Review Prompts Misinformation Flurry," *Inside the Pentagon* (1 March 2001); William M. Arkin, "Rumsfeld Stumbles," Washingtonpost.com, 26 March 2001.

67. James Kitfield, "A Small Study Carries a Heavy Burden," *National Journal* (3 March 2001): 644.

68. Ibid.

69. Ibid.

70. Arkin, "Rumsfeld Stumbles."

71. See, for example, Kenneth F. McKenzie Jr., "The Rise of Asymmetric Threats: Priorities for Defense Planning," QDR 2001: Strategy-Driven Choices for America's Security (Washington, D.C.: National Defense University Press, 2001), 75.

72. Commission to Assess the Ballistic Missile Threat to the United States, Executive Summary of the Report of the Commission to Assess the Ballistic Missile Threat to the United States (Washington, D.C.: Commission to Assess the Ballistic Missile Threat to the United States, July 1998), 1.

73. Jean-Michel Stoullig, "Rumsfeld Commission Warns against 'Space Pearl Harbor,'" Space Daily, 11 January 2001.

74. Vice Adm. Thomas R. Wilson, Statement for the Record, Hearing before the Armed Services Committee, United States Senate, 107th Cong., 2d sess., 19 March 2002.

75. Woodward, Bush at War, 318.

76. Barton Gellman, "A Strategy's Cautious Evolution: Before Sept. 11, the Bush Anti-Terror Effort Was Mostly Ambition," Washington Post, 20 January 2002, A1.

77. Daniel Benjamin and Steven Simon, The Age of Sacred Terror (New York: Random House, 2002), 343.

78. Ibid.

79. Alfred Goldberg, The Pentagon: The Fifty Years (Washington, D.C.: Historical Office, Office of the Secretary of Defense, 1992), 1.

Chapter 2. Locust Years

1. Caspar Weinberger, Fighting for Peace (New York: Warner Books, 1990), 21.

2. Caleb Carr, The Lessons of Terror (New York: Random House, 2002), 17. The FBI definition of terrorism is "the unlawful use of force or violence against persons or property to intimidate or coerce a government, the civilian population, or any segment thereof, in furtherance of political or social objectives." The State Department and the Department of Defense have slightly different definitions. More than one hundred possible definitions have been authored. See Walter Lacqueur, The New Terrorism: Fanaticism and the Arms of Mass Destruction (London: Phoenix Press, 2001), 5. Following the widely shared Mideastern concept that "one man's terrorist is another man's freedom fighter," another student of the definition issue has concluded that "Like beauty, . . . terrorism is in the eye of the beholder." Grenville Byford, "The Wrong War," Foreign Affairs (July/August 2002): 34.

3. Ian O. Lesser, Bruce Hoffman, John Arquilla, David Ronfeldt, and Michele Zanini, Countering the New Terrorism (Santa Monica, Calif.: RAND, 1999), iii.

4. George Schultz, Turmoil and Triumph (New York: Charles Scribner's Sons, 1993), 647 (emphasis added).

5. William Snyder and James Brown, eds., Defense Policy in the Reagan Administration (Washington, D.C.: National Defense University Press, 1988), 116.

6. George Schultz, *Turmoil and Triumph*, 647.

7. Ronald Reagan, Address to the Nation on the U.S. Air Strike in Libya, *Weekly Compilation of Presidential Documents* 22, 16 (14 April 1986): 491.

8. George Bush, *National Security Strategy of the United States* (Washington, D.C.: White House, August 1991), 3.

9. David C. Hendrickson, "The Recovery of Internationalism," *Foreign Affairs* (September/October 1994): 26–27.

10. Ibid.

11. A University of Georgia political scientist appointed by Clinton in 1994 to serve on an intelligence commission later reported that the president had paid little attention to either the commission or its final report. See Susan Page, "Why Clinton Failed to Stop Bin Laden," *USA Today*, 12 November 2001, A.01.

12. Ibid.

13. David Halberstam, *War in a Time of Peace* (New York: Scribner, 2001), 242.

14. George Stephanopoulos, *All Too Human* (Boston: Little, Brown and Company, 1999), 124.; Elizabeth Drew, *On the Edge: The Clinton Presidency* (New York: Simon and Schuster, 1994), 47–48.

15. William A. Manning, ed., "The World Trade Center Bombing: Report and Analysis," *U.S. Fire Administration* (26 February 1993).

16. Dick Morris, "While Clinton Fiddled," *Wall Street Journal*, 5 February 2002, A18.

17. Ibid.

18. Halberstam, *War in a Time of Peace*, 211.

19. Barton Gellman, "Struggles Inside the Government Defined Campaign," *Washington Post*, 20 December 2001, A30.

20. It had previously been thought that the risk of chemical attack was not great because of the difficulty in dispersing a chemical agent quickly and thoroughly enough to affect a significant number of people. Members of Japan's Aum Shinrikyo cult solved the problem by placing open bags of the lethal agent in the subway so that the toxic air would be spread quickly through the system by the push of rush-hour trains. Joshua Green, "Weapons of Mass Confusion," *Washington Monthly*, May 2001, 15.

21. "Clinton, Yeltsin, Castro Address U.N.," CNN World News, 22 October 1995. The president did not mention in the speech that his administration had shut down an investigation by law enforcement authorities of certain Islamic charities that same year. According to one account, the administration was "concerned that a public probe would expose Saudi Arabia's suspected ties to a global money-laundering operation that raised millions for anti-Israel terrorists." Jerry Seper, "Clinton White House Axed Terror-Fund Probe," *Washington Times*, 2 April 2002, 1.

22. Office of the Secretary of Defense, *Proliferation: Threat and Response*, (Washington, D.C.: Office of the Secretary of Defense, April 1996).

23. "Clinton Urges Anti-Terrorism Action," Online News Hour with Jim Lehrer, transcript, 6 August 1996.

24. Ibid.

25. Ibid.

26. Stephanopoulos, *All Too Human*, 416.

27. Dick Morris, "While Clinton Fiddled."

28. Green, "Weapons of Mass Confusion," 16.

29. Office of the Assistant Secretary of Defense (Public Affairs), news release, 19 May 1997, Washington, D.C., Reference No. 250-97.

30. William S. Cohen, Secretary of Defense, *Report of the Quadrennial Defense Review.*

31. Cited in Milton Leitenberg, "False Alarm," *Washington Post*, 14 August 1999, 15.

32. Ibid.

33. The mission of the Special Forces of Task Force Ranger is the subject of a book and subsequent movie. See Mark Bowden, *Black Hawk Down* (Thorndike, Maine: G. K. Hall and Company, 1999).

34. Halberstam, *War in a Time of Peace*, 418.

35. John G. Roos, "Who's in Charge?" *Armed Forces Journal International* (September 1999): 44.

36. "The Strike Briefing," News Hour with Jim Lehrer, transcript, 20 August 1998.

37. Advisory Panel to Assess Domestic Response Capabilities for Terrorism Involving Weapons of Mass Destruction, "Assessing the Threat," *First Annual Report to the President and the Congress* (Washington, D.C.: RAND, 15 December 1999), 3.

38. Commission to Assess the Ballistic Missile Threat to the United States, *Executive Summary.*

39. Hicks and Associates, Inc., *Homeland Defense: Threats and Policies in Transition* (McLean, Va.: Hicks and Associates, Inc., 23 July 1998), 9.

40. PDD-62 and PDD-63. The latter set goals for the protection of "critical infrastructures," defined as "those physical and cyber-based systems essential to the minimum operations of the economy and government."

41. Hicks and Associates, *Homeland Defense*, 9.

42. Ibid., 8.

43. U.S. Department of Justice, *Five-Year Interagency Counterterrorism and Technology Crime Plan* (Washington, D.C.: U.S. Department of Justice, 2000), 21.

44. Fred C. Ikle, "Defending the U.S. Homeland," *CSIS Homeland Defense Working Group Report* (Washington, D.C.: Center for Strategic and International Studies, January 1999).

45. Ibid.

46. Roos, "Who's in Charge," 48.

47. Ibid.

48. Ibid.

49. Commission to Assess the Organization of the Federal Government to Combat the Proliferation of Weapons of Mass Destruction, *Combating Proliferation of Weapons of Mass Destruction* (Washington, D.C.: Commission to Assess the Organization of the Federal Government to Combat the Proliferation of Weapons of Mass Destruction, 14 July 1999), v, 9.

50. Ibid.

51. Steven Lee Myers, "Federal Commission Predicts Increasing Threat of Terrorism," *New York Times*, 21 September 1999, A7.

52. As a matter of policy, DoD required the preparation and dissemination of after action reports for DoD-led exercises.

53. See Gen. Bruce Palmer Jr., "Commentary," in *The Second Indochina War: Proceedings of a Symposium Held at Airlie, Virginia, 7–9 November 1984*, ed. John Schlight (Washington, D.C.: U.S. Army Center of Military History, 1986), 155.

54. U.S. Commission on National Security/21st Century, *Road Map for National Security: Imperative for Change, Phase III Report* (Washington, D.C.: U.S. Commission on National Security/21st Century, 15 February 2001), 23.

55. Associated Press, "National Guard Anti-Terrorism Teams at Risk," *Washington Post*, 26 February 2001, 4; Tony Capaccio, "Pentagon Mismanaged Chemical and Bio Defense Team, Audit Says," Bloomberg.com, 4 February 2001. According to one account, National Guard officials convinced Congress to fund the civil support teams with help from defense contractors who came up with "a concept that was doomed to fail" and members of Congress "happy to let a bad idea go forward in exchange for their own slice of the funding pie." Green, "Weapons of Mass Confusion," 18.

56. *Congressional Record*, 106th Cong., 1st sess., 12 February 1999, S. Rept. 1634.

57. Rudyard Kipling, "Tommy," *Rudyard Kipling's Verse* (Garden City, N.J.: Doubleday and Company, Inc. 1940), 396.

58. Halberstam, *War in a Time of Peace*, 416. On the day before he left office, Clinton avoided criminal prosecution for perjury or obstruction of justice in connection with the Monica Lewinsky Grand Jury investigation by entering into a plea bargain agreement with the independent counsel. In return for the prosecutor's pledge not to seek an indictment, Clinton agreed to pay a $25 thousand fine to Bar officials in the state of Arkansas and to the suspension of his license to practice law for five

years. On 1 October 2001 he was suspended by the U.S. Supreme Court and given forty days to show cause why he should not be permanently disbarred by the court. On 9 November 2001 he resigned from the Bar of the Supreme Court rather than face disbarment.

59. Richard H. Kohn, "The Erosion of Civilian Control of the Military in the United States Today," *Naval War College Review* (summer 2002): 13.

60. Advisory Panel to Assess Domestic Response Capabilities for Terrorism Involving Weapons of Mass Destruction, "Assessing the Threat," *First Annual Report,* 3.

61. Advisory Panel to Assess Domestic Response Capabilities for Terrorism Involving Weapons of Mass Destruction, "Toward a National Strategy for Combating Terrorism," *Second Annual Report to the President and the Congress* (Washington, D.C.: RAND, 15 December 2000), iii.

62. The commission was established by the Omnibus Consolidated and Emergency Supplemental Appropriations Act of 1999 (Public Law 105-277, 105th Cong., 2d sess.) for the purpose of reviewing and assessing "the laws, regulations, policies, directives, and practices relating to combating international terrorism directed against the United States" and recommending "changes to improve U.S. counter-terrorism performance."

63. National Commission on Terrorism, *Countering the Changing Threat of International Terrorism* (Washington, D.C.: U.S. Government Printing Office, 7 June 2000), v.

64. Vernon Loeb, "After Counterterrorism Bill Fails, Nation's Preparedness is Debated," *Washington Post,* 9 October 2000, A21.

65. "Cohen Stresses the Need for Homeland Defense," InsideDefense.com, 3 October 2000.

66. Ibid.

67. Benjamin and Simon, *The Age of Sacred Terror,* 226, 239, 263, 319, 322, 387.

68. Ibid., 290–91.

69. In an interview aired on National Public Radio in May 2002, Clinton cited three accomplishments, including the criminal conviction of some terrorists, the move of Osama bin Laden's organization from Sudan to Afghanistan, and the 1998 strike against training camps in Afghanistan. His acknowledged failures included the scrapping of an operation that would have involved an effort by Pakistani opera-tives trained by the CIA to capture bin Laden, and his unsuccessful effort to per-suade Saudi Arabia to take custody of bin Laden after he was forced to leave Sudan. Associated Press, "Clinton Cites Anti-Terror Accomplishments," *Washington Post,* 11 May 2002, A18.

70. Gellman, "Struggles Inside the Government," A30.

71. Barton Gellman, "Broad Effort Launched after '98 Attacks," *Washington Post*, 19 December 2001, A26.

72. Charles Krauthammer, "Gore's Glass House," *Washington Post*, 27 September 2002, A23.

73. Gellman, "Broad Effort Launched," A27.

74. Ibid., A26.

75. Gellman, "Struggles Inside the Government," A30.

76. Ralph Peters, *Beyond Terror* (Mechanicsburg, Pa.: Stackpole Books, 2002), 331–32.

77. Napoleon I, *The Military Maxims of Napoleon* (New York: Macmillan Publishing Company, 1988), 85.

78. Stephen M. Duncan, "Catastrophic Terrorism: Are We Prepared?" Address to the Precision Strike Association, Johns Hopkins University, Laurel, Md., 11 October 2001.

79. Advisory Panel to Assess Domestic Response Capabilities for Terrorism Involving Weapons of Mass Destruction, "Assessing the Threat," *First Annual Report*, 3.

80. Theodore Roosevelt, *An Autobiography* (New York: MacMillan Company, 1914), 563.

81. Martin Gilbert, *Churchill: A Life* (New York: Hewey Holt and Company, 1991), 565.

82. Ibid.

83. Gen. Barry R. McCaffrey, "Challenges to U.S. National Security," *Armed Forces Journal International* (October 2001): 6.

84. Ibid.

Chapter 3. Counterterrorism Strategy on the Run

1. Woodward, *Bush at War*, 25.

2. James Carney and John F. Dickerson, "Inside the War Room," *Time*, 24 December 2001.

3. Woodward, *Bush at War*, 35. The other two threats were the increasing availability of weapons of mass destruction and the rising power of China.

4. Benjamin and Simon, *The Age of Sacred Terror*, 332.

5. Barton Gellman, "A Strategy's Cautious Evolution," *Washington Post*, 20 January 2002, A1, A16.

6. Ibid.

7. Ibid.

8. Ibid.

9. Woodward, *Bush at War*, 36.

10. Brian Hartman, "Steeling for War," abcNews.com, 14 September 2001.

11. Bernard Lewis, "A War of Resolve," *Wall Street Journal*, 26 April 2002.

12. George W. Bush, Address to Joint Session of Congress, *Weekly Compilation of Presidential Documents* 37, 38 (20 September 2001): 1347.

13. Ibid.

14. Ibid.

15. Mark Mazzetti and Richard J. Newman, "The Far Horizon," *U.S. News and World Report,* 8 October 2001, 14.

16. Michael E. O'Hanlon, "A Flawed Masterpiece," *Foreign Affairs* (May/June 2002): 49.

17. Carney and Dickerson, "Inside the War Room."

18. Woodward, *Bush at War,* 182.

19. John Barry, "A New Breed of Soldier," *Newsweek,* 10 December 2001, 28.

20. Vice Adm. John B. Nathan, "'We Were Great': Navy Air in Afghanistan," *U.S. Naval Institute Proceedings* (March 2002): 96.

21. Susan B. Glasser, "New Strategy's Success Leaves Much in Doubt," *Washington Post,* 14 March 2002, A14.

22. Eric Schmitt and Thom Shanker, "U.S. Raids Along Afghan Border Seen as Lasting Past Summer," *New York Times,* 6 May 2002, 1.

23. Anthony Lloyd, "British Officers Fear Five-Year War as Taliban Adopts Guerilla Tactics," *London Times,* 17 April 2002. The assistant commandant of the U.S. Marine Corps did not predict the length of the conflict. "We don't really even know how many countries the enemy's in. We're going to have to take him on in a way that will challenge all of us." But he did predict its likely nature. "We're probably going to be in a war of small units, a war of intelligence and a war of violent action in very short bursts of time." Mark Oliva, "Marines' Mobility Is Key to Fighting an Elusive Enemy, Says Assistant Commandant," *Pacific Stars and Stripes* (18 June 2002).

24. O'Hanlon, "Flawed Masterpiece," 47.

25. Philip Smucker, "As U.S. Coalition Debates Tactics, Taliban Fight On," *Christian Science Monitor,* 29 May 2002, 1.

26. Henry Kissinger, "Where Do We Go from Here?" *Washington Post,* 6 November 2001, A23.

27. Ibid.

28. Each country agreed to reduce the number of its nuclear warheads by the year 2012 to a total of between 1,700 and 2,200.

29. Jim Hoagland, "Cold War Afterthought," *Washington Post,* 15 May 2002, 27. Ironically, on 13 June the United States formally withdrew from the thirty-year-old Anti-Ballistic Missile (ABM) Treaty that had been signed with the Soviet Union. It had been argued for years that the ABM Treaty had terminated when one of the contracting parties— the Soviet Union—ceased to exist. Others predicted great

disruption of the U.S.-Russian relationship if the United States withdrew from the treaty. That did not occur.

30. Todd S. Purdum, "NATO Strikes Deal to Accept Russia in a Partnership," *New York Times*, 15 May 2002, A1.

31. David E. Sanger, "NATO Formally Welcomes Russia as a Partner," *New York Times*, 29 May 2002, 1.

32. Celia W. Dugger, "Wider Military Ties With India Offer U.S. Diplomatic Leverage," *New York Times*, 10 June 2002, 1.

33. Jim Hoagland, "No Easy Exit," *Washington Post*, 3 March 2002, B7.

34. Brian M. Jenkins, "The Organization Men: Anatomy of a Terrorist Attack," in James F. Hoge Jr. and Gideon Rose, eds., *How Did This Happen?: Terrorism and the New War* (New York: Public Affairs, 2001), 4–5.

35. Ibid., 5.

36. Walter Pincus, "Mueller Outlines Origin, Funding of Sept. 11 Plot," *Washington Post*, 6 June 2002, 1.

37. In June 2002 al Qaeda operations reportedly were increasingly teaming up with the Lebanon-based Hezbollah, an organization the United States had put on its terrorist list in 1997. Described as "the A-team of terrorism" by the chairman of the Senate Intelligence Committee, Hezbollah was responsible for the deaths of almost three hundred Americans during the past two decades; 241 marines and other service members died in the 1983 terrorist attack in Beirut—the largest loss ever sustained in peacetime by the U.S. Armed Forces. Dana Priest and Douglas Farah, "Terror Alliance Has U.S. Worried," *Washington Post*, 30 June 2002, A1.

38. These words are from a recent book by the former head of Egyptian Islamic Jihad who is considered to be Osama bin Laden's senior deputy and chief of policy and strategy. See Walter Pincus, "Al Qaeda Aims to Destabilize Secular Nations," *Washington Post*, 16 June 2002, A21.

39. Steve Hirsch, "The War against Terror Will Be Indefinite," *National Journal* (26 January 2002): 255.

40. Ibid.

41. Doyle McManus and Robin Wright, "Broad New U.S. Strategy to Fight Terror Emerging," *Los Angeles Times*, 16 September 2001, 1.

42. Woodward, *Bush at War*, 62, 126.

43. The informal and anonymous system of money transfers, known as hawala, has been used for hundreds of years to move money over great distances and to circumvent legal and financial obstacles in the Middle East and South Asia. A person desiring to send money gives it, a fee, and the name and location of the person to whom it

is being sent to a local hawala broker. The broker then contacts a counterpart in the recipient's country who contacts the recipient. According to one student of the system, "The money does not move, either physically or electronically. Brokers dole out money from the same pool that they take it in. They make money from the fees they charge for the transactions. The system is built on the trust between brokers, a trust built up between generations of hawala brokers." Kevin Anderson, "Hawala System under Scrutiny," BBC News Online, 8 November 2001.

44. Kimberly L. Thachuk, "Terrorism's Financial Lifeline: Can It Be Severed?" *Strategic Forum* (Institute for National Strategic Studies, National Defense University), no. 191 (May 2002).

45. The legislation is also known as the Uniting and Strengthening America by Providing Appropriate Tools Required to Intercept and Obstruct Terrorism Act of 2001.

46. Title III is known as the International Money Laundering Abatement and Anti-Terrorist Financing Act of 2001.

47. The advantage of such commodities is that they are small, thus easy to hide and ship. They are not subject to wide market fluctuations and they can be "released in small amounts on the market without arousing attention." See Karen DeYoung and Douglas Farah, "Al Qaeda Shifts Assets to Gold," *Washington Post*, 18 June 2002, A1. In December 2002 the West African governments of Liberia and Burkina Faso reportedly had hosted senior terrorist operatives who supervised an elaborate effort to purchase $20 million in diamonds. Douglas Farah, "Report Says Africans Harbored Al Qaeda," *Washington Post*, 29 December 2002, A1.

48. Carla Anne Robbins, "Post-Afghan Phase of War on Terror Begins Taking Shape in the Wings," *Wall Street Journal*, 29 November 2001, A20.

49. George W. Bush, Satellite Remarks to the Central European Counterterrorism Conference, *Weekly Compilation of Presidential Documents* 37, 45 (6 November 2001): 1604.

50. Robert D. Novak, "Not So Fast," *Washington Post*, 31 January 2002, 25.

51. Wesley Pruden, "When the Message Is Clear as a Bell," *Washington Times*, 1 February 2002, A4.

52. William Kristol, "Taking the War beyond Terrorism," *Washington Post*, 31 January 2002, 25.

53. Shlomo Nakdimon, *First Strike* (New York: Summit Books, 1987), 117.

54. The sale of the aircraft was governed by a mutual defense assistance agreement dated 23 July 1952.

55. Nakdimon, *First Strike*, 235.

56. Charles Krauthammer, "The Axis of Petulance," *Washington Post*, 1 March 2002, A25.

57. Asserting that Bush is not a unilateralist and certainly not an isolationist, Michael Kelly said that the president is properly focused on the question of what is good for the United States and that the "interests and sensibilities of other nations and other peoples are unapologetically of secondary concern." Michael Kelly, "A Victory for Bush," *Washington Post*, 15 May 2002, 27. He further argued that the new policy was not the realpolitik of the Cold War, but "a more complex realism—a realism rooted in morality," and that because Bush is solid on the ends he wishes to achieve, he "can afford to be limber on the means." Ibid.

58. Henry A. Kissinger, "Answering the 'Axis' Critics," *Washington Post*, 5 March 2002, A19.

59. George W. Bush, Commencement Address at the United States Military Academy in West Point, New York, *Weekly Compilation of Presidential Documents* 38, 23 (10 June 2002): 944. It has been rightly noted that the United States had no effective defense against a nuclear attack by the Soviet Union during the Cold War years. The "passive deterrent posture . . . a posture that made a virtue out of being defenseless against the greatest danger" was necessarily more important then that it is now. Loren B. Thompson, "The Bush Doctrine," *Wall Street Journal*, 13 June 2002. Today the threat is different and the potential originators of attacks against the United States are "too committed, or too accident-prone, or too irrational, or simply too obscure" to be effectively deterred. Ibid.

60. George W. Bush, Commencement Address at the United States Military Academy in West Point, New York.

61. David E. Sanger, "Bush to Formalize a Defense Policy of Hitting First," *New York Times*, 17 June 2002, 1.

62. Glenn Kessler and Peter Slevin, "Preempting Strikes Must Be Decisive, Powell Says," *Washington Post*, 15 June 2002, 16.

63. Thomas E. Ricks and Vernon Loeb, "Preemption to Be Military Policy," *Washington Post*, 10 June 2002, 1.

64. Ken Ringle, "A Duel with Tradition," *Washington Post*, 19 November 2002, C1. Arthur Schlesinger Jr., a former advisor to and biographer of President Kennedy, later wrote that the "policy of 'anticipatory self-defense' is alarmingly similar to the policy that imperial Japan employed at Pearl Harbor." Doug Struck, "In Japan, a Veteran Sees History Repeat," *Washington Post*, 7 April 2003, C1.

65. George W. Bush, Remarks on the Six-Month Anniversary of the September 11th Attacks, *Weekly Compilation of Presidential Documents* 38, 11 (18 March 2002): 390.

66. Cato Institute, "Future Enemies in the Expanding War on Terrorism: Iraq and Who Else?" Invitation to a Hill Briefing, June 2002.

67. Editorial, "Taking the Offensive," *Washington Post*, 4 June 2002, 16.

68. Dana Milbank, "Cheney's Venues Change But Message Doesn't," *Washington Post*, 20 February 2002, A4.

69. Senator Joseph Lieberman, "Winning the Wider War against Terrorism," excerpts of an address to the Georgetown University Lecture Fund that appeared in the *Officer* (March 2002): 36.

70. Milbank, "Cheney's Venues Change But Message Doesn't," A4.

71. Jim Hoagland, "Nuclear Preemption," *Washington Post*, 17 March 2002, B9.

72. Editorial, "The War's Next Stage," *Washington Post*, 12 March 2002, 20.

73. Ann Scott Tyson, "Philippines Deployment: Sign of U.S. Resolve," *Christian Science Monitor*, 22 January 2002.

74. Philip Pan, "Portrait of a Weakened, Desperate Abu Sayyaf," *Washington Post*, 11 June 2002, A16.

75. Sharon LaFraniere, "U.S. to Train 1,200 Georgian Soldiers in Terror Battle," *Washington Post*, 3 March 2002, A14.

76. Thomas E. Ricks, "U.S. Eyes Military Assistance for Yemen," *Washington Post*, 28 February 2002, A1.

77. Michael Slackman, "A Radicals' Haven Sets Out to Change Its Image," *Los Angeles Times*, 10 March 2002, A5; "Yemen Gets U.S. Surveillance Gear," *USA Today*, 24 June 2002, 9.

78. Robert D. Novak, "Ignoring Narco-Terror," *Washington Post*, 13 December 2001, A30.

79. Ibid.

80. Mary Jordan, "Terrorism Fight Hurts Drug War," *Washington Post*, 10 December 2001, A24.

81. Ibid.

82. Stephen M. Duncan, *Hearing before the Subcommittee on Defense, Appropriations Committee, United States House of Representatives*, 102d Cong., 2d sess., 1 April 1992.

83. Dana Milbank and Cheryl W. Thompson, "Bush Seeks Cut in Drug Use," *Washington Post*, 13 February 2002, A10.

84. A nine-month investigation by the U.S. House of Representatives' Committee on International Relations had just concluded that as many as fifteen members of the Irish Republican Army had been training the Marxist rebels in Colombia over the previous eighteen months. The expanded capability of the FARC had resulted in the deaths of four hundred military personnel and police officers and six hundred bombings of infrastructure targets such as pipelines, electrical towers, reservoirs, and bridges. Jerry Seper, "IRA Fuels Carnage of Colombian Terrorists," *Washington Times*, 29 April 2002, 1.

85. Editorial, *Chicago Tribune*, 6 May 2002, 14.

86. Nicholas Kralev, "Havana Pursues Biological Warfare," *Washington Times*, 7 May 2002, 1.

87. Judith Miller, "Washington Accuses Cuba of Germ-Warfare Research," *New York Times*, 7 May 2002, A6.

88. Kralev, "Havana Pursues Biological Warfare."

89. Bill Nichols, "U.S. Warns 3 More Nations: Weapons Efforts Must Stop," *USA Today*, 7 May 2002, 4.

90. Ibid.

91. David Wood, "An Ill-Defined Military Mission Gets Even More Complicated," Newhouse.com, 15 July 2002.

92. Thomas E. Ricks, "War Shifts from Combat Sweeps to Small Units Probing Shadows," *Washington Post*, 7 July 2002, A1, A13.

93. Ibid.

94. Rowan Scarborough, "Elite U.S. Unit Keeps Heat on Terrorists," *Washington Times*, 12 July 2002, 1.

95. Dexter Filkins, "F.B.I. and Military Unite in Pakistan to Hunt Al Qaeda," *New York Times*, 14 July 2002, 1.

96. Retired army colonel Robert Killebrew, a respected analyst of strategy and tactical issues, declared, "We are running the risk of letting our participation degenerate into continuous tactical scrapes without decisive action." See Ricks, "War Shifts from Combat Sweeps."

97. Donald H. Rumsfeld, Secretary of Defense, Remarks at DoD News Briefing at the Pentagon, Washington, D.C., 9 August 2002.

98. Glenn Kessler, "U.S. Fears Grow over Turmoil in Afghanistan," *Washington Post*, 8 August 2002, A1, A12.

99. Ibid.

100. James W. Crawley, "Terror War Will Expand Overseas," *San Diego Union-Tribune*, 31 July 2002, 2.

101. The U.S. Special Operations Command is one of the unified combatant commands. Headquartered in Tampa, Florida, the command includes U.S. Army Special Forces or Green Berets, U.S. Navy SEAL teams, U.S. Air Force combat controllers, the army's secret Delta Force, and search and rescue airmen.

102. Thomas E. Ricks, "Aggressive New Tactics Proposed for Terror War," *Washington Post*, 3 August 2002, 1.

103. Rowan Scarborough, "Pentagon Plan Seeks Countries' OK to Attack Cells," *Washington Times*, 5 August 2002, 1.

104. Woodward, *Bush at War*, 192.

105. "US Signals Afghan Policy Shift," *London Daily Telegraph*, 27 August 2002.

106. Cesar G. Soriano, "U.S. General: 'Long Ways to Go' in Afghanistan," *USA Today*, 26 August 2002, 6.

Chapter 4. Organizing at Home for a Long War

1. Dave McIntyre, "What Is Homeland Security? A Short History," ANSER Institute for Homeland Security, available at www.homelandsecurity.org; Judith Miller, Stephen Engleberg, and William Broad, *Germs: Biological Weapons and America's Secret War* (New York: Simon and Schuster, 2001).

2. McIntyre, "What Is Homeland Security?"; National Defense Panel, "Transforming Defense."

3. U.S. Department of Defense, *Dictionary of Military and Associated Terms*, Joint Publication 1-02 (Washington, D.C.: Joint Staff, 10 June 1998 as amended through 14 June 2000).

4. Bill Gertz and Rowan Scarborough, "Inside the Ring," *Washington Times*, 29 March 2002, 9.

5. Dave McIntyre has proposed that the term be defined to mean "those private and public actions at every level that ensure the ability of Americans to live their lives the way they wish, free from fear of organized attack." He has also offered a more detailed definition: "Homeland Security is the overarching concept, consisting of all actions taken at every level (federal, state, local, private, and individual citizen) to deter, defend against, or mitigate attacks within the United States, or to respond to other major domestic emergencies." McIntyre, "What Is Homeland Security?"

6. Ibid.

7. John G. Roos, "A New Beginning," *Armed Forces Journal International* (March 2001): 2.

8. "Rep. Thornberry Proposes New Homeland Security Agency," *Aerospace Daily*, 23 March 2001.

9. U.S. Commission on National Security/21st Century, *Road Map for National Security*, 10, 23.

10. "White House Said to Oppose New Homeland Security Agency Bill," InsideDefense.com, 28 March 2001.

11. National Commission on Terrorism, *Countering the Changing Threat of International Terrorism*, 34.

12. Center for Strategic and International Studies (CSIS), *Defending America in the 21st Century*, Executive Summary of Four Working Group Reports on Homeland Defense (Washington, D.C.: CSIS, 2000).

13. Advisory Panel to Assess Domestic Response Capabilities for Terrorism Involving Weapons of Mass Destruction, "Toward a National Strategy for Combating Terrorism," *Second Annual Report*, iii, v.

14. Ibid., vi.

15. U.S. Commission on National Security/21st Century, *Road Map for National Security*, viii.

16. Ibid.

17. Ibid.

18. Ibid., viii–ix.

19. See Bill Nichols, "Need for Homeland Defense Now 'Grim Reality,'" *USA Today*, 12 September 2001, 7A.

20. George W. Bush, Address to Joint Session of Congress, *Weekly Compilation of Presidential Documents* 37, 38 (20 September 2001): 1347.

21. Eric Pianin and Bradley Graham, "Ridge Is Tapped to Head Homeland Security Office," *Washington Post*, 21 September 2001, A1.

22. Ibid., A25.

23. Eric Pianin and Bradley Graham, "New Homeland Defense Plans Emerge," *Washington Post*, 26 September 2001, 4.

24. Dave McIntyre, "How to Start: Authority for the Homeland Security Advisor," ANSER Institute for Homeland Security, available at www.homelandsecurity.org.

25. The official title for the drug czar is director of the White House Office of National Drug Control Policy (ONDCP).

26. Dana Milbank and Bradley Graham, "With Crisis, White House Style Is Now More Fluid," *Washington Post*, 10 October 2001, A4.

27. Eric Pianin and Bradley Graham, "Ridge: Goal Isn't to Create Bureaucracy," *Washington Post*, 4 October 2001, 24.

28. Elizabeth Becker and Tim Weiner, "New Office to Become a White House Agency," *New York Times*, 28 September 2001, B5.

29. Ann Gerhart, "Tom Ridge, on High Alert," *Washington Post*, 12 November 2001, C1.

30. "Poor Tom," *Economist*, 20 April 2002, 33.

31. Elizabeth Becker and Elaine Sciolino, "A New Federal Office Opens," *New York Times*, 9 October 2001, 1.

32. Bonne Chance, "Bases Weigh Terror Risk, Security Costs," *Atlanta Journal and Constitution*, 4 July 2001, 8.

33. Donald H. Rumsfeld, Secretary of Defense, *Report of the Quadrennial Defense Review* (Washington, D.C.: U.S. Department of Defense, 30 September 2001), 18.

34. Ibid., 17.

35. Ibid., 19.

36. Ibid., iv.

37. Ibid.

38. Thom Shanker, "New Blueprint For Military Shifts Priority to U.S. Soil, Revising 2-War Strategy," *New York Times*, 2 October 2001, B6.

39. For several months it had been rumored that in order to pay for the long-term "transformation" of the military services, the current force structure would have to be cut significantly, especially the number of army ground combat units. By April 2002, however, the service chiefs had informed Congress that the war on terrorism and the resultant increase in troop deployments required an *increase* of as many as fifty-one thousand personnel.

40. The force structure of 1.37 million active personnel included 12 aircraft carriers, 108 active and 8 reserve surface combatant ships, 55 attack submarines, 12 amphibious ready groups, 10 active and 1 reserve naval air wings, 10 active and 8 Army National Guard divisions, 15 enhanced separate (National Guard) brigades, 1 active armored cavalry army regiment, 1 light cavalry army regiment, 3 active and 1 reserve marine corps divisions, 3 active and 1 reserve marine corps air wings, 3 active and 1 reserve marine corps force service support groups, 46 active air force fighter squadrons, 38 air force reserve (Air National Guard) fighter squadrons, 4 air force reserve air defense squadrons, and 112 air force bombers.

41. In late November Rumsfeld asked Congress to create two new under secretary of defense positions, one for homeland security and one for intelligence. The request was not approved before the first session of the Congress adjourned. A subsequent proposal recommended only one new under secretary (for intelligence) and an assistant secretary position for homeland defense.

42. Elaine M. Grossman, "Military Is Embroiled in Debate over Who Should Guard United States," *Inside the Pentagon* (20 September 2001).

43. The five regional unified combatant commands (composed of two or more military services) included the U.S. European Command, the U.S. Central Command, the U.S. Pacific Command, the U.S. Southern Command, and the U.S. Joint Forces Command.

44. Colin Powell and Joseph E. Persico, *My American Journey* (New York: Random House, 1995), 447.

45. Halberstam, *War in a Time of Peace*, 455.

46. Adm. William J. Crowe Jr., *The Line of Fire* (New York: Simon and Schuster, 1993), 160.

47. Gen. Wesley K. Clark, *Waging Modern War* (New York: Public Affairs, 2001), 452.

48. Halberstam, *War in a Time of Peace*, 454.

49. Ibid., 456.

50. Gen. Wesley Clark, "High Command Is No Place for Those Who Need Consensus" *Daily Telegraph (London)*, 30 October 2001, 22.

51. In November 2001 the four major regional CINCs asked that FBI and Treasury Department agents be assigned to their staffs for the purpose of improving the coordination between the civilian agencies and the armed forces.

52. Jim Garamone, "U.S. Northern Command to Debut in October," *Armed Forces Information Service* (17 April 2002).

53. The U.S. European Command previously had an area of responsibility (AOR) that included ninety-one nations in Europe, Africa, and the Middle East. Its CINC also serves as Supreme Allied Commander Europe—NATO's senior military commander, Its AOR was increased. It would now include the Atlantic area off the east coast to the shores of Europe and would be responsible for Russia and the Caucasus nations. The U.S. Pacific Command, which had an AOR that included forty-three countries, twenty territories and possessions, and ten U.S. territories stretching from the west coast of the U.S. mainland to the east coast of Africa and from the Arctic to the Antarctic, would help the European command with the eastern part of Russia and add Antarctica. The U.S. Joint Forces Command, which was responsible for both a geographic region (the northern Atlantic) and functional missions, would give up both its civil support function and related activities and its geographical responsibilities. It would continue to serve as a "force generator" to the regional commands and it would retain its mission of experimentation and helping the transformation of the armed forces. On 26 June 2002 the U.S. Space Command and the U.S. Strategic Command announced they would be merged in October 2002. The merged command is now responsible for both early warning of and defense against attack, as well as long-range conventional attacks. The AOR of the U.S. Central Command, which includes twenty-five nations located throughout the Horn of Africa, South and Central Asia, and Northern Red Sea regions, as well as the Arabian Peninsula and Iraq, would not be changed. The U.S. Southern Command's AOR, which encompasses thirty-two countries included within the land mass of Latin America south of Mexico, the waters adjacent to Central and South America, the Caribbean Sea, the Gulf of Mexico, and a portion of the Atlantic Ocean, would also remain the same. For the present, the other unified commands, which have such functional missions as space, transportation, special operations, and strategic warfare, would also remain unchanged.

54. Vince Crawley, "New Command to Focus on Homeland, Boss Says," *Navy Times* (23 September 2002): 33 (emphasis added).

55. Ibid.

56. Ibid.

57. David Wood, "War on Terror Pits Networks of Cells against Bureaucracies," Newhouse.com, 4 October 2001.

58. Ibid.

59. See the discussion of John Boyd's work in Chapter 1. Boyd believed that the ability to "operate at a faster tempo or rhythm than an adversary enables one to fold [the] adversary back inside himself so that he can neither appreciate nor keep up with what's going on." Coram, *Boyd: Fighter Pilot*, 344.

60. "Poor Tom," *Economist*, 20 April 2002, 33. Arguing that the war on terrorism was floundering, one observer expressed frustration, "[W]e as a nation can't seem to get ahead of the curve in avoiding the next catastrophe. . . . We lose our fingernail clippers when we board planes, but somebody could still detonate a dirty bomb in New York City and devastate the nation's economy or send out 100 anthrax letters around the country and close down the nation's postal system." Nicholas D. Kristof, "The War on Terror Flounders," *New York Times*, 10 May 2002, A35.

61. Jane Harman, "Securing American Homeland Requires a Strategy," *Hill*, 4 June 2002, available at www.house.gov/harman/press/op_ed.

62. George W. Bush, Address to the Nation on the Proposed Department of Homeland Security, *Weekly Compilation of Presidential Documents* 38, 23 (6 June 2002): 943.

63. Dana Milbank, "Plan Formed in Extraordinary Secrecy," *Washington Post*, 7 June 2002, 1A; David Von Drehle and Mike Allen, "Bush Plan's Underground Architects," *Washington Post*, 9 June 2002, A1.

64. Del Jones, "Homeland Security: a Tough Merger," *USA Today*, 11 June 2002, 3B.

65. Ibid.

66. "Wanted: Drill sergeant, manager, cheerleader, politician, guerrilla fighter, tent preacher, juggler, comedian, school principal, arm-twister, and multitasker for thankless job. Expertise necessary in: national defense; management of a large government agency, state, or company; law enforcement; intelligence analysis; and domestic threat assessment. Familiarity with corporate or government mergers, large computer systems, natural disasters, immigration law, industry lobbying, environmental protection, maritime safety, drug interdiction, and animal diseases a plus. Candidates under retirement age preferred." Siobhan Gorman, "Homeland Security Job May Require Larger-than-Life Figure," GovExec.com, 14 June 2002.

67. Newt Gingrich, "Congress's Tangled Purse Strings," *Wall Street Journal*, 10 June 2002, A16.

68. Louis Jacobson, "Merging Cultures of Homeland Security Agencies Will Be Big Challenge," GovExec.com, 13 June 2002.

69. Max Stier, "Homeland Security: Mega Merger," *Washington Post*, 25 June 2002, 19.

70. Ibid.

71. David M. Walker, "Homeland Security: A Framework for Addressing the Nation's Efforts" (GAO-01-1158T), *Hearing before the Committee on Governmental Affairs, United States Senate*, 107th Cong., 1st sess., 21 September 2001, 2.

72. Ibid.

73. Ibid., 4.

74. Ibid.

75. Center for Strategic and International Studies, *Combating Chemical, Biological, Radiological, and Nuclear Terrorism: A Comprehensive Strategy* (Washington, D.C.: CSIS Homeland Defense Project, May 2001).

76. Walker, "Homeland Security," 5.

77. Randall A. Yim, "National Preparedness: Integration of Federal, State, Local, and Private Sector Efforts Is Critical to an Effective National Strategy for Homeland Security" (GAO-02-62IT), *Hearings before the Committee on Transportation and Infrastructure, United States House of Representatives*, 107th Cong., 2d sess., 11 April 2002, 4.

78. Office of Homeland Security, *National Strategy for Homeland Security* (Washington, D.C.: White House, 16 July 2002), 1.

79. Ibid., 64.

80. Ibid., 44.

81. Ibid., 13.

82. Ibid., 48.

83. Peter Verga, Special Assistant for Homeland Security, Office of the Secretary of Defense, Remarks at the Homeland Security, The Civil-Military Dimensions Symposium, National Defense University, Fort Leslie J. McNair, Washington, D.C., 19 September 2002.

84. Office of Homeland Security, *National Strategy for Homeland Security*, 67.

85. Ibid.

86. Elizabeth Becker, "Yeas and Nays For Bush's Security Wish List," *New York Times*, 17 July 2002, A16.

87. Sebastian Mallaby, "Triage for Terrorism," *Washington Post*, 22 July 2002, A15.

88. Bill Miller and Juliet Eilperin, "House Approves Homeland Security Bill," *Washington Post*, 27 July 2002, A6.

89. Bill Miller, "Senate to Debate Homeland Plan," *Washington Post*, 4 September 2002, A10.

90. Ibid.

91. Miller and Eilperin, "House Approves Homeland Security Bill," A6.

92. "New Discord on Homeland Security," MSNBC News, 3 September 2002.

93. Bill Miller and Juliet Eilperin, "Obscure Labor Issues Block Homeland Security Agency," *Washington Post*, 23 September 2002, A8.

94. Bill Miller and Christopher Lee, "'A Massive Undertaking,'" *Washington Post*, 27 September 2002, A21.

95. George Washington, Farewell Address, 19 September 1796, in George Washington, *Writings* (New York: Library of America, 1997), 969.

96. Jackie Calmes, "Armey's Improbable Legacy," *Wall Street Journal*, 2 July 2002, A4.

Chapter 5. The Threat and the Bureaucratic Maze

1. Stephen E. Flynn, "America the Vulnerable," *Foreign Affairs* (January/February 2002): 60.

2. Maj. Gen. Malcolm R. O'Neill, *Hearing before the Subcommittee on Military Acquisition, Research, and Technology, Armed Services Committee, U.S. House of Representatives*, 103d Cong., 1st sess., 10 June 1993.

3. William J. Clinton, Letter to Congressional Leaders on Prevention of Importation of Weapons of Mass Destruction, *Weekly Compilation of Presidential Documents* 32, 45 (4 November 1996): 2346.

4. Richard A. Falkenrath, Robert D. Newman, and Bradley A. Thayer, *America's Achilles' Heel* (Cambridge: MIT Press, 2001), xviii, xxi. Falkenrath subsequently served in the White House Office of Homeland Security.

5. Office of Homeland Security, *National Strategy for Homeland Security*, 11.

6. Ibid., 9. As early as May 2002 the secretary of defense informed Congress, "[W]e have to recognize that terrorist networks have relationships with terrorist states that have weapons of mass destruction, and that they inevitably are going to get their hands on them, and they would not hesitate one minute in using them." Bill Miller and Christine Haughney, "Nation Left Jittery by Latest Series of Terror Warnings," *Washington Post*, 22 May 2002, A1; Office of Homeland Security, *National Strategy for Homeland Security*, 37.

7. Falkenrath et al., *America's Achilles' Heel*, 1.

8. It is generally recognized that not all consequences of a major terrorist attack using a weapon of mass destruction would be immediate. In addition to the massive destruction of human life, longer-term effects on the economy, the psychological health of the public, the nation's law and politics, and the government's ability to protect vital strategic interests around the world could be devastating. See, for example, Falkenrath et al., *America's Achilles' Heel*, 5–7.

9. Joby Warrick, "NRC Warns of Missing Radioactive Materials," *Washington Post*, 4 May 2002, A13. The theft of radioactive sources is a rather obvious threat. The

diversion of radioactive sources in the course of apparently legitimate activities is more difficult to detect and prevent.

10. A November 2001 report by the National Council on Radiation Protection and Measurements said that contamination from such a weapon would likely extend to several city blocks and that it would be "catastrophic but manageable." Michael Dobbs and Peter Behr, "Analysts Debate Next Weapon in Al Qaeda Arsenal," *Washington Post*, 16 November 2001, A18. A group of scientists has informed Congress that the greatest damage from a weapon would be the terror, panic and severe economic injury that would follow its use. James Glanz, "Some See Panic as Main Effect of Dirty Bombs," *New York Times*, 7 March 2002, 1.

11. Charles D. Ferguson, Tahseen Kazi, and Judith Perera, *Commercial Radioactive Sources: Surveying the Security Risks* (Monterey, Calif.: Center for Nonproliferation Studies, Monterey Institute of International Studies, January 2003). In May 2002 the United States and Russia did form a task force to improve security on materials in the former Soviet Union that might be used to produce dirty bombs. A major concern was a number of generators used in nuclear-powered radio beacons that the Soviet military had operated as navigational aids in the Arctic region and Siberia. The locations of the generators—each of which contained plutonium 238 or strontium 90— were not known.

12. Twenty-one U.S. nuclear reactors are located within five miles of an airport and 96 percent of all U.S. reactors were designed without any consideration of the effects of a crash by even a small aircraft. Josh Meyer, "Nuclear Plants Said to Face Big Attack Risk," *Los Angeles Times*, 26 March 2002, 1.

13. In December 2002, for example, Sultan Bashiruddin Mahmood, a leading Pakistani nuclear scientist, informed reporters through his son that prior to the 11 September 2001 attacks he had met with Osama bin Laden to discuss the building of nuclear weapons. Associated Press, "Bin Laden Said to Have Sought Nuclear Arms," *Baltimore Sun*, 30 December 2002.

14. Sam Nunn, William Perry, and Eugene Habiger, "Still Missing: A Nuclear Strategy," *Washington Post*, 21 May 2002, A17.

15. William J. Broad, Stephen Engleberg, and James Glanz, "Assessing Risks, Chemical, Biological, Even Nuclear," *New York Times*, 1 November 2001, A1. Over 225 million Americans live in metropolitan areas.

16. James V. Grimaldi and Guy Gugliotta, "Chemical Plants Are Feared as Targets," *Washington Post*, 16 December 2001, A1.

17. Ibid. While the data was intended to be more illustrative than a precise projection of likely casualties, a study by the army surgeon general has concluded that an attack

on a chemical plant in a densely populated area could result in as many as 2.4 million deaths. Eric Pianin, "Study Assesses Risk of Attack on Chemical Plant," *Washington Post*, 12 March 2002, A8.

18. John Mintz, "Bush Seeks Voluntary Chemical Plant Security Steps," *Washington Post*, 8 April 2003, A10.

19. "Special Report: The Spores of War—Biological Terrorism," *Economist*, 30 November 2002, 21.

20. The survey appeared in a special issue of the *Journal of the American Medical Association*. See the discussion of the survey in Walter Laqueur, *The New Terrorism: Fanaticism and the Arms of Mass Destruction* (New York: Oxford University Press, 1999), 258.

21. At the end of 2002 it was generally believed that as many as seventeen countries had retained some form of biological weapon capability including the seven countries—North Korea, Iraq, Iran, Libya, Sudan, Cuba, Syria—on the State Department's list of states that sponsor terrorism. Also, dozens of germ warfare scientists from the former Soviet Union were actively involved in weapons programs elsewhere. See Katherine McIntire Peters, "Behind in the Biowar," GovExec.com, 1 December 2001.

22. Ken Alibek and Stephen Handelman, "Bioterror: A Very Real Threat," *Wall Street Journal*, 11 October 2001. In July 2002 a military officer under the former white minority government of South Africa informed U.S. law enforcement officials that unique experiments with biological agents had been conducted and that plans had been prepared for epidemics to be sown in black communities. The question he could not answer was: Who controls the microbes now? Joby Warrick, "Biotoxins Fall into Private Hands," *Washington Post*, 21 April 2003, A1.

23. "Special Report: The Spores of War."

24. Rick Weiss, "Bioterrorism: An Even More Devastating Threat," *Washington Post*, 17 September 2001, 24.

25. Katherine McIntire Peters, "Behind in the Biowar."

26. Ibid.

27. Barton Gellman, "In U.S., Terrorism's Peril Undiminished," *Washington Post*, 24 December 2002, 1.

28. *The Public Health Security and Bioterrorism Preparedness and Response Act of 2000*, Public Law 107-188, 107th Cong., 2d sess., 12 June 2002, H.R. 3448.

29. See section 2811 of the act.

30. Office of the Assistant Secretary of Defense (Public Affairs), "DoD Announces Biological Defense Homeland Security Initiative," news release, 27 August 2002, Washington, D.C., Reference No. 444-02; Gerry J. Gilmore, "DoD Database

Provides Global Tripwire for Bio-Terror," *American Forces Press Service*, 17 December 2002.

31. The term "critical infrastructure" has been defined in various ways. A 1997 report used the following definition: "Infrastructures so vital that their incapacitation or destruction would have a debilitating impact on defense or economic security." President's Commission on Critical Infrastructure Protection, *Critical Foundations: Protecting America's Infrastructure* (Washington, D.C.: President's Commission on Critical Infrastructure Protection, October 1997). The Office of Homeland Security's *National Strategy for Homeland Security* lists the following "sectors" of the nation's critical infrastructure: agriculture, food, water, public health, emergency services, government, defense industrial base, information and telecommunications, energy, transportation, banking and finance, chemical industry, and postal and shipping.

32. The head of the government's Critical Infrastructure Protection Board has said that 98 percent of the administration's critical infrastructure protection effort is focused on cyberspace security and only 2 percent on the physical structures that support the computer networks. Joshua Dean, "Systems Failure," *Government Executive* (February 2002): 30. The danger of looking past the problems associated with the physical security of structures can be illustrated by the fact that many of the networks of the Defense Information Systems Agency are operated and located in a single compound in Arlington, Virginia, "which also houses the National Communications System, responsible for emergency operation of telephone and data systems, and the Defense's Joint Task Force–Computer Network Operations, dedicated to protecting Defense's computer networks and developing information war plans." Ibid.

33. Ariel Sabar, "NSA Still Subject to Electronic Failure," *Baltimore Sun*, 2 January 2003, 1.

34. Federal policy makers have declared that the American way of life involves five elements: our democratic political system, our freedom, our security, our economy, and our culture. Office of Homeland Security, *National Strategy for Homeland Security*, 8. A good discussion of the threats facing the nation and its vulnerabilities may be found at Advisory Panel to Assess Domestic Response Capabilities for Terrorism Involving Weapons of Mass Destruction, "Implementing the National Strategy," *Fourth Annual Report* (Washington, D.C.: RAND, 15 December 2002), 7–27.

35. Office of Homeland Security, *National Strategy for Homeland Security*, 2.

36. Ibid., 3.

37. Ibid., 13.

38. Ibid., 11–12.

39. Ibid., 41, 42.

40. Ibid., 44 (emphasis added).

41. Ibid., 13.

42. Ibid. (emphasis added).

43. Ibid.

44. Ibid.

45. Hart, *Strategy*, 320.

46. Jonathan Walters, "Frayed Connections," GovExec.com, 1 March 2002.

47. Thomas S. Foley and Newt Gingrich, "If Congress Were Attacked," *Washington Post*, 17 March 2002, B9.

48. Spencer S. Hsu, "Capitol's Emergency Plans Faulted," *Washington Post*, 26 November 2002, A2.

49. Office of Homeland Security, *National Strategy for Homeland Security*, 55 (emphasis added).

50. Shane Harris, "Disconnect," *Government Executive* (September 2002): 71.

51. Office of Homeland Security, *National Strategy for Homeland Security*, 56.

52. Harris, "Disconnect," 74 (emphasis added).

53. Gerry J. Gilmore, "Incompatible Info Systems Pose a Homeland Security Challenge, White House Info Czar Says," *American Forces Press Service*, 10 December 2002.

54. Office of Homeland Security, *National Strategy for Homeland Security*, 56.

55. Molly M. Peterson, "Homeland Defense Commander Stresses 'Need to Share' Information," GovExec.com, 3 December 2002.

56. In December 2002 NORTHCOM's Web site said that the command's mission "is homeland defense and civil support," specifically to (1) to "[c]onduct operations to deter, prevent, and defeat threats and aggression aimed at the United States, its territories, and interests within the assigned area of responsibility"; and (2) as directed by the president or secretary of defense, to "provide military assistance to civil authorities including consequence management operations."

57. Shortly after the 11 September attacks, the U.S. Joint Forces Command established the JFHQ-HLS to coordinate military support to civil authorities for both natural and man-made disasters.

58. Characterizing homeland security as "the most complex challenge ever undertaken by the U.S. government," David McIntyre, a former dean of the National War College, expressed great concern that the United States has no systematic preparation above training for first responders. "There is no nationally recognized program of higher education at all," he said. "In fact, there is no generally accepted body

of knowledge upon which to base an academic discipline. Precious little cross-disciplinary study has been published concerning how and why nations, local governments, and private industries work under normal conditions—and virtually no research is available concerning how they should function when under attack." David McIntyre, *Education for Homeland Security: The Critical Need*, Institute Commentary 012 (Washington, D.C.: ANSER Institute for Homeland Security, December 2002).

59. Walters, "Frayed Connections."

Chapter 6. Posse Comitatus and Military Force

1. *United States v. Harlley*, 796 F. 2d 112, 114 n. 3 (5th Cir. 1986).

2. See *Davis v. South Carolina*, 107 U.S. 597 (1883).

3. Paul Schott Stevens, *U.S. Armed Forces and Homeland Defense* (Washington, D.C.: CSIS, 2001), 23. A sponsor of the legislation declared that it was "designed to put a stop to the practice, which has become fearfully common, of military officers of every grade answering the call of every marshal and deputy marshal to aid in the enforcement of the laws." 7 Cong. Rec. 3846, 3849, quoted in 41 Op. Att'y Gen. 313, 330 n. 7 (1957), as cited in ibid.

4. See, e.g., *United States v. Chon*, 210 F. 3d 990, 993 (9th Cir. 2000).

5. U.S. Department of Defense Directive 5525.5, 20 December 1989, Washington, D.C.

6. A root cause of the American Revolution was the English maintenance of standing armies in America in peacetime without the consent of the colonial legislatures. The colonists had no need to project military force beyond their borders and were unwilling to pay for a significant professional army. Moreover, prior to the revolution, many colonists shared the belief of the English Whigs and Classical Republicans, "which stressed the role of the militia as the proper means of defense for a free republic." William S. Fields and David T. Hardy, "The Third Amendment and the Issue of the Maintenance of Standing Armies: A Legal History," *American Journal of Legal History* 35 (1991): 393.

7. *Perpich, et al. v. Department of Defense, et al.*, 496 U.S. 334, 340 (1990). The court also noted that at the Virginia ratification convention, Edmund Randolph stated that "there was not a member in the federal Convention, who did not feel indignation" at the idea of a standing army. Ibid., footnote 5.

8. See, for example, Allan R. Millett, *The American Political System and Civilian Control of the Military: A Historical Perspective* (Columbus: Ohio State University, 1979), 2.

9. See for example, Charles J. Dunlap Jr., "Welcome to the Junta: The Erosion of Civilian Control of the U.S. Military," *Wake Forest Law Review* 29 (1994): 341–42; Matthew Carlton Hammond, "The Posse Comitatus Act: A Principle in Need of Renewal," *Washington University Law Quarterly* (summer 1997).

10. Rowan Scarborough, "Record Deployments Take Toll on Military," *Washington Times*, 28 March 2000, 6.

11. Sam Walker, "A Few Good Men Are Being Stretched Too Thin," *Christian Science Monitor*, 19 August 1994, 1.

12. National Commission on Terrorism, *Countering the Changing Threat of International Terrorism* (Washington, D.C.: Government Printing Office, 2000), 39 (emphasis added).

13. H. R. McMaster, *Dereliction of Duty* (New York: Harper Collins, 1997), ix.

14. Gen. Douglas MacArthur, "Duty, Honor, Country," Address to the Corps of Cadets, U.S. Military Academy, West Point, New York, 12 May 1962.

15. U.S. Constitution, art. 2, sec. 2.

16. U.S. Constitution, art. 2, sec. 3.

17. U.S. Constitution, art. 1, sec. 8.

18. Ibid.

19. U.S. Constitution, art. 4, sec. 4 (emphasis added).

20. E. Corwin, *The President: Office and Powers, 1787–1957*, quoted in John Norton Moore, Frederick S. Tipson, and Robert F. Turner, *National Security Law* (Durham, N.C.: Carolina Academic Press, 1990), 822–23 (emphasis added).

21. Ibid.

22. President's Special Review Board, *Report of the President's Special Review Board* (Tower Commission Report) (Washington, D.C.: President's Special Review Board, 1987), II-1.

23. Ibid. (emphasis added).

24. *United States v. Curtiss-Wright Export Corp.*, 299 U.S. 304, 319–20 (1936) (emphasis added).

25. Thomas Jefferson, Letter to John Colvin, 29 June 1810, in Paul Ford, ed., *The Writings of Thomas Jefferson* (New York: Putnam, 1899), 9:276 (emphasis added).

26. *Youngstown Sheet and Tube Co. v. Sawyer*, 343 U.S. 579, 637 (1952) (Jackson, J., concurring).

27. Alexander Hamilton, *The Federalist Papers*, No. 23 (New York: New American Library, 1961), 153.

28. *Mitchell v. Harmony*, 54 U.S. (13 Howard) 115, 134 (1851).

29. Ibid.

30. *United States v. Russell*, 80 U.S. (13 Wallace) 623, 627 (1871).

31. Ibid.

32. Leonard W. Levy, Kenneth L. Karst, and Dennis J. Mahoney, *Encyclopedia of the American Constitution* (New York: MacMillan Publishing Company, 1986), 1:417.

33. Ibid.

34. Ibid.

35. *In re the Amy Warwick*, 67 U.S. (2 Black) 635 (1862).

36. Ibid., 668–69. In a recent case, a federal appellate judge, who quoted from the *Prize Cases*, wrote: "I read the *Prize Cases* to stand for the proposition that the President has independent authority to repel aggressive acts by third parties even without specific congressional authorization, and courts may not review the level of force selected." *Campbell v. Clinton*, 203 F.3d 19, 27 (D.C. Cir. 2000) (Silberman, J., concurring).

37. Theodore Roosevelt, *An Autobiography* (New York: MacMillan Company, 1913), 372.

38. Paul L. Murphy, *The Constitution in Crisis Times, 1918–1969* (New York: Harper and Row, 1972), 221.

39. Ibid.

40. For a discussion of "certain fundamental statutory authorities available to a president" in the context of a domestic emergency, including an attack involving a weapon of mass destruction, see Stevens, *U.S. Armed Forces and Homeland Defense*, 14–22, 24–25; see also Title 10 *U.S. Code*, sec. 382; Title 16, sec. 1861; Title 18, secs. 112, 351, 831, 1116, 1751, 3056; Title 25, sec. 180; Title 42, secs. 97, 1989; Title 43, sec. 1065; Title 48, secs. 1422, 1591; and Title 50, secs. 220.

41. Mark Thompson, "Soldier on the Beat," *Time*, 3 December 2001, 60.

42. Pentagon's Homeland Duties Have Checks and Balances," *CQ Daily Monitor*, 7 February 2002, 8.

43. David M. Shribman, "Next in the Debate over Security at Home, the Role of U.S. Military," *Boston Globe*, 23 July 2002, 3.

44. Office of Homeland Security, *National Strategy for Homeland Security*, 48, also available at www.whitehouse.gov./homeland/book/sect4.

45. Shribman, "Next in the Debate."

46. Joyce Howard Price, "Biden Backs Letting Soldiers Arrest Civilians," *Washington Times*, 22 July 2002, 1.

47. Ibid.

48. Edwin Chen and Nick Anderson, "Bush Sets Security Strategy," *Los Angeles Times*, 17 July 2002, 1.

49. Price, "Biden Backs Letting Soldiers Arrest Civilians."

50. Chen and Anderson, "Bush Sets Security Strategy."

51. Jeanne Cummings, "Homeland-Security Plan Roils Cabinet—Agencies Fear That Funds, Influence Will Be Diverted to Form New Department," *Wall Street Journal*, 17 July 2002, A4.

52. Shribman, "Next in the Debate."

53. Founded in 1977, the Cato Institute is a nonprofit public policy research foundation. The philosophy animating its work has, in its own words, "increasingly come to be called 'libertarianism.'" It involves a "strict respect for civil liberties and skepticism about . . . foreign military adventurism."

54. Gene Healy, "Misguided Mission for Military," *Washington Times*, 31 July 2002, 14.

55. NGAUS was created in 1878 for the express "purpose of providing united National Guard representation before Congress." The political clout of the organization can be illustrated by the almost identical words used by Secretary of Defense Dick Cheney and Chairman of the Joint Chiefs of Staff Colin Powell to describe their efforts to cut the number of guardsmen and reservists after the end of the Cold War. "We attempted to make some changes," Cheney said, "and we ran into a brick wall— the combination of the Guard and Reserve lobbies and the Congress." "When we tried to cut [the number of guardsmen and reservists] back to sensible levels," Powell recalled, "we had our heads handed to us by the National Guard and Reserve Associations and their congressional supporters. We were threatening part-time jobs, armories, money going into communities." See Brendan M. Greely Jr. and Fred L. Schultz, "About Fighting and Winning Wars: An Interview with Dick Cheney," *U.S. Naval Institute Proceedings* (May 1996): 34; Powell and Persico, *My American Journey*, 550.

56. Christopher Prawdzik, "Posse Comitatus Hits the Spotlight," ngaus.org/newsroom, 31 July 2002.

57. "The Army on the Home Front," *Christian Science Monitor*, 25 July 2002, 8.

58. Price, "Biden Backs Letting Soldiers Arrest Civilians."

59. Ibid.

60. Eric Schmitt, "Wider Military Role in U.S. Is Urged," *New York Times*, 21 July, 2002, 16.

61. Ibid.

62. Shribman, "Next in the Debate."

63. Schmitt, "Wider Military Role."

64. Joyce Howard Price, "Biden Backs Letting Soldiers Arrest Civilians."

65. Schmitt, "Wider Military Role."

66. *Perpich v. Department of Defense*, 496 U.S. 334, 345, 110 S. Ct. 2418, 2425 (1990).

67. *Reid v. Colvert*, 354 U.S. 1, 40 (1957).

68. Craig T. Trebilcock, "The Myth of Posse Comitatus," *Journal of Homeland Security* (October 2000).

69. John R. Brinkerhoff, "The Posse Comitatus Act and Homeland Security," *Journal of Homeland Security* (February 2002).

70. Ibid.

71. See, e.g., Title 10, *U.S. Code*, secs. 371–81.

72. See Stephen M. Duncan, *Hearing before the Subcommittees on Legislation and National Security and Government Information, Justice and Agriculture, House Committee on Government Operations, United States House of Representatives*, 101st Cong., 1st sess., 17 October 1989.

73. James Dao, "Leading the Military in a New Mission: A War at Home," *New York Times*, 8 October 2001, A12.

74. Bradley Graham and Bill Miller, "Pentagon Debates Homeland Defense Role," *Washington Post*, 11 February 2002, A6.

75. Eric Pianin, "Study Assesses Risk of Attack on Chemical Plan," *Washington Post*, 12 March 2002, A8.

76. Stevens, *U.S. Armed Forces and Homeland Defense*, 27.

77. The perceived deficiencies included the appearance of "selective justice" in ad hoc tribunals; delays which permit evidence to be destroyed, defendants to escape, and witnesses to be intimidated; excessive costs; and the limits of time and place.

78. George F. Will, "'Up from' Accountability," *Washington Post*, 11 July 2002, 21.

79. The technical objections are described with greater specificity in U.S. Department of State, "Fact Sheet: The International Criminal Court," Washington, D.C., 6 May 2002.

80. The concept of "universal jurisdiction," or at least the aggressive international effort to establish such a doctrine, is of relatively recent vintage. In 1993, Belgium adopted a law that purports to give that country jurisdiction over alleged war criminals regardless of where the alleged crimes are committed. A subsequent war crimes complaint against Prime Minister Ariel Sharon of Israel was dismissed by a Belgian appeals court in June 2002 on the ground that persons charged under the law have to be present in Belgium, but the law was sustained. The concept gained additional notoriety in 1998 when the former president of Chile was detained in Britain for almost a year and a half because a Spanish judge had issued an extradition request as part of an effort to try him for crimes allegedly committed against Spaniards on Chilean soil. For an informative discussion of the concept and its implications for U.S. foreign policy, see Henry Kissinger, *Does America Need a Foreign Policy?* (New York: Simon and Schuster, 2002), 273–82.

81. Will, "'Up from' Accountability."

82. Ruth Wedgewood, "An International Court Is Still a Bad Idea," *Wall Street Journal Online*, 15 April 2002.

83. Ibid.

84. Kissinger, *Does America Need a Foreign Policy*, 280.

85. Jeffrey T. Kuhner, "Balkans Tribunal Turns to Clinton," *Washington Times*, 8 July 2002, 1.

86. Wedgewood, "International Court Is Still a Bad Idea."

87. U.S. Department of State, "Fact Sheet: The International Criminal Court."

88. Donald H. Rumsfeld, Secretary of Defense, Statement on the ICC Treaty, Washington, D.C., 6 May 2002.

89. Ibid.

90. Ibid.

91. Ibid.

92. Jonathan Marcus, "Analysis: U.S. Treaty Turnaround," BBC News, 6 May 2002.

93. "U.S. Renounces World Court Treaty," BBC News, 6 May 2002.

94. Ibid.

95. "U.S. Seeks Exemption from Prosecution for U.N. Peacekeepers," *Baltimore Sun*, 21 May 2002.

96. Rumsfeld, Secretary of Defense, Statement on the ICC Treaty.

97. "The dispute," said the *London Daily Telegraph*, "is not about whether Washington supports human rights. America has an immeasurably better record . . . than most of the nations that have ratified the ICC. . . . The issue, rather, is: who has the authority to bring cases to trial? . . . [T]he Statute of Rome . . . destroys the understanding on which international law has rested for centuries. For the first time, it establishes the principle that treaties are binding not only on the states that are party to them, but also on non-signatories. . . . Hitherto, legal systems have been rooted in democratic assemblies. Laws are passed by national legislatures, which are responsible to their peoples, and treaties signed by accountable governments. But, from today, the ICC will cast off the guy-ropes that attach it to its constituent states. . . . From now on, it will function as an international body answerable to no one." "Lone Stand for Justice," *London Daily Telegraph*, 1 July 2002.

98. Rick Maze, "Reach of International Court Could Extend Beyond Troops," *Army Times* (19 August 2002): 19. Many U.S. officials also remember with concern the legal actions filed against former Secretary of State Henry Kissinger in Chilean courts for alleged support of the 1973 military coup in Chile that initiated seventeen years of military rule under Gen. Augusto Pinochet.

99. Bill Gertz and Rowan Scarborough, "Inside the Ring," *Washington Times*, 19 July 2002, 12.

100. Colum Lynch, "U.S. Wins 1-Year Shield from War Crimes Court," *Washington Post*, 13 July 2002, A16.

101. Nicholas Kralev, "U.N. Balks at ICC Compromise," *Washington Times*, 12 July 2002, 1.

102. George W. Bush, Remarks to the 10th Mountain Division at Fort Drum, New York, *Weekly Compilation of Presidential Documents* 38, 29 (22 July 2002): 1228.

103. Samuel Huntington, *The Soldier and the State* (New York: Vintage Books, 1957), 2.

104. Kissinger, *Does America Need a Foreign Policy*, 17.

Chapter 7. Mobilizing the Citizen Warriors

  1. The U.S. Army Reserve, U.S. Navy Reserve, U.S. Marine Corps Reserve, and U.S.
     Air Force Reserve are federal forces. The Army National Guard and Air National
     Guard are individual state forces when operating under state law or pursuant to Title
     32 of the *U.S. Code*. They become federal forces and operate pursuant to Title 10 of
     the *U.S. Code* only by the direction of the president. For the purposes here, the terms
     "reserve components" and "reserve forces" are generally meant to include the National
     Guard. Most individuals who serve in the reserve components are members of either
     the selected reserve or the individual ready reserve. The selected reserve (approxi-
     mately 863,000 in 2003) consists of units and individuals who are paid to train for a
     minimum of thirty-nine days each year and whose activation would likely be neces-
     sary for a large-scale contingency or wartime missions. The individual ready reserve
     (approximately 348,800 in 2002) is a pool of unpaid individuals who have prior mil-
     itary service; they are not required to train unless called to active duty.

  2. Mark Perry, *Four Stars* (Boston: Houghton Mifflin, 1989), 152. See also Lewis Sorley,
     Honorable Warrior (Lawrence: University Press of Kansas, 1998), 208–17.

  3. U.S. Department of the Navy, *A Report on the Navy's Total Force FY 90* (Washington,
     D.C.: U.S. Department of the Navy, 1990), ii.

  4. For a fuller discussion of the development of the base force, see Duncan, *Citizen
     Warriors*, 169–70, 180–83. See also Jaffe, *Development of the Base Force*.

  5. George Bush, Remarks at the Aspen Institute Symposium in Aspen, Colorado, *Weekly
     Compilation of Presidential Documents* 26, 31 (2 August 1990): 1190.

  6. The selected reserve consists of those units and individuals designated by their
     respective services and approved by the chairman of the Joint Chief of Staff as so
     essential to initial wartime missions that they have priority over all other reserves
     in terms of personnel, training, equipment, and readiness. When not employed on
     peacetime operational missions, members of the selected reserve typically spend
     at least thirty-nine days each year engaged in training. 10 *U.S. Code*, sec. 10143. The
     individual ready reserve/inactive National Guard is a manpower pool comprised
     principally of individuals who have received training while on active duty or in the
     selected reserve; they have some period of their military service obligations remain-
     ing. Generally, they do not perform regularly scheduled training.

  7. The story of the mobilization and performance of the reserve components in
     Operations Desert Shield and Desert Storm is told in Duncan, *Citizen Warriors*.

8. George Bush, Address before a Joint Session of the Congress on the Cessation of the Persian Gulf Conflict, *Weekly Compilation of Presidential Documents* 27, 10 (6 March 1991): 257.

9. William Matthews, "Pentagon Insists on Call-up Authority," *Army Times* (18 July 1994): 26.

10. William Matthews, "Reserves Get Larger Role in Battle on Domestic Ills," *Army Times* (25 July 1994): 22.

11. Deborah R. Lee, Remarks to the National Guard Association of the United States, Boston, Massachusetts, 2 September 1994.

12. William Matthews, "Call-up More Likely," *Army Times* (6 June 1994): 20.

13. William Matthews, "Call-Up Plan Hits Snag in Senate," *Army Times* (27 June 1994): 20.

14. Commission on Roles and Missions of the Armed Forces, *Directions for Defense: Report of the Commission on Roles and Missions of the Armed Forces* (Arlington, Va.: Commission on Roles and Missions of the Armed Forces, 24 May 1995).

15. William Matthews, "DoD Roles Review Rolls On," *Defense News* (28 August–3 September 1995): 4.

16. National Defense Panel, "Transforming Defense."

17. In the federal government's 1989 fiscal year, which was from 1 October 1988 to 30 September 1989, only 1,399,840 days of active duty were performed by reservists. That was consistent with the previous two years. In FY 1990, the year Iraq invaded Kuwait, reservists spent 5,463,966 days on active duty. In FY 1991, the year of combat operations against Iraq, 44,224,353 days of active duty were performed. When the armed conflict was over, the number of days of active duty performed in FY 1992 returned to the prewar range of 5,316,219. By FY 1996, however, reservists were required to perform 13,508,653 days of duty.

18. By February 2002 the number of selected reservists had been reduced to a total of 864,000, including 350,000 in the Army National Guard, 205,000 in the U.S. Army Reserve, 106,600 in the Air National Guard, 75,600 in the U.S. Air Force Reserve, 87,800 in the U.S. Naval Reserve, and 39,558 in the U.S. Marine Corps Reserve.

19. In his memorandum to each of the military services, Laird had highlighted his fiscal concerns: "Within the Department of Defense, . . . economies will require reductions in over all strengths and capabilities of the active forces and increased reliance on the combat and the combat support units of the Guard and Reserves. Emphasis will be given to the concurrent consideration of the Total Forces, Active and Reserve, to determine the most advantageous mix to support national strategy and meet the threat. A total force concept will be applied in all aspects of planning, programming, manning, equipping and employing National Guard and Reserve Forces."

Melvin B. Laird, Secretary of Defense, Memorandum to the Secretaries of the Military Departments, 21 August 1970, Pentagon, Washington, D.C.

20. Lewis Sorley, *Thunderbolt* (New York: Simon and Schuster, 1992), 361–66. By late 2002, and despite strong support for the all voluntary force among military leaders, some members of Congress were calling for a return to a draft on the ground that it would make members of Congress "think a little longer and harder before they send our nation's sons and our daughters into harm's way." Clarence Page, "Feeling a Draft Coming On," *Chicago Tribune*, 1 January 2003.

21. Duncan, *Citizen Warriors*, 220.

22. Ibid.

23. Steven Lee Myers, "Bush Warns against 'Overdeployment' of National Guard and Reserve Units," *New York Times*, 15 February 2001, A26.

24. The strength or total number of Army National Guard personnel is approximately 350,000. The strength of the U.S. Army Reserve is 205,000.

25. The strength of the Air National Guard is approximately 106,000. The strength of the U.S. Air Force Reserve is 75,600.

26. U.S. Commission on National Security/21st Century, *Road Map for National Security*, ix, 25 (emphasis added).

27. Don Edwards, "The National Guard's Enhanced Role in Homeland Security," *Journal of Homeland Security* (March 2001).

28. Bob Woodward and Dan Balz, "'We Will Rally the World,'" *Washington Post*, 28 January 2002, A10.

29. The executive order authorized the activation of members of the ready reserve "for not more than 24 consecutive months." George W. Bush, Executive Order 13223—Ordering the Ready Reserve of the Armed Forces to Active Duty and Delegating Certain Authority to the Secretary of Defense and the Secretary of Transportation, *Weekly Compilation of Presidential Documents* 37, 37 (17 September 2001): 1311. In 1976 Congress passed legislation that authorized a president to involuntarily activate members of the selected reserve without congressional approval "to augment the active forces for any operational mission." The statute was subsequently amended. During the 1990–91 Persian Gulf War, the law permitted the activation of as many as 200,000 selected reservists for no more than 180 days. In April 1992, I recommended to Secretary of Defense Dick Cheney that Title 10 of the *U.S. Code* be amended to permit a president to activate selected reservists for as long as 360 days. Cheney approved the recommendation. The statute was subsequently amended. In time of national emergency, it now authorizes the activation of as many as one million members of the ready reserve for as long as twenty-four consecutive months. Title 10, *U.S. Code*, sec. 12302.

30. George W. Bush, Remarks to Employees at the Pentagon and an Exchange with Reporters in Arlington, Virginia, *Weekly Compilation of Presidential Documents* 37, 38 (17 September 2001): 1319.

31. Mike Allen and Greg Schneider, "National Guard to Be Used at Airports," *Washington Post*, 28 September 2001, A1. National Guard personnel called up for duty at airports were activated by their respective states "in service of the United States." This permitted them to receive the same federal pay and benefits as those federalized for other duties, but they were governed by their state's military code, not the Uniform Code of Military Justice and they could not be deployed outside of the United States.

32. Matthew Cox, "Homeland Defenders," *Army Times* (22 October 2001): 13.

33. Bryan Bender, "National Guard Faces Drastic Overhaul," *Boston Globe*, 20 November 2001, 12.

34. C. Mark Brinkley, "First Line of Defense," *Army Times* (29 October 2001): 14.

35. Matthew Cox, "Stepping up," *Army Times* (12 November 2001): 18.

36. Stephanie Simon, "All the Readiness Money Can Buy," latimes.com, 26 December 2001. On the day of the terrorist attacks, it took a civil support team in New York twelve hours to arrive at the World Trade Center from a base near Albany. Ibid.

37. Ibid.

38. Barry McCaffery, former director of the White House Office of National Drug Control Policy, is of the opinion that the United States needs forty thousand agents on U.S. borders, not the ten thousand currently employed by the U.S. Border Patrol. Timothy B. Clark, "The Cost of Security," *Government Executive* (July 2002): 8.

39. "National Guard Troops to Aid Civilian Agencies in Securing U.S. Borders," *Inside the Pentagon* (31 January 2002): 1.

40. Since 1933 all persons enlisted in a state's National Guard unit have simultaneously enlisted in the National Guard of the United States. A member of the guard who is ordered to active duty in the federal service is relieved of his or her status in the state guard for the entire period of federal service. *Perpich, et. al. v. Department of Defense, et al.*, 496 U.S. 334, 345, 110 S. Ct. 2418 (1990).

41. "Identity Crisis," *Government Executive* (September 2002): 58, 60. Operations under state control, but funded by the federal government are authorized by Title 32 of the *U.S. Code*.

42. Ibid.

43. John Gittelsohn, "Guard's Border Role Delayed by Pentagon?" *Orange County Register*, 11 February 2002.

44. "Debate Swells over Sending Unarmed Troops to Guard U.S. Borders," *Inside the Pentagon* (7 March 2002): 1.

45. Christopher Thorne, "Officials Ask to Arm Guardsmen," *Los Angeles Times,* 24 March 2002, B6.

46. The adjutants general of the fifty states, three territories, and the District of Columbia are state military officials. They serve (unless federalized) in the Army National Guard or Air National Guard of their respective states and are the senior military officials of their states. Most are appointed by the state's governor. The adjutant general of South Carolina is elected in a statewide general election. Some hold a state rank that is not officially recognized by the Department of Defense. The adjutant general of Vermont, for example, had held the rank of lieutenant colonel for only eighteen months when she was promoted three ranks by her state to the rank of major general (state).

47. Adjutants General Association of the United States, "To the Governors and Legislators of the Several States, Territories and the District of Columbia and to the Congress and the President of the United States of America," letter, 25 February 2002, available at www.ngaus.org/adjutants/agaus. Even within the National Guard political loyalties vary. The adjutants general have stronger bonds to the state governor who appointed them. The military leaders of the National Guard bureau in the Pentagon are more sensitive to the army and air force chiefs of staff because they influence mission assignments and resource allocations.

48. Ibid., 4. Most governors share this view. The executive director of the National Governors Association told an audience at the National Defense University, "Governors feel that the Guard is theirs." Remarks of Dr. Raymond C. Scheppach at the Homeland Security: The Civil Military Dimensions Symposium, National Defense University, Fort Lesley J. McNair, Washington, D.C., 19 September 2002.

49. Adjutants General Association of the United States, "To the Governors and Legislators," 3.

50. Ibid., 4.

51. Ibid., 5.

52. Ibid.

53. As the senior counterdrug official in DoD during 1989–93, I established procedures for the review of each plan in depth to ensure that it was operationally feasible and that the costing methodology provided by the state was correct. The governing statute also required the secretary of defense to consult with the U.S. attorney general regarding the adequacy of each plan before funds could be released for pay, allowances, clothing, subsistence, gratuities, travel, the costs of the operation, the maintenance of equipment, and various other expenses. Perhaps more important, I

had the responsibility of deciding how much counterdrug funding each governor would receive and of defending my decisions before the governors and Congress.

54. Adjutants General Association of the United States, "To the Governors and Legislators," 5.

55. *Perpich, et al. v. Department of Defense, et al.*, 496 U.S. 334 at 353, 110 S. Ct 2418 (1990).

56. "The Citizens of each State shall be entitled to all Privileges and Immunities of Citizens in the several States." U.S. Constitution, art. 4, sec. 2.

57. *Nelson v. Geringer* and *Dillon v. Geringer*, 295 F.3d 1082, 1090, 1092 (10th Cir. 2002).

58. Ibid.

59. George Washington, General Orders, 4 July 1775, Cambridge, Mass.

60. Beth Shuster, "Call-up Worries Agencies," *Los Angeles Times*, 19 September 2001, B1.

61. Abraham McLaughlin, "U.S. Guard Call-up Hits Cities Hard," *Christian Science Monitor*, 28 January 2002, 1.

62. Rick Maze, "Officials Worry War Needs Erode Homeland Security," *Army Times* (21 April 2003): 26. To address the problem, the new commander of NORTHCOM has proposed having National Guard individuals volunteer to be federalized for specific missions with consent from their state governor. This would give governors more predictability in the use of certain elements of the state guard and give NORTH-COM a pool of available people with relevant skills and experience.

63. Associated Press, "General Says U.S. Troops Tired, Backs Forces Boost," *Washington Post*, 15 March 2002, A14.

64. Jim Tice, "More Soldiers?" *Army Times* (18 March 2002): 8.

65. Ibid.

66. David Postman, "Rumsfeld Says Guard Should Be Focused on War," *Seattle Times*, 20 April 2002, B1.

67. Sydney J. Freedberg Jr., "Weekend Warriors No More," *National Journal* (8 June 2002).

68. *Fishgold v. Sullivan Drydock and Repair Corp.*, 328 U.S. 275, 284 (1946).

69. The survey was conducted by William M. Mercer, Inc., New York, N.Y.

70. The survey was conducted by Ross Roy, Inc., Detroit, Mich.

71. Duncan, *Citizen Warriors*, 116.

72. Title 38, *U.S. Code*, sec. 4301.

73. George Edmonson, "U.S. Relies Heavily on Part-Time Warriors," *Atlanta Journal and Constitution*, 20 June 2002, 4B.

74. All of the seven reserve components now have established family readiness programs, which include such practices as issuance of predeployment checklists, printed guides and directories of resource contacts, Web sites that provide links to critical services, and volunteers who are trained to resolve family-related issues.

75. Matthew Cox, "Guarding Home," *Army Times* (15 April 2002): 16.

76. The early estimates of Pentagon officials were that at least 150,000 reservists would be required. "Advance Notice for Reserve Deployments?" *Army Times* (2 December 2002): 5. In fact, on 19 March 2003, the day on which hostilities against Iraq commenced in Operation Iraqi Freedom, the Pentagon announced that 212,617 citizen warriors were on active duty.

77. Gen. Wesley Clark, the former NATO commander, expressed the opinion that "even under the most optimistic scenarios, the troubles [would likely] begin" immediately after the fighting stopped. "Food distribution will break down. Health care will break down. There will be violence and revenge in the streets as Saddam's secret police melt-away." Wesley Clark, "A Quick War, Then Lots of Trouble," *International Harold Tribune*, 9 October 2002. Military authorities would be responsible for everything from ensuring order and stability to the management of oil production and humanitarian programs. Peter Slevin, "U.S. Mulls Military Rule after Hussein," *Washington Post*, 11 October 2002, A11.

78. Unique among military forces, civil affairs specialists bring to their military service their civilian experience as managers of local government, utilities, school systems, hospitals, and other civilian infrastructures. Fewer than four hundred of the army's civil affairs specialists in September 2002 were members of its regular (active) unit. David Wood, "Army's Civil Affairs Specialists Make Ready to Occupy Iraq," Newhouse.com, 8 October 2002.

79. Donald H. Rumsfeld, Secretary of Defense, *Report of the Quadrennial Defense Review* (Washington, D.C.: U.S. Department of Defense, 30 September 2001), 60.

80. Ibid., 63–64.

81. Donald H. Rumsfeld, Secretary of Defense, *Annual Report to the President and the Congress* (Washington, D.C.: U.S. Department of Defense, 2002), 63–64.

82. When the study—referred to as the Reserve Component Comprehensive Review—was completed, Rumsfeld asked the military services to consider changes in the active/reserve relationship. James Kitfield, "Reservists Guarded on Rumsfeld's Ideas," *National Journal* (8 February 2003). A House Armed Services Committee report called for a thirty-three-thousand-person increase in the active force to avoid a serious morale problem in the reserve components. Civilian officials in the Pentagon continued to assert that what was needed was not more troops, just some rearranging, namely, a shift of more jobs performed by active force personnel to civilians. Active personnel would thus be free to perform more pressing work that was currently assigned to reservists. Rick Maze, "It's All in the Balance, DoD Says of Force Levels," *Army Times* (24 March 2003): 24.

83. David S. Chu, Address to the National Guard Association of the United States, Long Beach, Calif., 9 September 2002.

84. The proposed legislation was referred to as the Defense Transformation for the 21st Century Act of 2003. As justification for the new training requirement, the Department of Defense declared, "Current laws governing the mobilization and training of the Reserve forces were fashioned to confront contingencies never experienced before 11 September 2001. These laws created processes built for wars in which we had some amount of warning and/or an identified state actor. Those factors allowed time for mobilizing and training large Reserve formations to prosecute the interests of our nation. Today, the unpredictable nature of future conflicts requires that both Active and Reserve forces must be able to respond quickly to threats at home and abroad. This means that Reserve forces must receive earlier, more effective training to ensure they are prepared to deploy immediately in response to imminent contingencies." U.S. Department of Defense, "Defense Transformation for the 21st Century Act of 2003," final recommendation, 10 April 2003, Washington, D.C., 64–65.

85. See, for example, "The Army on the Home Front," *Christian Science Monitor*, 25 July 2002, 8.

86. U.S. Commission on National Security/21st Century, *Road Map for National Security*, 25.

87. Ibid., 25–26.

88. L. Paul Bremmer III and Edwin Meese III, *Defending the American Homeland* (Washington, D.C.: Heritage Foundation, 22 January 2002), 9.

89. William Matthews and Christopher Prawdzik, "Price of Success?" *National Guard* (September 2002): 40.

90. Advisory Panel to Assess Response Capabilities for Terrorism Involving Weapons of Mass Destruction, "Implementing the National Strategy," *Fourth Annual Report* (Washington, D.C.: RAND, 15 December 2002), 101–7.

91. "Identity Crisis," *Government Executive*, 62.

92. "Homeland Security Not Just for Guard," *Army Times* (29 July 2002): 6.

93. Jackie Calmes, "Washington Wire," *Wall Street Journal*, 28 June 2002, 1.

94. "Identity Crisis," *Government Executive*, 62.

95. The director of the Air National Guard was quoted as saying, "If you *relegate* the Guard to homeland security only, there's the possibility that we'll lose relevance and we'll therefore lose priorities and partnering with modernization [and] future missions." The former chief of the National Guard bureau declared, "We are eager to help, . . . [but] we don't want to be 'rent-a-cops' on a permanent basis, nor do we

want to allow marginal mission creep to degrade our capabilities." Matthews and Prawdzik, "Price of Success," 41 (emphasis added).

96. See, for example, Calmes, "Washington Wire"; "Homeland Security Not Just for Guard," *Army Times*.

97. Office of the Assistant Secretary of Defense for Reserve Affairs, *Review of Reserve Component Contributions to National Defense* (Washington, D.C.: U.S. Department of Defense, 2003, draft), 34. The study did, however, propose a concept of rotational watch that had merit. Under this concept, specific reserve units would be identified for rotation for a ninety-day homeland security "watch" period every eighteen months. When not on watch, the units would be free to engage in training for more traditional operations. Ibid., 38.

98. The acting chief of the National Guard bureau expressed the opinion that nothing revolutionary will happen; whatever changes take place in the National Guard will be evolutionary. Remarks of Maj. Gen. Raymond Rees, ARNG (Army National Guard), Homeland Security: The Civil-Military Dimensions Symposium, National Defense University, Fort Lesley J. McNair, Washington, D.C., 19 September 2002.

Chapter 8. American Due Process and the Laws of War

1. In most circumstances, the U.S. government is represented in the lower courts, at both the trial and appellate levels, by a U.S. attorney or a representative of one of the other divisions of the Department of Justice. The solicitor general's primary responsibility is to represent the executive branch of the government in the U.S. Supreme Court. He does, however, have a special responsibility to the Court itself and its members rely on him to consider the long-term effect of each case upon the law generally and the jurisprudence of the Court, as well as the narrow, immediate result. As a result of this dual responsibility, he has been referred to as the "tenth justice." See Lincoln Caplan, *Tenth Justice* (New York: Alfred A. Knopf, 1987), 3. Since the 11 September 2001 attacks, the Office of the Solicitor General has assumed a much larger role in the Bush administration's assertion of executive authority in the war against terrorism. U.S. Solicitor General Theodore Olson, whose wife was aboard the jetliner that crashed into the Pentagon, explained the new policy. "There are certain cases that, if they look from the early stages as if they're going to possibly wind up in the Supreme Court, then we feel it's helpful to get involved at the early stage so we don't look back at the record that's been created later and say we wish we'd added that ingredient or wish we'd looked at that issue." Charles Lane, "Olson's Role in War on Terror Matches His Uncommon Clout," *Washington Post*, 3 July 2002, A21.

2. The holding facility for detainees at the naval base was activated on 11 January 2002 under the control of Joint Task Force 160. By the end of May 2002 there were 384 detainees at the facility.

3. 317 U.S. 1 (1942).

4. Associated Press, "DOD: Ruling Infringes on War Powers," abcNews.com, 19 June 2002.

5. The doctrine of the separation of powers has been addressed by the U.S. Supreme Court on several occasions. In *Kendall v. United States*, 37 U.S. (12 Pet.) 524, 610 (1838), the Court observed, "[T]he theory of the Constitution undoubtedly is, that the great powers of the government are divided into separate departments; and so far as these powers are derived from the Constitution, the departments may be regarded as independent of each other." In *Kilbourn v. Thompson*, 103 U.S. 168, 190–91 (1880), the Court declared that it is "essential to the successful working of [the U.S. system of government] that the persons entrusted with power in any one of these branches shall not be permitted to encroach upon the powers confided to the others, but that each shall by the law of its creation be limited to the exercise of the powers appropriate to its own department and no other." See also *Evans v. Gore*, 253 U.S. 245 (1920); *Myers v. United States*, 272 U.S. 106 (1926); *Youngstown Sheet and Tube Co. v. Sawyer*, 343 U.S. 579 (1952).

6. Michael D. Shear, "Judges Consider Suspect's Right to an Attorney," *Washington Post*, 26 June 2002, A14.

7. Katharine Q. Seelye, "Lawyers Argue over Rights of a Citizen Seized on Enemy Land," *New York Times*, 26 June 2002, A18.

8. Ibid.

9. Ibid.

10. The "next friend standing" doctrine provides a narrow avenue for entry into the federal courts by someone who does not meet the standing requirements of article 3, section 2 of the U.S. Constitution.

11. *Yaser Esam Hamdi v. Donald Rumsfeld, et al.*, 294 F.3d 598, 607 (4th Cir. 2002).

12. John Lancaster and Susan Schmidt, "U.S. Rethinks Strategy for Coping with Terrorists," *Washington Post*, 14 September 2001, A9.

13. John Ashcroft, *Hearing before the Committee on the Judiciary, United States House of Representatives*, 107th Cong., 1st sess., 24 September 2001.

14. Ibid.

15. The "pen register, trap and trace" rules of Title III of the existing Omnibus Crime Control and Safe Streets Act of 1968 covered the use of technology to track the origin and destination of telephone calls. Public Law 90-351, Title 18, *U.S. Code*, sec. 2510 et seq.

16. Ibid.

17. The statute is entitled the Uniting and Strengthening America by Providing Appropriate Tools Required to Intercept and Obstruct Terrorism Act (USA PATRIOT Act) of 2001. Public Law 107-56, 107th Cong., 1st Sess., 26 October 2001.

18. Jonathan Krim and Robert O'Harrow Jr., "Bush Signs into Law New Enforcement Era," *Washington Post*, 27 October 2001, A6.

19. John Lancaster and Susan Schmidt, "U.S. Rethinks Strategy for Coping with Terrorists," *Washington Post*, 14 September 2001, A9.

20. Spencer J. Crona and Neal A. Richardson, "Justice for War Criminals of Invisible Armies: a New Legal and Military Approach to Terrorism," *Oklahoma City University Law Review* (summer/fall 1996).

21. The Laws of War are a body of rules and principles observed by civilized nations— sometimes, but not exclusively included in treaties and agreements like the Geneva Conventions and the 1907 Hague Conventions—for the regulation of matters inherent or incidental to the conduct of a public war, such as the relations of neutrals and belligerents, blockades, captures, prizes, truces and armistices, capitulations, prisoners, and declarations of war and peace. Bryan A. Gardner, ed., *Black's Law Dictionary*, 7th ed. (St. Paul, Minn.: West Group, 1999), 895.

22. The actual language of the executive order said that it would apply to noncitizens who the president determined to be a present or former member of al Qaeda or who "has engaged in, aided or abetted, or conspired to commit, acts of international terrorism, or acts in preparation therefore, that have caused, threaten to cause, or have as their aim to cause, injury or adverse effects on the United States, its citizens, national security, foreign policy, or economy"; or those who knowingly harbored someone who engaged in the forbidden acts. George W. Bush, Military Order— Detention, Treatment and Trial of Certain Non-Citizens in the War against Terrorism, Executive Order, 13 November 2001, 66 *Federal Register* 57833 (16 November 2001).

23. Thomas Fleming, *Liberty! The American Revolution* (New York: Penguin Group, 1997), 312.

24. Ibid.

25. Stephen Young, "United States Military Commissions: A Quick Guide to Available Resources," LLRX.com, 1 March 2002.

26. 68 U.S. 243 (1863).

27. 71 U.S. 2 (4 Wall) (1866).

28. Ibid.

29. The twenty-four included several of the leading military and political figures of Hitler's Third Reich. Of the twenty-two individual defendants who were actually tried, eleven were sentenced to death by hanging, three were acquitted, three were given life imprisonment, and four were sentenced to terms of imprisonment ranging from ten to twenty years.

30. Seven of the twenty-five defendants were sentenced to hang, sixteen were sentenced to life imprisonment, and two received lesser terms.

31. "No bill of attainder of ex poste facto Law shall be passed." U.S. Constitution, art. 1, sec. 8.

32. John F. Kennedy, *Profiles in Courage* (New York: Harper and Brothers, 1961), 211–24.

33. 317 U.S. 1, 63 S. Ct. 1 (1942).

34. The Articles of War provided for the government of the army.

35. The writ of habeas corpus is the means by which a person who has been arrested or confined by government authority may ask a court to require the government representative to show cause why he or she is being held. Since it originated in the English common law, it has been regarded as a safeguard against tyranny by the executive branch of government and a critical safeguard of individual liberty. The writ may not be suspended "unless in Cases of Rebellion or Invasion the Public Safety may require it." U.S. Constitution, art. 1, sec. 9.

36. 317 U.S. at 25–27; 63 S. Ct. at 9–10 (emphasis added).

37. 317 U.S. at 28; 63 S. Ct. at 11.

38. 317 U.S. at 45–46; 63 S. Ct. at 19–20.

39. 317 U.S. at 30–31; 63 S. Ct. at 12.

40. Ibid.

41. 317 U.S. at 46; 63 S. Ct. at 20.

42. 317 U.S. at 45; 63 S. Ct. at 19.

43. 317 U.S. at 37–38; 63 S. Ct. at 15–16.

44. See, for example, *Application of Yamashita,* 327 U.S. 1 (1946); *Duncan v. Kahanamoku,* 327 U.S. 304 (1946); *Madsen v. Kinsella,* 343 U.S. 341 (1952); *United States Ex Rel. Toth v. Quarles,* 350 U.S. 11 (1955).

45. Capt. Alfred Dreyfus was a highly regarded French artillery officer from the prestigious Ecole Polytechnique. He was arrested in 1894 at age thirty-five on charges of espionage. He was court-martialed and sentenced to solitary confinement for life on Devil's Island, French Guyana. By 1898, however, the real guilty party had been identified. In response to a public outcry, Dreyfus was returned to France; he was retried in 1899. He received amnesty in 1900 and six years later was reinstated in the French army. He served with distinction in World War I and was promoted to colonel. He died in 1935.

46. William Safire, "Kangaroo Courts," *New York Times*, 26 November 2001, A17. A Star Chamber was an English court that had "broad civil and criminal jurisdiction at the King's discretion and noted for its secretive, arbitrary, and oppressive procedures, including compulsory self-incrimination, inquisitorial investigation, and the absence of juries." Garner, *Black's Law Dictionary*, 1414. It was abolished in 1641.

47. T. R. Reid, "Europeans Reluctant to Send Terror Suspects to U.S.," *Washington Post*, 29 November 2001, A23.

48. Laurence H. Tribe, "Why Congress Must Curb Bush's Military Courts," *New Republic Online*, 29 November 2001.

49. Ibid.

50. George F. Will, "Trials and Terrorists," *Washington Post*, 22 November 2001, A47.

51. CNN.com, 21 November 2001.

52. See Paul Wolfowitz, *Hearing before the Armed Services Committee, United States Senate*, 107th Cong., 1st sess., 13 December 2001.

53. Alberto R. Gonzales, "Martial Justice, Full and Fair," *New York Times*, 30 November 2001. Gonzales would later assert that while it wanted to respect constitutional protections, "at the end of the day" the administration's job is "to protect the country." "Ultimately," he said, "it is the job of the courts to tell us whether or not we've drawn the lines in the right place." Jeanne Cummings, "Gonzales Rewrites Laws of War— White House Counsel's Methods Outrage Military Legal Experts," *Wall Street Journal*, 26 November 2002, A4.

54. Ray Rivera, "Bush Looks to '42 Case to Justify Military Tribunals for Terrorism" seattletimes.com, 7 December 2001.

55. Wolfowitz, *Hearing before the Senate Armed Services Committee*.

56. George Terwilliger, Theodore Cooperstein, Shawn Gunnarson, Daniel Blumenthal, and Robert Parker, *The War on Terrorism: Law Enforcement or National Security?* (Washington, D.C.: Federalist Society, National Security White Papers, 2001), available at www.fed-soc.org.

57. Ibid.

58. In Germany, the United States prosecuted 1,672 individuals for war crimes before U.S. military commissions. Convictions were obtained in 1,416 cases. In Japan, 856 convictions of suspected war criminals were obtained in cases involving 996 individuals. Wolfowitz, *Hearing before the Senate Armed Services Committee*.

59. The first trial required five months of testimony, 207 witnesses, and 1,003 exhibits in addition to the time for legal argument and deliberation by the jury. The second trial involved two hundred witnesses and hundreds of exhibits. Crona and Richardson, "Justice for War Criminals."

60. See, for example, Will, "Trials and Terrorists,"

61. Laura Ingraham, "Military Tribunals Provide Streamlined Justice," *USA Today*, 26 November 2001, 15.

62. Wolfowitz, *Hearing before the Senate Armed Services Committee.*

63. Tribe, "Why Congress Must Curb Bush's Military Courts."

64. Ibid.

65. Ibid.

66. Richard A. Posner, "Security versus Civil Liberties," *Atlantic Monthly*, December 2001.

67. Ibid.

68. Jess Bravin, "Military-Tribunal Defendants Get Fewer Rights and Procedural Rules," *Wall Street Journal*, 22 March 2002, A4.

69. The rules granted the tribunals jurisdiction over war crimes, but not over broader categories of crime that might occur outside of an armed conflict, for example, genocide and crimes against humanity. After internal debate, the Bush administration decided not to permit prosecutions based solely on membership in al Qaeda. Critics of that proposal argued that it would criminalize political beliefs and undermine public perception of the legitimacy of the tribunals. U.S. Department of Defense, Military Commission Instruction No. 2, 30 April 2003, Washington, D.C.

70. International law permits indefinite detention, but only in cases of national emergency.

71. John Mintz, "U.S. Adds Legal Rights in Tribunals," *Washington Post*, 21 March 2002, A1.

72. See U.S. Constitution, art. 6, sec. 2: "This Constitution, and the laws of the United States which shall be made in pursuance thereof; and all Treaties made, or which shall be made, under the authority of the United States, shall be the supreme Law of the land."

73. Article 13 and Article 17, Geneva Convention Relative to the Treatment of Prisoners of War, adopted 12 August 1949 by the Diplomatic Conference for the Establishment of International Conventions for the Protection of Victims of War, held in Geneva, 21 April to 12 August 1949.

74. Vince Crawley, "Detainees or POWs?" *Army Times* (11 February 2002): 12.

75. Convention Respecting the Laws and Customs of War on Land, with Annex of Regulations, 18 October 1907, Annex art. 1, 36 stat. 2277, T.S. No. 539 (26 January 1910) (the "Hague Convention" and the "Hague Regulations").

76. *Yaser Easm Hamdi, et al. v. Donald Rumsfeld, et al.*, 296 F.3d 278, 282 (4th Cir. 2002).

77. Ibid.

78. Ibid., 283.

79. Ibid.

80. Ibid.

81. Ibid.

82. A "declaration" is a written statement submitted to a court in which the writer swears "under penalty of perjury" that the contents, usually assertions of fact, are true. The writer acknowledges that if he is lying, he may be prosecuted for perjury.

83. Tom Jackman, "Judge Demands More Facts on 'Combatant,'" *Washington Post*, 17 August 2002, A9.

84. Generally speaking, decisions of a trial judge may only be appealed after a trial is concluded and a final judgment or final order is entered. In certain limited circumstances, however, federal law permits an appeal before final judgment if an interim or "interlocutory" appeal may save time and expense for the judicial system and the litigants. When a district court (trial court) judge issues an order prior to or during trial and is of the opinion that an immediate appeal from the order may materially advance the ultimate termination of the litigation, he may so state in the order. The court of appeals may thereupon, in its discretion, permit an appeal to be taken from the order. Title 28, *U.S. Code*, sec. 1292(b).

85. Charles Krauthammer, "Invoking the Hamdi Rights," *Washington Post*, 16 August 2002, A25.

86. Ibid.

87. Toni Locy, "Al-Qaeda Suspect Could Face Military Panel," *USA Today*, 16 September 2002, 3.

88. Edward E. McNally, General Counsel, Office of Homeland Security, Remarks at the Homeland Security: The Civil-Military Dimensions Symposium, National Defense University, Fort Lesley J. McNair, Washington, D.C., 20 September 2002.

89. Associated Press, "Breyer Says Rights Need Guarding in Terror War," *Washington Post*, 15 April 2003, A10. In April 2003 the city of Arcata, California, passed an ordinance that purports to outlaw voluntary compliance with the USA PATRIOT Act of 2001.

90. Jeffrey Rosen, "Liberty Wins, So Far," *Washington Post*, 15 September 2002, B1.

91. Ibid.

92. William H. Rehnquist, *All the Laws But One* (New York: Alfred A. Knopf, 2001). It is of more than passing interest that he also wrote a book on Senate impeachment trials (*Grand Inquests*, New York: Random House, 1996) only seven years before he was called to preside over the Senate trial of President Clinton.

93. Chief Justice William H. Rehnquist, Remarks at 100th Anniversary Celebration of the Norfolk and Portsmouth Bar Association, Norfolk, Va., 3 May 2000.

94. Rehnquist, *All the Laws But One*, 222.

95. Rehnquist, Remarks at 100th Anniversary Celebration of the Norfolk and Portsmouth Bar Association.

96. Ibid.

97. Rosen, "Liberty Wins, So Far."

98. Ibid.

Chapter 9. Iraq—Again!

1. James R. Asker, ed., "Washington Outlook," *Aviation Week and Space Technology* (8 October 2001): 23.

2. Joby Warrick, "Uncertain Ability to Deliver a Blow," *Washington Post*, 5 September 2002, A1.

3. Marie Colvin and Nicholas Rufford, "Saddam's Arsenal Revealed," *London Sunday Times*, 17 March 2002. After the head of Iraq's military industries defected, Iraq admitted that it had produced "more than 30,000 liters of anthrax and other deadly biological agents." There was reason to believe that it had actually produced two to four times that amount. George W. Bush, Address to the Nation on Iraq from Cincinnati, Ohio, *Weekly Compilation of Presidential Documents* (7 October 2002): 1699. See also Carla Anne Robbins and Jeanne Cummings, "How Bush Decided That Hussein Must Be Ousted from Atop Iraq," *Wall Street Journal*, 14 June 2002, 1.

4. James Bone, "Iraqi Sites for Bio-War Revealed by Defector," *London Times*, 12 July 2002.

5. Tony Capaccio, "Iraq Chemical, Biological Weapons Elusive Target, Rumsfeld Says," Bloomberg.com, 29 July 2002.

6. Paul Martin, "Iraqi Scientist Says Materials for Nuclear Bombs in Hand," *Washington Times*, 16 September 2002, 1.

7. Douglas Farah and Colum Lynch, "Hussein Said to Exploit Oil-for-Food," *Washington Post*, 18 September 2002, A20.

8. R. Jeffrey Smith, "Iraq Reveals Bid to Build an A-Bomb," *Washington Post*, 24 August 1995, A1, A31; R. Jeffrey Smith, "U.N. Says Iraqis Prepared Germ Weapons in Gulf War," *Washington Post*, 26 August 1995, A1, A19; "Baghdad's Dirty Secrets," *U.S. News and World Report*, 11 September 1995, 41.

9. *Iraq Liberation Act of 1998*, Public Law 105-338, 105th Cong., 2d sess., 31 October 1998, sec. 2.

10. Ibid.

11. Ibid., sec. 3.

12. In 1995 Lt. Gen. Hussein Kamel al-Majid, Saddam Hussein's son-in-law and one of the original participants in Iraq's "unconventional weapons" program, defected to

Jordan with his wife, Saddam's favorite daughter. Believing that he had assurances of a pardon, Kamel returned to Baghdad. Within days of his return, he was killed. Some reports said that he died at the hand of Saddam's son, Uday.

13. Richard Norton-Taylor and Julian Borger, "Iraq Attack Plans Alarm Top Military," *London Guardian*, 30 July 2002, 1.

14. Ibid. The Center for Strategic and International Studies (CSIS) calculated that Iraq's armed forces included 424,000 men, 2,200 tanks, 3,700 other armored vehicles, 2,400 major artillery pieces, and 20 to 40 Scud missiles. Greg Miller and John Hendren, "Iraqi Strategy Centers on Cities," *Los Angeles Times*, 8 August 2002, 1. In testimony before a Senate panel in early August, Anthony Cordesman, a respected analyst with CSIS, noted that Iraq's ground forces may be weaker than at the beginning of Operation Desert Storm, but they still numbered over 400,000. It would be "foolish", he said, to assume that they would crumble in the face of a U.S. attack. "Saddam has been in power during the entire life of 80 percent of the Iraqi people," he added. "To say . . . that there are factions that will not follow him is reckless and dangerous." Peter Grier, "Scenarios Narrow for Attacking Iraq," *Christian Science Monitor*, 8 August 2002, 1.

15. Greg Miller and John Hendren, "Iraqi Strategy Centers on Cities," 1. An air campaign would present difficult new problems. Since the termination of Operation Desert Storm in 1991, Saddam Hussein had greatly improved Iraq's air defenses, particularly those in and around Baghdad. An underground fiber-optic network had greatly improved communications, mobile radar systems had been placed on truck beds, and new missiles had been secretly smuggled into the country.

16. Henry A. Kissinger, "Phase II and Iraq," *Washington Post*, 13 January 2002, B7.

17. Sig Christenson, "Ex-Drug Czar Sees U.S.-Iraq War over Hidden Nukes by January," *San Antonio Express News*, 10 May 2002.

18. Margaret Thatcher, *The Downing Street Years* (New York: Harper Collins, 1993), 824.

19. Margaret Thatcher, "Don't Go Wobbly," *Wall Street Journal*, 17 June 2002, A18.

20. Ibid.

21. Neil McFarquhar, "An Embrace of Baghdad Signals a Rebuff for Bush's Initiatives," *New York Times*, 29 March 2002, 1.

22. John Diamond, "Bush to Consult Congress on Iraq," *USA Today*, 8 August 2002, 1.

23. Ibid.

24. Robin Wright, "Jordan's King Sees Pitfalls in a Strike on Iraq," *Los Angeles Times*, 17 March 2002. It is worth noting that to the incredulity of the United States, Britain and even the larger Arab states, in 1990 King Hussein, the father of King Abdullah and then king of Jordan, sided with Saddam Hussein over the issue of Iraq's inva-

sion of Kuwait. Margaret Thatcher later characterized the king's action as one of clear calculation: "[H]e could not come out openly against Saddam Hussein and survive." Thatcher, *Downing Street Years*, 824.

25. In testimony before the House Armed Services Committee on 31 May Danielle Pletka, an analyst with the American Enterprise Institute, asserted, "Most Arab leaders do not agree with us as to what constitutes terrorism. Some have a vested interest in allowing it to continue and they know that 99 percent of the time they will not be called to account by the United States Government." Rick Maze, "Analysts: Defining Allies Is Difficult in War on Terrorism," *Army Times* (3 June 2002): 20.

26. Michael Evans, "NATO Talks on Nuclear Terrorism," *London Times*, 7 June 2002; Thom Shanker, "Defense Secretary Tells NATO to Beat Terrorists to Punch," *New York Times*, 7 June 2002; Stephen Castle, "Be Ready to Strike Terror States, Rumsfeld Tells NATO," *London Independent*, 7 June 2002.

27. Glenn Frankel, "Britons Grow Uneasy about War in Iraq," *Washington Post*, 7 August 2002, A14.

28. Tony Helm, "Rumsfeld Urges 'Offensive' NATO," *London Daily Telegraph*, 7 June 2002.

29. Simon Tisdall and Richard Norton-Taylor, "Bush and Blair Agree Terms for Iraq Attack," *London Guardian*, 27 July 2002.

30. Norton-Taylor and Borger, "Iraq Attack Plans Alarm Top Military."

31. Ibid.

32. Paul Reynolds, "Saddam's Tactics: Divide the Enemy," BBC News Online, 7 August 2002. The Suez crisis erupted in 1956 when Britain and France, supported by Israel, attacked Egypt after President Nasser nationalized the Suez Canal. The attack proved to be unsuccessful after the United States refused to support it.

33. Robert Kagan argued that Europeans believe that they are "moving beyond power into a self-contained world of laws and rules and transnational negotiation and cooperation." Europeans seek a world "where strength doesn't matter so much, where unilateral action by powerful nations is forbidden, where all nations . . . are protected by commonly agreed rules of behavior." For many Europeans, he asserted, "progress toward such a world is more important than eliminating the threat posed by Saddam Hussein." In contrast, the memory of Americans of the past fifty years "is of a Cold War struggle that was eventually won by strength and determination, not by the spontaneous triumph of 'moral consciousness'" and this experience is reflected in their exercise of power "in the Hobbesian world where international rules are unreliable and where security and the promotion of a liberal order shall depend on the possession and use of military might." See, Robert Kagan, "The U.S.-Europe Divide," *Washington Post*, 26 May 2002, B7. John Keegan, a respected European defense writer,

agreed. "Fifty years of peace have skewed the European outlook on the world," he wrote. "There can be no doubt that the American approach to the future is far more realistic than the European." John Keegan, "Resolve: The Right Response for Our Times," *Washington Post*, 6 October 2002, B1. Francis Fukuyama offered a similar analysis of the divergence of opinion. "Americans tend not to see any source of democratic legitimacy higher than the nation-state," he said. "To the extent that international organizations have legitimacy, it is because duly constituted democratic majorities have handed that legitimacy up to them in a negotiated, contractual process, which they can take back at any time. Europeans, by contrast, tend to believe that democratic legitimacy flows from the will of an international community much larger than any individual nation-state." In his view, there are three reasons for the divergence. First, weak states "understandably want stronger ones constrained by norms and rules, while the world's sole superpower seeks freedom of action." Second, Europeans, like "former smokers, . . . want everyone else to experience their painful withdrawal symptoms from sovereignty." Finally, "America's unique national experience and the sense of exceptionalism that has arisen from it" have made Americans believe in the "special legitimacy of their democratic institutions and . . . that they are the embodiment of universal values that have a significance for all of mankind." Francis Fukuyama, "U.S. vs. Them," *Washington Post*, 11 September 2002, A17.

34. A new study by the Center for Strategic and Budgetary Assessments concluded that the U.S. homeland had a greater chance of becoming a battleground in a war to oust Saddam Hussein than it did during the 1991 Persian Gulf War. "CSBA: U.S. Homeland Could Become Battleground in New War With Iraq," InsideDefense.com, 17 September 2002.

35. James Webb, former Reagan navy secretary, for example, worried that a long-term occupation of Iraq would require "an adjustment of force levels elsewhere, and could eventually diminish American influence in other parts of the world." James Webb, "Heading for Trouble," *Washington Post*, 4 September 2002, A21. Democrats on the House Budget Committee issued a report that concluded that the cost of ousting Saddam would be at least as much as $93 billion and could reach $200 billion. "Democrats Put War Cost Near $100 Billion," *Washington Post*, 24 September 2002, A3.

36. William Galston, former deputy assistant to President Clinton for domestic policy, asserted, "A global strategy based on the new Bush doctrine [of preemption] means the end of the system of international institutions, laws and norms that the United States has worked for more than half a century to build." He objected to an attack on Iraq because U.S. adversaries might redouble their efforts, cooperating nations

might stop arresting suspected terrorists, the United States might alienate European allies, and new generations of young people could grow up resenting their country. William A. Galston, "Why a First Strike Will Surely Backfire," *Washington Post*, 16 June 2002, B1.

37. Thomas E. Ricks, "Military Sees Iraq Invasion Put on Hold," *Washington Post*, 24 May 2002, 1.

38. Thom Shanker and Eric Schmitt, "Military Would Be Stressed by a New War, Study Finds, " *New York Times*, 24 May 2002, A8.

39. The Bush administration requested $30 million to develop a conventional warhead variant of the U.S. Navy's Trident D-5 submarine-launched ballistic missile. The new "penetrator" missile would be highly accurate, would be fired from a hidden submarine, would reach its target in only minutes from launch, and would have the capability to destroy underground facilities housing weapons of mass destruction, command and control systems, or ballistic missiles. "Pentagon Eyes Bunker-Busting Conventional Ballistic Missile for Subs," *Inside the Pentagon* (27 June 2002): 1.

40. Daniel Eisenberg, "We're Taking Him Out," *Time*, 13 May 2002.

41. Glenn Kessler, "Powell Treads Carefully on Iraq Strategy," *Washington Post*, 2 September 2002, 1.

42. The under secretary of defense for policy, for example, was quoted as saying, "These regimes that looked unchallengeable turn out to be highly brittle." Dave Moniz and Jonathan Weisman, "Military Leaders Question Iraq Plan," *USA Today*, 23 May 2002, 1. See also Michael O'Hanlon, "We're Ready to Fight Iraq," *Wall Street Journal*, 29 May 2002, A20.

43. Ricks, "Military Sees Iraq Invasion Put on Hold."

44. David Wood, "Administration Is Prepared to Go It Alone on Iraq," Newhouse.com, 6 May 2002.

45. Thomas E. Ricks, "Timing, Tactics on Iraq War Disputed," *Washington Post*, 1 August 2002, 1.

46. Thomas E. Ricks, "Some Top Military Brass Favor Status Quo in Iraq," *Washington Post*, 28 July 2002, 1; Norton-Taylor and Borger, "Iraq Attack Plans Alarm Top Military." As a general proposition, most students of civil-military relations agree that it is for military leaders to characterize and quantify the expected risk in conducting a particular operation. It is for civilian leaders to decide whether to accept the risk.

47. Rowan Scarborough, "Joint Chiefs Back Ouster of Saddam," *Washington Times*, 7 August 2002, 1.

48. Evan Thomas, "Rumsfeld's War," *Newsweek*, 16 September 2002, 26.

49. The Office of the Under Secretary of Defense for Policy was the target of particu-
    lar criticism. One former Pentagon official said that the policy shop was "completely
    broken." Another described it as "bureaucratic chaos." When a top deputy con-
    fronted the under secretary to say that he was abusing subordinates, the under sec-
    retary reportedly responded that he treated the subordinates just the way Secretary
    Rumsfeld treated him. Thomas E. Ricks and Vernon Loeb, "No. 3 Civilian Ruffles
    Feathers at the Pentagon," *Washington Post*, 8 December 2002, 8.

50. General of the Army (a five-star rank) George C. Marshall served as the army chief
    of staff and the officer upon whom Presidents Roosevelt and Truman relied most
    during World War II. He never was chairman of the Joint Chiefs of Staff because
    that position was not created until after the war. Powell and most former military
    leaders of his generation are suspicious of civilian policy makers who are ideologues;
    they feel most civilian policy makers are not sufficiently sensitive to political and
    combat realities. "Many of my generation," Powell wrote, "the career captains,
    majors, and lieutenant colonels seasoned in [the Vietnam] war, vowed that when
    our turn came to call the shots, we would not quietly acquiesce in halfhearted war-
    fare for half-baked reasons that the American people could not understand or sup-
    port." Powell and Persico, *My American Journey*, 149.

51. James Bainford, "Untested Administration Hawks Clamor for War," *USA Today*, 17
    September 2002, 15.

52. Ibid.

53. Eliot A. Cohen, *Supreme Command* (New York: Free Press, 2002), 1–14.

54. Eliot A. Cohen, "Hunting 'Chicken Hawks,'" *Washington Post*, 5 September 2002, 31.

55. Walter Pincus, "Hussein Tries to Mend Fences with Neighbors," *Washington Post*, 19
    July 2002, A22.

56. Reynolds, "Saddam's Tactics: Divide the Enemy."

57. Steven Mufson, "Scowcroft Urges Restraint against Iraq," *Washington Post*, 5 August
    2002, A4.

58. Miller and Hendren, "Iraqi Strategy Centers on Cities."

59. John Diamond, "Saddam Already Battling Invasion," *USA Today*, 8 August 2002, 4.

60. David B. Rivkin and Lee A. Casey, "No Declaration of War Needed," *Wall Street
    Journal*, 26 July 2002, A10.

61. The chairman of the House International Relations Committee was quoted, "As a prac-
    tical matter, the president would not and could not undertake such a dramatic move
    in foreign policy without congressional approval." Kathy Kiely, "Congress Leaders
    Cautious on Iraq," *USA Today*, 24 June 2002, 1. Senator John Warner, the ranking
    Republican on the Armed Services Committee, expressed similar sentiments.

62. A July 2002 Wall Street Journal/NBC News poll indicated that 54 percent of those surveyed supported military action against Iraq even if it was necessary to commit as many as 200,000 troops. Carla Anne Robbins, Leila Abboud, and Greg Jaffe, "Democrats to Pose Careful Questions on Iraq—Public Support for Bush Approach Means Political Risks in Senate Hearings," *Wall Street Journal*, 31 July 2002, A4.

63. George F. Will, "A Vote for War," *Washington Post*, 9 August 2002, A23.

64. David S. Cloud and Greg Jaffe, "Bush Faces Complex Gauntlet on the Path to War with Iraq," *Wall Street Journal*, 5 September 2002, 1.

65. Dana Priest and Joby Warrick, "Observers: Evidence for War Lacking," *Washington Post*, 13 September 2002, A33.

66. See, for example, "Senate Debate Heated on Iraq Military Action," *Washington Post*, 5 October 2002, A17. The phrase "clear and present danger" had its genesis in the 1919 Supreme Court decision in *Schenk v. United States*, 249 U.S. 47. The defendant had been prosecuted for distributing leaflets to men called for military service; the leaflets were allegedly calculated to cause insubordination. He challenged his conviction on the ground that it violated his First Amendment right to free speech. Writing for the Court in an opinion that affirmed the conviction, Justice Oliver Wendall Holmes declared, "But the character of every act depends upon the circumstances in which it is done. The most stringent protection of free speech would not protect a man in falsely shouting fire in a theatre and causing a panic. It does not even protect a man from an injunction against uttering words that may have all the effect of force. The question in every case is whether the words are used in such circumstances and are of such a nature as to create a clear and present danger that they will bring about the substantive evils that Congress has a right to prevent."

67. Jimmy Carter, "The Troubling New Face of America," *Washington Post*, 5 September 2002, A31 (emphasis added).

68. George F. Will, "Stuck to the U.N. Tar Baby," *Washington Post*, 19 September 2002, A27.

69. Alexander M. Haig Jr., "On Invading Iraq: Less Talk, More Unity," *Washington Post*, 29 August 2002, A31.

70. George Schultz, "Act Now," *Washington Post*, 6 September 2002, 25.

71. Todd S. Purdum, "Bush Officials Say the Time Has Come for Action on Iraq," *New York Times*, 9 September 2002, 1.

72. An unclassified version of the talking points used by Pentagon officials gave more weight to Iraq's "active and capable biological weapons program" and its "knowledge base and industrial infrastructure for quick, large-scale production." Tony

Capaccio, "Iraq's Immediate Threat Is Biological Weapons, Pentagon Says," Bloomberg.com, 11 September 2002.

73. George F. Will, "Improvised War Etiquette," *Washington Post*, 29 August 2002, A31.

74. Winston S. Churchill, *The Gathering Storm* (Boston: Houghton Mifflin Company, 1948), 320.

75. "Excerpts: Kofi Annan's Speech to the General Assembly," *New York Times*, 12 September 2002, B23.

76. Ibid.

77. Thomas E. Ricks, "War Plans Target Hussein Power Base," *Washington Post*, 22 September 2002, 1.

78. Ibid.

79. Kevin Whitelaw, "After the Fall," *U.S. News and World Report*, 2 December 2002, 20.

80. James Fallows, "The Fifty-First State?" *Atlantic Monthly*, November 2002, 58. When asked at a congressional hearing, the army chief of staff, who had commanded the NATO peacekeeping force in Bosnia, said that several hundred thousand troops might be needed for stabilization in Iraq. The deputy secretary of defense dismissed the estimate as "wildly off the mark." Bernard Weinraub and Thom Shanker, "Rumsfeld's Design for War Criticized on the Battlefield," *New York Times*, 1 April 2003, A1.

81. Linda Feldmann, "Why Bush's War Threats Have Extra Gravitas," *Christian Science Monitor*, 2 January 2003, 1.

82. John Keegan, *The Mask of Command* (New York: Penguin Books, 1988), 11.

83. Ibid.

Chapter 10. Building for Tomorrow

1. Michael Mandelbaum, "The Inadequacy of American Power," *Foreign Affairs* (September/October 2002): 61.

2. Ibid., 62–65.

3. Rumsfeld, Secretary of Defense, *Annual Report to the President and the Congress*, 9.

4. Michael Hirsh, "Bush and the World," *Foreign Affairs* (September/October 2002): 23.

5. David S. Broder, "Radical Conservatism," *Washington Post*, 25 September 2002, A27.

6. Karen DeYoung and Mike Allen, "Bush Shifts Strategy from Deterrence to Dominance," *Washington Post*, 21 September 2002, A1.

7. George W. Bush, *National Security Strategy of the United States of America*, 17 September 2002, 1, available at www.whitehouse.gov/nsc/nss.

8. Ibid., 11.

9. Ibid.

10. Ibid.

11. Ibid., 23, 3.

12. John Keegan, "The Radical at the Pentagon," *Vanity Fair,* 1 February 2003, 126.

13. Ibid.

14. George W. Bush, *National Security Strategy,* 21.

15. Ibid., 12, 21 (emphasis added).

16. Broder, "Radical Conservatism."

17. Peter Slevin, "Analysts: New Strategy Courts Unseen Danger," *Washington Post,* 22 September 2002, A1.

18. Stephen Murdoch, "Preemptive War: Is It Legal?" *Washington Lawyer* (January 2003): 23, 26. Conceding that the distinction between prevention and preemption is not always clear, Murdoch concluded that the 1981 strike by Israel on Iraq's Osirak nuclear reactor—a strike for which American troops in Operation Desert Storm were profoundly grateful—"is probably an example of an illegal preventive attack." Ibid.

19. Ibid., 20.

20. Reasons for European criticisms and suspicions are discussed in Chapter 9.

21. Clive Crook, "Let's Give International Law All the Respect It Is Due," *National Journal* (12 October 2002): 2955.

22. Glenn Frankel, "New U.S. Doctrine Worries Europeans," *Washington Post,* 30 September 2002, A15.

23. Ibid.

24. Agreeing that "countries that harbor terrorist headquarters or terrorist training centers cannot take refuge behind traditional notions of sovereignty," former Secretary of State Henry Kissinger asserted that preemption is merely the application of "a norm long recognized in international law: the right of self-defense. . . . What the argument is about is rules for lowering the threshold of when this principle can be applied." He has nevertheless argued that the United States "has an obligation to justify its actions by principles that transcend the assertions of preponderant power. It cannot be in either the American national interest or the world's interest to develop principles that grant every nation an unfettered right of preemption against its own definition of threats to its security." Henry A. Kissinger, "Consult and Control: Bywords for Battling the New Enemy," *Washington Post,* 16 September 2002, A19; Henry A. Kissinger, "A Dangerous Divergence," *Washington Post,* 10 December 2002, A29.

25. Jim Hoagland, "Wanted: An Argument Worth Having," *Washington Post,* 29 September 2002, B7.

26. The comment by Root in 1914 was noted by Secretary of State Cordell Hull, *Hearing before the Committee on Foreign Relations, United States Senate,* 77th Cong., 1st sess., 21 October 1941.

27. George Schultz, *Turmoil and Triumph,* 645–46 (emphasis added). Former British Prime Minister Margaret Thatcher was equally clear. "Terrorism . . . cannot ultimately be combated by concentrating on its 'causes', religious or secular, political or economic, social or ethnic," she said. "[I]t is the means adopted rather than the reasons—or excuses—given for violence that makes terrorists so feared and detested." Margaret Thatcher, *Statecraft* (New York: Harper Collins, 2002), 220. For months after the attacks Bush administration officials refused to discuss underlying root causes, but eventually the issue returned to the surface. On 11 December 2002, the director of central intelligence said, "[A]t the end of the day, we cannot hope to make lasting progress in the war against terrorism without serious steps to address 'the circumstances that give it rise.'" Two days later, Secretary of State Powell declared that it was necessary to bridge "the hope gap" that exists among young Arabs who are hostile to the United States. Barton Gellman, "In U.S., Terrorism's Peril Undiminished," *Washington Post,* 24 December 2002, A1.

28. "It's true," journalist Stuart Taylor asserted, "that the drafters of the U.N. Charter intended to outlaw the kind of preemptive attack that Bush now threatens unless authorized by the Security Council. Article 2 bans 'the threat or use of force against the territorial integrity or political independence of any state' without Security Council approval. Article 51 recognizes only a single, very limited exception: 'the inherent right of individual or collective self-defense if an armed attack occurs.'" Nevertheless, he concluded that accepted practice by several nations over the years has "superceded literal interpretation of the U.N. Charter." Stuart Taylor Jr., "The Hawks Are Scary, the Doves More Dangerous," *National Journal* (5 October 2002): 2859.

29. Ibid.

30. Fareed Zakaria, "We Need a Political Strategy," *Washington Post,* 22 October 2002, A27.

31. Ibid.

32. Richard G. Lugar, "Beating Terror," *Washington Post,* 27 January 2003, 19.

33. Ibid. Citing what he characterized as "parsimony between crises," Senator Lugar noted, "[I]n 2002, amid speculation about terrorists acquiring weapons of mass destruction, inaction by Congress effectively suspended for seven months new U.S. initiatives to secure Russia's immense stockpiles of nuclear, biological and chemical weapons. Congressional conditions also have delayed for years a U.S.-Russian proj-

ect to eliminate a dangerous proliferation threat: 1.9 million chemical weapons housed at a rickety and vulnerable facility in Russia." Ibid.

34. To Hart, the object in war is to attain a better peace—even if only from one's own point of view. Hence, "it is essential to conduct war with constant regard to the peace" desired. Grand strategy, therefore, is a nation's fundamental war policy or political goal. It should control war strategy that governs the conduct of operations. See Hart, *Strategy*, 353–60.

35. Donald H. Rumsfeld, *Hearing before the Armed Services Committee, United States Senate*, 107th Cong., 2d sess., 31 July 2002.

36. Ibid.

37. Brian Michael Jenkins, *Countering Al Qaeda* (Santa Monica, Calif.: RAND, 2002), vii–viii.

38. Charles Krauthammer, "The Hundred Days," *Time*, 31 December 2001–7 January 2002, 156.

39. One of my favorite memories of my testimony in approximately sixty congressional hearings during my service in the Reagan and Bush administration was a particular hearing before a House of Representatives committee in which I had presented recent data that indicated fewer seizures of illegal drugs in one particular area of the Caribbean that was more heavily patrolled than it had been the previous year. A congressman indignantly declared that the Department of Defense had been less successful than the prior year despite the use of more military units. I found it necessary to inquire whether he was familiar with the concept of deterrence.

40. The chairman of the Joint Chiefs of Staff described the operational success: "Operation Anaconda offers a useful comparison. In that case, 1,000 combat-tested enemy fighters occupied terrain of their choice—rugged mountains in eastern Afghanistan (at eight to nine thousand feet above sea level), the same area where the *mujahadeen* had often bloodied Soviet forces during the 1980s. . . . To defeat the Taliban and al Qaeda forces, the American ground commander integrated all elements of this joint team in a superb fashion. He incorporated our Afghan military partners on the tactical level to occupy key blocking positions. He had video and intelligence from various sources immediately available. Then a task force the size of a U.S. infantry battalion (some 500 soldiers) attacked and defeated a defending force twice its size." Richard B. Meyers, "A Word from the Chairman," *Joint Forces Quarterly* (summer 2002): 5.

41. Scott Baldanf, "Al Qaeda Massing for New Fight," *Christian Science Monitor*, 9 August 2002, 1. As late as December 2002 at least thirteen of twenty men on the government's classified list of "high value [al Qaeda] targets" remained unaccounted for. Gellman, "In U.S., Terrorism's Peril Undiminished."

42. Reuters, "Al Qaeda's Wealth Still Intact Says Swiss Official," *Washington Post*, 5 September 2002, A24.

43. According to former Secretary of Defense William J. Perry, in 1994 "the United States came to the brink of initiating war to stop North Korea from acquiring nuclear weapons." Ashton B. Carter and William J. Perry, "Back to the Brink," *Washington Post*, 20 October 2002, B1. The crisis ended with the negotiation of the so-called Agreed Framework, an agreement that required North Korea to abandon all efforts to establish a nuclear weapon program in return for assistance from the United States and its allies in the form of fuel, oil, and, ultimately, two nuclear reactors whose fuel would be under international control. Ibid., B5.

44. "Cuban Missile Crisis and Aftermath," *Foreign Relations of the United States, 1961–1963* (Washington: U.S. Government Printing Office, 1996), 11:31.

45. Vince Crawley, "Rumsfeld: North Korea Has Usable Nuclear Weapons," *Army Times* (28 October 2002): 22.

46. James A. Baker III, "No More Caving on North Korea," *Washington Post*, 23 October 2002, A27.

47. "Defense Threat Reduction Agency Director Warns of WMD Attacks," *Inside the Pentagon* (24 October 2002): 1.

48. Associated Press, "Rumsfeld: No Let-up in Terror Peril," *New York Daily News*, 23 October 2002.

49. Council on Foreign Relations, "America Still Unprepared—America Still in Danger," *Report of an Independent Task Force* (New York: Council on Foreign Relations, October 2002), 9.

50. David Johnston, "C.I.A. Puts Risk of Terror Strike at 9/11 Levels," *New York Times*, 18 October 2002, A1. In his testimony, George Tenet said that several terrorist plots had been interrupted before and after 11 September, but that Americans needed to know that "al Qaeda continues to plan and will attempt more deadly strikes" against the United States. "There will be more battles won," he said, "and sadly, more battles lost." Frank Davies, "Al Qaeda Poised to Attack U.S., Tenet Warns," Knight Ridder Newspapers, 17 October 2002.

51. Rumsfeld, Secretary of Defense, *Annual Report to the President and the Congress*, 30.

52. Thom Shanker, "Rumsfeld Favors Forceful Actions to Foil an Attack," *New York Times*, 14 October 2002, 1. Vince Crawley, "Rumsfeld Issues Guidelines for Sending Forces to War," *Army Times* (28 October 2002): 24. Former Secretary of Defense Caspar Weinberger believes the following conditions should exist before U.S. military force is employed: (1) a vital national interest at risk; (2) a determination to use overwhelming force to ensure success; (3) clear political, as well as military objectives;

(4) continuous reassessment to ensure that the military force is both necessary and sufficient; (5) reasonable assurance of public and congressional support; and (6) exhaustion of all other relevant instruments of power before military force is used. Caspar Weinberger, *Fighting for Peace* (New York: Warner Books, 1990), 433.

53. Rumsfeld, Secretary of Defense, *Annual Report to the President and the Congress*, 30–31.

54. Shanker, "Rumsfeld Favors Forceful Actions."

55. Ibid.

56. Ibid.

57. Ibid.

58. Ibid.; Rumsfeld, Secretary of Defense, *Annual Report to the President and the Congress*, 30.

59. Ibid.

60. Thom Shanker and Eric Schmitt, "Rumsfeld Orders War Plans Redone for Faster Action," *New York Times*, 13 October 2002, 1.

61. Ibid.

62. "9.11.02 What Has Changed," Special Report, *Business Week*, 16 September 2002, 26–27.

63. Lawrence K. Zelvin, "Homeland Security Challenges DoD," *U.S. Naval Institute Proceedings* (November 2002): 66.

64. Ibid.

65. Office of Homeland Security, *National Strategy for Homeland Security*, 13.

66. Ibid., i.

67. Rumsfeld, Secretary of Defense, *Report of the Quadrennial Defense Review*, 18.

68. For a discussion of the grounds that support this conclusion, see Advisory Panel to Assess Domestic Response Capabilities for Terrorism Involving Weapons of Mass Destruction, "Implementing the National Strategy," *Fourth Annual Report*, 91.

69. Council on Foreign Relations, "America Still Unprepared—America Still in Danger," 9.

70. Christopher Laszlo and Jean-Francois Laugel, *Large-Scale Organizational Change* (Boston: Butterworth-Heinemann, 2000), xv.

71. Ibid., 5.

72. T. Irene Sanders, "To Fight Terror, We Can't Think Straight," *Washington Post*, 5 May 2002, B2.

73. Ibid.

74. Andrew F. Krepinevich Jr., "A New War Demands a New Military," *Wall Street Journal*, 10 September 2002, A12.

75. John G. Roos, "Top-Level Makeovers," *Armed Forces Journal International* (February 2002): 2.

76. Woodward, *Bush at War,* 125.

77. Jenkins, "Countering Al Qaeda," 29.

78. David M. Walker, Comptroller General of the United States, interview, Washington, D.C., 22 October 2002.

79. Jefferson Morris, "OSD Striving to Define 'Transformation' for Military Personnel," *Aerospace Daily,* 6 September 2002. The new hand-picked commander of the U.S. Joint Forces Command, who had just completed duty as Rumsfeld's military assistant, said, "The best example of transformation since [he had] been in the military . . . [was] moving from Selective Service and the draft to an All Volunteer Force." Jack Dorsey, "Innovation Is the Job of Command in Norfolk," *Virginian-Pilot,* 2 January 2003. The chairman of the Joint Chiefs of Staff had his own ideas. "[T]ransformation is not necessarily a material thing," he said. "It is not buying things necessarily. . . . It is not necessarily more technology. . . . There is another huge piece of transformation that is the organization and doctrine, how you train, leadership . . . that are just as transformational." Hunter Keeter, "DoD to Stress Transformation in FY 04 Budget," *Defense Daily,* 23 January 2003, 2.

80. Ibid.

81. The comptroller general proposed a definition: "Creating the future of warfare and national defense while improving how the department [of defense], and all of its various component parts, does business in order to support and sustain our position as the world's preeminent military power within current and expected resource limits." David M. Walker, Comptroller General of the United States, interview.

82. David Isenberg and Ivan Eland, "Empty Promises: Why the Bush Administration's Half-Hearted Attempts at Defense Reform Have Failed," *Policy Analysis* (CATO Institute) (11 June 2002): 2.

83. Ibid., 1.

84. Andrew F. Krepinevich is the director of the Center for Strategic and Budgetary Assessments. See Vernon Loeb, "Billions, and It Can't Make Change," *Washington Post,* 13 September 2002, A37.

85. Amy Svitak, "Disjointed First Steps," *Defense News* (19–25 August 2002): 1.

86. Amy Svitak, "The New Department That Wasn't," *Navy Times* (23 September 2002): 28.

87. Ibid.

88. Svitak, "Disjointed First Steps." Six transformational goals had been set in earlier planning documents, but they were very general in nature. They included the protection of bases and critical infrastructure; denial of enemy sanctuaries; the leveraging of information technology; assurance of the security and productivity of information systems; and the leveraging of space systems and capabilities.

89. Ibid.

90. Elaine M. Grossman, "Rumsfeld Aide Sees 2004 Defense Budget as Pivotal 'Crossover Point,'" *Inside the Pentagon* (15 August 2002): 1.

91. The official said that more than $90 billion was being shifted from sustaining current systems to programs involving laser satellite transmissions and unmanned aerial vehicles. "FY 04 Budget Begins $90 Billion Shift Toward Defense Transformation Agenda, Official Says," *Aerospace Daily*, 20 December 2002. The proposed budget would seek $378 billion in defense spending for fiscal year 2004, including approximately $72 billion for new equipment. The recommendation was 6.5 percent larger than the previous budget, but it did not include funds for a possible war with Iraq.

92. George C. Wilson, "New Budget Gamble," *National Journal* (21 January 2003).

93. Leslie Wayne, "So Much for the Plan to Scrap Old Weapons," *New York Times*, 22 December 2002, 3.1.

94. See Jon R. Katzenbach, *Real Change Leaders* (New York: Time Books, 1995), 13. By September 2002, it was noted that Rumsfeld had "seized the bureaucratic initiative" by making subtle but key personnel changes. "He hasn't fired any generals, . . . but he has shifted some of those most opposed to change." Tom Donnelly, "Rumsfeld the Radical," *Weekly Standard* (9 September 2002).

95. James Belasco argues that the factors that produced today's success in a particular business often create tomorrow's failure. James A. Belasco, *Teaching the Elephant to Dance* (New York: Crown Publishers, Inc., 1990), 2. A private defense analysis firm asserts that the same danger exists in defense planning. "Militaries change because they lose wars or win them with difficulty," the firm's director argued. "They do not change when they win wars without hardly even trying." Ronald Brownstein, "Success in Afghanistan Clouds Military Transformation Plan," *Los Angeles Times*, 12 December 2001, A8.

96. Laszlo and Laugel, *Large-Scale Organizational Change*, 184. This asks a lot of military leaders who are personally responsible for the present security of the nation, but who will be long retired by the time future military capabilities come into play.

97. Tom Canahuate, "Told U.S. Military Transformation in 10 Years Not Realistic, Says Wolfowitz," DefenseNews.com, 17 August 2001.

98. Ibid.

99. Vernon Loeb and Thomas E. Ricks, "Rumsfeld's Style, Goals Strain Ties in Pentagon; 'Transformation' Effort Spawns Issues of Control," *Washington Post*, 16 October 2002, A1.

100. Ibid., A10. One service secretary did. The secretary of the navy left to become the new deputy secretary of the Department of Homeland Security. He later returned to DoD. On 25 April 2003 the secretary of the army resigned under pressure.

101. Dave Moniz, "Rumsfeld's Abrasive Style Sparks Conflict," *USA Today*, 10 December 2002, 1.

102. Ibid.

103. The Joint Staff is composed of approximately equal numbers of officers from each of the military services. It assists the chairman of the Joint Chiefs of Staff in accomplishing his responsibilities for the unified strategic direction of the combatant forces; for their operation under unified command; and for their integration into an efficient team of land, naval and air forces." The Joint Staff has recently been characterized as "the most powerful organization in the Department of Defense; frequently, by dint of its speed, agility, knowledge, and expertise, the Joint Staff frames the choices." Richard H. Kohn, "The Erosion of Civilian Control of the Military in the United States Today," *Naval War College Review* (summer 2002): 16.

104. "Rumsfeld Denies Ignoring Military Advice," *New York Times on the Web*, 17 October 2002.

105. Field Marshal Sir William Slim, William Queale Lecture to the Australian Institute of Management, Melbourne, Australia, 4 April 1957.

106. At his retirement ceremony on 11 June 2003 Gen. Eric Shinseki declared, "The Army has always understood the primacy of civilian control." But in words whose meaning escaped few, he said, "You must love those you lead before you can be an effective leader. You can certainly command without that sense of commitment, but you cannot lead without it. And without leadership, command is a hollow experience, a vacuum often filled with mistrust and arrogance." Thom Shanker, "Retiring Army Chief-of-Staff Warns against Arrogance," *New York Times*, 12 June 2003, A32.

107. Kohn, "The Erosion of Civilian Control," 9.

108. Ibid., 17.

109. Ibid., 22.

110. Lawrence D. Freedman, "Calling the Shots," *Foreign Affairs* (September/October 2002): 193.

111. In 1949 there were only five PAS (presidential appointee requiring Senate confirmation) positions in the Office of the Secretary of Defense. By 1999 there were twenty-three. In a similar manner, the number of PAS positions in the military departments has grown from eleven in 1947 to twenty-two today. "Most appointees . . . are rank amateurs in administering large organizations and budgets, supervising people, and *executing* (as contrasted with developing or promoting) policy." David M. Cohen, "Amateur Government: When Political Appointees Manage the Federal Bureaucracy" (Washington, D.C.: Brookings Institution, 1996), 1–2 (emphasis added). A former director of defense research and engineering has argued that can-

didates for senior defense positions should think about the following questions. "Have you managed a project? Have you run an organization, been a university president, run a company? Can you fire somebody? Can you do the things that a manager has to do?" Ibid.

112. Members of Congress agree. In February 2000 the House Committee on Government Affairs expressed "concern that some political appointees in the executive branch lack the requisite *leadership* and *management* skills and background to successfully address the challenges facing federal agencies." U.S. General Accounting Office, *Confirmation of Political Appointees*, GAO/GGD-00-174 (Washington, D.C.: Government Accounting Office, August 2000), 1 (emphasis added). A national commission also agrees. The National Commission on Public Service addressed several key areas of concern about the erosion of trust in government. One of the causal factors is the fact that the federal government "is not performing nearly as well as it can or should." The commission recommended that executive departments be run by managers selected for their operational skills. National Commission on Public Service, *Urgent Business for America: Revitalizing the Federal Government for the 21st Century* (Washington, D.C.: National Commission on Public Service, 7 January 2003).

113. Each of the 170 feet long vessels was to be manned by navy crews, but would carry small, specially trained teams of coast guard law enforcement personnel.

114. Jim Cowen, "CNO Stresses Need to Integrate Navy Resources in Homeland Security Challenge," *Navy Newsstand* (27 March 2002).

115. Ibid.

116. Marty Kauchak, "Navigating Seas of Change," *Armed Forces Journal International* (January 2002): 50.

117. Adm. Vern Clark, "Sea Power 21," *U.S. Naval Institute Proceedings* (October 2002): 35.

118. Vice Adm. Mike Bucchi and Vice Adm. Mike Mullen, "Sea Shield," *U.S. Naval Institute Proceedings* (November 2002): 56.

119. Gen. Charles C. Krulak, "The Three Block War: Fighting in Urban Areas," Address to the National Press Club, Washington, D.C., 10 October 1997.

120. Eric V. Larson, "U.S. Air Force Roles Reach Beyond Securing the Skies," *RAND Review* (summer 2002): 45.

121. Michael Sirak, "Gen. John Jumper: U.S. Air Force Chief of Staff," *Jane's Defense Weekly* (18 September 2002).

122. Larson, "U.S. Air Force Roles" (emphasis added).

123. See, for example, Antulio J. Echevarria II, "The Army and Homeland Security: A Strategic Perspective," pamphlet (Carlisle, Pa.: U.S. Army War College Strategic Studies Institute, March 2001), 7–9.

124. Richard Brennan, "U.S. Army Finds Its Role at Home up for Grabs," *RAND Review* (summer 2002): 47.

125. The atomic bomb dropped on Hiroshima, Japan, on 6 August 1945 was said by President Truman to have more power than twenty kilotons of TNT.

126. Echevarria, "The Army and Homeland Security."

127. Bruce R. Nardulli, "A Future of Sustained Ground Operations," *RAND Review* (summer 2002): 38.

128. Referred to as the "objective force," the army of the future would be designed with the goal of being able to deploy a combat-ready brigade in 96 hours, a division in 120 hours, and a corps of five divisions within 30 days. Each objective force unit would incorporate a yet-to-be designed future combat system (FCS) family of vehicles that would work together to perform reconnaissance, direct and indirect fire, command and control, and air defense functions. Army leaders hoped that the first unit of the objective force could be fielded as soon as 2008.

129. Sean D. Naylor, "Fort Lewis Stryker Brigade to Swap with Germany Unit," *Army Times* (23 September 2002): 12.

130. In 1967 the U.S. Coast Guard was moved from the Treasury Department to the newly created Transportation Department. Only one-third of its activities, however, are transportation related. Transportation-related activities include "ice breaking, safety inspections, and aiding navigation, which includes maintaining everything from buoys to signal systems." Matthew Weinstock, "Changing Course," *Government Executive* (December 2001): 58.

131. See, for example, Adm. James M. Loy and Capt. Robert G. Ross, "Meet the Homeland Security Challenge: A Principled Strategy for a Balanced and Practical Response," *Journal of Homeland Security* (September 2001).

132. Vice Adm. Howard B. Thorsen, "The Coast Guard in Review," *U.S. Naval Institute Proceedings* (May 2002): 93.

133. Ibid.

134. The U.S. Coast Guard has been described as "a combination of six different types of maritime agencies that in many other nations remain separate entities: (1) constabulary; (2) lifesaving; (3) navy; (4) safety and regulatory; (5) environmental protection; and (6) navigation agency." Capt. Bruce Stubbs, "We Are Lifesavers, Guardians, and Warriors," *U.S. Naval Institute Proceedings* (April 2002): 50. Its growing list of peacetime missions includes such diverse areas as enforcement of fishery, oil pollution, and immigration laws to drug interdiction and search and rescue operations.

135. U.S. Commission on National Security/21st Century, *Road Map for National Security*, 16–17.

136. See Capt. Bruce Stubbs, "Preparing for the New War," *Armed Forces Journal International* (February 2002).

137. Jason Peckenpaugh, "Sea Change," GovExec.com, 1 March 2002.

138. Weinstock, "Changing Course," 59.

139. John G. Roos, "Versatility Pays Off," *Armed Forces Journal International* (June 2002): 40.

140. Gordon I. Peterson, "9/11 Remembered," *Sea Power* (October 2002): 1.

Postscript: A Volatile Second Year

1. Hart, *Strategy*, 204.

2. The "Authorization for the Use of Military Force Against Iraq" required the president to notify Congress no later than forty-eight hours after he exercised the authority, that "(1) reliance by the United States on further diplomatic or other peaceful means alone either (A) [would] not adequately protect the national security of the United States against the continuing threat posed by Iraq or (B) is not likely to lead to enforcement of all relevant United Nations Security Council resolutions regarding Iraq, and (2) acting pursuant to [the] resolution [would be] consistent with the United States and other countries continuing to take the necessary actions against international terrorists and terrorist organizations, including those nations, organizations or persons who planned, authorized, committed or aided the terrorist attacks that occurred on September 11, 2001."

3. Jim Vandettei, Juliet Eilperin, "Congress Passes Iraq Resolution," *Washington Post*, 11 October 2002, A1.

4. Ibid.

5. Congress Approves Iraq Resolution," Fox News, 11 October 2002.

6. John Hendren, "High Degree of Terror Swayed Military To Act," *Los Angeles Times*, 17 October 2002; Gary Fields, "Rumsfeld Authorizes Use Of Military In Sniper Hunt," *Wall Street Journal*, 16 October 2002.

7. Paul Richter, "Military Is Easing Its War On Drugs," *Los Angeles Times*, 20 October 2002, 1. After 11 September 2001, AWACS (Airborne Warning and Control System) planes stopped flying counterdrug missions over the Caribbean and South America, as they had since the early 1990s, in order to participate in combat air patrols over certain U.S. cities and Afghanistan.

8. Ibid.

9. See chapter 3. Title XI of the FY 1989 National Defense Authorization Act gave the Defense Department major new counterdrug responsibilities. In September 1989, President George Bush announced his first *National Drug Control Strategy*. I had taken the lead in preparing the military elements of the *Strategy*, which established policies to unite federal counterdrug efforts with those of state, local, and private

entities. On 18 September 1989, then Secretary of Defense Dick Cheney issued guidance to the Armed Forces regarding the implementation of the president's *Strategy*, declaring that because the illegal traffic of drugs posed a direct threat to the sovereignty and security of the country. The detection and countering of the production, trafficking, and use of illegal drugs would, henceforth, be a "high priority national security mission" of the Department of Defense.

10. Dan Eggen, "U.S. Foils Swaps of Drugs for Weapons," *Washington Post*, 7 November 2002, A3.

11. Ibid.

12. *Hamdi v. Rumsfeld*, No. 02-7338, U.S. Court of Appeals for the Fourth Circuit, Brief for Respondents–Appellants, 12, 26–28, 4 October 2002.

13. *Hamdi v. Rumsfeld*, No. 02-7338, U.S. Court of Appeals for the Fourth Circuit, Brief of the Petitioners–Appellees, 23.

14. Ibid., at 51–52.

15. *Hamdi v. Rumsfeld, et al*, 316 F.3d 450, 464 (4th Cir. 2003).

16. Ibid., 473 (emphasis added).

17. Ibid., 474.

18. Ibid., 462, 474, 476.

19. If the U.S. Supreme Court exercises its discretion to review a case decided by a federal court of appeals or the highest court of a state, it issues a Writ of *Certiorari* directing the court below to send the record of the case to the Supreme Court. During each Supreme Court term, approximately eight thousand petitions for Writs of *Certiorari* are filed. Roughly seventy-five are granted. The Court exercises its discretion to review a particular case only if at least four of the nine justices vote to consider it. The unofficial, but traditional factors that determine discretionary review include such criteria as whether a conflict exists between the federal courts of appeal on an important point of law, whether the case has important national significance, and whether a request for review has been made by the government.

20. Eric Schmitt, "Pentagon Draws Up A 20-To-30 Year Anti-Terror Plan," *New York Times*, 17 January 2003, A10; Bradley Graham, "Troops Could Stay for Months Without Replacements," *Washington Post*, 23 January 2003, A12.

21. Rowan Scarborough, "Rumsfeld Seeks To Cut Three Top Posts," *Washington Times*, 23 January 2003, 1.

22. Joyce Howard Price, "Democrats Call For U.S. To Get Tough On Iraq," *Washington Times*, 9 December 2002, 1.

23. The bill establishing a Department of Homeland Security did not authorize the new department to collect intelligence or even have access to original or "raw" intelligence data except in special circumstances.

24. Vicki Allen, "Commission Calls for New Counter-Terror Agency," Reuters.com, 14 November 2002; The Associated Press, "Commission Recommends Terror Center," abcNews.com, 14 November 2002. The commission recommended that the new agency be independent of executive branch departments—much like NASA, GSA, the EPA, and others—so that it could "set priorities for its activities more objectively" and not be tied to a department with other responsibilities. Amy Svitak, "Panel Calls for New Agency to Gather Terrorism Info," *Army Times*, 25 November 2002, 29.

25. Ibid.

26. Molly M. Peterson, "Security Advisor Presses for New Intelligence Analysis Agency," GovExec.com, 14 November 2002.

27. BBC News Worldwide, 12 February 2003; Sarah El Deeb, "New Tape Promises Attacks on U.S.," *Washington Post*, 19 October 2003, A18.

28. Pursuant to a plan developed at the White House, the U.S. Coast Guard, the Secret Service, the Customs Service, the Immigration and Naturalization Service, and the new Transportation Security Administration were transferred to the new department on 1 March 2003. The other seventeen agencies were merged into the new department on 30 September 2003.

29. Rowan Scarborough, "Active-Duty Forces Taking Reserve, Guard Missions," *Washington Times*, 11 November, A1; Karen DeYoung, Thomas E. Ricks, "Iraqis Down Reconnaissance Drone," *Washington Post*, 24 December 2002, A11.

30. Vince Crawley, "Changing of the Guard," *Army Times*, 25 November 2002, 23.

31. At a town hall meeting in the Pentagon, Paul Wolfowitz declared that "one of the things that's remarkable about the way the system has worked over the last year is the uncomplaining way in which Reservists have answered a call and served for periods of time that they probably never imagined." Office of the Assistant Secretary of Defense (Public Affairs), "Secretary Rumsfeld Pentagon Town Hall Meeting," news transcript, 12 November 2002.

32. Vince Crawley, "A Balancing Act," *Army Times*, 9 December 2002, 31.

33. David S. C. Chu, *Hearing Before the Subcommittee on Total Force, Armed Service Committee, U.S. House of Representatives*, 108th Cong., 1st sess., 13 March 2003.

34. In order to maximize the "tooth-to-tail" ratio of combat units and combat support/combat service support units over the last three decades, the military services assigned most of the support missions to reserve units. Many functions performed by reservists, for example, civil affairs, military police, medical support, communications, and transportation, are precisely the functions necessary to the success of stability and peacekeeping operations in Iraq, Afghanistan, Bosnia, Kosovo, and the Sinai.

35. Vince Crawley, "CentCom's Next-in-Command Urges Mobilization Overhaul," *Army Times*, 7 July 2003, 34.

36. Dana Eggen, "Broad U.S. Wiretap Powers Upheld," *Washington Post*, 19 November 2002, A1; Jess Bravin, "U.S. Gains Powers in Terror Fight—Court Eases Requirements for Wiretaps, Warrants: Critics See Rights in Peril," *Wall Street Journal*, 19 November 2002, A2.

37. Susan Schmidt, "Patriot Act Misunderstood, Senators Say," *Washington Post*, 22 October 2003, A4.

38. Peter S. Goodman, "N. Korean Official Threatens 'Fight to the End' With U.S.," *Washington Post*, 24 December 2002, A20.

39. Michael Dobbs, "N. Korea Tests Bush's Policy of Preemption," *Washington Post*, 6 January 2003, Al, A9.

40. Rowan Scarborough, "Rumsfeld Says U.S. Can Win War In Two Theaters," *Washington Times*, 24 December 2002, 1.

41. According to the congressional testimony of a former commander of the U.S.-Korean Combined Forces Command, the North Korean weapons systems are capable of delivering up to five hundred thousand rounds per hour for several hours and many of the systems are armed with chemical and biological warheads. Bill Taylor, "Avoiding a Pyrrhic Victory," *Washington Times*, 10 January 2003, 17.

42. The navy base is situated in a forty-five-square-mile area on the southeastern tip of Cuba. Originally seized by the United States from Spain during the Spanish-American War, the property is leased, not owned by the United States, pursuant to a lease signed decades before the government of Fidel Castro came to power.

43. John Mintz, "6 Likely To Face Military Tribunals," *Washington Post*, 4 July 2003, A1.

44. United States Supreme Court, Order Nos. 03-334, 03-343, Order List, 540 U.S. (10 November, 2003).

45. 339 U.S. 763 (1950).

46. Most observers believed the court's decision would turn on the narrow issue of whether the naval base at Guantanamo Bay was within the territorial jurisdiction of the court: i.e., whether the petitioners were resident or nonresident aliens. Others focused on the question of whether, in the absence of a declaration by Congress, the United States was in a state of war. At least some were of the view that the court was merely protecting the fundamental doctrine established by the court in an 1803 opinion by Chief Justice John Marshall, who declared in *Marbury v. Madison* (5 U.S. 137) that "It is emphatically the province and duty of the [courts] to say what the law is." The U.S. Court of Appeals had ruled that "aliens detained by the military abroad" have only those rights that are "determined by the executive and the military, and not the courts."

47. According to its ambassador to the U.N., the goal of France was never to disarm Iraq. Rather, "the main and constant objective for France [was to] strengthen the role and authority of the Security Council." Michael J. Glennon, "Why the Security Council Failed," *Foreign Affairs* (May/June 2003): 25.

48. George W. Bush, Address to the Nation From the USS *Abraham Lincoln, Weekly Compilation of Presidential Documents,* 39, 18 (5 May 2003): 516.

49. Susan B. Glasser, "A Regime of Payoffs and Persecution," *Washington Post,* 17 April 2003, A1; Vince Crawley, "Less Is More" *Army Times,* 21 April 2003, 18.

50. George W. Bush, Remarks to Employees at the Boeing F-18 Production Facility in St. Louis, Missouri, *Weekly Compilation of Presidential Documents,* 39, 16 (16 April 2003): 435.

51. Three days after the fall of Baghdad, North Korea suddenly dropped its demand for direct, one-on-one negotiations with the United States about its nuclear problem. The president of South Korea expressed the view that the U.S. military success in Iraq had terrified North Korea, which feared that it might be the next U.S. target. Doug Struck, "North Korea Drops Its Demand For One-On-One Talks with U.S.," *Washington Post,* 13 April 2003, 22. The head of the Russian Defense Ministry's official think tank on strategic nuclear policy was quoted as saying that "The gap between our capabilities and those of the Americans has been revealed, and it is vast." The Russian author of a book on military reform declared that "The Americans have rewritten the textbook, and every country had better take note." Fred Weir, "Iraqi Defeat Jolts Russian Military," *Christian Science Monitor,* 16 April 2003, 6.

52. In October 2003 the commander of the Joint Forces Command informed Congress that the main reason for the victory was the new level of teamwork, of joint operations. A preliminary army study disagreed. An 18 August report of the study—based upon 176 interviews with the personnel from all of the military services—concluded that victory was the result of the combined effect of U.S. technological superiority and an incompetent Iraqi military. "Iraqi ineptitude" was the "key determinant," the report said, and the authors cautioned against using the war as a model for planning future conflicts against foes who are more capable and more determined. Tom Bowman, "U.S. Technology, Inept Enemy Led to Iraq Victory, Army Says," *The Sun,* 13 October 2003, 11A.

53. "Nation-building is not principally about economic reconstruction," argues one student of the issue, "but rather about political transformation." He defines the term as "the use of armed force in the aftermath of a conflict to underpin an enduring transition to democracy." James Dobbins, "Nation Building: The Inescapable Responsibility of the World's Only Superpower," *RAND Review* (Summer 2003):17.

54. Vince Crawley, Sean Naylor, "What Next?," *Army Times*, 21 April 2003, 10. The U.S. Agency for International Development estimated that two thousand miles of road would have to be built or repaired, six thousand schools repaired, one hundred bridges rehabilitated, five airports restored to operation, and the railway returned to service. Ibid.

55. Dana Milbank, "U.S. Faces Long Stay In Iraq, Bush Says," *Washington Post*, 2 July 2003, A1.

56. Two multinational divisions totaling more than 20,000 troops, one under British command and a second under Polish command, were already serving in Iraq with approximately 128,000 American troops. The Polish-led division included 9,200 troops from twenty-one different countries.

57. Texas Republican Senator Kay Bailey Hutchison, who chaired the Senate Appropriations subcommittee on military construction, wrote in the *Washington Times* that "We need more troops or fewer missions." Her view was shared by senators John McCain, Joe Biden, and many other powerful members of Congress. One analyst noted that even if the deployments to Afghanistan, Bosnia, and Kosovo were terminated, the number of troops saved would not be sufficient to make the current deployment in Iraq sustainable. Frederick W. Kagan "Now You See It, Now You Don't," *Weekly Standard*, 22 September 2003.

58. The issue appeared to be primarily a question of cost. Before asking for funds to enlarge the armed forces, Rumsfeld said, he wanted to transfer to civilians some three hundred thousand military positions—which he characterized as involving "administrative" tasks—and reduce the number of less-urgent foreign assignments. He also pointed out that the addition of end-strength was not a near-term solution to the problem since it would take at least one to two years to recruit, organize, train, and equip new troops. Critics continued to believe that Rumsfeld's concept of military transformation, including a fondness for air power, technology, and smaller, faster land forces, was the real reason. A normally friendly analyst at the American Enterprise Institute expressed the opinion of many: "Now, the kingdom may be lost for want of a nail. The goal of creating a stable environment in Iraq is a moving target. The longer decisive action is postponed, the harder it will be to achieve. Transforming our military for the future is a secondary concern when there's a war to be won today." Tom Donnelly, "Secretary of Stubbornness," *Weekly Standard*, 15 September 2003. On 17 October the Senate voted to increase the end-strength of the active army by ten thousand soldiers, who would be trained in "constabulary" duty skills, including civil affairs, military police, special operations, and light infantry.

59. According to Rumsfeld, rapid increases in the number of Iraqi security forces could

be expected, reaching a total of 221,000 by the fall of 2004. That goal, however, could only be reached by accelerating the training of the Iraqi forces, a risky proposition. Few Iraqis had any experience in conducting counterterrorism operations. Declaring that Iraqification is less a winning strategy than an exit strategy for a president who wants to demonstrate in the election year that "Iraqis are governing their affairs and Americans are coming home," a *Newsweek* columnist argued that "Accelerating the training schedule (which has already been accelerated twice before) will only produce an ineffective Iraqi army and police force." Fareed Zakaria, "Iraqification: Losing Strategy," *Washington Post*, 4 November 2003. Members of Congress also expressed concern that a premature transfer of political authority could leave the appearance that the United States is anxious to "cut and run," and result in an Iraqi government that is more of a Muslim theocracy or a new dictatorship than a democracy. Such a development could leave the country in the kind of unstable circumstances that permit the growth of new terrorist elements.

60. The Marines were expected to send a force of twenty-one thousand troops, most of which would come from the 1st Marine Division, the unit which had taken Baghdad on 10 April 2003, only twenty days after the war began and after fighting its way north from the Kuwait border. It would be the first time since the Vietnam War that Marines were used for long-term stabilization duties, rather than for expeditionary operations.

61. James R. Helmly, "A Streamlined Army Reserve," *Washington Post*, 22 September 2003, 23.

62. Jeff Jacoby, "The Media Ignored The Real WMD News," *Boston Globe*, 9 October 2003; Charles Krauthammer, "WMD In A Haystack," *Washington Post*, 10 October 2003, A27.

63. See a discussion of four "reasons" for the war in Thomas L. Friedman, "Because We Could," *New York Times*, 4 June 2003, A31.

64. John Diamond and Bill Nichols, "Bush's War Doctrine Questioned," *USA Today*, 6 June 2003, 8.

65. For a good discussion of both points, see M. Elaine Bunn, "Preemptive Action: When, How, and to What Effect?" *Strategic Forum* (Institute for National Strategic Studies, National Defense University, No. 200, July 2003).

66. In remarks on the president's *National Security Strategy* at the Waldorf-Astoria Hotel, New York, on 1 October 2002, Dr. Condoleezza Rice, the president's national security advisor, declared that "new technology requires new thinking about when a threat actually becomes 'imminent' . . . . We must adapt the concept of imminent threat to the *capabilities* and *objectives* of today's adversaries" (emphasis added).

67. On this subject, Dr. Rice declared that the use of preemption "must be treated with great caution. It does not give a green light—to the United States or any other nation—to act first without exhausting other means, including diplomacy. The threat must be very grave. And the risks of waiting must far outweigh the risks of action." Ibid.

68. Sophie Lambroshchini, "Russia: Moscow Struggles To Clarify Stance On Preemptive Force," *Radio Free Europe/Radio Liberty*, 14 October 2003.

69. "Transformation is 'a process that shapes the changing nature of military competition and cooperation through new combinations of concepts, capabilities, people and organizations that exploit our nation's advantages and protect against our asymmetric vulnerabilities to sustain our strategic position, which helps underpin peace and stability in the world.'" U.S. Department of Defense, *Transformation Planning Guidance* (Washington, D.C.: Department of Defense, April 2003), 3.

70. Ibid.

71. Perhaps the most controversial proposed legislative changes would eliminate mandatory terms of office for certain flag and general officers, permit flag and general officers to serve until age sixty-eight, and authorize the secretary of defense to retain—at his discretion—certain flag and general officers until age seventy-two. *The Defense Transformation for the 21st Century Act of 2003*, Sections 112-120. Opposition to the proposal in the House of Representatives was led by first-term Rep. John Kline, a Republican from Minnesota. Kline, a twenty-five-year veteran of the Marine Corps, argued that the proposal would unnecessarily age the officer corps, slow the promotion of highly qualified younger officers—with an attendant loss of morale—and politicize the appointments of senior officers by permitting the secretary of defense to surround himself with "like-minded" officers.

72. Dave Moniz and Tom Squitieri, "Defense Memo: A Grim Outlook," *USA Today*, 22 October 2003, 1.

73. Ibid.

74. Vince Crawley, "U.S. Troops Go on Offensive in Troubled Iraqi Provinces," *Army Times*, 6 October 2003, 20.

75. Council on Foreign Relations, "Nearly Two Years After 9/11, the United States is Still Dangerously Unprepared and Underfunded for a Catastrophic Terrorist Attack, Warns New Council Task Force," Press Release, 29 June 2003.

76. The "Topoff 2" (for top government officials) exercise involved eight thousand emergency workers, federal agents, and scientists and it simulated (radiological) dirty bomb and bioterror attacks in Seattle and Chicago. The weaknesses that the exercise revealed were made more significant by the fact that it was heavily scripted. See Robert Block, "FEMA Points To Flaws, Flubs In Terror Drill," *Wall Street Journal*, 31

October 2003, B1.

77. John Mintz, "Government's Hobbled Giant," *Washington Post*, 7 September 2003, A1.

78. U.S. General Accounting Office, *Homeland Security: Management Challenges Facing Federal Leadership* (Washington, D.C.: GAO, No. GAO-03-260, December, 2002), 3–4.

79. *Bob Stump National Defense Authorization Act for Fiscal Year 2003*, 107th Cong., 2d sess., Conference Report on H.R. 4546, sec. 1404.

80. The Defense Science Board was established in 1956. Its thirty-two members and seven ex-officio members are appointed for terms ranging from one to four years and are selected "on the basis of their preeminence in the fields of science, technology and its application to military operations, research, engineering, manufacturing and acquisition process."

81. E. C. Aldridge Jr., "Memorandum for Chairman, Defense Science Board," 6 January 2003.

82. Office of the Assistant Secretary of Defense (Public Affairs), "Secretary Rumsfeld Pentagon Town Hall Meeting" news transcript, 12 November 2002, Washington, D.C., (emphasis added).

83. Office of the Assistant Secretary of Defense (Public Affairs), "Pentagon Town Hall Meeting with Secretary Rumsfeld," news transcript, 6 March 2003, Washington, D.C., (emphasis added). In the fall of 2003 it was reported that in order to implement the concept of "forward defense and the related policy of preemption, the DoD was considering major changes in the U.S. military basing policy. On the assumption that future threats to U.S. security were likely to emerge from identifiable areas of volatility and instability, it was being proposed that U.S. troops be moved away from the DMZ in South Korea, and that large numbers of troops garrisoned in Germany be moved to remote, spartan, forward operation bases near potential flash points. "Taken together," said analysts at the Center for Strategic and International Studies, the moves would "constitute the most sweeping changes in the U.S. military posture abroad in half a century." Kurt M. Campbell and Celeste Johnson Ward, "New Battle Stations?" *Foreign Affairs*, September/October 2003, 95.

84. George W. Bush, *The National Security Strategy of the United States of America; op. cit.*, Introduction, chapter III.

85. Michael Vlahos, "Perspectives on Military Transformation: Towards a Global Security Force," April 2003.

86. Office of Homeland Security, *The National Strategy for Homeland Security* (Washington, D.C.: The White House, 16 July 2002), Letter from the President.

87. *The National Security Strategy of the United States of America*, chapter V (emphasis added).

88. Commenting on the remarks in his 16 October 2003 memorandum that relatively little effort had been made to develop a long-range plan to fight terrorism, Rumsfeld blamed the lace of cooperation among government departments and agencies. "The hardest things to do," he said, "are things that are between agencies." Bill Gertz, "Rumsfeld Pushes 'New Sense Of Urgency,'" *Washington Times*, 24 October 2003, 1.

89. Rick Atkinson, "The Lessons of Global War," *Washington Post*, 6 October 2003, B07.

90. Ibid.

91. In the spring, 76 percent supported the war effort and the president's performance in office. A *CNN-USA Today-Gallup* Poll released on 6 November 2003 showed that 54 percent of the respondents disapproved of his policies in Iraq.

92. Dana Milbank, Thomas E. Ricks, "Survey Shows Skepticism About Iraq," *Washington Post*, 5 November 2003, A13.

93. The conflict in Vietnam involved a general uprising by a large percentage of the Vietnamese people and a much higher casualty rate. Referring to a suicide bomber who had driven an ambulance full of explosives into a Baghdad Red Cross office a few days earlier, one editorialist described the primary difference between the two wars. "The people who mounted the attacks on the Red Cross are not the Iraqi Vietcong," he said. "They are the Iraqi Khymer Rouge—a murderous band of Saddam loyalists and Al Qaeda nihilists, who are not killing us so Iraqis can rule themselves. They are killing us so they can rule Iraqis." Thomas L. Friedman, "It's No Vietnam," *New York Times*, 30 October 2003.

94. The so-called "Sunni Triangle" is bounded by Baghdad, Tikrit (Saddam Hussein's hometown), and Ramadi.

95. Long a weak point in U.S. intelligence operations, human intelligence was critically needed in Iraq. Tips about potential attacks could only be obtained through infiltration into the groups of anti-American insurgents making the daily attacks by residents who were familiar with the neighborhoods and who did not need translators.

96. Vernon Loeb, "Fighting a 'Battle Of Perceptions,'" *Washington Post*, 10 November 2003, A20; Robin Wright, Thomas E. Ricks, "New Urgency, New Risks In Iraqification," *Washington Post*, 14 November 2003, 1.

97. "Fickle Interventionists," *Wall Street Journal*, 31 October 2003, A12.

98. Doyle McManus, "Less Bravado, More Frank Talk," *Los Angeles Times*, 3 November 2003, 1.

99. In a speech a few days later, which was designed to again explain the aggressive nature of his global war on terrorism and to elevate the conflict in Iraq to the status of a moral cause, the president characterized it as part of a national commitment

to advance democracy. "The failure of Iraqi democracy," he said, "would embolden terrorists around the world and increase dangers to the American people and extinguish the hopes of millions in the region." But, he added that "The establishment of a free Iraq at the heart of the Middle East will be a watershed event in the global democratic revolution." George W. Bush, Address Marking the 20th Anniversary of the National Endowment for Democracy, *Weekly Compilation of Presidential Documents* (November, 2003).

100. Alec Russell, David Rennie, "'We Are At War For Freedom,'" *London Daily Telegraph*, 14 November 2003, 1.

101. Thomas E. Ricks, "U.S. Tolerance of Deaths Tested," *Washington Post*, 16 November 2003, A20.

102. Glen Frankel, "Blair Defends Bush Partnership," *Washington Post*, 12 November 2003, A19.

103. Henry A. Kissinger, "Needed: A Sense of Common Purpose," *Washington Post*, 2 November 2003, B7.

104. Associated Press, "France: U.S. Exit Would Be Mistake," *Dallas Morning News*, 31 October 2003.

105. Jim Hoagland, "Our Crucible Year," *Washington Post*, 8 September 2002, B07.

106. See, for example, David S. Broder, "A Lump of Coal From the President," *Washington Post*, 4 December 2002, A23.

107. Ibid.

Index

About the Author

Stephen M. Duncan served as assistant secretary of defense in two presidential administrations and as the Pentagon's senior drug war official. A decorated Vietnam veteran with more than forty years of active and reserve naval service, he is the recipient of two awards of the Department of Defense Medal for Distinguished Public Service. A former federal criminal prosecutor, trial counsel in major public policy cases and commercial litigation, and chief executive officer of a defense industry technology company, Duncan is the author of *Citizen Warriors*, an account of the use of the National Guard and U.S. Reserve forces in the 1990–91 Persian Gulf War. He received his bachelor of science degree from the U.S. Naval Academy, a master of arts degree in U.S. Government from Dartmouth College, and a juris doctor degree from the University of Colorado. He is currently a Distinguished Fellow at the National Defense University, Fort McNair, Washington, D.C.

The **Naval Institute Press** is the book-publishing arm of the U.S. Naval Institute, a private, nonprofit, membership society for sea service professionals and others who share an interest in naval and maritime affairs. Established in 1873 at the U.S. Naval Academy in Annapolis, Maryland, where its offices remain today, the Naval Institute has members worldwide.

Members of the Naval Institute support the education programs of the society and receive the influential monthly magazine *Proceedings* and discounts on fine nautical prints and on ship and aircraft photos. They also have access to the transcripts of the Institute's Oral History Program and get discounted admission to any of the Institute-sponsored seminars offered around the country.

The Naval Institute also publishes *Naval History* magazine. This colorful bimonthly is filled with entertaining and thought-provoking articles, first-person reminiscences, and dramatic art and photography. Members receive a discount on *Naval History* subscriptions.

The Naval Institute's book-publishing program, begun in 1898 with basic guides to naval practices, has broadened its scope to include books of more general interest. Now the Naval Institute Press publishes about one hundred titles each year, ranging from how-to books on boating and navigation to battle histories, biographies, ship and aircraft guides, and novels. Institute members receive significant discounts on the Press's more than eight hundred books in print.

Full-time students are eligible for special half-price membership rates. Life memberships are also available.

For a free catalog describing Naval Institute Press books currently available, and for further information about subscribing to *Naval History* magazine or about joining the U.S. Naval Institute, please write to:

Membership Department
U.S. Naval Institute
291 Wood Road
Annapolis, MD 21402-5034
Telephone: (800) 233-8764
Fax: (410) 269-7940
Web address: www.navalinstitute.org